ANCIENT RECORDS OF EGYPT

HISTORICAL DOCUMENTS

FROM THE EARLIEST TIMES TO THE PERSIAN CONQUEST, COLLECTED
EDITED AND TRANSLATED WITH COMMENTARY

BY

JAMES HENRY BREASTED, Ph.D.

PROFESSOR OF EGYPTOLOGY AND ORIENTAL HISTORY
IN THE UNIVERSITY OF CHICAGO

VOLUME III
THE NINETEENTH DYNASTY

ISBN: 978-1-63923-644-2

All Rights reserved. No part of this book maybe reproduced without written permission from the publishers, except by a reviewer who may quote brief passages in a review to be printed in a newspaper or magazine.

Printed: January 2023

Published and Distributed By:
Lushena Books
607 Country Club Drive, Unit E
Bensenville, IL 60106
www.lushenabks.com

ISBN: 978-1-63923-644-2

TABLE OF CONTENTS

VOLUME I

	§§
THE DOCUMENTARY SOURCES OF EGYPTIAN HISTORY	1–37
CHRONOLOGY	38–57
CHRONOLOGICAL TABLE	58–75
THE PALERMO STONE: THE FIRST TO THE FIFTH DYNASTIES	76–167
I. Predynastic Kings	90
II. First Dynasty	91–116
III. Second Dynasty	117–144
IV. Third Dynasty	145–148
V. Fourth Dynasty	149–152
VI. Fifth Dynasty	153–167
THE THIRD DYNASTY	168–175
Reign of Snefru	168–175
Sinai Inscriptions	168–169
Biography of Methen	170–175
THE FOURTH DYNASTY	176–212
Reign of Khufu	176–187
Sinai Inscriptions	176
Inventory Stela	177–180
Examples of Dedication Inscriptions by Sons	181–187
Reign of Khafre	188–209
Stela of Mertityôtes	188–189
Will of Prince Nekure, Son of King Khafre	190–199
Testamentary Enactment of an Unknown Official, Establishing the Endowment of His Tomb by the Pyramid of Khafre	200–209
Reign of Menkure	210–212
Debhen's Inscription, Recounting King Menkure's Erection of a Tomb for Him	210–212
THE FIFTH DYNASTY	213–281
Reign of Userkaf	213–235

	§§
Testamentary Enactment of Nekonekh	213–215
I. The Priesthood of Hathor	216–219
II. The Mortuary Priesthood of Khenuka	220–222
III. Nekonekh's Will	223–225
IV. Nekonekh's Mortuary Priesthood	226–227
V. Nekonekh's Mortuary Statue	228–230
Testamentary Enactment of Senuonekh, Regulating His Mortuary Priesthood	231–235
Reign of Sahure	236–241
Sinai Inscriptions	236
Tomb Stela of Nenekhsekhmet	237–240
Tomb Inscription of Persen	241
Reign of Neferirkere	242–249
Tomb Inscriptions of the Vizier, Chief Judge, and Chief Architect Weshptah	242–249
Reign of Nuserre	250–262
Sinai Inscription	250
Tomb Inscriptions of Hotephiryakhet	251–253
Inscription of Ptahshepses	254–262
Reign of Menkuhor	263
Sinai Inscription	263
Reign of Dedkere-Isesi	264–281
Sinai Inscriptions	264–267
Tomb Inscriptions of Senezemib, Chief Judge, Vizier, and Chief Architect	268–277
Mortuary Inscription of Nezemib	278–279
Tomb Inscription of the Nomarch Henku	280–281
THE SIXTH DYNASTY	282–390
Reign of Teti	282–294
Inscriptions of Sabu, Also Called Ibebi	282–286
Inscription of Sabu, Also Called Thety	287–288
Inscription of an Unknown Builder	289–290
Inscription of Uni	291–294
I. Career under Teti (l. 1)	292–294
II. Career under Pepi I (ll. 2–32)	306–315
III. Career under Mernere (ll. 32–50)	319–324
Reign of Pepi I	295–315
Hammamat Inscriptions	295–301

	§§
I. The King's Inscriptions	296
II. The Expedition's Inscription	297–298
III. Chief Architect's Inscription	299
IV. Inscription of the Treasurer of the God Ikhi	300–301
Sinai Inscription	302–303
Inscription in the Hatnub Quarry	304–305
Inscription of Uni: II Career under Pepi I	306–315
Reign of Mernere	316–336
Inscriptions at the First Cataract	316–318
I. Northern Inscription	317
II. Southern Inscription	318
Inscription of Uni: III Career under Mernere	319–324
Inscriptions of Harkhuf	325–336
Inscriptions of Harkhuf (continued)	350–354
Reign of Pepi II	337–385
Conveyance of Land by Idu, Called Also Seneni	337–338
Sinai Inscription	339–343
Stela of the Two Queens, Enekhnes-Merire	344–349
Inscriptions of Harkhuf (continued from § 336)	350–354
Letter of Pepi II	350–354
I. Dates and Introduction	351
II. Acknowledgment of Harkhuf's Letter	351
III. Harkhuf's Rewards	352
IV. King's Instructions	353–354
Inscriptions of Pepi-Nakht	355–360
Inscriptions of Khui	361
Inscriptions of Sebni	362–374
Inscriptions of Ibi	375–379
Inscription of Zau	380–385
Reign of Ity	386–387
Hammamat Inscription	386–387
Reign of Imhotep	388–390
THE NINTH AND TENTH DYNASTIES	391–414
Inscriptions of Siut	391–414
I. Inscription of Tefibi	393–397
II. Inscription of Kheti I	398–404
III. Inscription of Kheti II	405–414

TABLE OF CONTENTS

	§§
THE ELEVENTH DYNASTY	415–459
The Nomarch, Intef	419–420
Mortuary Stela	419–420
Reign of Horus-Wahenekh-Intef I	421–423
Royal Tomb Stela	421–423
Reign of Horus-Nakhtneb-Tepnefer-Intef II	423A–423G
Stela of Thethi	423A–423G
Reign of Nibhotep-Mentuhotep I	423H
Temple Fragments from Gebelen	423H
Reigns of Intef III and Nibkhrure-Mentuhotep II	424–426
Relief near Assuan	424–426
Reign of Senekhkere-Mentuhotep III	427–433
Hammamat Inscription of Henu	427–433
Reign of Nibtowere-Mentuhotep IV	434–459
Hammamat Inscriptions	434–459
I. The First Wonder	435–438
II. The Official Tablet	439–443
III. The Commander's Tablet	444–448
IV. The Second Wonder	449–451
V. Completion of the Work	452–456
Stela of Eti	457–459
THE TWELFTH DYNASTY	460–750
Chronology of Twelfth Dynasty	460–462
Reign of Amenemhet I	463–497
Inscription of Khnumhotep I	463–465
Hammamat Inscription of Intef	466–468
Inscription of Nessumontu	469–471
Inscription of Korusko	472–473
The Teaching of Amenemhet	474–483
Dedication Inscription	484–485
The Tale of Sinuhe	486–497
Reign of Sesostris I	498–593
The Building Inscription of the Temple of Heliopolis	498–506
Inscription of Meri	507–509
Wadi Halfa Inscription of Mentuhotep	510–514
Inscription of Amenemhet (Ameni)	515–523
Stela of Ikudidi	524–528
Inscription of Intefyoker	529

TABLE OF CONTENTS

	§§
Inscriptions of Mentuhotep	530–534
The Contracts of Hepzefi	535–538
I. First Contract	539–543
II. Second Contract	544–548
III. Third Contract	549–553
IV. Fourth Contract	554–558
V. Fifth Contract	559–567
VI. Sixth Contract	568–571
VII. Seventh Contract	572–575
VIII. Eighth Contract	576–581
IX. Ninth Contract	582–588
X. Tenth Contract	589–593
Reign of Amenemhet II	594–613
Inscription of Simontu	594–598
Inscription of Sihathor	599–605
Sinai Inscription	606
Stela of Khentemsemeti	607–613
Reign of Sesostris II	614–639
Inscription of Hapu	614–618
Inscription of Khnumhotep II	619–639
Reign of Sesostris III	640–748
The Conquest of Nubia	640–672
I. The Canal Inscriptions	642–649
I. First Inscription	643–645
II. Second Inscription	646–648
II. The Elephantine Inscription	649–650
III. The First Semneh Stela	651–652
IV. The Second Semneh Stela	653–660
V. Inscription of Ikhernofret	661–670
VI. Inscription of Sisatet	671–673
See also	676 ff. and 687
Hammamat Inscription	674–675
Stela of Sebek-Khu, called Zaa	676–687
Inscriptions of Thuthotep	688–706
Hammamat Inscriptions	707–712
Inscriptions of Sinai	713–738
I. Wadi Maghara	713–723
I. Inscriptions of Khenemsu	714–716

			§§
	II.	Inscription of Harnakht	717–718
	III.	Inscription of Sebekdidi	719–720
	IV.	Inscription of Ameni	721–723
II.	Sarbût el-Khadem		724–738
	I.	Inscription of Sebek-hir-hab	725–727
	II.	Inscription of Ptahwer	728–729
	III.	Inscription of Amenemhet	730–732
	IV.	Inscription of Harurre	733–738

Turra Inscription 739–742
Inscription of Sehetepibre 743–748
Reign of Amenemhet IV. 749–750
    Kummeh Inscription 749
    Sinai Inscriptions 750

FROM THE THIRTEENTH DYNASTY TO THE HYKSOS . . 751–787
  Reign of Sekhemre-Khutowe 751–752
    Records of Nile-Levels 751–752
  Reign of Neferhotep 753–772
    Great Abydos Stela 753–765
    Boundary Stela 766–772
  Reign of Nubkheprure-Intef 773–780
    Coptos Decree 773–780
  Reign of Khenzer 781–787
    Inscriptions of Ameniseneb 781–787

VOLUME II

			§§
THE EIGHTEENTH DYNASTY			1–1043
Reign of Ahmose I			1–37
Biography of Ahmose, Son of Ebana			1–3
I.	Career under Ahmose I (ll. 1–24)		4–16
II.	Career under Amenhotep I (ll. 24–29)		38–39
III.	Career under Thutmose I (ll. 29–39)		78–82
Biography of Ahmose-Pen-Nekhbet			17–25
I.	Ahmose's Campaigns [Continued § 40]		18–20
II.	Ahmose's Rewards		21–24
III.	Ahmose's Summary		25

TABLE OF CONTENTS

	§§
Quarry Inscription	26–28
Karnak Stela	29–32
Building Inscription	33–37
Reign of Amenhotep I	38–53
Biography of Ahmose, Son of Ebana	38–39
II. Career under Amenhotep I (ll. 24–29)	38–53
Biography of Ahmose-Pen-Nekhbet	40–42
Career under Amenhotep I	40–42
Biography of Ineni	43–46
I. Career under Amenhotep I	44–46
II. Career under Thutmose I	99–108
III. Career under Thutmose II	115–118
IV. Career under Thutmose III and Hatshepsut	340–343
Stela of Harmini	47–48
Stela of Keres	49–52
Reign of Thutmose I	54–114
Coronation Decree	54–60
Biographical Inscription of Thure	61–66
Tombos Stela	67–73
Inscriptions at the First Cataract	74–77
I. Sehel Inscription	75
II. Sehel Inscription	76
III. Assuan Inscription	77
Inscription of Ahmose, Son of Ebana	78–82
III. Career under Thutmose I (ll. 29–39)	78–82
Biography of Ahmose-Pen-Nekhbet	83–85
Career under Thutmose I	83–85
Karnak Obelisks	86–89
Abydos Stela	90–98
Biography of Ineni	99–108
II. Career under Thutmose I (ll. 4–14)	99–108
Stela of Yuf	109–114
Reign of Thutmose II	115–127
Biography of Ineni	115–118
III. Career under Thutmose II	115–118
Assuan Inscription	119–122
Biography of Ahmose-Pen-Nekhbet	123–124
IV. Career under Thutmose II	123–124

TABLE OF CONTENTS

	§§
Campaign in Syria	125
The Ebony Shrine of Der el-Bahri	126–127
Reign of Thutmose III and Hatshepsut	128–390
Introduction	128–130
Inscription of the Coronation; Buildings and Offerings	131–166
Semneh Temple Inscriptions	167
I. Renewal of Sesostris III's List of Offerings	168–172
II. Dedication to Dedun and Sesostris III	173–176
Biography of Nebwawi	177
I. The Statue Inscription	178–183
II. Abydos Stela	184–186
The Birth of Queen Hatshepsut	187–191
I. The Council of the Gods	192
II. Interviews Between Amon and Thoth	193–194
III. Amon with Queen Ahmose	195–198
IV. Interview Between Amon and Khnum	199–201
V. Khnum Fashions the Child	202–203
VI. Interview Between Thoth and Queen Ahmose	204
VII. Queen Ahmose is Led to Confinement	205
VIII. The Birth	206–207
IX. Presentation of the Child to Amon	208
X. Council of Amon and Hathor	209
XI. The Nursing of the Child	210
XII. Second Interview of Amon and Thoth	211
XIII. The Final Scene	212
Statue of Enebni	213
Vase Inscription	214
The Coronation of Queen Hatshepsut	215
I. The Purification	216
II. Amon presents the Child to All the Gods	217–220
III. The Northern Journey	221–225
IV. Coronation by Atum	226–227
V. Reception of the Crowns and the Names	228–230
VI. Proclamation as King before Amon	231
VII. Coronation before the Court	232–239
VIII. Second Purification	240–241
IX. Concluding Ceremonies	242
Southern Pylon Inscription at Karnak	243–245

TABLE OF CONTENTS

The Punt Reliefs 246-295
   I. Departure of the Fleet 252-253
   II. Reception in Punt 254-258
   III. The Traffic 259-262
   IV. Loading the Vessels 263-265
   V. The Return Voyage 266
   VI. Presentation of the Tribute to the Queen by the Chiefs of Punt, Irem and Nemyew . . . 267-269
   VII. The Queen Offers the Gifts to Amon . . . 270-272
   VIII. Weighing and Measuring the Gifts to Amon . 273-282
   IX. Formal Announcement of the Success of the Expedition before Amon 283-288
   X. Formal Announcement of the Success of the Expedition to the Court 289-295
Inscription of the Speos Artemidos 296-303
The Karnak Obelisks 304-307
   I. Shaft Inscriptions; Middle Columns . . . 308-311
   II. Shaft Inscriptions; Side Columns 312-313
   III. Base Inscription 314-321
Reliefs of Transportation of Obelisks 322
   I. Transport 323-329
   II. Reception in Thebes 330-335
   III. Dedication of the Obelisks 336
Rock Inscription in Wadi Maghara 337
Building Inscription of Western Thebes 338-339
Biography of Ineni 340-343
   IV. Career under Thutmose III and Hatshepsut . 340-343
Biography of Ahmose-Pen-Nekhbet 344
Conclusion of Summary 344
Inscriptions of Senmut 345-368
   I. Inscriptions on the Karnak Statue . . . 349-358
   II. Assuan Inscription 359-362
   III. Inscriptions on the Berlin Statue . . . 363-368
Inscription of Thutiy 369-378
Inscriptions of Puemre 379
   I. Statue of Inscription 380-381
   II. Tomb Inscriptions 382-387
Inscriptions of Hapuseneb 388-390

	§§
Reign of Thutmose III	391–779
The Annals	391–405
The Annals: Conspectus of Campaigns	406
I. Introduction	407
II. First Campaign (Year 23)	408–443
Wadi Halfa Inscription	411–437
Fragment on the Siege of Megiddo	438–443
III. Second Campaign (Year 24)	444–449
IV. Third Campaign (Year 25)	450–452
V. Fourth Campaign	453
VI. Fifth Campaign (Year 29)	454–462
VII. Sixth Campaign (Year 30)	463–467
VIII. Seventh Campaign (Year 31)	468–475
IX. Eighth Campaign (Year 33)	476–487
X. Ninth Campaign (Year 34)	488–495
XI. Tenth Campaign (Year 35)	496–503
XII. Eleventh Campaign (Year 36)	504
XIII. Twelfth Campaign (Year 37)	505
XIV. Thirteenth Campaign (Year 38)	506–515
XV. Fourteenth Campaign (Year 39)	516–519
XVI. Fifteenth Campaign	520–523
XVII. Sixteenth Campaign	524–527
XVIII. Seventeenth Campaign	528–539
XIX. Conclusion	540
Feasts and Offerings from the Conquests	541–573
Biography of Amenemhab	574–592
Fragments of Karnak Pylon VII	593–598
Great Karnak Building Inscription	599–608
Building Inscription of the Karnak Ptah-Temple	609–622
Obelisks	623
I. Karnak Obelisks	624–625
II. Lateran Obelisks	626–628
III. Constantinople Obelisk	629–631
IV. London Obelisk	632–633
V. New York Obelisk	634–636
Medinet Habu Building Inscriptions	637–641
Heliopolis Building Inscriptions	642–643
Nubian Wars	644–654

		§§
I.	Canal Inscription	649–650
II.	Inscriptions of Nehi, Viceroy of Kush	651–652
III.	Offerings from the South Countries	653–654

Hymn of Victory 655–662
Tomb of Rekhmire 663–759
    I. Appointment of Rekhmire as Vizier . . . 665–670
    II. Duties of the Vizier 671–711
    III. The Sitting of the Vizier 712–713
    IV. Reception of Petitions 714–715
    V. Inspection of Taxes of Upper Egypt . . . 716
        A. Above Thebes 717–728
        B. Below Thebes 729–745
    VI. Reception of Dues to the Amon-Temple . . 746–751
    VII. Inspection of Daily Offerings and of Monuments 752
    VIII. Inspection of Craftsmen 753–755
    IX. Inspection of Sculptors and Builders . . . 756–759
    X. Reception of Foreign Tribute 760–761
    XI. Accession of Amenhotep II 762
Stela of Intef the Herald 763–771
Tomb of Menkheperreseneb 772–776
Stela of Nibamon 777–779
Reign of Amenhotep II 780
    Asiatic Campaign 780–798
        I. Karnak Stela 781–790
        II. Amâda and Elephantine Stelæ . . . 791–798
        III. Karnak Chapel 798A
    Turra Inscription 799–800
    Tomb of Amenken 801–802
    Karnak Building Inscription 803–806
    Biography of Amenemhab 807–809
Reign of Thutmose IV 810–840
    Sphinx Stela 810–815
    Asiatic Campaign 816–822
    Konosso Inscription 823–829
    Lateran Obelisk 830–838
    Stela of Pe'aoke 839–840
Reign of Amenhotep III 841–931
    Birth and Coronation 841

TABLE OF CONTENTS

	§§
Nubian War	842–855
I. Stela at First Cataract	843–844
II. Stela of Konosso	845
III. Bubastis Inscription	846–850
IV. Semneh Inscription	851–855
Tablet of Victory	856–859
The Commemorative Scarabs	860–869
I. Marriage with Tiy	861–862
II. Wild Cattle Hunt	863–864
III. Ten Years Lion-Hunting	865
IV. Marriage with Kirgipa	866–867
V. Construction of a Pleasure Lake	868–869
Jubilee Celebrations	870–874
Quarry and Mine Inscriptions	875–877
Building Inscription	878–892
I. Introduction (ll. 1–2)	882
II. Temple of the (Memnon) Colossi (ll. 2–10)	883–885
III. Luxor Temple and Connected Buildings	886–887
IV. Sacred Barge of Amon (ll. 16–20)	888
V. Third Pylon of Karnak (ll. 20–23)	889
VI. Temple of Soleb (ll. 23–26)	890
VII. Hymn of Amon to the King (ll. 26–31)	891–892
Building Inscriptions of the Soleb Temple	893–898
Great Inscription of the Third Karnak Pylon	899–903
Dedication Stela	904–910
I. Speech of the King (ll. 1–13)	905–908
II. Speech of Amon (ll. 14–20)	909
III. Speech of the Divine Ennead (ll. 20–24)	910
Inscriptions of Amenhotep, Son of Hapi	911–927
I. Statue Inscription	913–920
II. Mortuary Temple Edict	921–927
Statue of Nebnefer	928–931
Reign of Ikhnaton	932–1018
Quarry Inscription at Silsileh	932–935
Tomb of the Vizier Ramose	936–948
The Tell El-Amarna Landmarks	949–972
Assuan Tablet of the Architect Bek	973–976
The Tell El-Amarna Tombs	977–1018

TABLE OF CONTENTS

	§§
Tomb of Merire II	981
Tomb of Merire I	982–988
Tomb of Eye	989–996
Tomb of Mai	997–1003
Tomb of Ahmose	1004–1008
Tomb of Tutu	1009–1013
Tomb of Huy	1014–1018
Reign of Tutenkhamon	1019–1041
Tomb of Huy.	1019–1041
I. Investiture of the Viceroy of Kush	1020–1026
II. Tribute of the North	1027–1033
III. Tribute of the South	1034–1041
Reign of Eye	1042–1043

LIST OF FIGURES

	PAGE
Plan of Punt Reliefs	105

VOLUME III

	§§
THE NINETEENTH DYNASTY	1–651
Reign of Harmhab	1–73
Tomb of Harmhab	1–21
I. Leyden Fragments	2–9
I. Stela with Adoration Scene	2–5
II. Reward of Gold	6–9
II. Vienna Fragment	10–12
III. Alexandria Fragments	13
IV. British Museum Fragments	14–19
I. Doorposts	14–17
II. Stela with Three Hymns	18–19
V. Cairo Fragments	20–21
Coronation Inscription	22–32
Graffiti in the Theban Necropolis	32A–32C
The Wars of Harmhab	33–44
I. In the North	34–36
II. In the South	37–44
Edict of Harmhab	45–67

		§§
I.	Introduction (ll. 1–10)	49
II.	Introduction: The King's Zeal for the Relief of the People (ll. 10–14)	50
III.	Enactment Against Robbing the Poor of Dues for the Royal Breweries and Kitchens (ll. 14–17)	51
IV.	Enactment Against Robbing the Poor of Wood Due the Pharaoh (ll. 17–18)	52
V.	Enactment Against Exacting Dues from a Poor Man Thus Robbed (ll. 18–20)	53
VI.	Against Robbing the Poor of Dues for the Harem or the Gods by the Soldiers (ll. 20–24) . .	54
VII.	Enactments Against Unlawful Appropriation of Slave Service (ll. 22–24)	55
VIII.	Enactment Against Stealing of Hides by the Soldiers (ll. 25–28)	56–57
IX.	Against Connivance of Dishonest Inspectors with Thievish Tax-Collectors, for a Share of the Booty (ll. 28–32)	58
X.	Enactment Against Stealing Vegetables Under Pretense of Collecting Taxes (ll. 32–35) . .	59
XI.	Enactments too Fragmentary for Analysis (ll. 35–39) and Right Side (ll. 1, 2)	60–62
XII.	Narrative of the King's Reforms, Containing Also an Enactment Against Corrupt Judges (ll. 3–7)	63–65
XIII.	Narrative of the King's Monthly Audiences and Largesses (ll. 7–10)	66
XIV.	Laudation of the King, and Conclusion (Left Side)	67
	Tomb of Neferhotep	68–73
	Reign of Ramses I	74–79
	Wadi Halfa Stela	74–79
	Reign of Seti I	80–250
	Karnak Reliefs	80–156
	Scene 1. March through Southern Palestine . .	83–84
	Scene 2. Battle with the Shasu	85–86
	Scene 3. Capture of Pekanan.	87–88
	Scene 4. Capture of Yenoam	89–90

TABLE OF CONTENTS

	§§
Scene 5. Submission of the Chiefs of Lebanon	91–94
Scenes 6 and 7. Binding and Carrying Away Prisoners	95–97
Scene 8. Reception in Egypt	98–103
Scene 9. Presentation of Shasu Prisoners and Precious Vessels to Amon	104–108
Scene 10. Presentation of Syrian Prisoners and Precious Vessels to Amon	109–112
Scene 11. Slaying Prisoners Before Amon	113–119
Scene 12. First Battle with the Libyans	120–122
Scene 13. Second Battle with the Libyans	123–132
Scene 14. Return from Libyan War	133–134
Scene 15. Presentation of Libyan Prisoners and Spoil to Amon	135–139
Scene 16. Capture of Kadesh	140–141
Scene 17. Battle with the Hittites	142–144
Scene 18. Carrying off Hittite Prisoners	145–148
Scene 19. Presentation of Hittite Spoil and Prisoners to Amon	149–152
Scene 20. Slaying Prisoners before Amon	153–156
Wadi Halfa Stela	157–161
Inscriptions of Redesiyeh	162–198
I. First Inscription	169–174
II. Second Inscription	175–194
III. Third Inscription	195–198
Building Inscriptions	199–250
I. First Cataract Inscription	201–204
1. Assuan Inscription	201–202
2. Elephantine Stela	203–204
II. Silsileh Quarry Stela	205–208
III. Gebelên Quarry Inscription	209–210
IV. Mortuary Temple at Thebes (Kurna)	211–221
V. Temple of Karnak	222–224
VI. Mortuary Temple at Abydos	225–243
VII. Temple Model of Heliopolis	244–246
VIII. Miscellaneous	247–250
Reign of Ramses II	251–568
Great Abydos Inscription	251–281
Kubbân Stela	282–293

	§§
The Asiatic War	294–391
I. Beginning of the Hittite War	296–351
I. First Campaign	297
II. Second Campaign: The Battle of Kadesh	298–351
a. Poem of the Battle of Kadesh	305–315
b. Official Record of the Battle of Kadesh	316–327
c. The Reliefs of the Battle of Kadesh	328
I. The Council of War	329–330
II. The Camp	331–332
III. Ramses' Messengers	333–334
IV. The Battle	335–338
V. The Defense of the Camp	339–340
VI. After the Battle	341–347
VII. Presentation of Captives to Amon	348–351
III. Palestinian Revolt	352–362
I. Reconquest of Southern Palestine	353–355
II. Reconquest of Northern Palestine	356–362
IV. Campaign in Naharin	363–391
I. Conquest of Naharin	364–366
II. Treaty with the Hittites	367–391
Relations of Egypt with the Hittites after the War	392–491
I. The Blessing of Ptah	394–414
II. Marriage Stela	415–424
III. Message of the Chief of Kheta to the Chief of Kode	425–426
IV. Coptos Stela	427–428
V. Bentresh Stela	429–447
Nubian Wars and References to Northern Wars	448–491
I. Abu Simbel Temple	449–457
II. Bet el-Walli Temple	458–477
III. Assuan Stela	478–479
IV. Luxor Temple	480–484
V. Abydos Temple	485–486
VI. Tanis Stelæ	487–491
Building Inscriptions	492–537
I. Great Temple of Abu Simbel	495–499
II. Small Temple of Abu Simbel	500–501
III. Temple of Serreh	502

TABLE OF CONTENTS

			§§
		Temple of Derr	503
IV.		Temple of Sebûʿa	504
VI.		Temple of el Kab	505
VII.		Temple of Luxor	506–508
VIII.		Temple of Karnak	509–513
IX.		The Ramesseum	514–515
X.		Temple of Kurna	516–522
XI.		Seti I's Temple at Abydos and Great Abydos Inscription	262–267
XII.		Ramses II's Temple at Abydos	524–529
XIII.		Memphis Temples	530–537
	1.	Great Abydos Inscription (l. 22)	260
	2.	Blessing of Ptah (ll. 32, 35)	412–413
XIV.		City of Tanis (Blessing of Ptah (ll. 16–18))	406
		Stela of the Year 400	538–542
		Royal Jubilee Inscriptions	543–560
I.		First Gebel Silsileh Inscription	552
II.		Bigeh Inscription	553
III.		Second Gebel Silsileh Inscription	554
IV.		Third Gebel Silsileh Inscription	555
V.		Fourth Gebel Silsileh Inscription	556
VI.		Sehel Inscription	557
VII.		El Kab Inscription	558
VIII.		Fifth Gebel Silsileh Inscription	559
IX.		Sixth Gebel Silsileh Inscription	560
		Inscription of Beknekhonsu	561–568
		Reign of Merneptah	569–638
		The Invasion of Libyans and Mediterranean Peoples	569–617
I.		The Great Karnak Inscription	572–592
II.		The Cairo Column	593–595
III.		The Athribis Stela	596–601
IV.		The Hymn of Victory	602–617
		Inscriptions of the High Priest of Amon, Roy	618–628
		Daybook of a Frontier Official	629–635
		Letter of a Frontier Official	636–638
		Reign of Siptah	639–650
		Nubian Graffiti	639–650

LIST OF FIGURES

	PAGE
Fig. 1. Plan of the Reliefs of Seti I, on the North Wall of the Great Hall of Karnak	39
Fig. 2. Seti I on the Route through Southern Palestine (Scene 1)	44
Fig. 3. Showing Two Superimposed Figures	61
Fig. 4. Inserted Figure of "First King's-Son"	61
Fig. 5. An Unknown Prince Following the Chariot of Seti I (Scene 14)	66
Fig. 6. Figure of an Unknown Prince Inserted in a Fragmentary Scene (§ 130)	66
Fig. 7. Map of the Orontes Valley in the Vicinity of Kadesh	126
Fig. 8. March to Kadesh: First Positions	128
Fig. 9. Battle of Kadesh: Second Positions	130
Fig. 10. Battle of Kadesh: Third Positions	130
Fig. 11. Battle of Kadesh: Fourth Positions	130
Fig. 12. Battle of Kadesh: Fifth Positions	130
Fig. 13. The Modern Mound of Kadesh	152

VOLUME IV

	§§
THE TWENTIETH DYNASTY	1–603
Reign of Ramses III	1–456
Medinet Habu Temple	1–150
Building and Dedication Inscriptions	1–20
Historical Inscriptions	21–138
I. Treasury of Medinet Habu Temple	25–34
II. First Libyan War, Year 5	35–58
1. Great Inscription in the Second Court (Year 5)	36–58
III. Northern War, Year 8	59–82
1. Great Inscription on the Second Pylon, Year 8	61–68
2. Relief Scenes Outside North Wall and in Second Court, Year 8	69–82
IV. Second Libyan War	83–114

		§§
1. Great Inscription on the First Pylon (Medinet Habu)		85–92
2. Poem on Second Libyan War		93–99
3. Relief Scenes on First Pylon and Outside North Wall (Medinet Habu)		100–114
4. Papyrus Harris		405
V. The Syrian War		115–135
VI. The Nubian War		136–138
Medinet Habu Temple Calendar		139–145
Act of Endowment of the Temples of Khnum		146–150
Papyrus Harris		151–412
Discussion of		151–181
Content:		
I. Introduction		182–183
II. Theban Section		184–246
III. Heliopolitan Section		247–304
IV. Memphite Section		305–351
V. General Section (Small Temples)		352–382
VI. Summary		383–396
VII. Historical Section		397–412
Record of the Royal Jubilee		413–415
Records of the Harem Conspiracy		416–456
I. Appointment of the Court		423–424
II. The Condemned of the First Prosecution		425–443
III. The Condemned of the Second Prosecution		444–445
IV. The Condemned of the Third Prosecution		446–450
V. The Condemned of the Fourth Prosecution		451–452
VI. The Acquitted		453
VII. The Practicers of Magic		454–456
Reign of Ramses IV		457–472
Hammamat Stela		457–468
I. The First Stela		457–460
II. The Second Stela		461–468
Abydos Stela		469–471
Building Inscription of the Khonsu Temple		472
Reign of Ramses V		473
Tomb Dedication		473
Reign of Ramses VI		474–483

	§§
Tomb of Penno	474–483
Reign of Ramses VII	484–485
Stela of Hori	484–485
Reign of Ramses IX	486–556
Inscriptions of the High Priest of Amon, Amenhotep	486–498
I. Building Inscriptions	488–491
II. Records of Rewards	492–498
The Records of the Royal Tomb-Robberies	499–556
I. Papyrus Abbott	509–535
II. Papyrus Amherst	536–541
III. Turin Fragment	542–543
IV. Mayer Papyri	544–556
Reign of Ramses XII	557–603
The Report of Wenamon	557–591
Records of the Restoration of the Royal Mummies	592–594
Letter to the Viceroy of Kush	595–600
Building Inscriptions in the Temple of Khonsu	601–603
THE TWENTY-FIRST DYNASTY	604–692
The Twenty-First Dynasty	604–607
Reign of Hrihor	608–626
Inscriptions of the Temple of Khonsu	608–626
Reign of Nesubenebded	627–630
Gebelên Inscription	627–630
Reign of the High Priest and King Paynozem I	631–649
I. Paynozem I as High Priest	631–635
Building Inscriptions	631–635
Records on the Royal Mummies	636–642
II. Paynozem I as King	643 ff.
Records on the Royal Mummies	643–647
Building Inscriptions	648–649
High Priesthood of Menkheperre	650–661
Stela of the Banishment	650–658
Record of Restoration	659
Karnak Graffito	660
Records on the Royal Mummies	661
High Priesthood of Paynozem II	662–687
Records on the Priestly Mummies	662–663
Records on the Royal Mummies	664–667

	§§
Record of Paynozem II's Burial	668
Stela of the "Great Chief of Me," Sheshonk	669–687
High Priesthood of Pesibkhenno	688–692
Records on Mummy-Wrappings	688
Burial of Nesikhonsu	689
Records on the Royal Mummies	690–692

THE TWENTY-SECOND DYNASTY 693–792
  Records of Nile-Levels at Karnak 693–698
  Reign of Sheshonk I 699–728
    Records on Mummy-Bandages of Zeptahefonekh . 699–700
    Building Inscription 701–708
    Great Karnak Relief 709–722
    Presentation of Tribute 723–724
    Karnak Stela 724A
    Dakhel Stela 725–728
  Reign of Osorkon I 729–737
    Record of Temple Gifts 729–737
  Reign of Takelot I 738–740
    Statue of the Nile-God Dedicated by the High Priest, Sheshonk 738–740
  Reign of Osorkon II 742–751
    Flood Inscription 742–744
    Statue Inscription 745–747
    Jubilee Inscriptions 748–751
  Reign of Takelot II 752–755
    Graffito of Harsiese 752–754
    Stela of Kerome 755
  Reign of Sheshonk III 756–777
    Annals of the High Priest of Amon, Osorkon . 756–770
      I. East of Door 760–761
      II. West of Door 762–770
    First Serapeum Stela of Pediese 771–774
    Record of Installation 775–777
  Reign of Pemou 778–781
    Second Serapeum Stela of Pediese 778–781
  Reign of Sheshonk IV 782–792
    Stela of Weshtehet 782–784

Serapeum Stela of Harpeson	§§ 785–792
THE TWENTY-THIRD DYNASTY	793–883
Records of Nile-Levels at Karnak	793–794
Reign of Osorkon III	795
Will of Yewelot	795
Reign of Piankhi	796–883
The Piankhi Stela	796–883
THE TWENTY-FOURTH DYNASTY	884
Reign of Bocchoris	884
Serapeum Stelæ	884
THE TWENTY-FIFTH DYNASTY	885–934
Records of the Nile-Levels at Karnak	885–888
Reign of Shabaka	889
Building Inscription	889
Reign of Taharka	892–918
Tanis Stela	892–896
Building Inscription in Large Cliff-Temple of Napata	897–900
Inscription of Mentemhet	901–916
Serapeum Stela	917–918
Reign of Tanutamon	919–934
Stela of Tanutamon	919–934
THE TWENTY-SIXTH DYNASTY	935–1029
Reign of Psamtik I	935–973
Adoption Stela of Nitocris	935–958
Statue Inscription of the Chief Steward, Ibe	958A–958M
First Serapeum Stela	959–962
Second Serapeum Stela	963–966
Statue Inscription of Hor	967–973
Reign of Necho	974–980
Serapeum Stela	974–979
Building Inscription	980
Reign of Psamtik II	981–983
Statue Inscription of Neferibre-Nofer	981–983
Reign of Apries	984–995
Serapeum Stela	984–988
Stela of the Divine Consort Enekhnesneferibre	988A–988J
Inscription of Nesuhor	989–995

	§§
Reign of Amasis (Ahmose II).	996–1029
Elephantine Stela	996–1007
Serapeum Stela	1008–1012
Statue Inscription of the General Ahmose	1013–1014
Statue Inscription of Pefnefdineit	1015–1025
Mortuary Stelæ of the Priest Psamtik	1026–1029

LIST OF FIGURES

	PAGE
Plan of Scenes and Inscriptions in Medinet Habu Temple	5
INDEX	521

EXPLANATION OF TYPOGRAPHICAL SIGNS AND SPECIAL CHARACTERS

1. The introductions to the documents are in twelve-point type, like these lines.

2. All of the translations are in ten-point type, like this line.

3. In the footnotes and introductions all quotations from the documents in the original words of the translation are in *italics*, inclosed in quotation marks. *Italics* are not employed in the text of the volumes for any other purpose except for titles.

4. The lines of the original document are indicated in the translation by superior numbers.

5. The loss of a word in the original is indicated by —, two words by — —, three words by — — —, four words by — — — —, five words by — — — — —, and more than five by ————. A word in the original is estimated at a "square" as known to Egyptologists, and the estimate can be but a very rough one.

6. When any of the dashes, like those of No. 5, are inclosed in half-brackets, the dashes so inclosed indicate not lost, but uncertain words. Thus ⌜—⌝ represents one uncertain word, ⌜— —⌝ two uncertain words, and ⌜————⌝ more than five uncertain words.

7. When a word or group of words are inclosed in half-brackets, the words so inclosed are uncertain in meaning; that is, the translation is not above question.

8. Roman numerals I, II, III, and IV, not preceded by the title of any book or journal, refer to these four volumes of Historical Documents. The Arabic numerals following such Romans refer to the numbered paragraphs of these volumes. All paragraph marks (§ and §§, without a Roman) refer to paragraphs of the same volume.

9. For signs used in transliteration, see Vol. I, p. xv.

THE NINETEENTH DYNASTY

REIGN OF HARMHAB

TOMB OF HARMHAB[a]

1. This splendid limestone tomb was built by the general, Harmhab, who afterward became King Harmhab. His career before he gained the throne is openly narrated in his Coronation Inscription (§§ 22 ff.); but the first step in the study of his life is the demonstration of the identity of the general and the king. This was first proved by the observation that the Vienna fragment may be fitted upon the Leyden blocks[b] (§§ 2–13). The construction of the tomb and execution of the reliefs belong to a period either just before or just after the Aton heresy of Ikhnaton; for Harmhab, in praising King Ikhnaton, states that he owes his kingdom to Amon[c] (§ 8); furthermore, the gods of Heliopolis—Horus, Osiris, Isis, Nephthys, and Hathor—are mentioned. As Amon is not erased in the tomb, this, with the mention of the other gods, would indicate that the tomb was constructed under Ikhnaton's weak successors, after the resumption of the Amon-worship, at a time when the commemoration of Harmhab's favor under Ikhnaton was not yet a political *faux pas*. But this is not certain.

---

[a]It originally stood in Sakkara, but has been ruthlessly destroyed. The few fragments which have survived are now in six different museums.

[b]See my remarks, *Zeitschrift für ägyptische Sprache*, 38, 47 ff.

[c]This has little or no bearing on the date of the event depicted in the relief, but only on the date of the execution of the relief. The later insertion of the uraeus shows that an anachronism like the assumed mention of Amon in Ikhnaton's presence might easily be perpetrated after the worship of Amon had been resumed.

I. LEYDEN FRAGMENTS[a]

1. STELA WITH ADORATION SCENE[b]

2. The hawk-headed Re, enthroned, is worshiped by the deceased, standing, who "shows in his body exactly those deformities by which the king Chu-en-Aten is to be recognized. The belly projects forward prominently, and heavy masses of fat are distributed along the entire body. His hair is curled, and about the neck he wears the braided necklace with which Chu-en-Aten was accustomed to reward his most faithful servants." The inscription of twelve very short vertical lines over the heads of the figures, is as follows:

Over the God

3. 1. Harakhte! Great god, lord of heaven, lord of earth; who cometh forth from the horizon. He illuminateth the Two Lands, the sun of darkness, as the great one, as Re.

Over Harmhab

4. Praise to thee! Re, lord of truth, great god, sovereign of Heliopolis!, May he grant a fortunate life, ⌜—⌝ in eternity, glory in heaven, favor in earth, for the ka of the commander in chief of the army, Harmhab, triumphant.

5. The content of the inscription, like the reliefs, shows plain traces of the influence of Ikhnaton's movement; although Aton is not mentioned. The following reliefs show clearly the relation of Harmhab to Ikhnaton.

---

[a]These fragments have never been published entire.

[b]Leyden Museum, V, 29; a rectangular tablet, the text of which was published by Wiedemann (*Zeitschrift für ägyptische Sprache*, 1885, 80, 81) without the reliefs of which he offers the above description.

2. REWARD OF GOLD[a]

6. These reliefs are in two series,[b] both representing Harmhab receiving the reward of gold from his king.

7. In the first series, the figure of the king (at the extreme right) is lost. Harmhab, wearing the uraeus, and with hands raised in rejoicing, is loaded with collars of gold; behind him (at the left) approach two long double lines of Asiatics, each pair led by two Egyptians; over these were lines of horsemen![c]

8. In the second series, the lower portion of the king's figure (at the extreme left) is preserved and shows unmistakably the peculiar characteristics found only in the representations of Ikhnaton. His queen stands behind him, as in the similar scenes at Amarna, and showing the same peculiarities of style. Below is Harmhab alone,[d] his neck loaded with golden collars, having before him the lower ends of three lines of inscription, as follows:

¹[Speech] ─────── in his presence, by the hereditary prince, count, sole companion, king's-scribe, Harmhab, triumphant. He says, while he answers ²[the king] ─────── [ᶠThe kingdom is thineᶫ] forever and ever; Amon has assigned it to thee. They muster [every] country ³─────── in their heart as one. Thy name is a fire ⁴───────.

9. Adjoining this scene on the right is a continuation,

---

[a]These reliefs have never been published. I secured photographs of them through the kindness of Dr. Pleyte. They are described by Leemans, *Description raisonnée des monuments égyptiens*, 40–41, C, 1–3; see also Leemans, *Monuments du Musée d'Antiquités*, I, 31–34.

[b]The upper portion, containing the inscriptions in each series, is unfortunately lost, and the extreme lower ends of a few lines remain.

[c]Only a long line of prancing horses' feet are visible; as there are no chariot wheels among them, and no human feet of men leading them (except at the extreme front), we may suppose that we have here a unique scene on an Egyptian monument—a troop of Asiatic horsemen. That the horses are being driven in a loose herd in the presence of the king is also possible.

[d]The head is lost, but of course it would show the uraeus, as everywhere else in the tomb.

showing Harmhab (on the left) received with acclamation by his household servants[a] (on the right), as he returns wearing his newly received collars of gold. Besides his two Egyptian servants appears a group of Asiatics,[b] like those in the first scene, all in postures of extravagant joy.[c]

II. VIENNA FRAGMENT[d]

10. The block contains a text of eight vertical lines above a relief scene, representing a group of Egyptian officials bowing (toward the left) to their superior, Harmhab (his figure is lost on the left), who is giving them instructions regarding the disposition of certain Asiatics, whose town has been attacked, plundered, and destroyed. The whole description shows that we have in these Asiatics, fugitives from the conditions in Palestine described in the Amarna Letters at this time. The arrival of these people must have fallen under the reign of Ikhnaton or his immediate successors. They desire a home in Egypt, as they say, "*after the manner of your fathers' fathers since the beginning.*" This, with the letter in Papyrus Anastasi[e] (VI, 4, 13 ff., and 5, 1 ff.), makes quite certain the custom of allowing the Asiatic Bedwin the privilege of settling in Egypt, to pasture their herds in the eastern Delta in times of distress, and is

---

[a]The same in the tomb of Eye at Amarna.

[b]Two Libyans are among them.

[c]One of them is on his back, and one on his belly. This explains the greeting in the Amarna letters: "At the feet of my lord the king ...... seven times and seven times with breast and back, I throw myself" (ed. Winckler, p. 285, No. 158, ll. 9–13). No. 157 has: "with belly and back."

[d]In the imperial collection; published by Wiedemann, *Proceedings of the Society of Biblical Archæology*, XI, 425; and Bergmann, *Zeitschrift für ägyptische Sprache*, XXVII, 125–27. Neither publishes the reliefs, for which I had my own photograph and collation of the original. I have published the photograph showing the relief in *ibid.*, 38, 47.

[e]§§ 637 ff.

an interesting parallel to the similar favor shown to Abraham and the kindred of Joseph.

11. These seven lines read:

¹———ᵃ Asiatics; others have been placed in their abodes ²——— they have been destroyed, and their town laid waste, and fire has been thrown ³———;ᵇ [ʳthey have come to entreatʳ] the Great in Strength to send his mighty sword before ⁴———. Their countries are starving, they live like goats of the mountain, [their] childrenᶜ ⁵——— saying: "A few of the Asiatics, who knew not how they should live, have come ⁶[ʳbeggʳ]ing [ʳa home in the domainʳ]ᵈ of Pharaoh, L. P. H., after the manner of yourᵉ fathers' fathers since the beginning, under ⁷———. Now, the Pharaoh, L. P. H., gives them into yourᵉ hand, to protect their borders."

12. Behind the officials receiving these instructions stood the Asiatics mentioned, as is shown by the fragment of one line of their inscription still surviving. It reads:

——— their boundaries — — ʳLordʳ of the Two Lands. They give praise to the Good God, the Great in Strength, Zeserkheprure (Harmhab).

Now, as this Vienna block has been shown to belong to the Leyden reliefs,ᶠ the conclusion would be that the royal figure in the Leyden reliefs must be King Harmhab. But the royal figure is clearly that of Ikhnaton. The difficulty is solved by the explanation of another incongruity in the tomb. Throughout its reliefs the figure of the general, Harmhab, wears the uraeus. This uraeus, as has been

---

ᵃAn uncertain amount is lacking at the beginning of each line; this is left unindicated by Wiedemann.

ᵇProbably, "*fire has been thrown* [*into their grain*];" see I, 658, ll. 15, 16.

ᶜAn obvious emendation.

ᵈThe restoration is exceedingly uncertain, but something similar must be supplied.

ᵉPlural.

ᶠI have published the Vienna block and the adjoining Leyden fragments in *Zeitschrift für ägyptische Sprache*, 38, 47.

clearly proved,[a] is a later insertion after the reliefs were finished. Hence the name of King Harmhab is a similar later insertion, and the Asiatics bowing, of course, like the officials, originally to the general Harmhab, are now represented as giving praise to the king Harmhab. The identity of the general and the king is thus demonstrated.

III. ALEXANDRIA FRAGMENTS[b]

13. The text recounted a journey of Harmhab to the upper Nile, as messenger of some king—a journey from which he returned successfully, bringing tribute which the king publicly inspected. Under this text is the figure of Harmhab wearing the uraeus and leaning on a staff.

¹——— ²⌜—⌝ He was sent as royal messenger as far as Aton shines, coming ³⌜———⌝ no land stood before him; ⁴he captured it in the passing of a moment. His name shall be remembered in ⁵the land of ⌜———⌝ He sailed northward. Behold, his majesty ⁶appeared upon a dais (used) at the bringing[c] in of tribute ⁷and the [tribute] ⁸of south and north was brought in. ⁹Behold, the prince, ¹⁰Harmhab, triumphant, ¹¹stood by the side of ———.

IV. BRITISH MUSEUM FRAGMENTS

1. DOORPOSTS[d]

14. These monuments are chiefly of a religious nature, but the movement of Ikhnaton was so largely religious that

---

[a]*Zeitschrift für ägyptische Sprache*, 38, 49, 50. The fan which Harmhab carries in his hand, has been shifted to one side and distorted. The old lines still visible show that in its original position, the top of the fan would have interfered with the uraeus; hence it was shifted aside to insert the uraeus.

[b]In the Collection Zizinia; published by Wiedemann, *Proceedings of the Society of Biblical Archæology*, XI, 424; it contains portions of eleven lines, the first and last very broken, and the beginning of all the lines wanting.

[c]Egyptian idiom, "*a dais of the bringing in of tribute.*"

[d]Nos. 550 and 552; Birch, *Guide to the Egyptian Galleries*, 36; Sharpe, *Egyptian Inscriptions*, II, 92; excellent photographs by Clark and Davies, London; I had also my own copy.

such texts from the transition period are historically important. Furthermore, the titles of Harmhab which they contain indicate unusual powers and connect the owner of this tomb with the Harmhab of the Turin inscription (§§ 22 ff.), thus confirming the identity of the general and the king, Harmhab.

15. Each of the doorposts has below a figure of Harmhab in adoration, wearing the uraeus as usual, and having strapped to his back his fan, as insignium of his office. His form clearly shows traces of the style of art which prevailed under Ikhnaton, e. g., the thin ankles, above which the limbs thicken too suddenly.

16. The texts are in six vertical lines above and before the figures, one being a Sun-Hymn, as follows:

[1]Utterance of the hereditary prince, Harmhab, triumphant, when he worships Re at his rising, saying:

"Praise to thee! who becomest[a] every day,
"Who begettest thyself[a] each morning,
"Who comest[a] forth from the body of thy[a] mother without ceasing.
"The two regions come to thee bowing down,
"They give to thee praise, when thou risest,
"When thou hast illuminated the earth with brightness.
"[2]Thy divine limbs flame as a mighty one in the heavens,
"Excellent god, eternal king,
"Lord of brightness, ruler of light,
"Upon his throne in the Morning-Barque,
"Great in brilliance in the Evening-Barque,
"Divine youth, heir of eternity,
"Who begetteth himself, who generateth himself.
"The great ennead worship thee,
"[3]The lesser ennead exult to thee;
"They praise thee in thy beautiful forms,
"With thy brilliance in the Evening-Barque,
"As when the sacred apes spy thee.

---

[a]The Egyptian idiom requires third person here.

"⁴Rise thou, thy heart glad,
"With thy diadems in the horizon of heaven;
"Grant thou glory in heaven,
"Power in earth,ª
"That I may go forth among thy followers ⁵of every day;
"That my heart may be satisfied with all offerings,
"May receive flower-offerings, from the sanctuary (ẖ· t-bnbn),
"Upon the table of the lords of Heliopolis."
⁶By the hereditary prince, count, wearer of the royal seal, sole companion, privy councilor of the palace, superior in the whole land, fan-bearer at the right of the king, general of the Lord of the Two Lands, real king's-scribe, his beloved, the hereditary prince, Harmhab.

17. The other doorpost bears the usual prayer to Osiris (but is important for the titles of Harmhab), as follows:

¹Praise to thee! Presider over the west; Osiris, ruler of eternity; Wennofer, lord of Tazoser; Anubis, lord of Rosta; the gods, lords of the necropolis. May they grant bread, beer, oxen, fowl, libations of water, wine and milk for the hereditary prince, the general in chief of the Lord of the Two Lands, king's-scribe, ²scribe of recruits, fan-bearer at the right hand of the king, overseer, giving satisfaction in the whole land, great in his office, great in rank, the two eyes of the king in the Two Lands, favorite of Horus in the palace, satisfying the heart of the king, ³with all monuments, overseer of works in the mountain of gritstone,ᵇ deputy of the king, presiding over the Two Lands, Harmhab, triumphant; he saith: "Homage to thee! Presider over the west, Osiris in the midst of Abydos. ⁴I have come to thee (extending) my two hands in adoration of the beauty of thy majesty. Set thou me among thy followers, like the glorious ones who enter ⁵the nether world, who live in truth every day. May I be one among them, (for) my abomination was lying, I executed ⁶truth upon earth without neglecting it.

"For the ka of the hereditary prince, real king's-scribe, his beloved, deputy of the king in the whole land, general in chief, Harmhab, triumphant."

ªCf. the prayer on the second Leyden fragment.
ᵇCf. Inscription of Amenhotep, son of Hapi (II, 917, l. 40).

2. STELA WITH THREE HYMNS[a]

18. Above, occupying about one-third of the stela, is a relief showing the divinities Harakhte, Thoth, and Mat, standing, before whom stands Harmhab worshiping. His head is (in the photograph) almost wholly destroyed, and the uraeus, if present, cannot be discerned. Over Re are the words: "*Harakhte, only god, king of the gods; he rises in the west, he sendeth his beauty——.*" Thoth and Mat bear the usual titles, while before Harmhab is a magical prayer.

19. The text of twenty-five lines addresses one after the other, Re, Thoth, and Mat, with the usual praise and prayers. These show clearly that the old traditional views are in full sway, although Aton is mentioned in l. 2: "*Thou art beautiful, youthful, as Aton before thy mother Hathor.*" The hymn is very interesting, but not historically important.

V. CAIRO FRAGMENTS

20. Two blocks,[b] apparently doorposts, contain the following important titles of Harmhab above his figure on each block seated at an offering-table and wearing the uraeus. Each column begins with: "*Hereditary prince, count, wearer of the royal seal, sole companion;*" and then proceeds with the further titles:

[1]Privy councilor of the palace (*pr-stny*), great in love with his lord, chief prophet of Horus, lord of Sebi (*Sby*);[c] for the ka of the general in chief, Harmhab. [2]Prince of the greatest of the companions, confidant of especial confidants (conclusion as in l. 1); [3]king's-follower on his expe-

---

[a]Published by Meyer, *Zeitschrift für ägyptische Sprache*, 1877, 148 ff.; photograph by Clark and Davies; I had also my own copy from the original.

[b]Mariette, *Monuments divers*, 74 = Rougé, *Inscriptions hiéroglyphiques*, CVII–CVIII.

[c]The place is unknown, but is probably connected, if not identical, with Alabastronpolis, the patron deity of which was also Horus; this Horus is the one whom the king claims as his special patron at his coronation (§ 27). The title, "*chief prophet,*" is an old nomarch title, and of course descended to Harmhab from his ancestors at Alabastronpolis.

ditions in the south and north country (conclusion as in l. 1). ⁴Greatest of the great, mightiest of the mighty; great lord of the people (conclusion as in l. 1). ⁵King's-messenger at the head of his army, to the south and north country (conclusion as in l. 1). ⁶Chosen of the king, presider over the Two Lands, in order to carry on the administration of the Two Lands, general of generals of the Lord of the Two Lands; for the ka of the real king's-scribe, his beloved, Harmhab. ⁷Giving satisfaction in the entire land, privy councilor of the palace, unique in his qualities, recorder of the troops; for the ka of the chief steward, Harmhab. ⁸Companion of the feet of his lord upon the battlefield on that day of slaying the Asiatics ($S\underline{t}\cdot tyw$)ᵃ (conclusion as in l. 1).

21. Several other fragments in Cairo contain the conventional mortuary prayersᵇ and show Harmhab wearing the uraeusᶜ and kneeling before various divinities, chiefly Osiris, Isis, and Nephthys. Finally there are two fragments in Bologna not noted heretofore; oneᵈ shows him wearing the uraeus, and plowing in the fields of Yaru in the hereafter; the otherᵉ contains part of an historical scene, showing the presentation of Negro captives, and mentioning the tribute of Palestine.

CORONATION INSCRIPTION

22. This important inscription relates: (1) the youth (ll. 1–5); (2) career at court (ll. 5–12); (3) coronation in

---

ᵃIt is impossible to suppose that Ikhnaton is the king meant here; it must be one of his successors, probably Tutenkhaton, by whom tribute was received from the north.

ᵇRougé, *Inscriptions hiéroglyphiques*, CIV–CVI.

ᶜMariette, *Monuments divers*, 75 = Rougé, *Inscriptions hiéroglyphiques*, XXXVI f.

ᵈNo. 1885. The fragment does not bear the name of Harmhab anywhere, but is identical in style with the known fragments of his tomb, and as the uraeus is clearly a later insertion throughout the fragment (six lines), it is undoubtedly another hitherto unnoticed wanderer from Harmhab's tomb.

ᵉNo. 1165. The style is unquestionably sufficient to identify this piece as belonging to the same tomb.

ᶠEngraved "on the back of a black granite group of two seated statues in the

Thebes (ll. 12-21); and (4) the early reign (ll. 21-26) of Harmhab. It shows clearly this king's obscure origin and his rise, through continued favor at court, to the kingship. The king who favored him is not mentioned; but the Leyden tomb reliefs (§§ 2 ff.) show that he was a favorite of Ikhnaton. It is possible that he is to be found among Ikhnaton's favorites at Amarna as Patonemhab.[a] He also enjoyed the favor of Tutenkhamon,[b] and it must have been one of these two kings of whom he speaks; probably the latter. He was the descendant of an old nomarchical house at Alabastronpolis. Rising from such beginnings, throughout the precarious reigns of Ikhnaton's successors, Harmhab skilfully maintained himself, and gradually gained a position of such power that by conciliating the priestly party of Amon, which was then again in the ascendant, he finally succeeded in seizing the throne. Thus, after their long struggle with the Aton heresy, we see the Amonite priests seating a second Pharaoh on the throne, as they had seated Thutmose III. From his home in Alabastronpolis he is led by Horus, as the piously veiled language of the inscription puts it, into the presence of Amon at Thebes, where he is crowned and his

---

Museum of Turin," representing Harmhab and his wife, Mutnezmet. The two sides also contained texts, which have disappeared, with the exception of nineteen signs on the lady's side, among which her name occurs. The statues are described by Birch (*Transactions of the Society of Biblical Archæology*, III, 486 ff.), who gives other references. The text of twenty-six lines was published by Birch (*ibid.*, facing p. 486) from a sketch by Bonomi, which the latter made from a squeeze taken by himself. It is very inaccurate, as Birch evidently worked from the squeeze in translating, and did not revise Bonomi's sketch. It was published again by Brugsch (*Thesaurus*, V, 1073-78), also very inaccurately. I have copied the original in Turin and collated the copy with the Berlin squeeze (No. 1253). This I again collated with the original in Turin.

[a]*Recueil*, XV, 50. The tomb of this man is at Amarna. Such a change of name, involving the substitution of Atou for Horus (Har), is common at this time. But I am more inclined to find in Patonemhab the man who was won to Harmhab's cause and became high priest of Re at Heliopolis, with the name Premhab (*Recueil*, XVI, 123 f.).

[b]Sayce, *Proceedings of the Society of Biblical Archæology*, XXI, 141.

titulary fixed by the gods. To make his claim on the crown legitimate, however, he next proceeds to the palace of the princess, Mutnezmet, the sister of Ikhnaton's queen, Nefernefruaton-Nofretete, who, although advanced in years, was a princess of the royal line, and is there recognized as her husband.

23. After the celebration of a feast in Luxor, the king proceeds northward, to restore the temples of the gods— an interesting indication of the destructive work of Ikhnaton's reform, in abolishing the old cults. Thus the old order and, particularly, the unchecked domination of Amon are restored. The calendar of feasts was immediately resumed and before he left Thebes, he celebrated the Feast of Ptah in his Theban temple. He left a record[a] of it in the Ptah-temple there:

> Year 1, fourth month of the first season, day 22, of the King Harmhab,[b] the day of the feast of "Ptah-South-of-His-Wall," lord of "Life-of-the-Two-Lands" in Thebes; at his feast were founded [the offerings] of the ancestors ————."[c]

This record enables us to determine that Harmhab remained in Thebes at least two months; for it is to be inferred that he was present at the above feast, which is about two months later than the Feast of Opet, during which he arrived at Thebes for his coronation.

Youth

24. [1]————[d] [Horus: Mighty Bull, Ready in Plans; Favorite of the Two Goddesses: Great in Marvels in Karnak; Golden Horus: Sat-

---

[a]Mariette, *Karnak*, Pl. 47, D; Legrain, *Annales*, III, 100.

[b]Double name.

[c]Doubtless a list of the restored offerings followed. A stela commemorating Harmhab's pious works in this temple has suffered too much to discern its content (*Annales*, III, 111, 112).

[d]The lacuna contained either: (1) the date, followed as usual by "*under the majesty of*" and the royal titulary; or (2) the frequent opening formulary, "*Live the Horus*," followed by the titulary.

is]ᵃfied with Truth, Creator of the Two Lands;ᵇ King of Upper and Lower Egypt, Lord of the Two Lands: Zeserkheprure, Setepnere;ᶜ Son of Re, Lord of Diadems: Beloved of Amon, Harmhab,ᵈ [Beloved of] Horus, lord of Alabastronpolisᵉ —— ᶠ ²———— ᵍ Bull of his mother, Amon, king of gods, was the one who brought him up; Har-si-ese, his guardian was the protector of his limbs. He came forth from the body, clothed with strength; the hue of a god was upon him; he made —— ³———— ʰ the arm was dropped to him as a child, obeisance among great and small, ⌜—⌝ him food and eatables, while he was a child, without his counsel ⁴———— ⁱ great before all the land; the form of a god was in his color, before the beholder of his form, the strength of his father, Horus. He set himself behind him; he that created him exerted his protection. The people brought all ⌜—⌝ — ⁵———— ʲ he knew the day of his satisfaction, to give to him his kingdom.

Appointment to Office

25. Behold, this god exalted his son before all the land;ᵏ he desired to extend his steps, until the coming of the day of his receiving his office, that he might give ⁶———— ˡ of his time. The heart of the king was satisfied with his affairs; (he) rejoiced at his choice; he appointed him to be chief (*r ᵓ -ḥry*) of the land, to administer the laws of the Two Lands as hereditary prince of all this land; he was unique, without his second. The plans ⁷———— ᵐ. [⌜He astonished⌝] the people, by that which came out of his mouth. When he was summoned before the king, the palace, it began to fear. When he opened his mouth, when he replied to the king, he pleased him with that which came out of his mouth. The only excellent one, without ⁸[his ⌜second⌝] ————.ᵐ

ᵃThe lacking portion of the full titulary is restored from the Karnak pylons of Harmhab, cf. Brugsch-Bouriant, *Le livre des rois*, 56, 57.

ᵇIncorrectly copied as a *t* by Birch.

ᶜMeaning: "*Splendid* (*is*) *the being of Re, Chosen of Re.*"

ᵈMeaning: "*Horus at the feast.*"

ᵉThis shows that the statue came from Alabastronpolis; it is omitted by Brugsch.

ᶠBirch adds "*Good God*," but it is not in his text.   ʰAbout one-third line.

ᵍAbout one-third line.   ⁱOver one-quarter line.

ʲOver one-quarter line. The subject of the verb is some god, as is evident from the next sentence.

ᵏWith the determinative of people.

ˡOver one-quarter line.   ᵐAbout one-quarter line.

His every plan was in the footsteps of the Ibis.ᵃ His decisions wereᵇ in accord withᵇ the Lord of Hesret;ᵃ rejoicing in accustomed usage like Thoth, pleased of heart therewith like Ptah. When he woke in the morning, he presented her ⌜due⌝; ⌜the way⌝ ⁹———ᶜ his affairs. As for one who walks in herᵈ way, it is she who protects him on earth forever.

Appointed Deputy

26. Behold, he administered the Two Lands during a period of many years; there reported [to him]ᵉ ¹⁰———ᶜ there [bowed down] to him the council in obeisance at the front of the palace, there came to him the chiefs of the Nine Bows, South as well as North; their hands were spread out in his presence, they offered praise to his face as (to) a god. All that was done was done under command ¹¹[from him]ᶠ ———ᶜ. When he came, the fear of him was great in the sight of the people; prosperity and healthᵍ were besought for him; he was greeted: "Father of the Two Lands, excellent counsel of divine gift,ʰ in order to administer ¹²——— "ᶜ

Coronation in Thebes

27. [Now, when many days had]ⁱ passed by, while the eldest son of Horus was chief and hereditary prince in this whole land, behold, this august god, Horus, lord of Alabastronpolis, his heart desired to establish his son upon his eternal throne, and [he] commanded ¹³——— of the —ʲ of Amon. Horus proceeded with rejoicing to Thebes, city of the lord of eternity, (and with) his son in his embrace to Karnak, to introduce him before Amon, to assign to him his office of king, to pass his life (as such). Behold, ¹⁴———ᵏ [⌜they came⌝ with rejoi]cing at his beautiful feast in Luxor. Heˡ saw the majesty of this god, Horus, lord of Alabastronpolis, his son being with him as king, introduced in

---

ᵃThoth.   ᵇLit., "*a part of.*"   ᶜAbout one-quarter line.
ᵈThe feminine pronoun in this passage refers to "*usage*" (l. 8).
ᵉCompare the duties of the vizier, Rekhmire, § 692, l. 22, and § 706, l. 29.
ᶠOr only the suffix, "*his.*"   ᵍA greeting accorded only to royalty.
ʰLit., "*of that which the god gives.*"
ⁱThe phrase so common in the folk-tales.
ʲBirch has "house," but it is not to be gotten from his text.
ᵏAbout one-eighth line.   ˡAmon.

order to give to him[a] his office and his throne. Behold, Amon-Re was filled[b] with joy when he saw [15][him coming] on the day of giving his offerings. Then he presented himself to this prince, the hereditary prince, head (ḥr-ḏ⸗ ḏ⸗) of the Two Lands, Harmhab.

Marriage to Mutnezmet

28. He proceeded to the palace, he brought him before him to the shrine[c] of his revered eldest daughter [16]— — —. [She did] obeisance to him, she embraced his beauty, and placed herself before him.

Rejoicing of the Gods

The gods, the lords of the ⌈fire-chamber⌉ were in exultation because of his coronation; Nekhbet, Buto, Neit, Isis, Nephthys, Horus, Set, all the ennead of gods who preside over the great throne [17]lifted praises to the height of heaven, rejoicing at the satisfaction of Amon: "Behold, Amon hath come, his son before him, to the palace, to set his crown upon his head, to lengthen his whole life. We have gathered together, that we might establish for him [18]—. Let us count for him the adornments[d] of Re; let us praise Amon on his behalf: "Thou hast brought to us our protector; grant to him the royal jubilees of Re, the years of Horus as king; for it is he who shall satisfy thy heart in the midst of Karnak, likewise Heliopolis and Memphis; it is he who shall make them splendid."

The Gods Fix the Titulary

29. [19]Let the great name of this Good God, and his titulary be made like (that of) the majesty of Re, as follows:
 1. Horus: Mighty Bull, Ready in Plans;
 2. Favorite of the Two Goddesses; Great in Marvels in Karnak;
 3. Golden Horus: Satisfied with Truth, Creator of the Two Lands;
 4. King of Upper and Lower Egypt: Zeserkheprure, Setepnere;
 5. Son of Re: Mernamon, Harmhab, given life.

---

[a]The ambiguity of the pronouns in this and following sentences is also in the original.

[b]Lit., "*permeated*."

[c]*Pr-wr.* There was, therefore, a shrine or chapel of the "*Divine Consort*" in the king's palace.

[d]Which Re once wore as King of Egypt.

Festival in Luxor

30. Then came forth to the ²⁰⌈rear⌉ in the palace the majesty of this august god, Amon, king of gods, his son being before him. He embraced his beauty crowned with the royal helmet, in order to assign to him the circuit of the sun.[a] The Nine Bows are beneath his feet. Heaven is in festivity, earth hath joy. The ennead of gods of Egypt, their hearts are happy. ²¹Behold, all the land was in joy, they cried out to heaven; great and small, they took up the jubilation; the whole land was rejoicing. After the completion of this feast in Luxor, Amon, king of gods, returned in peace to ²²Thebes[b] ($W^{\supset} \check{s} \cdot t$).

Restoration of the Temples

31. His majesty sailed down-stream as the image of Harakhte. Behold, he organized this land; he adjusted according to the time of Re. He restored the temples (from) the pools of the marshes[c] to Nubia ($T^{\supset}\text{-}pd \cdot t$). He shaped all their images ²³⌈in number⌉ more than before, increasing the beauty in that which he made. Re rejoiced when he saw them, which had been found ruined aforetime. He raised up their temples. He fashioned 100 images with all (their) bodies correct, and with all splendid costly stones. ²⁴He sought the precincts[d] of the gods, which were in the districts in this land; he furnished them as they had been since the time of the first beginning. He established for them a daily offering every day; all the vessels of their temples ²⁵were wrought of silver and gold. He equipped them with priests ($w^c b \cdot w$), with ritual priests, and with the choicest of the army. He transferred to them lands and cattle, supplied with all equipment.

Prayer for the King

32. They rise early to sing to Re in the morning ²⁶every day: "Mayest thou exalt ᵉfor usᵉ the kingdom of thy son who satisfies thy heart, Zeserkheprure, Setepnere (Harmhab). Mayest thou give to him a

---

[a]Aton.

[b]The palace was therefore at Luxor; the god has been at Luxor during the feast; he went in procession to the palace, and now returns from Luxor to Karnak.

[c]In the Delta; hence, from the Delta to Nubia. These temples had been neglected since the reform of Amenhotep IV.

[d]This rare word ($b^{\supset} k^{\supset} y \cdot t$) will be found applied to the sacred precinct of the cemetery at Abydos (Mariette, *Abydos*, I, Pl. 19, *e*).

[e]Birch has *m* (for *nn*), but as he also renders "*for us*," it shows clearly that he never revised Bonomi's text of the inscription for publication.

myriad of royal jubilees, and cause him to be victorious over all lands, like Har-si-ese, according as he satisfied thy heart in Heliopolis, united with thy divine ennead."

GRAFFITI IN THE THEBAN NECROPOLIS[a]

32A. The significance of these graffiti does not consist alone in the light which they throw upon the history of the robbery of the royal tombs at Thebes, showing that their violation began at least two centuries earlier than we had supposed; but they reveal to us also the state of anarchy which followed the religious revolution of Ikhnaton. It is only at that time that such an act could have taken place at Thebes, and we thus discern the turbulent conditions from which Harmhab rescued the country.

32B. Year 8, third month of the first season (third month), day 1, under the majesty of the King of Upper and Lower Egypt, Zeserkheprure-Setepnere, Son of Re, Harmhab-Mernamon.

Command of his majesty, L. P. H., to commission the fan-bearer on the king's right hand, king's-scribe, overseer of the treasury, chief of works in the "Eternal Seat" (necropolis), leader of the feast(s) of Amon in Karnak, Meya ($My^{\jmath}$), son of the judge, Yui (Ywy), born of the matron, Weret, to restore the burial of King Menkheprure ($M\bar{n}$-$ḫprw$-R^c, Thutmose IV), triumphant, in the august house[b] on the west of Thebes.

32C. Beneath is the name of Meya's assistant and the latter's parents:

His assistant, steward of the Southern City (Thebes), Thutmose, son of Hatey ($Ḥ^{\jmath \cdot} t$-$y^{\jmath} y$). His mother, Yuh (Ywh), of the City (Thebes).

---

[a]Written with ink on the wall of one of the lower chambers in the tomb of Thutmose IV in the Valley of the Kings' Tombs at Thebes; published in *The Tomb of Thutmose IV* (Mr. Theodore M. Davis' excavations), by Carter and Newberry, London, 1904, pp. xxxiii–iv, Figs. 7 and 8.

[b]His tomb.

THE WARS OF HARMHAB

33. Very little is recorded of Harmhab's relations with the foreign world. The scattered references on the surviving monuments are gathered here, recording his wars: I, in the North (§§ 34–36); II, in the South (§§ 37–44).

I. IN THE NORTH

34. The character and extent of these wars are very uncertain. The only sources are: (1) a list[a] of names, of which remains of eleven are preserved, among which appears Kheta; and (2) a relief [b]showing Harmhab leading three lines of captives and presenting them to Amon, Mut, and Khonsu. The costumes of the captives and their physiognomy indicate Asiatics. The inscription[c] with the middle[d] row is as follows:

35. The wretched princes of the Haunebu; [they say: "Hail to] thee! Thy name has encircled the two ends of the earth, among all lands; every land fears because of thy fame; thy fear is in their heart."

36. The lower row has the following:

The wretched princes of —; [they say: "Hail to thee! like the great ———; [fear] has entered into their bodies, terror is in their hearts."

II. IN THE SOUTH

37. An expedition to Punt, probably of a peaceful nature, is recorded on the wall connecting Harmhab's two Karnak pylons.[e] A relief shows the king at the right, holding

---

[a]On the north side of Karnak Pylon XI; Champollion, *Notices descriptives*, II, 178, and *Recueil*, XVI, 42. See Müller, *Mittheilungen der Vorderasiatischen Gesellschaft*, 1897, III, 276–78.

[b]*Recueil*, XVI, 42 f.

[c]Published also by Wiedemann, *Proceedings of the Society of Biblical Archæology*, XI, 423.

[d]That of the upper row is lost.

[e]Relief and inscriptions on the inside (west side) of the wall north of the door in the middle.

audience, receiving the chiefs of Punt approaching from the left, bearing sacks of gold dust, ostrich feathers, etc.[a] Their words are given in an accompanying inscription[b] as follows:

38. Speech of the great chiefs of Punt: "Hail to thee, King of Egypt, Sun of the Nine Bows! By thy ka! We knew not Egypt; our fathers had not trodden it. Give us the breath which thou givest. All lands are under thy feet."

39. Another scene[c] represents Harmhab presenting the newly acquired products of Punt to Amon, as indicated in the accompanying inscription:

Bringing the tribute, by his majesty, to his father Amon; being the tribute of Punt. "———[d] by thy victorious might. Thou hast set their chiefs in tumult, because of thy terror ——— bearing all their tribute upon their backs. Great is thy might in every country."

40. A campaign in Kush is recorded in a series of superb reliefs in the temple which the king had cut in the rocks at Silsileh.

Scene[e]

41. The king, accompanied by a fan-bearer and two sunshade-bearers, is seated on his throne, which is borne upon the shoulders of six soldiers. Before him march a priest offering incense, the Negro captives, and three lines of soldiers, whose trumpeter blows a fanfare in salutation of the king.

---

[a]Only the line of Puntite chiefs is published (Mariette, *Monuments divers*, 88).

[b]Mariette, *Monuments divers*, 88; Brugsch, *Recueil de monuments*, II, 57, 3 = *Recueil*, XVII, 43.

[c]Nowhere published; Wiedemann (*Proceedings of the Society of Biblical Archæology*, XI, 424) says: "a fragment lying quite near the wall alludes to them [Harmhab's victories], showing flowers and other gifts." He then adds the lower ends of the inscription long ago published, Champollion, *Notices descriptives*, II, 180, but without comment. It is translated above, § 39.

[d]An address of Amon to the king begins in the lacuna.

[e]Lepsius, *Denkmäler*, III, 121, *a–b*.

Words of the Bearers

42. "All health is with thee, O Lord of the Two Lands! Re is the protection of thy limbs."

Description of the Scene

The Good God comes, he triumphs over the princes of every country. His bow is in his hand like the lord of Thebes (Montu), puissant king, mighty in strength, who carries away the princes of wretched Kush, King Zeserkheprure (Harmhab),[a] given life. His majesty came from the land of Kush, with the captives which his sword had made, according as his father Amon commanded him.

Scene[b]

43. The king stands before Amon, both grasping a wand between them.

Inscription: Words of Amon

I have given to thee triumph over the South, victory over the North.

Scene[c]

44. A line of Negro captives advancing toward the first scene.

Words of the Negroes

"Hail to thee, King of Egypt, Sun of the Nine Bows! Thy name is great in the land of Kush, thy battle-cry is in their abodes. It is thy might, O good ruler, that makes the countries into heaps, O Pharaoh, L. P. H.! Thou Sun!"

EDICT OF HARMHAB[d]

45. This is the most important edict which has come down to us from ancient Egypt, and it is much to be regretted

---

[a]Usual double name and titles.
[b]Below at the left, Lepsius, *Denkmäler*, III, 20, b.
[c]Below at the right; Lepsius, *Denkmäler*, III, 120, a.
[d]A large stela discovered by Maspero in February or March, 1882. It is, or when complete was, about five meters high by three wide, and stands against one

that its very fragmentary state, together with the execrable manner in which it has been published, has deprived us of so many of its important data.

The edict contains the practical legislation of Harmhab by means of which he intended to prevent the oppressive abuses connected with the collection of taxes from the common people, who were continually robbed and impoverished by the fiscal officers. This legislation consists of a series of enactments, each of the following form:

a) Statement of the abuse as it existed before this legislation and the king's displeasure at it.

b) Statement of a hypothetical commission of the offense by the officials concerned.

c) Declaration of the penalty to be inflicted.

46. A very interesting question is whether these enactments have preserved on the stela the form and language of the original edict in the royal archives. It seems probable that, beginning with l. 13 (§ 50), we have the *ipsissima verba* of the original document, and that it continued to and included l. 2 (§ 62), although Müller is doubtful on this point.[a]

47. The content of the entire inscription is as follows:

---

of the pylons of Harmhab at Karnak. Over a third of the stone has broken off. The inscription occupies the face and the side edges. It has been copied and published very inaccurately by Bouriant, *Recueil*, VI, 41 ff.; important corrections, which unfortunately include only part of the inscription, by Piehl, *Zeitschrift für ägyptische Sprache*, 1885, 86 f.; see also *Revue égyptologique*, VIII, 106–9. I am greatly indebted to my friend, Mr. A. H. Gardiner, for a careful copy of the original on the spot. His copy corrects the incredibly numerous errors of Bouriant's publication, and fills out many of the lacunæ therein, though the stone shows loss since Bouriant's copy. Some fragments still surviving when Bouriant made his copy, Mr. Gardiner states, are now missing entirely. An exhaustive study by Müller, with translation and notes, in *Zeitschrift für ägyptische Sprache*, 1888, 70–94. The present translation owes much to Müller, for which I make general acknowledgment here.

[a]*Zeitschrift für ägyptische Sprache*, 1888, 75.

Front

Above was an adoration scene,[a] showing Harmhab worshiping before Amon.

I. Introduction (ll. 1–10, § 49).

II. Introduction: the king's zeal for the relief of the people (ll. 10–14, § 50).

III. Enactment against robbing the poor of dues for the royal breweries and kitchens (ll. 14–17, § 51).

IV. Enactment against robbing the poor of wood due the Pharaoh (ll. 17, 18, § 52).

V. Enactment against exacting dues from a poor man thus robbed (ll. 18–20, § 53).

VI. Enactment against robbing the poor of dues for the harem or the gods by the soldiers (ll. 20–22, § 54).

VII. Enactment against unlawful appropriation of slave service (ll. 22–24, § 55).

VIII. Enactment against stealing of hides by the soldiers (ll. 25–28, §§ 56, 57).

IX. Enactment against connivance of dishonest inspectors with thievish tax-collectors for a share of the booty (ll. 28–32, § 58).

X. Enactment against stealing vegetables under pretense of collecting taxes (ll. 32–35, § 59).

XI. Enactments too fragmentary for analysis (ll. 35–39; right side, ll. 1, 2, §§ 60–62).

XII. Narrative of the king's reforms, containing also an enactment against corrupt judges (ll. 3–7, §§ 63–65).

XIII. Narrative of the king's monthly audiences and largesses (ll. 7–10, § 66).

XIV. Laudation of the king, and conclusion (left side, § 67).

---

[a]Very fragmentary; it is the only source from which we gain the name of the king who issued the edict; Pl., *Recueil*, VI. Mr. Gardiner states that it is now missing.

48. In the translation it has been necessary to indicate the connection between the beginnings of the lines, a large portion of the ends having been lost.[a] These connecting insertions contain only what was probably the intervening thought, without any attempt to reproduce the lost words.[b]

I. INTRODUCTION

49. ⌜........¹⁰........⌝[c]

II. INTRODUCTION: THE KING'S ZEAL FOR THE RELIEF OF THE PEOPLE (LL. 10–14)

50. His majesty took counsel with his heart ⌜how he might¹⌝ ———[d] ¹¹[exp]el evil and suppress lying. The plans of his majesty were an excellent refuge,[e] repelling violence behind ———[d] ⌜and delivering the Egyptians from ¹²ᶠthe oppressions¹⌝ which were among them. Behold, his majesty spent the whole time seeking the welfare of Egypt and searching out instances ᵍ[of oppression in the land].ᵍ ———[d] ⌜came the scribe¹⌝ ¹³of his majesty. Then he seized palette and roll; he put it into writing according to all that his majesty, the king himself said. He spoke as follows: "[My majesty] commands ——— ⌜concerning all¹⌝ ¹⁴instances of oppression in the land.

ᵃBouriant says: "Des lignes visibles aujourd'hui les quatre premières ne présentent plus que quelques signes très mutilés et ne pouvant fournir aucun sens; les vingt-deux suivantes ont perdu environ les deux tiers de leur longueur primitive, quelques-unes même ont perdu plus encore. A partir de la vingt-sixième, les lignes gagnent en longueur mais elles sont coupées de lacunes fréquentes......" This is verified by Mr. Gardiner's scale copy. After l. 31 they rapidly decrease in length, and become so fragmentary that a coherent rendering is impossible.

ᵇThey often follow Müller, but I have carefully verified his conclusions in every case.

ᶜSee Bouriant's remark above (note a); the lines contained the usual eulogistic introduction with names and titles of the king. Its length, one-fourth of the entire inscription, is unusual.

ᵈAbout two-thirds of a line.

ᵉSame phrase applied to Amenhotep III (II, 916, l. 35).

ᶠMüller inserts here a fragment containing the ends of three lines, which should conclude ll. 11, 12, and 13. These ends fit 13 very well, 11 fairly, and 12 not at all; for some reason Müller has ignored the end of l. 12, or it would have been apparent that the alleged fragment of the end of l. 12 does not connect with the beginning of l. 13.

ᵍRestored from l. 14.

III. ENACTMENT AGAINST ROBBING THE POOR OF DUES FOR THE ROYAL BREWERIES AND KITCHENS (LL. 14-17)

51. If the poor man made for himself a craft with its sail, in order to be able to serve the Pharaoh, L. P. H., ⌜loading it with the dues for the breweries and kitchens of the Pharaoh, and he was robbed of the craft and⌝] ¹⁵the dues, the poor man stood reft of his goods and stripped of his many ⌜labors⌝. [⌜This is wrong, and the Pharaoh will suppress it by⌝] ¹⁶his excellent measures. If there be[a] a [⌜poor man⌝] who pays the dues of the breweries and kitchens of the Pharaoh, L. P. H., ⌜to the two⌝ deputies, [⌜and he be robbed of his goods and his craft, my majesty commands: that every officer who seizeth the dues⌝] ¹⁷and taketh the craft of any citizen (ᶜ nḥ) of the army or of any person who is in the whole land, the law shall be executed against him, in that his nose shall be cut off, and he shall be sent to Tha[ru].[b]

IV. AGAINST ROBBING THE POOR OF WOOD DUE THE PHARAOH (LL. 17, 18)

52. [⌜Furthermore, concerning the impost of wood, my majesty commands that if any officer find⌝] ¹⁸a poor man without a craft, then let him bring to him a craft for his impost from another, and let him send him to bring for him the wood; thus he[c] shall serve [the Pharaoh].

V. AGAINST EXACTING DUES FROM A POOR MAN THUS ROBBED (LL. 18-20)

53. [⌜Furthermore, my majesty commands that if any poor man be oppressed by⌝] [robbe]ry, ¹⁹his cargo be emptied by theft of them, and the poor man stand reft of hi[s good]s, [⌜no further exactions for dues shall be made from him⌝] ²⁰when he has nothing. For it is not good, this report of very great injustice. My majesty commands that restitution be made to him; behold, ————.

---

[a]Text has "*stand.*"

[b]This is a remarkable corroboration of Strabo, who mentions Rhinocolura as "so called from the colonists, whose noses had been mutilated. Some Ethiopian invaded Egypt and, instead of putting the malefactors to death, cut off their noses and settled them at Rhinocolura......" (XVI, II, § 31; translation of Hamilton and Falconer, III, 176). See also Herodotus, II, 137, and Diodorus, I, 60 and 65; and Müller, *Zeitschrift für ägyptische Sprache*, 1888, 81.

[c]The ambiguity of the pronouns is also in the original.

VI. AGAINST ROBBING THE POOR OF DUES FOR THE HAREM OR THE GODS BY THE SOLDIERS (LL. 20–22)

54. [ᶦFurthermore, as for those whoᶦ] ——— ²¹and those who bring to the harem, likewise for the offerings of all gods, paying dues to the ᶦtwoᶦ deputies of the army and ——— [ᶦmy majesty commands that if any officer is guilty of extortions or theftsᶦ], ²²the law [shall be executed] against him, in that his nose[a] shall be cut off, and (he) shall be sent to Tharu [Tᵓ-rw] likewise.

VII. AGAINST UNLAWFUL APPROPRIATION OF SLAVE SERVICE (LL. 22–24)

55. When the officers ($sḏm·w$) of the Pharaoh's house of offerings have gone about tax-collecting in the towns, to take [katha (kᵓ-tᵓ)-plant], [ᶦthey have seized the slaves of the people, and kept them at workᶦ] ²³for 6 days or 7 days, without one's being able to depart from them ᶦafarᶦ, so that it was an excessive detention indeed. It shall be done likewise[b] ᶦagainst themᶦ. If there be any place [ᶦwhere the stewards shall be tax-collecting, and any oneᶦ] ²⁴shall hear, saying: "They are tax-collecting, to take katha-plant ᶦfor themselves,ᶦ" and another shall come to report, saying: "My man slave (or) my female slave has been taken away [ᶦand detained many days at work by the stewards;" it shall be done likewise against themᶦ].

VIII. AGAINST STEALING OF HIDES BY THE SOLDIERS (LL. 25–28)

56. ²⁵The two divisions[c] of troops which are in the field, one in the southern region, the other in the northern region, stole hides in the whole land, not passing a year, without applying the ᶦbrandᶦ[d] of [ᶦthe

---

[a] See note on l. 17.

[b] The same punishment inflicted as in §§ 51 and 54; this is not the place for the penalty, which heretofore has followed, not after the narrative of the crime, but after a second, hypothetical statement of the crime. It is therefore anticipatory, and hence the full statement of the penalty, as in §§ 51 and 54, may have been repeated in the lacuna at the end.

[c] This important statement defines the two great divisions of the army, and shows that Herodotus' division of the Egyptian army of his time into Kalasiries and Hermotybies is not a late arrangement. See Müller, *Zeitschrift für ägyptische Sprache*, 1888, 82–84, and Wiedemann, *Herodots Zweites Buch*, 573–77.

[d] Text has "*fire*."

royal house to cattle which were not due to them, thereby increasing⌐] ²⁶⌐their⌐ number, and stealing that which was stamped from them. They went out from house to house, beating and ⌐plundering⌐ without leaving a hide for ⌐the people ———. Then the officer⌐] of Pharaoh went about ⌐to each one,⌐] ⌐to collect the hides charged against him, and came to the people demanding⌐] ²⁷⌐them⌐, but the hides were not found with them (⌐although⌐) the ⌐amount charged⌐ against them could be established. They satisfied them,[a] saying: "They have been stolen from us." A wretched case is this, ⌐therefore⌐ it shall be [done] likewise.[b]

57. When the overseer of the cattle of Pharaoh, L. P. H., goes about to attend to the loan-herds[c] in the whole land, and there be not brought to him the hides of the —[d] which are on the ⌐lists⌐,[e] ⌐he shall not hold the people responsible for the hides if they have them not, but they shall be released by command of his majesty,⌐] ²⁸according to his just purposes.[f] As for any citizen (ᶜ nḫ) of the army, (concerning) whom one shall hear, saying: "He goeth about stealing hides," beginning with this day, the law shall be executed against him, by beating him a hundred blows, opening five wounds, and taking from him by force the hides which he took.[g]

IX. AGAINST CONNIVANCE OF DISHONEST INSPECTORS WITH THIEVISH TAX-COLLECTORS, FOR A SHARE OF THE BOOTY (LL. 28-32)

58. Now, as for this other instance of evil which the ⌐official staff [h] were accustomed to commit, when they held inspection⌐][i] in the land, of that which happened[i] [⌐against the law⌐], [the table-scribe of] ²⁹the queen and the table-scribe of the harem went about after the official staff,

---

[a]The officers, here pluralized.
[b]The same punishment inflicted as in §§ 51 and 54.
[c]Herds of the Pharaoh which were contracted to be maintained by private individuals; see also Ameni (I, 522, ll. 16, 17; cf. Müller, *Zeitschrift für ägyptische Sprache*, 1888, 85 86).
[d]Only the determinative of the fallen enemy or criminal is preserved.
[e]Only an *r* is visible; perhaps to be read *rḫ·t*, "*list*."
[f]The meaning probably is that the cattle loaned on contract by the Pharaoh sometimes died, in which case the people must show the hides. These the corrupt officials often stole before the overseer of cattle arrived.
[g]Lit., "*thievishly*;" but see Spiegelberg, *Studien*, 68.
[h]Ḳnb·t? [i]Fragment placed by Müller.

punishing[a] them and investigating the ⌈affair⌉[b] —— of the one who sailed down- or up-river. One investigated it among the officials in the time of the King Menkheperre (Thutmose III).[c] Now, when the one who sailed down- or up-river whom they took; and when [⌈the superior officials of⌉] [the king],[d] Menkheperre, went about[d] [⌈after these officials⌉] ³⁰⌈each year,⌉ [⌈that they might make an⌉] expedition to the ⌈city,⌉ and that these superior officials might come to these officials; saying: "Give thou [to us] the consideration for the careless expedition;"[e] then, behold, the Pharaoh, L. P. H., made the expedition at the feast of Opet[f] each year without carelessness. One prepared the way before the Pharaoh [⌈and questioned the local magistrate, wherever he⌉] landed,[d] [⌈concerning the ³¹corrupt official⌉] causing him to ⌈— —⌉ what he (the corrupt official) was like. As for the one who goes about again, afterward, to seek the consideration — —, then these officials shall go about with the expedition[g] concerning the affairs of these poor people ——————— ³²———————.[h] My majesty commands to prevent that one shall do thus, beginning with this day ——————[i] the landing; he is the one against whom one shall prosecute it.

X. AGAINST STEALING VEGETABLES UNDER PRETENSE OF COLLECTING TAXES (LL. 32–35)

59. Likewise the ⌈collection⌉ of vegetables for the breweries [and kitchens of the Pharaoh and] ——————— [⌈Extortion was practiced, ³³and the officials plundered⌉] the poor, taking the best of their vegetables, saying: "They are for the impost [of the Pharaoh]." [Thus they] robbed the poor of their ⌈labors,⌉ so that a double [⌈impost was levied. Now, my majesty commands that as for any officials who come to⌉] collect vegetables [for] the impost of Pharaoh, L. P. H., in the

---

[a]Read ▸◂◂ and see Gardiner, *Inscription of Mes*, 21, note 59; also p. 40.
[b]Müller supplies *nkt*, "*affair*," which is exceedingly probable.
[c]The following is a description of the conditions under Thutmose III.
[d]Fragment.
[e]The meaning is: "We have gone about carelessly, intentionally overlooking your extortions; now divide with us."
[f]Early in October, when he had returned from the summer's campaign in Syria (see II, 409, 410).
[g]Meaning perhaps the expedition of the king, thus preventing collusion.
[h]About ten or twelve words.   [i]Eight or ten words.

arbors,[a] and the — houses of the estates of Pharaoh, L. P. H., and the — of Pharaoh which contain vegetables,[b] (concerning whom[c]) one shall hear, saying: "They — for any ⌜—⌝[d] of any citizen (ʿnḫ) of the army, or [any] people, [beginning with this day, the law shall be executed against them][e] ——— 35— — — transgressing commands.

XI. ENACTMENTS TOO FRAGMENTARY FOR ANALYSIS (LL. 35–39, AND RIGHT SIDE, LL. 1 AND 2)

60. The fragmentary condition of ll. 35–39 makes any coherent rendering impossible. They contain, however, a new enactment of the greatest interest regarding taxation of grain, in which there is an apparent contrast between the property owners, or citizens of the city, and the poor, thus:

61. Now as for these officials of the ⌜herds⌝, who go about ⌜— —⌝ in the southern region or the northern region collecting grain from the [citizens][f] of the city[g]. . . . . . . 36. . . . . going about . . . . in the southern region or northern region collecting . . . . .[g] from the poor. . . . .[h]

62. [i]——— going about taking possession to bring every citizen,[j] to cause them to see ——— (concerning whom) one shall hear, (saying) "ᵃ——— a crime, . ——— collectors of the harem who go about in the [⌜towns tax-collecting⌝] ——— the ⌜—⌝ of the fishermen ——— carrying the ———.

---

[a]Doubtless to be read: ʿwt n(t)-ḥt, like the ʿt-nt-ḥt of IV, 194, 264; and IV, 1021.

[b]Vegetable products in general are thus designated.

[c]The antecedent is "*officials*" (end of l. 33); see l. 28.

[d]Judging from l. 28, one would expect: "They steal vegetables, etc.," but Mr. Gardiner's copy clearly forbids.

[e]After l. 28.   [f]The following context shows that we must read ʿnḫ·w.

[g]Indications of measurements are given here, which need special study.

[h]Fragments of three lines more are visible.

[i]Proceeding to the right side (miscalled left by Bouriant). This text is so fragmentary that I have made no attempt to indicate the length of the lost portions, or my own omissions.

[j]Tw ɔ.

XII. NARRATIVES OF THE KING'S REFORMS, CONTAINING ALSO AN ENACTMENT AGAINST CORRUPT JUDGES (LL. 3–7)

Appointment of Two Judges

63. [3]I have improved this entire land — — — I have sailed it, as far as south of the wall,[a] I have given —————, I have learned its whole interior, I have traveled it entirely in its midst,[b] I have searched in —————— [4]⌜and I have sought two officials[1]⌝[c] perfect in speech, excellent in good qualities, knowing how to judge the innermost heart,[d] hearing the words of the palace, the laws of the judgment-hall. I have appointed them to judge the Two Lands, to satisfy those who are in ————. [⌜I have given to each one[1]⌝] his seat; I have set them in the two great cities[e] of the South and the North; every land among them cometh to him[f] without exception; I have put before them regulations in the daily register [of the palace][g] ————— [5]⌜— —⌝ I have directed [them] to the way of life, I lead them[h] to the truth, I teach them,[h] saying: "Do not associate with others of the people;[i] do not receive the reward of another, not hearing — — — —. ⌜How, then, shall those⌝ like you judge others, while there is one among you committing a crime against justice.

Now, as to the obligation of silver and gold — [6]— — [my] majesty remits it, in order that there be not collected an obligation of anything from the official staff (<u>knb·t</u>) of the South and North.[j]

---

[a]Probably not a reference to Ptah, but to some southern limit of the kingdom.

[b]See similar statements by Amenemhet III (I, 482, ll. 10, 11).

[c]The reference to "*him*" (in l. 4) shows that there were but two of these judges, one in each of the two cities. The two viziers must be meant. Mr. Gardiner, however (*Inscription of Mes*, 34), regards the passage as referring to the two great courts of the South and North (<u>knb·t</u> ⸦⸧·t).

[d]Lit., "*that which is in the body*" (Coptic *maht*, "viscera"), meaning the thoughts of a man.

[e]Thebes and either Memphis or Heliopolis, probably the latter.

[f]That is, every man with a complaint comes for redress to the official in whose jurisdiction he lives.

[g]Restored from Annals,(year 31, II, 472, l. 13).   [h]Omitted by Müller.

[i]Just what misdeed is implied in this first admonition is not clear. See l. 35 of the front, and Müller, *Zeitschrift für ägyptische Sprache*, 1888, 92.

[j]Müller thinks this refers to a percentage paid the state by the judges from the income of their office. (This is shown to be a fact by the inscriptions of Rekh-

Punishment of Bribery

64. Now, as for any official or any priest (concerning whom) it shall be heard, saying: "He sits, to execute judgment among the official staff (*ḳnbˑt*) appointed for judgment, and he commits a crime against justice therein;" it shall be against him a capital crime.[a] Behold, my majesty has done this, to improve the laws of Egypt, in order to cause that another should not be — — [b7]———.

Appointment of Local Courts

65. [⌜Behold, my majesty appointed⌝] the official staff (*ḳnbˑt*) of the divine fathers, the prophets of the temples, the officials (*ḥꜣtyw*) of the court (*ḥnw*) of this land and the priests of the gods who comprise the official staff (*ḳnbˑt*) out of desire that they shall judge the citizens (*ꜥnḫˑw*) of every city. My majesty is legislating for Egypt, to prosper the life of its inhabitants; when he[c] appeared upon the throne of Re. Behold, the official staffs (*ḳnbˑt*) have been appointed in the whole land — all — to comprise the official staffs (*ḳnbˑt*) in the cities according to their rank.

XIII. THE KING'S AUDIENCES AND LARGESSES (LL. 7–10)

66. [8]——— They[d] went around — times a month, ⌜which⌝ he ⌜made⌝ for them like a feast; every man sat down at a portion of every good thing, of good bread, and meat of the storehouses, of royal provision ———;[e] their voices reached heaven, praising all benefits — the heart of all the soldiers of the army. [9]⌜The king appeared to the people⌝ — — throwing (gifts) to them from the balcony[f] while every man was called by his name by the king himself. They came forth from the presence rejoicing, laden[g] with the provision of the royal

---

mire, II, 716 ff.) Owing to the strict prohibition of bribery, the king now remits this payment, allowing the judges to keep all their income from the people.

[a]Lit., "*a great crime of death.*" [b]See Spiegelberg, *Studien*, 50 f.

[c]As the king is speaking, the first person is to be expected here.

[d]These must be the inspecting officials who are thus so liberally provided for that they have no occasion to accept bribes, etc.

[e]Five or six broken words.

[f]The palace balcony; cf. Great Karnak Inscription of Merneptah (§ 587, l. 48, and note).

[g]Lit., "*victualed.*"

house; yea, they took ⌜grain-heaps⌝ in the granary, every one of them ⌜bore⌝ barley and spelt, there was not found one who had nothing ———— ¹⁰their cities. ⌜If⌝ they did not complete the circuit therein within three days, ⌜— —⌝ their khetkhet-officers hastened after them to the place where they were immediately. They were found there ————.

XIV. LAUDATION OF THE KING, AND CONCLUSION[a]

67. Little can be made out of these nine lines. In line 9, the conclusion of the whole edict can be discerned:

Hear ye these commands which my majesty has made for the first time governing the whole land, when my majesty remembered these cases of oppression[b] which occur before this land.

TOMB OF NEFERHOTEP[c]

68. This beautiful tomb, so well known to the tourist visitors at Thebes, contains wall scenes and inscriptions of great importance for the study of religious and mortuary customs. But it also contains one scene of historical importance, depicting the honors received by Neferhotep at the hands of his king, Harmhab.

Scene

69. At the right, in a balcony, stands King Harmhab, wearing a helmet, and carrying the royal scourge. He is accompanied by two attendants. Before him is a court

---

[a]Nine lines on the left side (incorrectly called right by Bouriant). According to Mr. Gardiner, there were originally ten lines.

[b]See ll. 12 and 14 (front), § 50.

[c]In the cliff of Assasîf at Thebes; published by Bénédite in *Mémoires de la mission française au Caire*, V, 489–540, and Pls. I–VI; partially by Dümichen, *Historische Inschriften*, II, xl, to xl, *e*, and *Flotte*, XXX and XXXIII; and Brugsch, *Recueil de monuments*, I, Pl. 37. This tomb is not to be confused with that of another Neferhotep in the cliff of Shekh Abd-el-Kurna, and published by Champollion, *Notices descriptives*, I, 546–51, 853 f.; Champollion, *Monuments*, 172 ff.; Rosellini, *Monumenti Civili*, 130, 131, 134; and Wilkinson, *Manners*.

marshal, accompanied by the two viziers, and behind these Neferhotep, with arms uplifted in rejoicing, is being decorated with golden collars by two attendants. Golden collars and bracelets, also intended for him, are lying on a table before the balcony. The accompanying inscriptions are these:

Over King's-Attendants

70. Superintendant of a royal domain, king's-butler, king's-attendant in every place.

Before King

71. Year 3 under the majesty of the King of Upper and Lower Egypt, Zeserkheprure-Setepnere (Harmhab).

Lo, his majesty appeared, like the sun in his palace of satisfying life, after offering bread to his father, Amon. At his coming forth from the Gold-House, acclamation passed through the whole land; and rejoicing, it reached heaven. The divine father of Amon, Neferhotep was summoned to receive the favor of the king's-presence: myriads of everything, of silver, gold, garments, ointment, bread, beer, meat, and cakes, at the command of my lord Amon, who secures my favor in the (royal) presence.

72. The ritual priest, pleasing the heart of Amon, Neferhotep; he says: "How many are the possessions of him who knows the gifts of that god, the king of gods. Wise is he who knows him, favored is he who serves him, there is protection for him who follows him, he is the sun of his body, the Aton who is his, [forever]a and ever.

73. After the presentation, Neferhotep, wearing his collars of gold, is met by his brother, Amenemyenet. Over his head is his name with the words: "*Rewarded with silver and gold by the king himself.*" He is followed by another priest, wearing similar collars, and accompanied by the following words:

Arrival in peace, bearing the favor of the king, by the divine father of Amon, Perennefer, triumphant.

---

a*Nḥḥ* must have fallen out here, but it is lacking in both publications.

REIGN OF RAMSES I

WADI HALFA STELA[a]

74. This stela was erected by Ramses I in commemoration of his pious works at the temple of Horus of Bohen (Halfa). These works consisted of new offerings, an increase in the number of priests and servants, and an addition to the temple building. Seti I, in recording on a second stela his own works in this temple, uses the identical form and words of his father's stela,[b] with the exception of the new building record which Seti, who built nothing here, omits. The occurrence of Seti I's name as king at the bottom shows that he was coregent with his father in the latter's second year. His father died not more than six months after the erection of this stela (§ 157), and reigned a maximum of two and a half years.

75. The reference to the *"captivity of his majesty"* (l. 8) would indicate that Ramses I had somewhere in Nubia carried on war; but as the inscription places him in Memphis, the occurrence of Seti I's name at the bottom may indicate that he (Seti) carried on the campaign, evidently in Nubia.

Introduction

76. [1]Year 2, second month of the second season, twentieth day. Live the Horus: Mighty Bull, Flourishing in Kingship; Favorite of the

---

[a]Discovered by Champollion in 1829 in the southernmost of the two temples at Wadi Halfa (Champollion, *Notices descriptives*, I, 32), and published by him (*Monuments*, I, 1, No. 2, and partially, *Notices descriptives*, I, 32–34); again by Rosellini (*Monumenti Storici*, 45, No. 1), and finally by Brugsch (*Thesaurus*, V, 1233 f.). Now in the Louvre (C 59), where I made the copy of it used in the accompanying translation.

[b]As both monuments are fragmentary, it is possible to fill up all the lacunæ in Ramses I's monument by reference to Seti's, except one. The brackets in the translation therefore represent restorations from Seti's stela.

Two Goddesses: Shining as King, like — [Golden Horus]: ———
²in the Two Lands; King of Upper and Lower Egypt: Menpehtire; Son of Re: Ramses (I), beloved of Amon, lord of Thebes and Min-si-ese, ³appearing upon the Horus-throne of the living, like his father, Re, every day.

Establishment of Offerings

77. Lo, his majesty was in the city [of Memphis ($Ḥ·t$-$k^{\jmath}$-$Ptḥ$)] performing the cerem]onies ⁴of his father, Amon-Re, Ptah-South-of-His-Wall, lord of "Life-of-the-Two-Lands," and all the gods of Egypt ($T^{\jmath}$-mry), according as they gave to him [might and victory over all lands], ⁵united with one heart in praising thy ka. All lands, all countries, the Nine Bows are overthrown ———. ⁶His majesty, the King of Upper and Lower Egypt: Menpehtire (Ramses I), given life, commanded to establish divine offerings for his father, Min-Amon, residing in B[ohen, the first[a] of] his [establishment] ⁷in his temple: 12 ($pr·t$-s) loaves; 100 ($by^{\jmath}·t$) loaves; 4 (ds) jars of beer; 10 bundles of vegetables.

Establishment of Priests

78. Likewise [this temple was filled with prophets, ritual priests] ⁸and priests ($w^c b$); his storehouse was filled with male and female slaves, of the captivity of his majesty, the King of Upper and Lower Egypt, Menpehtire (Ramses I), [given life, like Re, forever and ever].

New Building

79. ⁹His majesty was — watchful, he was not slothful in seeking exce[llent things to do them for his father] ¹⁰Min-Amon, residing in Bohen (*Bhny*), making for him a temple like the horizon of heaven, wherein Re [rises].

Here follows the double name of Seti I without connection with the preceding; it concludes the inscription.

---

[a]This was possibly not "*first*" in Ramses I's inscription; but it probably was so, or the number of his establishment would not be mentioned at all.

REIGN OF SETI I

KARNAK RELIEFS[a]

80. These reliefs form the most important document surviving from Seti I's reign, being practically our only source for his wars. Unfortunately, their function was a religious one; they furnish us a series of scenes presenting the wars of Seti I in their religious aspect, accompanied by a few meager explanatory inscriptions annexed to the principal actors in each scene. These scenes, like the Annals of Thutmose III, again illustrate the nature of the compact between the Pharaoh and his god: on the one hand, the god grants the Pharaoh the might which prevails over all the nations; on the other, the Pharaoh offers to the god the captives and the plunder thus gained. According to these scenes, the wars of Seti have but one aspect, and that is religious. Even in the arrangement of the scenes on the wall this is evident. Distributed symmetrically on each side of the temple door (see Fig. 1), the action of the suc-

---

[a]This, the most extensive series of war reliefs in Egypt, occupies the exterior of the entire northern wall of the great hypostyle hall in Karnak, and extends also eastward around the corner onto the eastern face of the eastern wall of the hall. The reliefs are arranged in three rows, one above the other, all of the top row being lost except one scene (see Fig. 1). They have been often published, and a statement of the publications will be found inserted in each scene (Fig. 1). But none of the publications meets the demands of modern epigraphic accuracy. I arranged all the inscriptions as given by the several publications in parallel columns, and checked these to some extent by photographs; but my photographs were unfortunately made after the lower row was again encumbered by débris. What purports to be an accurate publication of the inscriptions collated with photographs is given by Guieysse (*Recueil*, XI, 52–77). I collated over half of Guieysse's publication, and found it so excessively inaccurate that it was useless to insert its variants, and I did not employ it further. (See my note, *Zeitschrift für ägyptische Sprache*, 37, 139, n. 5.) On the princes in these reliefs, see my remarks, *ibid.*, 37, 130–39.

cessive scenes converges on that door, until the final scenes on each side of it represent the culminating sacrifice in the temple itself in the presence of the god. At the two extreme ends, as far from the door as possible, are the battles and marches of the war in distant lands; moving toward the door follow the capture and deportation of prisoners, the arrival in Egypt, the presentation of prisoners and spoil to Amon, and finally on either side of the door itself the slaying of captive princes, who are thus sacrificed in the temple by the king himself in the presence of Amon.

81. The only date in these reliefs is that of the year 1, which occurs only with the reliefs of the Shasu campaign. It is absurd to suppose that Seti I completed a war with the Libyans, a campaign against the Shasu, the conquest of Palestine and some of southern Syria, and a war with the Hittites, and finally accomplished the return to Thebes, all in one year.

In the opinion of the present writer, the arrangement above described indicates at least two great periods of war, each made by the artist to culminate in a human sacrifice before Amon.[a] The first (east of the door, Scenes 1–11) is a war in the year 1[b] against the Shasu, followed by a

---

[a]This does not overlook the fact that the geographical list accompanying each sacrificial scene is identically the same. The whole series of scenes was planned after the completion of Seti's conquests, and the total territory gained could not, of course, then be cut up and assigned to different campaigns. Moreover, these two lists are only intended to convey the impression of vast conquest, and are so full of mistakes and repetitions as to show clearly that their compiler had no definite idea of the territory covered.

[b]This date occurs only on the east side of the door (thrice, Scene 3, Scene 8, and Scene 9, all in the Shasu row), and dates both beginning and end of of Seti's first campaign. There is no more reason for supposing that the Syrian campaign on the west side of the door, which bears no date, necessarily took place in year 1, than that two contiguous undated campaigns of Thutmose III must belong to the same year.

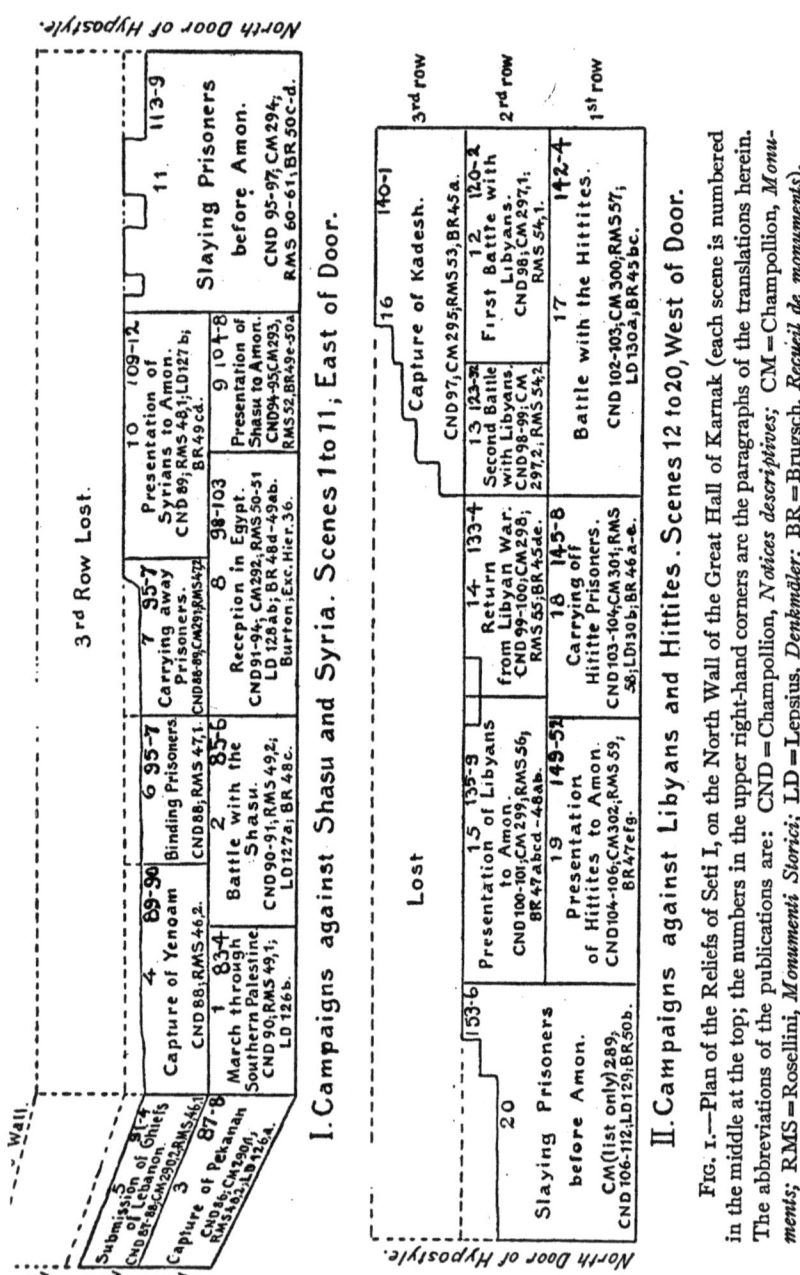

FIG. 1.—Plan of the Reliefs of Seti I, on the North Wall of the Great Hall of Karnak (each scene is numbered in the middle at the top; the numbers in the upper right-hand corners are the paragraphs of the translations herein. The abbreviations of the publications are: CND=Champollion, *Notices descriptives*; CM=Champollion, *Monuments*; RMS=Rosellini, *Monumenti Storici*; LD=Lepsius, *Denkmäler*; BR=Brugsch, *Recueil de monuments*).

campaign to the north as far east as the Hauran;[a] thence westward along the Phœnician coast, perhaps as far as Simyra, and Ullaza; the second, preceded by a subordinate campaign against the Libyans, is the further prosecution of the Syrian conquest. The method pursued is exactly that of Thutmose III in his conquest of 130 years before (II, 396), viz., first to gain control of the Phœnician coast, and thoroughly establish connection with Egypt by sea, so that reinforcements and supplies for the next campaign might land at one of the Phœnician harbors from which as a base he could move upon the interior of Syria, especially the Orontes valley.[b] From the coast the war was now carried inland and northward between the Lebanons, where the Egyptians met the Hittites for the first time in battle.[c] It

---

[a]Professor G. A. Smith discovered a monument showing Seti I worshiping Amon and Mut in the Hauran, in 1901, at "Tell-esh-Shihâb" (*Athenæum*, July 6, 1901; *Académie des Inscriptions*, October 18, 1901). But see § 140.

[b]That Seti follows the method of Thutmose III is evident at every step. His first campaign, like that of Thutmose III, is through southern Palestine; then, like Thutmose III, he moves northward through Palestine and subdues the Lebanon. Before Thutmose III can move upon Kadesh, he secures the Phœnician coast (fifth campaign), and attacks Kadesh the next season. It can be no accident that the campaign of Seti's first year subdues Lebanon and the Phœnician coast, while the (undated) campaign west of the door shows him in the Hittite country on the Orontes. The undated Hittite campaign here clearly bears the same relation to the coast campaign as in the case of Thutmose III.

[c]A glance at Fig. 1 will show that the arrangement of the wars on each side of the door strikingly indicates that they fall into two groups. One row on each side is a preliminary campaign near home, while the other rows on each side are the more important distant battles and conquests, thus:

Lost		Lost	Kadesh
Syria (without date)	Door	Libya (without date)	
Shasu (year 1)		Hittites (without date)	

We thus get two groups of wars: (1) Shasu-Syrian wars; (2) Libyan-Hittite wars. The further question now arises, whether each row does not represent a separate war. This is clearly the case with the two lower rows on the right-hand

is possible that Seti at this time reached even as far north as Naharin, as he claims in his lists;[a] but the Hittite power was evidently not broken, and Seti could not push his permanent northern boundary beyond an east-and-west line running through the Phœnician coast (probably well south), eastward into the Hauran, and his son, Ramses II, was obliged to spend long years in the struggle for the upper Orontes valley (§§ 294 ff.).[b]

82. 1. In harmony with the supposition of several campaigns in Asia is the fact that Seti numbered his campaigns, or at least began to do so. Furthermore, on returning from the campaign of the year 1, a rebellion is announced to him, as in the case of Thutmose IV (II, 826) for example, calling for a further campaign. A stela,[c] erected in the Ptah-temple at Karnak in his first year after his return from the first campaign, runs thus:

---

side of the door; on the left-hand side it is probable, for only the Shasu war is dated, and he returns from that war (Scene 8) by land, of course, whereas he would more probably return by sea (as did Thutmose III), had he pushed on directly from the Shasu war into Syria, and gained possession of the Phœnician coast. If, therefore, each row represents a different war, Seti fought at least four Asiatic campaigns (besides the Libyan war), of which one is in the south and three in the north.

[a]It must not be forgotten that, with the exception of the scene of the capture of Kadesh (Scene 16, Fig. 1), the entire uppermost row of Seti's reliefs (that is, about one-third of them) is lost. As the capture of Kadesh shows, this uppermost row dealt with his northernmost advance inland. We may therefore have lost in this row full corroboration of the northern advance claimed in the lists.

[b]Other references to Seti's conquests are few in number: (1) The Wadi Halfa Stela (§§ 157 ff.). (2) The stela of Hori from Abydos (Mariette, *Abydos*, II, 51, which is incorrectly numbered 57), where Seti is seen before Osiris saying: "*I have made for thee great herds of cattle from the captivity of my might.*" Hori's titles were: "*Overseer of herds of the house ($ḥ·t$) of Menmare*, (named:) '*The-Heart-is-Satisfied-in-Abydos*,' and mayor, Hori, belonging to '*The-Tower ($bḫn$)-of-Ramses.*'" The last is some fortified place (cf. Scene 3) established or named by Seti's father, Ramses, from which Hori came. (3) The Elephantine Stela (§§ 203, 204); (4) He is called: "*Slayer of Palestine, smiter of Kush*," in a rock inscription at Silsileh (Lepsius, *Denkmäler*, III, 141, g). (5) The list on the north wall, Karnak (*loc. cit.*, III, 144; see note on Scene 11, § 114, note).

[c]Legrain, *Annales*, III, 112, 113.

¹Year 1 under the majesty of Seti I ..... ⁵...ᵃ His majesty returned with glad heart from his first victorious campaign, ⁶when his onset passed over every country, and he took captive the rebellious countries by the puissance of his father, Amon, who decreed to him victorious might. He puts himself before him with glad heart ⁷furnishing ⌈protection⌉ for his son, assigning to him South, North, West, and East. They who invade his border are gathered together and delivered into his hand. There is none that thrusts aside his hand, carrying away their chiefs ⁸as living captives, with their tribute upon their backs, presenting them to his august father, Amon, and his associate gods, in order to fill their storehouse with male and female slaves, ⁹the captivity of every country. Lo, his majesty was at the Southern City (Thebes), performing the pleasing ceremonies of his father, Amon-Re, lord of Thebes ———.

2. The announcement of hostilities,ᵇ by a messenger who found the king thus engaged, unquestionably followed. This cannot be the announcement of the Shasu invasion of the year 1, which is already past. It can only be that of the Libyans, who are now invading the Delta. This supposition becomes extremely probable, if not a certainty, when we note that Seti I spent the next year in the Delta, as proved by the billsᶜ for the maintenance of his court during year 2 and part of year 3. They show that Seti spent practically the whole of the year 2 in the Delta,ᵈ Memphis, or Heliopolis. This would indicate that he fought the Libyan war in that year.

ᵃFull title and several lines of conventional encomium.

ᵇAs so frequently in such inscriptions, e. g., II, 826.

ᶜPapyri in the Bibliothèque Nationale at Paris, published by Spiegelberg, *Rechnungen aus der Zeit Seti I*. The numbers used are his.

ᵈIn year 2 he was at Memphis from the second to the fourth of the first month (Bill 2); in the eastern Delta on the seventh, and in the same place from the fourteenth of the first month to the thirtieth of the fourth month (Bill 2), with the exception of the twenty-third and twenty-eighth of the fourth month, when he was in Memphis (Bill 5). On the sixteenth of the sixth month he was in Heliopolis (Bill 7); and from the seventh of the fourth month (with the above exceptions) to the seventeenth (?) of the eleventh month he was in the eastern Delta (Bill 3).

In the following treatment each scene is numbered as in Fig. 1, where its position on the wall can be instantly determined.

SCENE I. MARCH THROUGH SOUTHERN PALESTINE[a]

83. On leaving Tharu, his last station in Egypt, Seti strikes into the desert south of and merging into Palestine. Here he finds only fortified water stations[b] at intervals along the way, which are depicted (Fig. 2), each with its name added, in the relief. The interspersed inscriptions are these:

Over King, Left of Sun

Lord of the Two Lands: Menmare; Lord of Diadems [Seti-Merneptah].

In Fortress

84. Town (*dmy*) ——.

Over Horses

Great first span of his majesty: "Amon-Assigns-to-Him-the-Victory," also called: "Anath (ᶜ *n-ty-t*)-is-Satisfied."

Over Horses Each Side of Fortress

¹The Good God achieving with his arms, an archer like Montu, residing in Thebes, ————, smiting ²the Asiatics, making his boundary as far as his desire places it; his arm is not repulsed ³in all the lands; the king who protects ⁴Egypt, who pierces ⁵the wall ⁶in the rebellious countries. ⁷He causes the chiefs of Kharu ($Ḥ$ ᵓ-*rw*) ⁸to cease every contradiction of their mouths. His mighty sword ⁹is his[c] valor; his might is like the son of Nut.

Over Princes, behind Chariot

———— every country beneath [thy] sandals ————.

---

[a]Bibliography in Fig. 1.

[b]See Müller (*Asien und Europa*, 134).

[c]The second arm is probably to be corrected to the possessive *f*, as Guieysse has done.

Fig. 2.—Seti I on the Route through Southern Palestine (Scene I, §§ 83, 84). (This example may serve to illustrate the character of this series of reliefs.)

In Fort, over Horses

Town [*dmy*], which his majesty built anew at the well of Hu — ti (*Ḥw — ty*).[a]

Under Fort, over Horses

The victory ——— Menmare, heir of Re.

——— [H]arabat (⌈H⌉ ꜣ -r ꜣ -b ꜣ -ty, with determinative of a well.)

Under Fort, under Horses

The well: "Menmare-is-Great-in-Victory."

In Pool, under Horses

The pool: "Sweet."

SCENE 2. BATTLE WITH THE SHASU[b]

85. Pushing along this road in the Negeb, the king scatters the Shasu, who from time to time gather in sufficient numbers to meet him. One of these actions is depicted in this relief as taking place on the desert road, with the neighboring fortified stations indicated as in the preceding scene (§§ 83, 84).

In King's Bow

86. Menmare, Seti-Merneptah.

In Fortress, Right End

The stronghold (*bḫn*) of Menmare (called): "The-——-His-Protection."

Under Same

"The Fortress (*nḫtw*) of Seti-Merneptah."

---

[a] The restoration of Guieysse, viz., *bw-r* ꜣ between *Ḥw* and *ty*, is merely a guess. It is more likely we should restore according to the broken line under the fort, where a word of which the beginning is lacking has also the determinative of a well (like the broken word in the fortress), thus: [*H*] ꜣ -r ꜣ -b ꜣ -ty (and determinative of well). The *H* is uncertain, but exceedingly probable. Thus our word in the fortress is probably *Ḥw-*[*r* ꜣ -*b* ꜣ]-*ty*, though two of the copies (Champollion, *Notices descriptives*, and Lepsius, *Denkmäler*) show the beginning of a bird with a stroke (*b* ꜣ ?), as the sign after *ḥw*. This is surely חָרְבָה, "desert" or "ruin."

[b] For bibliography, see Fig. 1.

Middle Fortress
Town (*dmy*) which [his] majesty [buil]t a[new].

In Pool
The pool: "Ibsekeb" (*Yb-s ᵓ -k ᵓ -b ᵓ*).

Under Fortress, Left End
The well of Seti-Merneptah.

Over Battle
The Good God, Sun of Egypt, Moon of all lands, Montu in the foreign countries; irresistible, mighty-hearted like Baal, there is none that approaches him on the day of drawing up the battle-line. He has extended the boundaries of Egypt as far as the heavens on every side. The rebels, they know not how they shall [flee];[a] the vanquished of the Shasu, who were —, — — his majesty; [becoming like] that which exists not.

SCENE 3. CAPTURE OF PEKANAN[b]

87. The fighting with the Shasu, as depicted in the preceding scene, continued until Seti reached Canaan. Somewhere on the frontier, not far into Asia, Seti apparently meets a fortified town, to which the relief gives the name "*Pekanan*" or "*the Canaan.*" Exactly what this name means here is not certain. Pekanan is used in the text (§ 88) to indicate the limits of the war with the Shasu since the king has left Tharu, his last stop in Egypt. "*The town of Pekanan*" would seem, therefore, to indicate the place of his arrival in Canaan, as Müller thinks (*Asien und Europa*, 205); but this is not certain. The Egyptians called the entire west of Syria-Palestine "Canaan,"[c] and it

---

[a]Determinative of legs is preserved.

[b]For publications, see Fig. 1, to which may be added Sharpe, *Egyptian Inscriptions*, II, 48.

[c]*Pekanan;* "*Pe*" is the article, the whole being "*the Canaan*" as we say "the Levant."

is only certain that Seti is now fighting somewhere in that country.

Over King

88. King of Upper and Lower Egypt: Menmare, Son of Re: Seti-Merneptah, given life, like Re, beloved of Menhyt.

Fortress

Town (*dmy*) of Pekanan (P°-k°-n^{c}-n°).

Over Horses

Great first span of his majesty: "Victory-in-Thebes."

Over Enemy

¹Year 1. King of Upper and Lower Egypt, Menmare (Seti I). The destruction ²which the mighty sword of Pharaoh, L. P. H., made among the ³vanquished of the Shasu ($Š^{\circ}$-sw) from ⁴the fortress of Tharu (T°-rw) to ⁵Pekanan (P°-k°-n^{c}-n°), when his majesty ⁶marched against them like a fierce-eyed lion, ⁷making them carcasses in their ⁸valleys, overturned in their blood like ⁹those that exist not. Everyone that escapes his fingers ¹⁰says: "His might toward distant countries is ¹¹the might of his father, Amon, who hath assigned to him[a] ¹²victorious valor in the countries ($ḫ^{\circ}s\cdot wt$)."

SCENE 4. CAPTURE OF YENOAM

89. Seti has now traversed the entire length of Palestine. His lists (§ 114) show that after crossing Carmel he captured Peher and Bethshael, both in the plain of Jezreel, and then proceeded to Akko, whence he marched along the Phœnician coast to Tyre and Othu. Our relief represents the capture of Yenoam, which lies a short distance inland from the last two cities. It is depicted surrounded by forest, as we should expect.

Name in Fortress

90. Town of Yenoam (Y-nw-$^{c\circ}$-mw).

---

[a] Guieysse, "*to thee.*"

SCENE 5. SUBMISSION OF THE CHIEFS OF LEBANON[a]

91. Leaving Tyre and Othu, Seti now pushed northward, and advanced along the coast of Phœnicia, as indicated by his lists (§ 114). As he passes Lebanon, he receives the submission of its local dynasts, and secures cedar[b] for his temples in Egypt. This the Syrians are depicted as felling, while one of Seti's officers assures him of their submission. The name of this officer is not given, but he has been identified by Wiedemann with the prince appearing in the Libyan campaign, for which there is no evidence.[c]

92. According to Seti's lists (§ 114), he advanced northward along the coast past Simyra and Ullaza, but the upper row of reliefs, which contained the northernmost conquests,[d] has unfortunately been lost, and we are unable to control the lists or trace this coast march in detail. If Seti really reached Simyra and Ullaza, it was only the intervening mountains on the east which prevented a collision with the Hittites.

93. Having secured the coast,[e] as did his great ancestor, Thutmose III, Seti returned home with his plunder. He was now certain of a harbor for his sea connection with Syria on the next campaign—a connection which would greatly facilitate future operations in the North.

In Fortress

94. Town (*dmy*) of Kader ($K^{\flat}$-*dw-rw*) in ⌐Pemehtem ($P^{\flat}$-*mḫ-t*$^{\flat}$-*m*$^{\flat}$)⌐.[f]

---

[a]For bibliography, see Fig. 1.   [b]See my *New Chapter*, 28, 29.
[c]See my remarks, "Ramses II and the Princes in the Karnak Reliefs of Seti I," *Zeitschrift für ägyptische Sprache*, 37, 136, 137.
[d]As shown by the one scene (the capture of Kadesh) preserved in this uppermost row.
[e]It is difficult to say just where Seti attempted to fix his northern boundary in Phœnicia; if Ramses II's stelæ at Beyrut are boundary marks, as seems probable, then Seti's boundary is almost certain to have been south of Beyrut, as Ramses would probably not mark off less than his father held.
[f]So Guieysse, but Champollion, *Notices descriptives*, omits *t*$^{\flat}$, and Champol-

Before and behind King

[Inspection of the chiefs of] Lebanon; who are cutting down [cedars for]^a the great barge of the "Beginning-of-the-River," ———— likewise for the great flagstaves of Amon, ———— building ———— with satisfying life ———— [like] Re, every day ————, Favorite of the Two Goddesses: Uhem-mesut. ———— Mightiest of Bows ———— Seti-Merneptah, given life.[b] ————satisfied with victory; the chiefs ———— his might ———— his ———— [he loves an hour of battle] more than a day [of rejoicing] ———— he sees ⌜them⌝, his lord ———— his heart is satisfied, making the boundaries of Egypt ———— to fill the storehouses ———— heir — ———— in —.

Before Egyptian Officer

Said the fan-bearer at the right of the king in his answer to the Good God: "It shall be done according to all that thou hast said, O Horus, Vivifier of the Two Lands. Thou art like Montu in every country; when the chiefs of Retenu (*Rṯnw*) see thee, the fear of thee is in their limbs.

Over Chiefs of Lebanon

The great chiefs of Lebanon; they say in praising the Lord of the Two Lands, in magnifying his might: "Thou seemest like thy father, Re; there is life in seeing thee."

SCENES 6 AND 7. BINDING AND CARRYING AWAY PRISONERS[c]

95. The return to Egypt has begun, and we see the king in two symbolical scenes binding and carrying away the captives.

Before and behind King

96. 6. ———— ———— all countries; he carries them off as living captives ———— Hartema, Lord ———— felling ———— his enemies.

---

lion, *Monuments*, and Rosellini, *Monumenti Storici*, have $P\ni$-ḥn-m$\ni$. On Kader, which is the Hebrew "Gader," a "stockade" or "inclosure," see Müller, *Asien und Europa*, 202, 203.

[a] For the restorations, see my *New Chapter*, 29, note a.

[b] These fragments of Seti I's complete titulary may be restored from Redesiyeh (§§ 169, l. 1).

[c] For bibliography, see Fig. 1.

Over Horses

97. 7. Great first span of his majesty: "Great-in-Victory."

Over Prisoners

Great chiefs of Retenu (*Rṯnw*), whom his majesty carried off as living captives.

SCENE 8. RECEPTION IN EGYPT[a]

98. Seti has now reached Egypt, and nears the frontier city, Tharu, driving and leading his prisoners. On the Egyptian side of the canal which passes by the city stands a body of officials acclaiming the victorious Pharaoh.[b]

99. The most important item in this scene is the long inscription (§ 101), which informs us of the reason of Seti's chastisement of the Shasu. It was reported to him that the Bedwin (Shasu) were making common cause against the Palestinians (Kharu), and that this invasion had resulted in the complete overthrow of all authority in Palestine. That these Bedwin are the Khabiri[c] of the Amarna Letters there can be no doubt. The conditions which confronted Seti I in Palestine are exactly those which we should expect in view of what we learn from the letters of Abdkhiba of Jerusalem. There is also further evidence of the same conditions, in the tomb of Harmhab (§§ 10 ff.). The attempt of the Hebrews to gain a footing in Palestine is undoubtedly involved in the larger movement of the Bedwin, which Seti here records.[d]

---

[a]For bibliography, see Fig. 1, to which may be added Brugsch, *Geographische Inschriften*, I, Pl. 48.

[b]The prince who marches behind the Pharaoh whose name is lost (§ 102 *infra*), has been identified by Wiedemann with the crown prince of Scene 13; for which there is no evidence, and against which there is conclusive evidence. See *Zeitschrift für ägyptische Sprache*, 27, 136, 137.

[c]See Ed. Meyer, *Festschrift für Georg Ebers*, 75, 76.

[d]See Meyer, *loc. cit.*

Over King

100. King of Upper and Lower Egypt, Lord of the Two Lands. Menmare; Son of Re, Lord of Diadems: Seti-Merneptah, given life, like Re.

Under Vulture

Nekhbet, the white goddess of Nekhen, may she give life, stability, and satisfaction, like Re.

In Canal

The bridge.

In Fort, by Canal

The fortress ($ḫtm$) of Tharu ($T^{ꜣ}$-rw).

Fort under Horses

The store-chamber: "The Lion."

In Fort behind Horses

The Tower (M-k-ty-$r^{ꜣ}$) of Menmare.

Beside Pool of Fort

The Pool of Hepen ($Ḥw$-$p^{ꜣ}$-$n^{ꜣ}$).[a]

Fort behind Horses

Buto of Seti-Merneptah.

Pool under Fort

The pool of the water-⌈supply⌉.

Over Horses

Great first span of his majesty, L. P. H.: "Amon-He-Giveth-Might."

Over Horses at Top

101. Year 1 of Uhem-mesut[b] ²King of Upper and Lower Egypt, Lord of the Two Lands, Menmare, given Life.

---

[a]This occurs in two places according to Champollion, *Notices descriptives*, and Lepsius, *Denkmäler*, 128, but the one placed by these two authorities on the right side of the canal is not to be found in my photograph. The reading $Ḥw$-$ṯ^{ꜣ}$-y-$n^{ꜣ}$ (Anast., I, 27) would indicate that we should read $Ḥw$-$ṯ^{ꜣ}$-na here, but the texts all have $p^{ꜣ}$. See Müller (*Asien und Europa*, 134), who, however, has not gone back of the publications.

[b]Part of the second name in Seti I's fivefold titulary, see *infra*, Redesiyeh, § 169, l. 1.

³One came to say to his majesty: ⁴"The vanquished Shasu (*Šʾ-sw*), they plan ⁵ᶠrebellion¹. Their tribal chiefs ⁶are gathered together, risingᵃ against the Asiatics of Kharuᵃ (*Ḥʾ-rw*). ⁷They have taken to cursing, and quarreling, each of them ⁸slaying his neighbor, and they disregard the laws of the ⁹palace."

The heart of his majesty, L. P. H., was glad on account of it. ¹⁰Lo, as for the Good God, he rejoices ¹¹to begin battle, he is delighted to ¹²enterᵇ into it, his heart is satisfied ¹³at seeing blood, he cuts off ¹⁴the heads of the rebellious-hearted, he loves ¹⁵an hour of battle more than a day of rejoicing. His majesty slays them at one time. He leaves not a limb among them, and he that escapes his hand as a living captive, is carried off to Egypt.

Over Princeᶜ behind Chariot

102. Following the king on his marches in the countries of Retenu (*Rṯnw*), by the hereditary prince, great in invocationᵈ by ——— real king's-scribe, his beloved ——— king's-son, of his body, his beloved ——— ᵉ

Over Rejoicing Egyptians

103. Prophets, nobles, and officials (*hʾ·tyw*) of the South and North, coming to acclaim to the Good God, at his return from the country of Retenu (*Rṯnw*) with very numerous captivity. ²Never was seen the like of it, since ³the time of the god. They say, in ⁴praising his majesty, in magnifying ⁵his might: "Welcome art thou, from ⁶the countries which thou hast subdued; ⁷thou art triumphant, and thy enemies are ⁸beneath thee. Thy duration as king ⁹is like Re in heaven, while gratifying thy heart ¹⁰on the Nine Bows. When Re made thy

---

ᵃOr: "*standing (gaining a foothold) in the Kharite (Horite) regions of Asia.*"

ᵇOr: "*when one transgresses against him.*"

ᶜSee also Lepsius, *Denkmäler*, Text, III, 19.

ᵈMy explanation in *Zeitschrift für ägyptische Sprache* (XXXVII, 136, n. 5) is incomplete, if not incorrect; *sh*, or *swh ʾ*, means "*to bless or curse*," these meanings being derived from a common idea, viz., "*to invoke divine powers*," a meaning used in magical texts.

ᵉThis fragmentary name contained the syllable *nb* or *ḥb;* hence Lefebure restores Harmhab (*Proceedings of the Society of Biblical Archæology*, XII, 447); while Wiedemann at first favored Nebwa (*Nb-wʾ*) (*Proceedings of the Society of Biblical Archæology*, XII, 258 ff.), and later thinks it was Amon-nefer-nebef (*Recueil*, XVIII, 121). See my note, *Zeitschrift für ägyptische Sprache* (37, 137, note 1).

boundary, his two arms ¹⁰were a protection behind thee. Thy sword was in the midst of ¹¹every land, and their chiefs fell by thy blade."

SCENE 9. PRESENTATION OF SHASU PRISONERS AND PRECIOUS VESSELS TO AMON.[a]

104. Seti appears before Amon presenting him with slaves and costly vessels from his campaign against the Shasu, though the victories are stated to have been in Retenu, and the upper row of captives is affirmed to be from Retenu.

Over Amon

105. Utterance of Amon-Re, Lord of Thebes: "O my beloved son, Lord of the Two Lands: Menmare, I have caused that thou shouldst be [ʳvictoriousʸ] over every country, that thou shouldst rule over their chiefs, so that they come to thee, gathered together with a burden (tribute) upon their backs, for fear of thee."

Over Tribute

106. [Presentation of the tribute by his majesty to his father, Amon],[b] at the return from the country of Retenu ($R\underline{t}nw$). The chiefs of the country are living prisoners, their tribute upon their back, consisting of every vessel, the choicest of their countries, of gold, silver, lapis lazuli | — — which thou givest me in every country ———.

Over Prisoners, Upper Line

107. Chiefs of countries which knew not Egypt, which his majesty carried away, from his victories in the country of Retenu ($R\underline{t}nw$) the wretched. They say, in magnifying his majesty, in acclaiming his victories: "Hail to thee! How great is thy name, how mighty thy power! The countries rejoice to be subject to thee, and they that transgress thy boundary are bound. By thy ka! We knew not Egypt, nor had our fathers trodden it. Give to us the breath that thou givest."

Over Prisoners, Lower Line

108. Captivity which his majesty carried off from the Shasu ($\check{S}$ʾ-sw), whom his majesty himself overthrew, in the year 1 of Uhem-mesut (Seti I).

---

[a]For bibliography, see Fig. 1.   [b]Restored from Scene 10.

SCENE 10. PRESENTATION OF SYRIAN PRISONERS AND PRECIOUS VESSELS TO AMON

109. A scene like that in the preceding relief, but with Syrians in place of Shasu.

Over Amon

110. Utterance of Amon-Re, lord of Thebes: "Thou comest in peace, O Good God, Lord of the Two Lands: Menmare, I have set thy might in every country, thy fear in the hearts of the Nine Bows. Their chiefs come to thee as one man, with a burden (viz., tribute) on their backs. I have placed for thee the lands under thy fear, bowing down in terror of thee."

Over Vessels

111. Presentation of the tribute by his majesty, to his father, Amon, at his return from the country of Retenu (*R*ṭ*nw*), the wretched; consisting of silver, gold, lapis lazuli, malachite, ⌜—⌝, and every splendid, costly stone. The chiefs of the countries are inclosed in his grasp, in order to fill the storehouse of his father, Amon, by the might that thou hast given to me (sic!).

Over Prisoners, Upper Row

112. Arrival of his majesty from Retenu (*R*ṭ*nw*) the Upper, ex[tend-ing the boun]daries of Egypt ─────.

Over Prisoners, Lower Row

Chiefs of countries that knew not Egypt, whom his majesty carried off as living captives.

SCENE 11. SLAYING PRISONERS BEFORE AMON[a]

113. This bloody ceremony, which is of very ancient origin, is the king's final recognition of his power as coming from the god, before whom he now sacrifices a number of the foes, whom the god has enabled him to vanquish. The fulsome praise and promises of the god are taken from earlier sources. The first portion (§ 116) is plagiarized

---
[a]For bibliography, see Fig. 1.

from the great stela of Amenhotep III recounting his buildings (II, 891, 892). Seti I had restored this splendid stela after its defacement by Ikhnaton (II, 878), and apparently at its restoration it was found to be so pleasing by Seti that he appropriated its form for his own use, but with many changes. Seti's form of it was then again used by Ramses III on his Medinet Habu temple (IV, 137). The other part of Amon's discourse (§ 117) is taken from a still earlier composition, the great Hymn of Victory of Thutmose III (II, 658 ff.), but again with some changes.

114. The title over the captive towns and countries led by Amon and a Theban genius, is restored from Scene 20, where it is repeated. This list of the towns and countries gained in these conquests was appended to each of the two sacrificial scenes (11 and 20) concluding the two great series. Both lists are totally confused, even the stereotyped "Nine Bows" being broken up into two fragments. Evidently little reliance can be placed upon them, as they are placed here to serve a conventional function, viz., merely to convey the idea of vast conquests. Fortunately, a more careful list of Seti's conquests is preserved upon a sphinx in his temple at Kurna,[a] which is as follows: 1–9, the "Nine Bows;" 10, Kheta ($ḫt^{ʾ}$); 11, Naharin (N-h-r-ny); 12, Alasa (^{ʾ}-$r^{ʾ}$-$s^{ʾ}$); 13, Akko (^{c}-k-^{ʾ}); 14, Simyra ($ḏ^{ʾ}$-my-$^{b}r^{ʾ}$); 15, Peher ($P^{ʾ}$-$ḥ$-$r^{ʾ}$); 16, Bethshael ($B^{ʾ}$-t-$š^{ʾ}$-$r^{ʾ}$); 17, Khamehem ($^{r}ḫ^{ʾ}$-my-h-mw); 18, Yenoam (Y-nw-^{cʾ}-mw); 19, Ullaza (^{ʾ}n-n-$r^{ʾ}$-$ṭ^{ʾ}$); 20, Kemed ($K^{ʾ}$-my-dw); 21, Tyre ($ḏ^{ʾ}$-rw); 22, Othu (Yw-tw); 23, Bethanath ($B^{ʾ}$-t-^{c}-n-t); 24, Keremim ($k^{ʾ}$-$r^{ʾ}$-my-mw);[c] The remaining

---

[a]Lepsius, *Denkmäler*, III, 131, a. See Müller, *Asien und Europa*, 191–95.

[b]Text "*ty*," which is clearly to be corrected to *r*ʾ (Müller, *Asien und Europa*, 187, n. 2).

[c]Perhaps to be corrected, as Müller does (*Asien und Europa*, 195), to $K^{ʾ}$-$r^{ʾ}$-t-^{c}-n-t.

names (25–43) are haphazard selections[a] of the famous towns and districts, chiefly of Asia, familiar to the Egyptians from earlier conquests. Only the towns in the northern plain of Jezreel, and in Phœnicia are grouped together (Nos. 13–24), but within the group they occur at haphazard. Not even such a grouping can be discovered in the aimless, confused conclusion (Nos. 25–43).[b]

115. In harmony with the claims of these lists the words accompanying the king's action claim for him the great domain of his predecessors of the Eighteenth Dynasty, viz., from the "*Horns of the Earth*,"[c] on the south, to the "*marshes of Naharin*," (§ 118) on the north. This is still literally true for the southern boundary, but is unquestionably an exaggeration in the case of the northern boundary. If Seti ever carried his arms as far as Naharin, he was unable to establish his boundary there, or hold anything inland, north of Galilee.

Over Amon

116. [1]Utterance of Amon-Re, lord of Thebes: "O my son, of my body, [2]my beloved, Lord of the Two Lands: Menmare, lord of might in every country! [3]I am thy father; I set thy terror in Retenu, the Upper and [4]the Lower. The Nubian Troglodytes are slain beneath thy feet.

I bring [5]to thee the chiefs of the southern countries, that they may

---

[a]They do not seem to be taken from Scenes 11 and 20, as Müller states (Müller, *Asien und Europa*, 191, n. 1), but are equally orderless and methodless selections from the names known to the compiler.

[b]A relief on this same north wall of Karnak shows Amon presenting to an uncertain king a series of thirty captured towns. Müller (*Asien und Europa*, 164-66) has shown that this list includes some towns in the west of central Palestine. He has attributed the relief to Ramses II, but the location of the document, where only Seti I's inscriptions are found would indicate that it belongs to the latter.

[c]A stela at Ibrim contains similar references (Sayce, *Recueil*, 16, 170 f.); the southern boundary is given as the "*Horns of the Earth*," and, referring to the northern, the king is called the "*crusher of Retenu, carrying off their chiefs as living prisoners*." Then follow the conventional references to the submission of South and North.

make thee to receive the tribute, being ⁶every good product of their countries, to hasten ⁷————.

[I turn] my face to the north,ᵃ I work a wonder ⁸[for thee] — — — snaring the rebels in their nests by the power of thy might. I bring to thee ⁹countries that know not Egypt, with their tribute borne, consisting of silver, gold, lapis lazuli, every splendid costly stone of God's-Land.

¹⁰I turn my face to the east, I work a wonder for thee, I bind them all for thee, gathered in thy grasp. I gather together all the countries ¹¹of Punt, all their tribute, of gum of myrrh (ᶜ*nty*), cinnamon, and all the pleasant sweet woods of God's-Land, ¹²⌜fragrant⌝ before thee, and thy uraeus.

I turn my face to the west, I work a wonder for thee, consuming for thee every land of Tehenu (*Tyḥnw*). ¹³They come bowing down [to thee],ᵇ falling upon their knees for terror of thee. The chiefs of ¹⁴———— to give to thee praise.

I turn my face to heaven, I work a wonder for thee; the gods of the horizon of heaven acclaim ¹⁵to thee, when Re is born every morning; thou flourishest like Re, when he has brought midday.

I turn my face to the earth, ¹⁶[I work a wonder for thee, I appoint for thee victories in every country]. The gods rejoice in thee, in their temples; thou shalt spend eternity as king upon the throne of Keb.

Before Amon

117. ¹I have caused them to see thy majesty as lord of radiance, so that thou hast shone in their faces like my image.

²I have caused them to see thy majesty, arrayed in thy regalia, when [thou] takest the weapons of war in the chariot.

³I have caused them to see thy majesty like a circling star, which scatters its flame in fire and gives forth its dew.

⁴I have caused them to see thy majesty as a young bull, firm of heart, ready-horned, irresistible.

⁵I have caused them to see thy majesty as a crocodile, terrible on the shore, unapproachable.

ᵃThe god should first face south, as in the original text of Amenhotep III (II, 891), from which our text of Seti I is plagiarized.

ᵇCorrected from Medinet Habu; Guieysse has totally confused the two texts, his Medinet Habu text being incorrect.

⁶I have caused them to see thy majesty like a flame of fire, like the very being of Sekhmet, in her tempest.

⁷I have caused them to see thy majesty as [a fierce-eyed lion, so that thou makest] them corpses in their valleys.

⁸I have caused them to see thy majesty as a —, great in strength, irresistible in heaven or in earth.

Before Amon's Sword

Take to thyself the sword ($ḫpš$), O mighty king, whose mace smites the Nine Bows.

Before the King

118. Slaying of the Asiatic Troglodytes (Ynw-$Mn·t·yw$), all inaccessible countries, all lands, the Fenkhu of the marshes of Asia, the Great Bend ($pḫr\ wr$) of the sea ($w\ ᵓ\ ḏ$-wr).

Over King

Smiting the Troglodytes, beating down the Asiatics ($Mn·t·yw$), making his boundary as far as the "⌈Horns⌉ of the Earth," as far as the marshes of Naharin (N-h-r-n).

Line below King

119. List of those southern and northern lands, which his majesty smote, making a great slaughter among them, of unknown number. [Their subjects are][a] carried away [as living captives, to fill the storehouse of his father, Amon-Re, lord of Thebes, all countries] ———.

SCENE 12. FIRST BATTLE WITH THE LIBYANS[b]

120. With this scene we pass to the other side of the door (cf. Fig. 1), to a group of nine scenes where there is no date preserved; and as shown above (§§ 80 ff.), they do not necessarily belong to the wars of year 1 on the east side of the door, but may have occurred at any time subsequent to the year 1. As we have shown above (§ 82), Seti spent practically his entire second year in the Delta, and he may well have fought the Libyan war in that year.

---

[a]Restored from Scene 20.   [b]For bibliography, see Fig. 1.

§ 123]   KARNAK RELIEFS   59

121. As Seti's first war in Asia was introduced by a minor campaign against the Bedwin of Sinai and the Negeb, so now his second Asiatic war is preceded by a campaign against the Libyans. It is evident that the pressure of the Libyans into the Delta, which became so serious under Seti's grandson, Merneptah (§§ 569 ff.), already began under Seti himself. He was, therefore, unable to continue his conquests in Asia without chastising them. Unfortunately, the scene is purely conventional, and the descriptive texts contain nothing but general terms.

Before King

122. Lord of the Two Lands: Menmare; Lord of Diadems: Seti-Merneptah.

Behind King

Hartema, Lord of achievement.

Over Horses

¹——— ²devastating, seizing in every country, ³brave without his like, achieving with his ⁴sword, till the Two Lands know it, till the ⁵whole earth sees it. He is like Baal, ⁶he traverses the mountains, ⁷his terror has penetrated the countries, his name ⁸is victorious, ⁹his sword ¹⁰is mighty, ¹¹there is none ¹²that stands before him.

SCENE 13. SECOND BATTLE WITH THE LIBYANS[a]

123. This second battle scene in addition to the strength and vigor which give it value as an artistic composition, is of great importance because of the two princes, whom it represents as participating in the battle. One of them (behind Seti) bears the name of Ramses, and is of course, he who later became Ramses II. This fact has had great weight in the study of the reigns of Seti and of Ramses II, and has

---

[a]For bibliography, see Fig. 1, to which Prisse, *Histoire de l'art égyptien* (plates unnumbered), may be added.

materially modified the chronology of both reigns.[a] But let it be noted, in the first place, that this figure of Ramses is in a scene of the Libyan war, without a date, far from the scenes of the Shasu war of year 1, on the other side of the door. This appearance of Ramses with his father was therefore not necessarily in his father's first year, as has been so often assumed.

124. Furthermore, a close examination of the accompanying figures will show, first, that this scene is no proof that Ramses ever appeared with his father in battle at all; and, second, that Ramses was not the first heir to Seti's throne.[b] Behind the Libyan chief whom Seti hurls backward stands an Egyptian prince (Fig. 4, broken lines), facing toward the left, and watching, or possibly taking part in, the conflict. Behind Seti stands Prince Ramses (Fig. 3, dotted lines), facing toward the right, and likewise watching the conflict. Fig. 4 cannot also be Ramses, for he could not appear twice in the same scene. Its accompanying inscription[c] is as follows: "*Hereditary prince, first king's-son, of his body* ———," in which, unfortunately, the name is wanting; where it could have stood before its disappearance is a question, for the skirt of the prince projects under the titles, and the name must therefore have been pushed to

---

[a]Thus Maspero (*Struggle of the Nations*, 369, n. 3) concludes that Seti I married Ramses II's mother, Tuya, under Harmhab, and (*ibid.*, 387, n. 5) that Seti I could not have reigned longer than fifteen to twenty years (possibly only twelve or fifteen), because Ramses II appears "as a stripling in the campaign of Seti's first year."

[b]A full discussion of these questions by the present writer will be found in *Zeitschrift für ägyptische Sprache*, 37, 130–39, from which the accompanying figures are taken.

[c]It is very faint and has been overlooked in Champollion, *Monuments*, 297, 2, and in Rosellini, *Monumenti Storici*, 54, 2; the only publication containing it is Champollion, *Notices descriptives*, 99. Every sign is traceable in the photograph which I used for making the drawing.

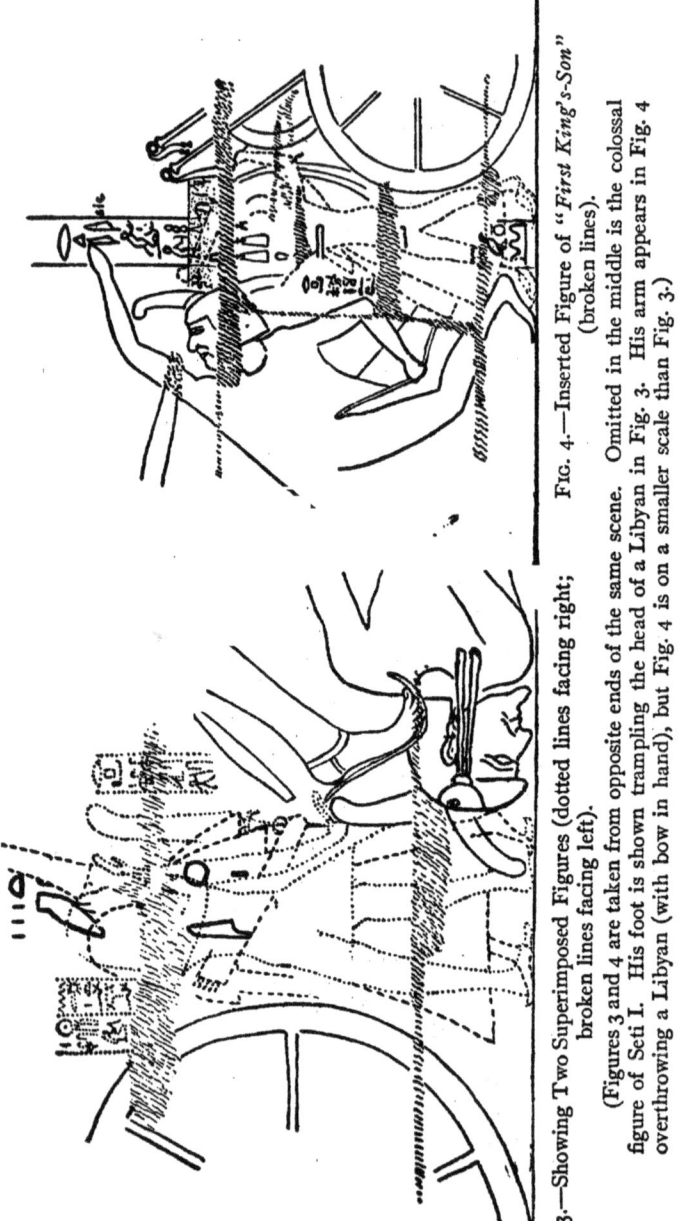

FIG. 3.—Showing Two Superimposed Figures (dotted lines facing right; broken lines facing left).

FIG. 4.—Inserted Figure of "*First King's-Son*" (broken lines).

(Figures 3 and 4 are taken from opposite ends of the same scene. Omitted in the middle is the colossal figure of Seti I. His foot is shown trampling the head of a Libyan in Fig. 3. His arm appears in Fig. 4 overthrowing a Libyan (with bow in hand), but Fig. 4 is on a smaller scale than Fig. 3.)

the left (under the Libyan chief's elbow).[a] The historical conclusion here is important: the "*first king's-son*" of Seti I was not his successor, Ramses; that is, that Ramses II had an older brother, who did not reach the throne.

125. But a further examination of this scene discloses the fact that this figure of Ramses' elder brother (Fig. 4) is not original and does not belong where it stands. The first glance shows that the contracted space between the chariot wheel (belonging to the next scene to the right) and the leg of the falling Libyan is too narrow for another figure, and the artist has barely been able to squeeze the prince in. Thus he is as much in one scene as the other, an anomalous arrangement! He stands with fan upraised in his right hand, as if to smite the falling Libyan. The fan runs directly across the vertical line of text! It is difficult to say where the right arm is; it seems to have been raised, and it may be that he was seizing his father's foe, as his father is doing. Passing through the fan, the large column of text extends down through the prince's head and body, to the bottom. It is clear, therefore, that at some time after Seti had completed these reliefs his eldest son had himself inserted here, as taking part in Seti's Libyan campaign. It is clear also that someone desired his removal, for his figure has been rudely chiseled away. Champollion speaks of him[b] as a "prince martelé et surchargé avec débris de légende" (his titles follow), showing that also his accompanying inscription has been hammered out. The person to whom the figure of the eldest son would be most unwelcome, and who

---

[a]There is now no trace of it there, owing to a large fissure in the stone. I am unfortunately obliged to work from photographs, as I did not study these reliefs when at Karnak, and the figures of the princes are now nearly covered with débris again.

[b]*Notices descriptives*, II, 99.

would therefore be most desirous to remove it, is of course, the other prince in the same scene, Ramses. We are certainly correct in attributing the mutilation to him. Moreover, it is quite certain that he did this in order to have the figure of himself inserted in the same scene, for his own figure (Fig. 3, dotted lines) is not original to this scene.

126. In the first place, we notice in Fig. 3, as in Fig. 4, the narrowness of the space into which the prince's figure has been squeezed, so that his left foot passes through the feather of the fallen Libyan, whom Seti is trampling, and his left hand collides with the other feather. Further, we again notice a column of text extending down through the prince's head into his body.[a] Ramses stands with right hand raised palm outward, as usual in salutation, and carrying his fan vertically before him in the left hand. A joint in the masonry has obliterated shoulders and face. The accompanying text is partly in one scene and partly in the next. It is as follows: *"Prince ($rp^c \cdot ty$), king's-son, crown prince, of his body, his beloved, Ramses."* The historical conclusions to be derived from this text will be taken up later.

127. A closer inspection of Ramses' figure shows that, in having himself inserted here, he at the same time improved the opportunity to efface another figure, which we will call X, over which his own has been cut. The motives for this second effacement are undoubtedly the same as for the first, and X was therefore Ramses' elder brother. But, as the elder brother has already been once effaced in this scene, we should expect that this second occurrence of his figure belonged to another scene, and such is clearly the case. Under Ramses' figure appears a second pair of feet striding in the

---

[a]These signs are so clear that they were copied by Rosellini, but in his publication (*Monumenti Storici*, 54, 2) he has shifted the column above too far to the right.

opposite direction (the left; see broken lines); behind Ramses is the front point of a skirt; behind him is a third arm; across his figure is a quiver[a] with the opening to the left; above him is a fan[b], with the tip of the feather turned to the left.[c] All these belong, of course, to the figure X (broken lines), facing to the left. A comparison of X with the prince in Fig. 5 shows clearly that X was striding in the same way after the chariot behind which he is. Especially characteristic are his left foot poised for the next step, the arm hanging down in front, and the fan over the shoulder. X therefore belongs to the scene to the left, representing Seti's triumphant return (Scene 14) from the Libyan war, riding in his chariot and driving his prisoners before him, like the prince following Seti in his return from the first Syrian war (Fig. 5). This is what we should expect; before Ramses' interference, the figure of his elder brother appeared once in each of the two scenes: the battle with the Libyans (Fig. 4) and the return (Fig. 3). Ramses preferred to appear in the battle and had himself inserted facing the right.

128. But if the figure of Ramses is a later insertion, that of his brother (X) is equally so; the latter's fan, quiver, and indeed his whole figure cut directly into the original column of text, as the figure of Ramses does. X has had himself inserted here. It is this fact which renders certain the identity of X and Seti's eldest son (Fig. 4); both desired

---

[a]The quiver was always carried on the left side, with the opening in front; hence in this case belonging to a person facing the left.

[b]The fan was always borne with the tip of the feather pointing toward the front, as in Ramses' figure and in Fig. 5.

[c]The feet and the quiver were seen and copied by Rosellini and Champollion, and appear in their publications (Rosellini, *Monumenti Storici*, 54; Champollion, *Monuments*, 297, 2), but seem to have remained unnoticed since.

to appear in Seti's Libyan war, both were the object of Ramses' hatred, and both were effaced by him.

129. To recapitulate, we find thus far three stages on this wall:

1. An uninterrupted column of text on each side of the battle scene; and no princes in either it or the scene of the return.

2. Seti's eldest son inserts his own figure at the right of the battle scene and at the right of the return.

3. Prince Ramses effaces the figure of his elder brother in both places, but over that of his brother in the return scene he inserts his own figure, so facing as to belong to the battle scene.

130. There are evidences of a similar insertion (Fig. 6) at the top of this same wall, on a few isolated blocks at the left of the capture of Kadesh (Scene 16). Here we see a figure (Fig. 6, broken lines) with uplifted arm, like that of Ramses in the battle scene, and wearing a quiver. Before this figure are the arms of a captive bound behind his back, showing that the man follows the king's chariot (as in Fig. 5), behind which, however, the king leads a line of captives. But this figure is likewise a later insertion, for a column of text extends down through it, and the head of the Syrian, who has fallen beneath the chariot, projects into the skirt. It is impossible to decide whether this figure is that of Ramses or his brother.

131. The historical results to be drawn from the above facts are not numerous, but are important. It is clear, in the first place, that these reliefs offer no evidence whatever that Ramses II ever took part in any campaign of his father, of whatever year. It is therefore no longer necessary to shorten the reign of Seti in order that Ramses may be sufficiently young at his (Ramses') accession, as Maspero con-

FIG. 5.—An Unknown Prince Following the Chariot of Seti I (Scene 14).

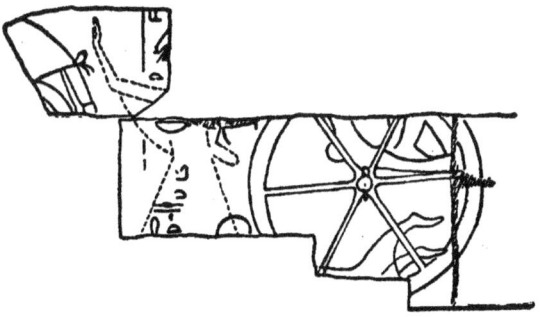

FIG. 6.—Figure of an Unknown Prince Inserted in a Fragmentary Scene (§ 130).

sidered unavoidable. As far as these reliefs are concerned, Ramses might even have been born after Seti's accession. The fact alone that Ramses was obliged to insert his own figure in his father's battle scenes, in order to appear there at all, of course creates a strong suspicion that he had nothing to do with the events they depict;[a] and thus Seti's reign may have been considerably longer than is usually attributed to him. He was about to celebrate his jubilee when he died, having left an obelisk unfinished, so that it was completed by his son, Ramses II (§§ 544 ff.). If his father reigned two and a half years, Seti's jubilee might have fallen in the middle of his twenty-eighth year. But as he did not live to complete the obelisk and celebrate the jubilee, he may have died a few years before the jubilee, after a reign of over twenty years. A greater maximum is improbable, for the reason that Setau, viceroy of Kush in Seti I's second year,[b] is known also in Ramses II's thirty-eighth year, which, if Seti reigned twenty years, makes Setau's term of office at least fifty-seven years—an extraordinary tenure of office. For the extensive building which Seti I accomplished, twenty years are none too long a reign.

Over the Foe

132. [1]——— [overth]rowing his enemies, smiting [2]——— among them, [3]——— their chiefs fall [4]——— [beneath] the two feet of Horus, [5][the King of Upper and Lower Egypt], Men[mare]; [6][the Son of Re, Seti-Me]rn[eptah], given satisfying life, like Re.

Before King

Smiting the chiefs of Tehenu (*Tyḥnw*).

---

[a]See the discussion of Ramses II's youth, §§ 254, 283.

[b]Papyrus in Bibliothèque Nationale, 209, in Spiegelberg, *Rechnungen*, Pl. X, col. 4, l. 3.

Over Fan

Hartema, Lord of the Two Lands, Lord of Offering, smiting every country.

Under Fan

All protection, life, stability, satisfaction are behind him, like Re, lord of might, smiting the Nine Bows.

Left of Fan

The King, Lord of the Two Lands, Lord of Might, Menmare, smites the chiefs of the countries.

With Prince behind King

The hereditary prince (rp ͨ ˙ ty), the king's-son, crown-prince, of his body, his beloved, Ramses.

With Prince behind Enemy

Prince (rp ͨ ˙ ty), first king's-son, of his body ———.

Over Horses

Great first span of his majesty (named): "Smiter-of-Foreigners."

SCENE 14. RETURN FROM LIBYAN WAR[a]

133. We here see Seti returning from the Libyan war in the same manner as he is shown returning from his Syrian war of the year 1. Behind Seti's chariot, in this scene, his eldest son had himself inserted following the chariot, as does the prince behind the chariot in the return from Syria (Scene 8). The prince's figure is here cut in over a column of inscription (see Fig. 3), showing that it is not a part of the relief as left by Seti. It was afterward erased and replaced by the figure of Ramses II, who faces the other way and belongs to the preceding scene (13).

Over King

134. Lord of the Two Lands: Menmare, Lord of Diadems, Seti-Merneptah, given life.

---

[a]For bibliography, see Fig. 1.

Over Horses
Great first span of his majesty:—"Mighty-is-Amon."

Over Prisoners, Upper Line
———— he causes them to cease standing upon the meadow, unable to take up the bow, passing the day in the caves, hidden like wolves for fear of his majesty ———— their hearts ———— might.

Over Prisoners, Lower Line
———— as living prisoners in the country of Tehenu (*Tyḥny*), by the might of his father, Amon.

SCENE 15.   PRESENTATION OF LIBYAN PRISONERS AND SPOIL TO AMON[a]

135. This presentation does not differ from those depicted east of the door. The inscription over the Libyan prisoners in the upper line referring them to "*Retenu*" and calling them "*Asiatics*"(!), only shows the subordinate character of the Libyan campaign, and the exclusive importance of the Asiatic victories. It may also indicate that this presentation of Libyan spoil did not take place till after the second Asiatic war; but as these reliefs were not put on the temple wall until the close of Seti's wars, all the campaigns in Retenu are then past, and could be referred to.

Over Amon
136. [1]Utterance of Amon-Re, lord of Thebes: [2]"O Son of my body, my beloved, Lord of the Two Lands, [3]Menmare; my heart is glad [4]for love of thee, I rejoice to look on [5]thy beauty. I set the terror of [6]thy majesty in every country ———— [7]over their chiefs, [they] come [8]to thee together, to Egypt, [9]with all their possessions [10]borne upon their backs.

Before Mut
Mut, mistress of Ishru ———— mistress of heaven, queen of all gods, ———— eternity as king of the Two Lands, while thou appearest as Re.

---
[a]For bibliography, see Fig. 1.

Before Khonsu

Khonsu in Thebes, Beautiful Rest, Horus, lord of joy (and) Thoth, lord of Karnak.

Below

I give to thee might against the south, victory against the north.

Over Spoil

137. Presentation of tribute by his majesty ²to his father, Amon-Re, consisting of silver, gold, lapis lazuli, malachite, ³every splendid costly stone, from the might which thou givest to me in every country. ⁴King of Upper and Lower Egypt. Lord of Offering: Menmare; ⁵Son of Re, Lord of Diadems: Seti-Merneptah, given life, like Re.

Before King

138. ¹Presentation of tribute by the Good God to his father, Amon, from the rebellious chiefs of the countries that knew not ²Egypt. Their tribute is upon their backs, in order to fill thy storehouse with slaves, male and female; ³from the victories which thou givest me in every country.

With Prisoners, Upper Line

139. ¹His majesty arrived from the countries ——— when he had desolated ²Retenu (*Rṯnw*) and slain their chiefs, causing ³the Asiatics (`ꜥ ꜣ mw`) to say: ⁴"See ⁵this! He is ⁶like a flame ⁷when it goes forth and ⁸no water is brought." He causes ⁹all rebels to cease ¹⁰all contradiction ¹¹of their mouths, ¹²when he has taken away¹³ their breath. ¹⁴——— When one approaches the boundaries, he is like Montu, ¹⁵———, he is like the son of Nut; no country stands before ¹⁶[him].

Over Prisoners, Lower Line

Chiefs of the countries of Tehenu (*Tyḥnw*) ———.

SCENE 16. CAPTURE OF KADESH[a]

140. The campaign against Libya being concluded, we find Seti again in Syria. Like the Annals of Thutmose III, the campaigns of which so often begin, "*His majesty was in the land of X,*" so our reliefs offer no statement of the

---

[a]For bibliography, see Fig. 1.

route of the army, but show it at once in the midst of the enemy's country, where he attacks the Galilean Kadesh.[a] The crossing of the Jordan valley and the erection of a boundary stela in Hauran (see §81) may perhaps be connected with this campaign instead of with that against the coast cities.

Beside City

141. Town (*dmy*) of Kadesh (*Ḳdš*).

In Fortress

The charge which Pharaoh, L. P. H., made to devastate the land of Kadesh (*Ḳdš*), of the land of the Amor (*Y-m-r*).

Over Battle

1——— rage 2—— heaven, Montu upon 3—— his right, valor 4—— battle of myriads 5—— his army; a wall for millions 6—— when he sees multitudes, [he does] not 7[consider][b] myriads united, charging 8—— of the Asiatics, making them 9—— smiting the towns 10—— destroying the settlements 11—— his [w]ay, smiting ———.

SCENE 17. BATTLE WITH THE HITTITES[c]

142. Seti's advance between the Lebanons necessarily brings him into collision with the Hittites, and we see him here in the first battle between Egyptians and Hittites known to us. Unfortunately, no details of the conflict are given.

---

[a]Müller sees in this city the Kadesh on the Orontes (*Asien und Europa*, 217); but there seem to me conclusive reasons against this identification: (1) The relief shows a city on rocky heights, while Kadesh is in a low valley surrounded by moats (Müller thinks this due to the artist's looseness). (2) It is said to be "*of the land of Amor.*" Now, Kadesh on the Orontes clearly did not belong to the land of the Amorites (see Meyer, *Festschrift für Georg Ebers*, 69), and the purpose of the addition, "*of the land of Amor*," is precisely to distinguish the Galilean Kadesh from its more powerful neighbor in the north. (3) Müller's argument that Seti failed to capture the city, which would be impossible if it were a small Galilean town, is refuted by the fact that *fḫ* is used by Ramses II of a whole list of captured cities (Lepsius, *Denkmäler*, III, 156, with metathesis *ḫf*).

[b]See §148, l. 8; and Champollion, *Notices descriptives*, II, 76, 77.

[c]For bibliography, see Fig. 1.

Over King

143. The Good God, the mighty Lord of the Two Lands; Menmare; Lord of Diadems: Seti-Merneptah, chosen of the favor of Re.

Over Enemy

The wretched land of the Hittites ($Ht^{\ni}w$), among whom his majesty, L. P. H., made a great slaughter.

Over Battle

144. ¹Horus: Mighty Bull, Shining in Thebes, Vivifier of the Two Lands, ²King of Upper and Lower Egypt, Lord of the Two Lands: Menmare; Son of Re: Seti-Merneptah; ³Good God, mighty in strength, brave like Montu, ⁴mightiest of the mighty, like him that begat him, illuminating the Two Lands like the horizon-god, ⁵great in strength like the son of Nut, victorious, the double Horus ⁶by his ⌜own⌝ hand, treading the battlefield like Set, ⁷great in terror like Baal in the countries. Favorite of the Two Goddesses, ⁸while he was in the nest, (for) his might protected Egypt. Re made ⁹for him his boundary as far as the limits of that which Aton illuminates. ¹⁰Divine Hawk, bright of plumage, sailing the heavens ¹¹like the majesty of Re; prowling Wolf circling this land ¹²within an hour; fierce-eyed Lion, tramping the inaccessible ways of every ¹³country; mighty Bull, [ready]-horned, [⌜mighty⌝]-hearted, smiting the Asiatics, ¹⁴beating down the Hittites ($Ht^{\ni}(w)$), slaying ¹⁵their chiefs, overthrown in ¹⁶their blood, charging ¹⁷among them like a tongue of ¹⁸fire, making them as that which is not.

SCENE 18. CARRYING OFF HITTITE PRISONERS[a]

145. As in the other wars, Seti now carries off his prisoners. The reference to Tehenu (Libya, § 147) would indicate that, as we have already concluded, the Libyan war preceded the Hittite campaign.

Before King

146. Lord of the Two Lands: Menmare; Lord of Diadems: Seti-Merneptah.

---

[a]For bibliography, see Fig. 1.

Over Horses

Great first horse of his majesty (called): "Amon-Giveth-to-Him-the-Might."

Over Prisoners in Front, Upper Line

147. Good God, mighty in being, great in strength like Montu, residing in Thebes, youthful Bull, ready-horned, ⁵firm-hearted, smiting myriads; mighty Lion, tramping the inaccessible ¹⁰ways in every country; the prowling southern Wolf, circling this land within an hour, sm[iting] his [enem]ies in every country, mighty warrior without his like, ¹⁵an archer skilful of hand, setting his fame like a mountain of copper, furnishing their nostrils with his breath. Retenu ($Rṯnw$) comes to him bowing down, the land of Tehenu ($Tyḥy$, sic) on its knees. He establishes ²⁰seed as he wishes in this wretched land of Kheta ($Ḥtʾ$ -$tʾ$, sic); their chiefs fall by his blade, becoming as that which is not. His prowess is among them ²⁴like fire, (when) he destroys their towns (dmy).

Over Prisoners in Front, Lower Line

148. Chiefs of the countries that knew not Egypt, whom [his] majesty brought as living captives. They bring upon their backs of all the choicest of their countries.

Over Prisoners Behind

¹Victorious king, great in strength; his terror is like (that of) the son of ²Nut. The victor returns, when he has devastated the countries. He has smitten ³the land of Kheta ($Ḥy$-$tʾ$), causing the cowardly rebels ⁴to cease. Every country has become peaceful, ⁵(for) the fear of his majesty has entered ⁶among them, his ⌜odor⌝ has penetrated into their hearts. ⁷The chiefs of the countries are bound ⁸before him, he considers not myriads united together.

SCENE 19. PRESENTATION OF HITTITE SPOIL AND PRISONERS TO AMON[a]

149. The captive Hittites and their spoil are now presented to Amon, as in the other wars; but there is unfortunately no additional information in the inscriptions as to the character or extent of the campaign.

---

[a]For bibliography, see Fig. 1.

Over King

150. Good God, great in victory, King of Upper and Lower Egypt: Menmare; Son of Re: Seti-Merneptah, chosen of Re, in the barque of Re.

Over Amon

¹[Utterance: "I give to thee] all might and all victory."
²Utterance: "I give to thee all lands, all countries beneath thy sandals."
³Utterance: "I give to thee the duration of Re, the years of Atum."
⁴Utterance: "I give to thee an eternity of jubilees, like Re."
⁵Utterance: "I give to thee all food-offerings."
⁶Utterance: "I give to thee all life, stability, satisfaction; all health."
⁷Amon-Re, lord of Thebes, presider over Karnak.

Over Bast

¹Mut, the great Bast, ruler of Karnak, mistress of amiability and love.

Over Khonsu

Khonsu in Thebes, Beautiful Rest, Horus, lord of joy.

Over Mat

Utterance of Mat, daughter of Re: "O my son, of my body, my beloved, Lord of the Two Lands, lord of might, Menmare."

Over Spoil

151. ¹[Presentation of] the tribute by the Good God, ²to his father, Amon-Re, lord of Thebes, when he returned from the country of Kheta (*Ḥt*ʾ), ³devastating the [rebellious] countries, smiting the Asiatics, ⁴[taking] their possessions of silver, gold, lapis lazuli, malachite, ⁵and [every] splendid, [costly stone], according as he decreed to him might and victory against every country.

Over Prisoners, Upper Lines

152. ¹Great chiefs of Retenu (*Rṯnw*) the wretched, whom his majesty ²carried off in his victories in the country of Kheta (*Ḥt*ʾ),³in order to fill the storehouse of his august father, Amon-Re, lord of Thebes, ⁴according as he has given to him might against the south and victory against the north. ⁵The chiefs of the countries, they say in acclaiming his majesty, L. P. H., ⁶in magnifying his might: "Hail to thee, O king of

[§ 154] KARNAK RELIEFS 75

Egypt, Sun [7]of the Nine Bows. Great is thy fame, O lord of gods, (for) thou hast carried away all[a] the countries, [8]thou bindest them beneath the two feet of thy son Horus, Vivifier of the Two Lands."

Over Prisoners, Lower Line

Great is thy fame, O victorious king; how great is thy might! Thou art Montu in every country; thy strength is like his form.

SCENE 20. SLAYING PRISONERS BEFORE AMON[b]

153. This scene on the right of the door forms the symmetrical pendant of the like scene (11) on the left of the door, from which it differs only in the inscriptions. The account of Scene 11 (§§ 113 ff.) may serve equally well for this scene.

Before King

154. Good God, great in might, Lord of the Two Lands, Lord of Offering: Menmare, achieving with his sword —; Son of Re, smiting myriads, Lord of Diadems: Seti-Merneptah, smiter of —, given life, like Re.

Behind King

All protection, life, stability, satisfaction, all health, are behind him, like Re. The living king's-ka, Lord of the Two Lands, presiding over the $ḏb^{ꜣ\cdot}t$-hall, presiding over the $dw^{ꜣ\cdot}t$-hall;[c] he is given all life. Mighty Bull, Shining in Thebes, Vivifier of the Two Lands.

Over King

Hartema, lord of offering, smiting the countries, overthrowing his enemies.

Under Vulture

She gives victory, like Re; she gives all life, and satisfaction, like Re.

---

[a]On the use of r^c, see my *De Hymnis in Solem sub Rege Amenophide IV Conceptis*, 22–25; but my explanation of the phrase in the sun-hymn, "$yn\cdot k\ r^c\ -\dot{s}n$" (*ibid.*), is to be modified in view of this Seti passage. R^c is here clearly equivalent to "*number*," as so often in the great Papyrus Harris, and is used like *ṯnw*, "*number*," in the sense of "*all*." "*Yn*," being parallel with "$w^c\ f$, *seize or bind*," is clearly used as usual with the meaning: "*carry away captive*."

[b]For bibliography, see Fig. 1.   [c]See IV, 410, l. 1.

Before and behind Amon

155. ¹[Utterance of Amon:] ——— the Two Lands, my son, of my body, my beloved, Lord of the Two Lands: Menmare, brilliant in diadems ——— ² ——— his enemies. Thou hast carried away all countries; he who approaches [thy] boundaries ——— ³ ——— it is on the north of him; thy excellent fame is all that he (the sun) encircles; thy fear has penetrated ——— ⁴ ——— thy victories. I put the fear of thee in their hearts so that thou cuttest down the Curly-Haired^a ——— ⁵ ——— thy — in order to make me lord of their heads. The Sand-dwellers ($Hry\ w\text{-}š$ ᶜ) ——— ⁶ ——— I — my mace as ⁷ ——— thee, subduing for thee the rebe⁸[llious-hearted] ——— ⁹ ——— their chiefs [come] to thee with all their good tribute of their countries. I have given to thee Egypt ($T^\ni\text{-}mry$) ¹⁰ ——— [capti]ves for thy treasury. I cause the South to come to thee, doing obeisance, and the North bowing down. ¹¹ ——— before thy face. I have given to thee a kingdom established on earth, I make thy terror to circulate in ¹² ——— the sea ⌜bring⌝ his ⌜wealth⌝; I have opened for thee the highways of Punt. ¹³ ——— who is there. I give to thee Inmutef^b ($Yn\text{-}mw^\cdot t^\cdot[f]$) to lead thee, Khonsu and Horus-Soped, ¹⁴ ——— as thy followers, I make for thee his two hands as a cool retreat of the countries, ¹⁵ ——— [the countries that knew] not Egypt. I cause thy majesty to tread it like one — faced, like the wolf ¹⁶ ———. I give to thee the possessions of Horus and Set, and their victories. The portions of the two gods are made thy portions.

Over List of Captives

156. List of those southern and northern lands, which his majesty smote, making a great slaughter among them of unknown number. Their subjects are carried away as living captives to [fill] the storehouse of his father, Amon-Re, lord of Thebes, all countries —.

Under Amon's Foot

——— I give to thee all lands, every country is beneath thy sandals.

ᵃFor *rdb* read *ndb*, as in Tombos Inscription, l. 8 (II, 71).
ᵇLit., "*Pillar of his Mother*." See II, 133 and 138, note.

WADI HALFA STELA[a]

157. As stated above (§ 74), this monument is practically a duplicate of a stela erected by Seti I at the same place six months before, recording his father's pious works in the southernmost of the two temples at Wadi Halfa. It was perhaps erected by Seti after his campaign of the first year, as it is dated in that year, and refers at the same time to "*the captivity of his majesty*."[b] The king is only confirming the offerings established by his father, as they are identical with those on Ramses I's stela (§§ 74 ff.), and this identity, and the absence of Ramses I's name, make it certain that Ramses I had died in the interval between the two stelæ. Moreover, both stelæ are of Seti I's first year; on the first his father is still living; on the second, six months later, he is not mentioned. Hence he died in Seti's first year, and probably in his own second year; at most he reigned two and a half years.

Introduction

158. ¹Year 1, fourth month of the third season, the last day. Live Seti I[c] .... ². .... given life, beloved of ³Amon, lord of Thebes, and Min-si-ese, appearing upon the Horus-throne of the living, like his father, Re, every day.

Establishment of Offerings

159. Lo, his majesty was ⁴i[n the c]ity of Memphis ($Ḥ·t-k^ꜣ-Ptḥ$) performing the ceremonies of his father, Harakhte, Ptah, the great, South-of-His-Wall, lord of Life-of-the-Two-Lands, Atum, lord of the

---

[a]Sandstone stela in the British Museum (No. 1189); published by Turajeff, St. Petersburg, 1902. The above translation is from my own copy of the original; the brackets contain restorations from Ramses I's stela (§§ 74 ff.).

[b]This captivity might possibly refer to some raid of Seti's among the Nubians, for in an inscription at Silsileh (Rougé, *Inscriptions hiéroglyphiques*, 165–67), otherwise consisting of conventional phrases only, he is called: "*bringer of the limits of the land of the Negroes as living captives.*" Moreover, as the stela reproduces that of his father merely, the phrase may be only an inadvertent repetition.

[c]The full fivefold titulary, as at Redesiyeh (§ 169).

Two Lands of Heliopolis ⁵and all [the gods] of Egypt (T ͗ -mry), according as they gave [to him] might and victory over all lands, united with one heart under thy sandals. ⌜— — —⌝ ⁶[His majesty^a commanded] to found [divine offerings for his father Min-] Amon residing in Bohen (Bhn˙t), his first foundation in his temple: 12 (pr˙t-s) loaves; ⁷[100 (by ͗˙t) loaves; 4 (ds) jars of beer; 10 bundles of vegetables.]^b

Priests and Servants

160. [Likewis]e this temple was filled with prophets, ritual priests, priests (w ᶜ b); ⁸his storehouse was filled with male and female slaves from the captivity of his majesty, L. P. H., [the King of Upper and Lower Egypt] Menmare (Seti I), given life, like Re, forever and ever.

161. ⁹Lo, his majesty sought excellent things to do them for his father Min-A[mon] ¹⁰residing in Bohen; he made a great, august stela of good sandstone for the — place ——— ¹¹of [his father], Amon, for the beautiful birth-house of the ennead, where appears the lord of gods, the King of Upper and Lower Egypt ———.

INSCRIPTIONS OF REDESIYEH^c

162. The reliefs in the vestibule contain two stereotyped scenes, showing the king overthrowing the people of the north and south. These evidently do not refer to specific victories of Seti, but are of the conventional order. They are as follows:

163. ^dAmon, leading ten peoples captive, extends the

---

^aThere is not room for the cartouche, as on Ramses I's stela (l. 6).

^bDeterminative preserved, showing with the first item that Seti's list was identical with Ramses I's (l. 7). Turajeff inserts all the items and numbers, probably from the stela of Ramses I.

^cIn the temple usually given the same name, although it is located in the desert thirty-seven miles east of the modern Redesiyeh (Baedeker, 347 f.), which is on the Nile about five miles above Edfu. It was discovered by Cailliaud in 1816. The inscriptions have never been completely published; the most important ones by Lepsius (*Denkmäler*, III, 139–41, *d*, copied thence by Rheinisch, *Chrestomathie*, Taf. 9); the long ones much better by Golénischeff (*Recueil*, XIII, Pl. I and II). See also Lepsius, *Denkmäler*, Text, IV, 75–84.

^dLepsius, *Denkmäler*, III, 139, *a*.

(ḫpš-) sword to Seti, who slays a group of Kushites before the god. Interspersed are the following inscriptions:

Over Amon

164. Utterance of Amon: "Take to thyself the sword, O mighty king, Horus of the bows, in order to overthrow the chiefs of Kush, the wretched; in order to cut off their heads. Thy terror enters into their bodies, like Sekhmet when she rages."[a]

By the King

Smiting the chiefs of Kush the wretched.

Scene[b]

165. Same as above, only with Horus[c] in place of Amon, and Asiatics in place of Kushites; inscriptions as follows:

Over Horus

Utterance of Horus of Edfu: "Take to thyself the sword, O mighty King, Horus, shining in Thebes, in order to smite the rebellious countries, that violate thy boundaries. Thy fame is among them forever; (they) fall in their blood by the might of thy father, Amon, who hath decreed thee might and victory."

166. In addition to these unimportant scenes, the temple contains three inscriptions[d] of great importance as indicating the revival of intercourse with the Red Sea region, and the exploitation of the gold mines in the Gebel Zebâra district[e]. According to these inscriptions, the road to the mines eastward though the desert, was so lacking in water that the working of the mines in Seti's time had languished. Seti undertook to establish communications by digging a well on

---

[a]The list of ten names in the ovals of the captives is entirely conventional.
[b]Lepsius, *Denkmäler*, III, 140, a.
[c]The god here leads only six countries, of which Shinar, Shasu, Kadesh, Ashur, and Megiddo are certain.
[d]Cut on the face of the rock in which the temple is excavated.
[e]See Lepsius, *Metalle*, 36, 37.

this road thirty-seven miles from the Nile, claiming that he was the first to do so, although the name of a *"king's-son"* under Amenhotep III, named *"Mermose,"*[a] still surviving, cut on the rocks in the vicinity, proves the use of the station already in the Eighteenth Dynasty.

167. The first inscription, dated in the year 9, narrates the successful completion of the well and also the erection of a temple and establishment of a settlement at this station. The heretofore unnoticed motive for all this elaborate equipment is stated in the king's words to be (l. 13): *"on behalf of my beautiful house in Abydos."* This is, of course, Seti's famous temple at Abydos, which he says was erected *"by oracle of the god"* (l. 13). It is to endow the king's mortuary service in this temple that he is now restoring communications with the eastern gold regions. He therefore prays, as he worships for the first time in the new temple at the newly established station on the road to the mines, that the god may instruct coming generations of kings and princes to respect his establishment, presumably both at Abydos, and at the new station by which communication with the source of revenue for Abydos was to be maintained. This explains why the next inscription of nineteen lines, the longest of the three, is devoted almost exclusively to warnings and curses addressed to those who may in future interfere with the arrangements by which Seti hopes to perpetuate the income of his Abydos temple from the gold mines. Hence at its close (l. 19) he calls down the vengeance of Osiris, Isis, and Horus upon the person, wife, and children of any official of the necropolis (of course, at Abydos) who shall disregard (*"avert the face from"*) *"the command of Osiris."* But, notwithstanding these solemn adjurations of Seti, he had

---

[a] *Recueil*, XIII, 79, and Pl. IV, No. 1.

not been dead a year when his mortuary endowments at Abydos were suspended (§ 263). They were then re-enacted by his son, Ramses II (§ 271, ll. 73-75; § 272, 77-89).

168. The third inscription records the gratitude of the king's people who use the new station and the road thus rendered easy. They call him "*the good shepherd*"[a] (l. 2), and it is not accidental that in the dedicatory inscription of Seti's Abydos temple, he is likewise called the "*mighty shepherd*,"[b] indicating that particular activity of the king, to which the temple owed its income.

I. FIRST INSCRIPTION[c]

Introduction

169. ¹Year 9, third month of the third season, the twentieth day, under the majesty of Horus: Mighty-Bull-Shining-in-Thebes-Vivifier-of-the-Two-Lands; Favorite of the Two Goddesses: Uhemmesut,[d] Mighty of Sword, Expelling-the-Nine-Bows; Golden Horus: Repeating-Coronations, Mightiest-of-Bows-in-All-Lands; King of Upper and Lower Egypt: Menmare (Mn-m ᵓ ᶜ · t-R ᶜ); Son of Re: Seti-Merneptah, given life forever and ever.

Seti's Excursion in the Desert

170. On this day, lo, as his majesty inspected the hill-country as far as the region of the mountains, his heart desired ²to see the mines from which the electrum[e] is brought. Now, when his majesty had

---

[a] Read the standing man, with the staff and sack (?), as s ᵓ, e. g., Brugsch, *Thesaurus*, VI, 1435. The same phrase (s ᵓ n/r) applied to the king occurs in Mariette, *Karnak*, 35, l. 62 (corrected from photo); and compare also Libyan war of Merneptah (§ 580, l. 16). See also Bergmann, *Zeitschrift für ägyptische Sprache*, 1890, 40, n. 2.

[b] Lepsius, *Denkmäler*, III, 138, d.

[c] Lepsius, *Denkmäler*, III, 140, b = Golénischeff, *Recueil*, XIII, Pl. 1.

[d] Whm-msw · t = "Begetting again," or "Begotten (or born) again."

[e] Gold was commonly found with so large an admixture of silver as often to be thus spoken of; and in this same temple the god says to Seti: "*I have given to thee the gold-countries, giving to thee what is in them of electrum, lapis lazuli and malachite.*" Lepsius, *Metalle*, 45, and *Denkmäler*, III, 141, b. The same in Ramses III's treasury (IV, 28).

ascended from the signs of numerous water courses, he made a halt in the road, in order to devise counsel with his heart, and he said: "How evil is the way without water! It is as with a traveler ³whose mouth is parched. ⌈How⌉ shall their (sic!) throats ⌈be cooled⌉, how shall he (sic!) quench their thirst; for the lowland is far away, and the highland is vast. The thirsty man cries out for himself against a fatal country. Make haste! Let ⁴me take counsel of their needs. I will make for them a supply ᵃfor preserving them alive, so that they will thank god in my name, in after years. They shall come, and the generations which are to be, shall come to charm by me, because of my might and because that, lo, I am kind-hearted, inclining toward ⁵the circuit runners."

The Successful Well

171. Now, after his majesty had spoken these his words, in his own heart, he coursed through the highland seeking a place to make a water-station. Lo, the god led him, in order to grant the request which he desired. Then were commanded workmen ⁶in stone, to dig a well upon the mountains, that he might sustain the fainting, and cool for him the burning heart in summer. Then this place was built in the great name of Menmare ($Mn\text{-}m^{\jmath\,c\cdot}t\text{-}R^c$, Seti I), and the ⁷water inundated it in very great plenty like the two caves^b of Elephantine.

Plan for a Settlement and Temple

172. Said his majesty: "Behold, the god has performed my petition and he has brought to me water upon the mountains. Since the gods the way has been dangerous, (but) it has been made pleasant in my glorious reign. ⁸The districts of the colporteurs are refreshed, the land is extended, my reign is with might in every respect. It has not been known —— —— —— under me. Another good thought has come into my heart, at command of the god, even the equipment of a town, ⁹in whose august midst shall be a resting-place, a settlement, with a temple. I will build a resting-place in this spot, in the great name of my fathers, the gods. May they grant that what I have wrought abide, that my name prosper, circulating through the hill-country."

ᵃThis is the same as *ᶜ-mw*, "*water-supply*," in the Assiut inscriptions (I, 407), but the *mw* is here omitted, as also sometimes elsewhere. See also II, 698.

ᵇText has *tph·t* and *krty*, from which the Krophi and Mophi, given by Herodotus as the Nile sources, were doubtless corrupted.

Construction of the Temple

173. Then his majesty commanded ¹⁰that the leader (*ḫrp*) of the king's workmen be commissioned, and with him the quarrymen, that there should be made by digging (š ᵓ d)ᵃ in this mountain, this temple, wherein is Amon, in whose midst is Re, in whose great house are Ptah, Osiris, Horus, Isis, Menmare (Seti I), and the divine ennead ¹¹belonging in this temple.

Seti Worships in the New Temple

174. Now, after the stronghold was completed, adorned and its paintings executed, his majesty came to worship his fathers, all [the gods]. He said: "Praise to you, O great gods! who furnished heaven and earth according to their mind. May ye favor me ¹²forever, may ye establish my name eternally. As I have been profitable, as I have been useful to you, as I have been watchful for the things which ye desire, may ye speak to those who are still to come (*yw·ty·sn*), whether kings, or princes or people (*rḫy·t*), that they establish ¹³for me my work in the place, on behalf of my beautiful house in Abydos, made by the oracle of the god, the existent one, that they may not subvert his plan. Say ye, that it was done by your oracle, for that ye are the lords. I have spent my life and my might for you, ¹⁴to attain my acceptability from you. Grant that my monuments may endure for me, and my name abide upon them."

II. SECOND INSCRIPTION[b]

Address to Earlier Kings

175. ¹King of Upper and Lower Egypt: Menmare (Seti I), Son of Re: Seti-Merneptah. He saith to his fathers, all the Kings of Upper Egypt, the Kings of Lower Egypt, the rulers[c] and the people (*rḫy·t*): "Hearken to me, ye chiefs of bowmen of the Land of Egypt (*T ᵓ -mry*); may ye hear ²the things, O may ye —. I have desired to requite your virtues alike, ye being like gods; a lord is counted among the divine ennead. I have said this for the ⸢guidance⸣ of my caravaneers of the gold-washers to my temple, to set them carrying ³for my house ———— my temple."

ᵃAll except the vestibule of the temple is excavated in the side of the mountain.
ᵇLepsius, *Denkmäler*, 140, *c* = Golénischeff, *Recueil*, XIII, Pl. II.
ᶜIt is possible to render also: "*rulers of the people.*"

Warning to Caravaneers on the Inviolability of Gold

176. As for gold, it is the limbs of the gods;[a] not your possession. Take care lest ye say ⌈that which⌉ Re said at his beginning of speech: "My skin is of pure electrum."

Warning to Caravaneers concerning Earlier Endowments

177. "Now, Amon, the lord of my temple 4————. His two eyes are upon his possessions. They do not desire to be deprived of their belongings. Take heed against the incursions of their people, because they are like them that taste his —. Make not 5joy————. As for the one who trespasses upon the matter of another, there shall come to him an end, by doing likewise; the monument of the violator shall be violated, and there shall not remain an example of the deceivers — — 6the king."

Seti's New Plans

178. "———— to let you know that I have inaugurated a way, in order to save you; I have made the caravaneers into gold-washers in — 7in my name ———— my — by my virtues. I have made them into caravaneers anew, in order that they might remain under me. I have not brought from other 8caravaneers ———— among the children of my temple, or among the mountaineers of my sanctuary."

Exhortation and Good Wishes to Future Kings

179. "As for any king who shall be after me, he shall establish my work, 9in order to cause to abide ———— conveying his impost to the house of Menmare (Seti I), to gild all their images, made by Amon, Harakhte, Ptah-10Ta[te]nen ———— they flourish. May they rule the lands with gladness of heart, may they overthrow the Red Lands and Nubia; may their ka's abide; may their food-offerings endure. May he satisfy 11those who are upon earth; may Re hear ————."

Warning to Kings Who Shall Disregard Seti's Establishments

180. ———— saying: "Now, as for any king, who is to come, who shall overthrow any of my plans with me, he is one of whom the lands after me shall say, that I and they were as they are 12with him; an evil

---

[a]Compare the words of Ptah in his address to Ramses II (Lepsius, *Denkmäler*, III, 194; § 401, l. 7).

matter for the heart of the gods. Behold, one shall answer him in Heliopolis ———. They shall make answer concerning their affairs. They shall redden like flame of fire, and they shall consume their limbs, (because) they ¹³hearkened not to me. They shall consume the violator of my plans, in order to place him in the dungeon of the gate."ᵃ

Good Will for the King Who Respects Seti's Establishments

190.ᵇ "[ᴵAs for him who respects] our affairs, cause to save him, void of his offense; ᴵfor he isᴵ another who derives ¹⁴understanding from the divine ennead; they shall abide with him."

Blessing on Seti's Officials, Who Shall Survive Him

191. Now, as for any official who shall survive to (the time of) a king after me, he shall cause to remember good, in order to establish the matter which I have done in my name. May the god give reverence for him on earth; may his end be satisfaction ¹⁵brought to his ka.

Curse on Disregardful Officials Surviving Seti

192. Now, as for any official who shall bring near this thought to his lord, in order to take away the (ḥsb·w) people,ᶜ to give them to another, ᴵ—ᴵ by counsels of evil testimony; the fire shall burn his glowing limbs, the flame shall ¹⁶devour his members, because his majesty made all these things for their ka, the lords of my house. An abomination of the god is the transgression against his people. None turns away the violating hand except it be the caravaneers ¹⁷of the gold-washing, which I have made for the house of Menmare, protected and defended. It shall not be made to fall by any people who are in the whole land, by any chief archer of the gold, or by any inspector of the highlands.

Further Warning to Respect Endowment

193. Now, as for anyone who shall transgress against the people therein, ¹⁸putting (them) into another place, the gods and goddesses, the lords of my house shall execute upon him the appropriate penalty. (For) there is none ᵈto oppose that any of my property in the inventory

---

ᵃThe prison at Thebes was at the gate of the temple of Amon (IV, 541).

ᵇIntentional omission of nine in numbering sections.

ᶜSome kind of official people in Seti's new establishment, whom Seti now warns their superiors not to take away, in disregard of his endowment.

ᵈThe negative *n* is to be read.

should be beneath their feet, forever and ever; except it be the chief archer of the caravaneers of the gold-washing of the house of ¹⁹Menmare, by his hand, presenting their impost of gold to the house of Menmare.

Curse on One Disregarding Command of Osiris

194. As for anyone who shall avert the face from the command of Osiris, Osiris[a] shall pursue[b] him, Isis shall pursue his wife, Horus shall pursue his children, among all the princes of the necropolis, and they shall execute their judgment with him.

III. THIRD INSCRIPTION[c]

195. ¹Horus: Mighty-Bull-Shining-in-Thebes, Vivifier-of-the-Two-Lands; King of Upper and Lower Egypt [Menmare (Seti I)]; he made (it) as his monument for his father, Amon-Re, and his divine ennead; making for them a temple anew:[d] wherein the gods are satisfied; before which he dug a well. Never was made ²the like of it by any king, save by the king, the maker of glorious things, the Son of Re, Seti-Merneptah, the good shepherd,[e] who preserves his soldiers alive, the father and mother of all. They say from mouth to mouth: "O Amon, give to him eternity; double to him everlastingness. Ye gods dwelling in the well,[f] ³give ye to him your duration; for he hath opened for us the way to march in; (when) it was closed up before us. We proceed[g] and are saved; we arrive and are preserved alive. The difficult way, which is in our memory, ⁴has become a good way. He (the king) has caused the mining of the gold to be like the sight of the Horus-hawk.[h] All generations that are to be, beseech for him eternity, that he may celebrate jubilees like Atum, that he may flourish like the Edfuan Horus,

---

[a]A second *ws*-throne has been omitted in the original; "Osiris" must be read twice, as the parallels following show.

[b]Lit., "*be behind;*" cf. English "be after."

[c]Lepsius, *Denkmäler*, III, 140, *d* = Golénischeff, *Recueil*, XIII, Pl. II.

[d]Or: "*for the first time.*"   [e]See § 168 and note.

[f]The formal name of each god, as patron of the temple and well, was: "*Amon or Horus (or any god in the ennead) dwelling in the well of Menmare*" (see Lepsius, *Denkmäler*, III, 139, *b, c, e, f*).

[g]"*T ꜣ wnn ḥr,* etc.," and "*Twn ḥr,* etc.," are parallel, the first being a miswriting of the auxiliary verb.

[h]An obscure comparison; Golénischeff thinks it refers to the swiftness of the hawk's eye.

⁵for he has made monuments upon the highlands for all the gods; he hath dug for water upon the mountains, (although) far[a] from men, the supply of every messenger that traverses the highlands, with the life, stability, and satisfaction[b] of the King of Upper and Lower Egypt, Menmare (Seti I), beloved of Amon-Re, king of gods.

196. On the neighboring rocks three of the officials intrusted by Seti with the establishment or administration of the station have left inscriptions. In the first two[c] the official's name is no longer legible, though in the second one may discern the words:

197. "Made by the officer of marines ———— commissioned to dig (*šd·t*) 'The Well of Seti-Merneptah.'"

198. The third[d] was made by Iny (*Yny*), an official of high rank, who is shown praising Seti I, thus:

"Praise to thy ka, O good and beautiful ruler, child of Amon, the sun (*Šw*), in seeing whom one lives. O ka of every house, my god, who fashioned me, in order to make me; grant thou the food of the great. How prosperous is he who follows thee daily. [For the] ka of the chief of the stable, of the 'Stable of Seti-Merneptah,' charioteer of [his] majesty, king's-son of Kush —, chief of the gendarmes, Ini (*Yny*) ————."

BUILDING INSCRIPTIONS

199. Seti I has not left us any long record of his buildings, like those which we find in the Eighteenth Dynasty. Of his notable activity as a builder the only inscriptional witnesses are several quarry stelæ, and the architrave and other dedication formulæ still to be found in the buildings themselves. Besides erecting new temples, Seti was active in

---

[a] Meaning the water; it was formerly far from men in this place.
[b] That is, "*in the service*" of the king.
[c] Golénischeff, *Recueil*, XIII, Pl. III.
[d] Lepsius, *Denkmäler*, III, 138, *n;* corrections by Golénischeff, *Recueil*, XIII, 79.

restoring the old. Throughout the country he had his sculptors at work restoring the defacement of the gods' names which had taken place under Ikhnaton, especially that of Amon. Examples of these restorations will be found frequently, as in the temple of Amenhotep III at El Kab,[a] on the great building record of Amenhotep III at Thebes (II, 878); or on the obelisks of Hatshepsut (II, 312). They are usually recorded thus:

200. Restoration of the monument which King Seti I made in the house of — (name of a god).

Taking up first the quarry stelæ, the following are the building inscriptions of Seti I:

I. FIRST CATARACT INSCRIPTIONS

1. ASSUAN INSCRIPTION[b]

201. In his ninth year, Seti I sent an expedition to Assuan, to obtain granite for his obelisks and colossi; the expedition left a record of its work on the rocks, showing Seti offering to Khnum, Satet, and Anuket, in a relief at the top, below which is the following inscription:

202. Year 9 under the majesty of[c] .... Seti I. .... [d]

His majesty, L. P. H., commanded to execute numerous works, in order to make very great obelisks[e] and great and marvelous statues, with the name of his majesty. .... [f]

---

[a]Lepsius, *Denkmäler*, III, 138, *g*, and Text, IV, 45.

[b]On the rocks on the route from Philæ to Assuan; published from inaccurate copies in de Morgan, *Catalogue des monuments*, I, 7. The text is, according to de Morgan, "très mal gravée," so that the concluding lines are untranslatable in his publication.

[c]Full titulary.   [d]A series of conventional epithets of the king are omitted.

[e]See his only surviving obelisk, from Heliopolis (§§ 544 ff.), and the mention of them on his temple model (§ 246).

[f]The remainder is totally unintelligible in the publication. A mutilated and badly copied rock inscription of Seti from the same locality (Lepsius, *Denkmäler*, III, 141, *i*), doubtless contained similar information as the above text, for it is also dated in "*year 9*" and begins: "*His majesty, L. [P.] H., commanded to make great obelisks for Egypt. Then his majesty found* ———" (remainder lost).

2. ELEPHANTINE STELA[a]

203. Above, Seti I worships Amon and Khnum; below, an inscription of eighteen lines, containing a prayer of the king to Khnum. It is very fragmentary, and the only data of historical importance are these:

204. [14]——— Thou hast flooded thy temple with their food-offerings ——— [15]——— of silver, gold, lapis lazuli, and malachite; thou hast filled [thy] storehouse ——— [16]———. Thou hast given to me the South as well as the North, the West and the East, beneath [my sandals].[b]

II. SILSILEH QUARRY STELA[c]

205. In his sixth year Seti I sent an expedition of one thousand men to Silsileh to procure blocks of sandstone for his temples. He records with pride his humane treatment

---

[a]A stela set up at one corner of one of the Elephantine temples; copied and published by Champollion (*Notices descriptives*, I, 223, 224), but since probably covered up again, as it was not copied by de Morgan's expedition.

[b]These are conventional terms, and may not apply to any particular conquests of Seti. A neighboring rock shows him in the ancient traditional style smiting the southern enemy, while the viceroy of Kush adores him. The latter is accompanied by the following inscription: "*Fan-bearer on the king's right hand, governor of the Southern Country, king's-son, Amenemopet*" (Lepsius, *Denkmäler*, III, 141, $h =$ de Morgan, *Catalogue des monuments*, 28–5). This viceroy of Kush has left his name several times in this locality, e. g., on the island of Sehel (*ibid.*, 103, No. 53; also Mariette, *Monuments divers*, No. 53). Farther up the river he has left a considerable inscription (Sayce, *Recueil*, 16, 170 ff.). "Above the inscription is a representation of the Pharaoh in the act of slaying an enemy; behind him is a chariot drawn by two horses which are galloping away from the scene of combat, while to the left is a standing human figure. On the left-hand side of the last seven lines of hieroglyphic text are three vertical lines of inscription recording the name of Amen-mapet, the royal son of Kush, to the left of which again is the figure of a man kneeling on one knee and holding a 'fan' in his hand." This is Amenemopet, as the inscription beside him shows: the long inscription referred to contains only conventional praise of Seti I, in which occur the phrases: "*Valiant king, making his boundary to the limits in the 'Horns of the Earth.'* ..... *hacking up their town* ..... *The Southerners come to him in obeisance, and the Northerners with prostrations.*"

[c]On the east shore at Silsileh in the sandstone quarry, published by Rougé, *Inscriptions hiéroglyphiques*, 263–65, and Griffith, *Proceedings of the Society of Biblical Archæology*, XI, Pl. IV; Lepsius, *Denkmäler*, Text, IV, 98; cf. Lepsius, *Denkmäler*, III, 141, *e* (also *f* and *g*) and Text, IV, 97.

of his workmen, and the bountiful character of the rations which he issued to them.

Dispatch of the Expedition

206. ¹Year 6, fourth month of the first season, first day, under the majesty of Seti I.[a] .... ⁴....... On this day, lo, his majesty, L. P. H., was in the Southern City,⁵ performing the pleasing ceremonies[b] of his father, Amon-Re, king of gods, spending the night awake in pursuit of benefactions for the gods, the lords of Egypt. When the land brightened ⁶and ⌜day⌝ came, [his majesty], L. P. H., commanded to send a king's-messenger of [his] majesty, L. P. H., with a body of citizens of the army, being 1,000 men ⁷——————— in troops to transport the monuments of his father Amon-Re-Osiris and his divine ennead, of fine sandstone.

Rations of the Troops

207. His majesty, L. P. H., ⁸increased that which was furnished to the army in ointment, ox-flesh, fish, and plentiful vegetables without limit. ⁹Every man among them had 20 deben[c] of bread daily, ⌜2⌝ bundles of vegetables, a roast of flesh; and ⌜2⌝ linen garments monthly. (Thus) they worked ¹⁰with a loving heart for his majesty, L. P. H., his plans were pleasing in the mouth of the people who were with the king's-messenger of his majesty, L. P. H.

Rations of the King's-Messenger and Standard-Bearers

208. ¹¹That which he had: good bread, ox-flesh, wine, sweet oil, (⌜olive⌝) oil, ⌜fat⌝, honey, figs, ⌜—⌝, fish, and vegetables every day. Likewise the wreath[d] ¹²of his majesty, L. P. H., which was paid him from the House of Sebek, lord of Silsileh, daily; 20 linen garments were paid to the magazine of the standard-bearers of his army ¹³in like manner. ......[e]

---

[a]After the date nearly four lines are occupied by the names, titles, and epitheta of Seti I; they are very much mutilated.

[b]The original is corrupt; it must contain the usual *ḥr· yr t ḥss· t*, etc., occurring in this connection, e. g., on the Assuan stela of Thutmose IV (II, 826).

[c]Nearly four pounds.

[d]Mr. Alan Gardiner has called my attention to the occurrence of this word (ᶜ *nḫ*) here.

[e]Usual conventional phrases attached to the names of the king in conclusion.

III. GEBELÊN QUARRY INSCRIPTION[a]

209. The fragmentary record of Seti's quarrying operations at Gebelên shows that he took out stone there for his mortuary temple at Thebes, on the west side by Kurna.

210. [b]⸺ to search out ⌜—⌝ ⸺ Hathor, in order to cut out very much stone therein, (for) the "House-of-Menmare (Seti I)-of-Millions-of-Years-upon-the-West-of-Thebes." Then he came to his majesty, L. P. H., saying ⸺ an opportunity of making his name to flourish in the whole land. On this day, the overseer of [⌜the treasury⌝], Thutmose — who ⸺ gave silver and gold of one time,[c] to prosecute his work ⸺ to cut out very much stone (for) the "House-of-Menmare (Seti I)," while working ⸺. He said: "— plan — the king protect —" — regulation of the impost, to assign their [⌜overseer⌝] who is in charge of "Lord-of-Life;"[d] the people — the work. It is his father, Amon ⸺ telling thee the desires of the heart ⌜since⌝ the time of the god. For the ka of the scribe, who conducts the monuments of the Lord of the Two Lands, the chief of works, Hui.

IV. MORTUARY TEMPLE AT THEBES (KURNA)

211. Besides the quarry inscription at Gebelên, Seti has recorded the erection of his beautiful mortuary temple at Kurna in a series of dedication inscriptions in the building itself. Several show that the temple was also dedicated to the mortuary ritual of his deceased father:

212. [e]Seti I; he made (it) as his monument for his father, Osiris-Ramses I [triumphant; making for him a house] of millions of years, the "Temple-of-the-Spirit-of-Seti-Merneptah-in-the-House-of-Amon-on-the-West-of-Thebes;" and fashioning his barque, ⌜built⌝ of electrum, in

---

[a]In one of the quarries, on the rocks at Gebelên; found there and published by Daressy, *Recueil*, X, 134.

[b]Here are visible the fragments of Seti I's titulary, which was doubtless preceded by the date and followed by the words: "His majesty commanded, etc."

[c]A kind of gold.

[d]The name of the mountain on the west of Thebes; also the word for "*sarcophagus lid*."

[e]Champollion, *Notices descriptives*, I, 705.

order to carry his beauty in the procession of the lord of gods, at his feast of the valley.

213. ᵃSeti I; he made (it) as his monument for his father, the Good God, Menpehtire (Ramses I), making for him a place of coolness forever.

ᵇ........ making for him a Great House of silver, wrought with electrum ———.

ᵇ........ making for him an august palace of eternity.

ᵇ........ᶜ making for him a house of millions of years on the west of Thebes.

214. The name of the temple: "*Temple-of-the-Spirit-of-Seti-Merneptah-in-the-House-of-Amon-on-the-West-of-Thebes*"ᵈ shows clearly that it was also Seti's own mortuary temple. Hence I have also found six dedications to himself alone or to Amon:

215. 1.ᵉ Seti I; he made (it) as his monument for his father, Amon-Re, lord of Thebes, —— of Karnak, making for him a great palace, an august holy of holies, for the divine ennead, a place of rest for the lord of the gods at his beautiful feast of the valley; which the son of Re, Seti I, given life, like Re, forever, made for him.

216. 2.ᵉ Seti I; he made (it) as his monument for his father, Amon-Re, king of gods, making for him a house of millions of years, on the west of Thebes, over against Karnak, of fine white sandstone, made very high and great, which the son of Re, etc........ᶠ

217. 3.ᵍ Seti I; he made it as his monument for his father, Amon-

---

ᵃLepsius, *Denkmäler*, III, 131, *b;* Champollion, *Notices descriptives*, I, 707.

ᵇBrugsch, *Recueil de monuments*, 52, 3; Lepsius, *Denkmäler*, III, 132, *g, h*. Usual introduction omitted.

ᶜLepsius, *Denkmäler*, III, 131, *c* and *d;* also *ibid.*, 132, *h*.

ᵈSeti I's temple at Memphis was also called: "*Temple-of-the-Spirit-of-Seti-Merneptah-in-the-House-of-Ptah*" (Brugsch, *Thesaurus*, V, 1223).

ᵉLepsius, *Denkmäler*, III, 132, *a;* Champollion, *Notices descriptives*, I, 696, 697.

ᶠAs in No. 1; but the name here is that of Ramses II, according to Champollion, *Notices descriptives*, I, 696.

ᵍLepsius, *Denkmäler*, 132, *e*, and again 152.

Re, lord of Thebes, residing in the "Temple-of-the-Spirit-of-Seti-Merneptah-in-the-House-of-Amon-on-the-West-of-Thebes," making for him a house of millions of years, of fine, white sandstone, a place of appearance for the lord of gods, to behold the beauty of Thebes. The doors thereof are of real cedar, wrought with Asiatic copper, made high and large.

218. 4.[a] .... making for him a wide hall, shining in the midst of his house, a place for the appearance of his august image at his beautiful "Feast of the Valley." The great divine ennead who are in Tazeser, their hearts are satisfied ———.

219. 5.[b] He made (it) as his monument for his fathers, the gods and goddesses residing in the temple (called): "Spirit (y.$ḥ$)-of-Seti-Merneptah-in-the-House-of-Amon-on-the-West-of-Thebes," making for them an august palace as a house of the holy of holies for the gods. When they rest in its palace, Amon-Re is at the front ———."

220. 6.[c] .... making for him a house of millions of years on the west of Thebes, over against Karnak, of fine white sandstone, made very high and large. ....[d]

221. The temple was not finished at Seti's death, but was completed by his son, Ramses II, who has left in it more dedication inscriptions (§§ 516–22) than did his father.

V. TEMPLE OF KARNAK

222. The northern half of the great hypostyle hall, including the nave, with both its rows of columns and also the first row south of the nave, are the work of Seti I. The pylon in front of the hall was at least begun under Ramses I. Seti's portion of the hall contains architrave inscriptions and dedications, recording the building as his work, though it was finished under his son, Ramses II. Its name was:

---

[a]Lepsius, *Denkmäler*, III, 132, *d;* and 152, *d;* the latter is fuller and better preserved; the omitted introduction is the same as No. 3.

[b]"Chambre latérale, côté est de la grande salle" (Brugsch, *Recueil de monuments*, 51, 4).

[c]Champollion, *Notices descriptives*, I, 697; usual introduction is omitted.
[d]Conclusion as in No. 1.

"*Temple-of-the-Son-of-Seti-Mernamon-in-the-House-of-Amon.*"

223. ªSeti I; he made (it) as his monument for his father, Amon-Re, lord of Thebes (*Ns· wt-t ͗ wy*); making for him a great and splendid temple of fine sandstone. . . . . . ————. Utterance of Amon-Re, king of gods: "O my son, of my body, my beloved, lord of the Two Lands, Menmare (Seti I), Begotten of Re. How beautiful is this monument which thou hast made! O Uhem-mesut! Thou hast made festive my house a[new]; how exalted, how greatly extended are the august precincts,[b] which existed before the kings of Upper and Lower Egypt. No god put it into their hearts to make ⌈the like of that which thou hast made⌉."

224. Seti I, king, shining upon the steed like the son of Isis; archer, mighty of arm like Montu; a great wall of bronze, protecting his army; ⌈—⌉ upon the ⌈field⌉ in the day of battle; he did not consider[c] millions gathered together, by the might of Amon, who assigns to him victory and might over every land. . . . .[d]. . Seti I, maker of monuments in the House of Amon ⌈—⌉, in order to make for him who begat him in the great and august precinct of Karnak, a beautiful, divine resting-place wherein Amon might rest, a place of appearance for the lord of the gods at his feast of the First of the Year.

Other references like: "*maker of monuments with a loving heart in the house of his father, Amon,*"[e] occur in several places.

VI. MORTUARY TEMPLE AT ABYDOS

225. This, in decoration the most beautiful temple in Egypt, was chiefly the work of Seti I.[f] While serving as a

---

ªArchitrave inscription over the columns of the north side; Champollion, *Notices descriptives*, II, 79, 80.

[b]*S ͗ tw*, lit., "*ground, pavement;*" it is possible that we should understand it literally here, the reference being to the rise and extension of the site, which, according to Legrain, rose over a meter from Sesostris I to Seti (*Annales*, IV, 32, 33).

[c]Meaning "he despised." [d]Fuller titulary.

[e]Champollion, *Notices descriptives*, II, 78.

[f]Views of the temple, Mariette, *Voyage dans la haute Egypte*, I, Pls. 19–34, and the author's *Egypt through the Stereoscope* (Nos. 43–45).

mortuary temple for himself, sacred to all the gods of Egypt, it was also closely identified with the mortuary cult of the remote kings of the earliest dynasties, with whose tombs in the desert behind, it was connected by a pylon and a causeway. All Egypt was conceived as participating in and contributing to this service of the gods and the early kings; hence the nomes of all Egypt are represented at its doors in personified form.

226. The first and second pylons, with all of the first and most of the second court, have perished, and with them the dedication inscriptions of the architraves.[a] Those which remain are connected with the seven chapels devoted to the king and six great divinities, which form a row across the rear of the second hypostyle hall. In the center is Amon; on the right, Osiris, Isis, and Horus; on the left, Harakhte, Ptah, and the king himself. Thus the right is devoted to the Osirian triad, and the center and left to the three great state-gods of Thebes, Heliopolis, and Memphis, with whom is naturally associated the king himself as head of the state. The seven aisles leading to these chapels each bear inscriptions devoted to the divinity to whose chapel the respective aisle leads. These aisles pass through the first and second hypostyle, and the connecting doors between the two hypostyles bore dedications each to the divinity to whose chapel the respective aisle leads. These dedications of Seti I were erased by Ramses II, who inserted his own;[b] only four[c] are still legible:

---

[a]A long inscription in one of the rear chambers represents the goddess Safkhet-abui as describing the temple, but it can hardly be called a dedication or building inscription (Mariette, *Abydos*, I, Pl. 50, 51), being chiefly of religious significance. On the foundation ceremony in this inscription, see Brugsch (*Thesaurus*, VI, 1268 f.).

[b]He erased the name of Seti throughout the first hypostyle (Mariette, *Abydos*, I, 14, 37).

[c]Mariette, *Abydos*, I, Pl. 13, c, d, e. The fourth (b), not read by Mariette,

227. King Seti I, given life. He made (it) as his monument for his mother Isis, the great, the divine mother; making for her a doorway of electrum (named): "Menmare-is-Rich-in-Food."

228. This formula was repeated at each of the doors, with only the necessary change in the name of the god and the door. The recesses for the opened double doors also bore each a dedication of the chapel itself, which was six times repeated on each doorway, varying only in the name of the chapel:

229. [a]Seti I; he made it as his monument for his father, Horus, residing in "House ($h \cdot t$)-of-Menmare;" making for him a Great House ($h \cdot t$- ^{c} $^{\supset \cdot}$ t) of gold, that he may be given life.

230. In the five repetitions on this door we find in place of "*Great House*" above: (2) *Doorway;* (3) *Divine Monument;* (4) *Great House (pr wr);* (5) *August Palace;* and (6) *Place of the Heart's Rest.* In the aisle of Ptah the chapel is called:[b]

(1) Great House (*pr wr*) Adorned with Electrum; (2) Splendid Palace like the Horizon of Heaven; (3) Temple made Festive with Provisions; (4) Glorious Temple upon the Excellent Seat; (5) August Temple of Gold; (6) Great Seat by the Side of ⌜Rosta⌝.

231. The chapels themselves also bear dedications. Three[c] of these refer to the temple as a whole, and mention only Osiris:

232. 1. He made (it) as his monument for Osiris, residing in "House ($h \cdot t$)-of-Menmare;" making for him a temple like heaven; its

---

is furnished by Borchardt's copies. The four are dedicated to Horus, Isis, Osiris, and Harakhte. Another dedication to Amon-Re, king of gods, Harakhte, Ptah of Memphis, and Osiris is published partially by Daressy (*Recueil*, 21, 6). See also Lepsius, *Denkmäler*, III, 138, *b–j*.

[a]*Ibid.*, Pl. 14, *a*.

[b]*Ibid.*, *b*. The designations may, of course, apply to the second hypostyle. Mariette published only the two given above.

[c]Along the ceilings; Mariette, *Abydos*, I, Pl. 19, *b, c, d*, and p. 17, § 49.

divine ennead are like the stars in it; its radiance is in the faces (of men) like the horizon of Re rising therein at early morning ———.

233. 2. . . . .[a] making for him an august temple, the most pure [house] of eternity, splendid seat of everlastingness, fronted by images and figures of all gods.

234. 3. . . . .[a] making for him a temple, beautiful, pure, glorious and excellent upon the divine soil of the lords of Tazeser, the cool seat of Wennofer, the rest — —.

235. The dedications on the chapel doorposts refer to the individual chapels, and mention on each one only the divinity to whom the respective chapel was devoted. The six[b] are as follows:

236. 1*a*. HORUS. He made (it) as his monument for his father, Horus, son of Isis, residing in "House-of-Menmare;" making for him a great seat shining in the faces (of men), its door is like a great illumination, by the side of his mother, Isis, (named): "Menmare-is-the-Protector-of-His-Father."

237. 1*b*. . . . .[c] in his house of millions of years; door (named): . . . . . .[d]

2*a*. ISIS. . . . . making for her a Great Seat, its door glittering with every splendid costly stone, its door is gilded with electrum, giving forth radiance like the sun; (named): "Menmare-is-Enduring-in-Monuments."

2*b*. . . . . . . making for her a great house — ⌜—⌝ house of millions of years; (named): . . . .

3*a*. OSIRIS. . . . . making for him a Great Seat, over against the lord of Tazeser, a great house (*pr wr*), gilded with electrum, its door [⌜expels⌝] darkness like the sun, when he appears in the morning; (named): "Menmare-is-the-Enricher-of-Abydos."

3*b*. . . . . making for him a very radiant —, its doorway gilded with electrum, its door — — adorned with every splendid, costly stone; (named): . . . .

---

[a]Same as No. 1.

[b]Mariette, *Abydos*, I, Pl. 18, *a–f*. Each dedication is double, one on each doorpost. One is fuller than the other. I have rendered the fuller form (*a*), adding the shorter as a variant (*b*).

[c]Same as 1*a*, as far as "*Isis*." [d]As in 1*a*.

4a. AMON. (Lost.)
4b. (Only fragments.)
5a. HARAKHTE......... making for him a Great Seat, adorned with electrum, its door gilded with electrum (named): "Menmare-the-Emanation-of-Re-is-the-Satisfier-of-Re-in-Abydos."
5b. (The same.)
6a. PTAH........ making for him a Great Seat, a chapel of the august ⌜god⌝, its door gilded with electrum (named): "Menmare-Ruler-of-Thebes-is-Great-in-Might."

238. In each of the chapel doorways is a further fivefold dedication, each formula containing a different name for the respective chapel.[a]

239. The colonnaded hall behind the Osiris-chapel contains a series of dedications inscribed on the columns. They begin with the usual formulary as above, but continue with various designations[b] of the temple as a whole, each beginning with "*making for him;*" thus:

240. 1. a pure palace anew, of fine limestone of Ayan.
2. a temple anew in the glorious seat of eternity.
3. a divine palace in the place which his heart loved.
4. an august adytum in the district of the lords of Tazoser.
5. an august adytum in the nome of the lord of Tazoser.
6. a great house ($h \cdot t^{c \, \supset} \cdot t$), a splendid seat of the lords of eternity.
7. horizon of eternity, place for performing the pleasing ceremonies in the presence.
8. a pure audience-hall, excellent forever.
9. a palace, a door of the dwellers in the Nether World.
10. the great seat of the ⌜sanctuary⌝.
11. a pure dwelling in the precinct of Tazoser.
12. a house like the heavens, its beauty illuminating the Two Lands.
13. a glorious seat, excellent for giving jubilees to the king.
14. this monument, beautiful, pure, flourishing, and excellent.
15. the favorite place of Wennofer by the side of Tazoser.

---

[a]These thirty dedications were not copied by Mariette; but from Borchardt's copies it is evident that they contain for the most part the conventional designations, and need not be repeated here. There are some repetitions.
[b]Mariette, *Abydos*, I, Pl. 19, *e*.

241. The seventh chapel, devoted in large measure to the king, was, after all, sacred to the gods in general, as the following dedications[a] show:

242. He made (it) as his monument for his fathers, the gods residing in "House-of-Menmare," making for them an august Great House (*pr wr*) in my house of millions of years, my great seat beside their majesties; (named): "Menmare-Equips-Abydos."

243. The other dedication begins with the same words, and proceeds: *making for them — — my door of millions of years (named): "King Menmare — —."*

VII. TEMPLE MODEL[b] OF HELIOPOLIS

244. This unique monument was the base block of a model temple and accessory monuments executed by Seti I at Heliopolis. It shows the sockets in which were set up the side walls, the pylons, colossal statues, a pair of obelisks, and the last pair of the avenue of sphinxes between which are the steps leading up to the temple. It was clearly not an architect's working model, but served some religious purpose in the temple, like the model tools and implements always found in the temple foundation deposit, or the model temple offered by the kings to the gods. Supplementing the model, the inscriptions on the right and left edge mention the making of a holy of holies, which by metonymy may mean an entire temple; two pylons, doorways, two "*pairs*," and two obelisks. Now the materials given are such as are never used for such purposes in a real temple, and the inscriptions therefore unquestionably refer to the model

---

[a]Mariette, *Abydos*, I, Pl. 28, *e*.

[b]A single block of gritstone about $34\frac{1}{2}$ by $44\frac{1}{4}$ inches, and $9\frac{1}{4}$ inches thick, "discovered at a village near Cairo in 1875," now in the possession of Commander H. H. Gorringe, U. S. N. It was published by Emil Brugsch in *Recueil*, 7–9, Pls. III and IV, and by Gorringe in his *Egyptian Obelisks* (New York, 1882), Pl. XXXII.

itself and to its parts. The model itself is the "*holy of holies*" (*sḥm*), also called "*temple*" (*ḥ·t-ntr*) of conglomerate; the two miniature pylons were of some costly white stone, the doorways of bronze, the flagstaves (the "*pairs*") of mesdet stone, and the obelisks of diorite. These valuable materials have long since been stolen, but the base block of conglomerate has survived, because of its ordinary material.

245. Although this model, as the inscriptions show,[a] had its own religious function, it suggests real buildings of Seti I, at Heliopolis. As a matter of fact, he did erect at least one obelisk there, which now stands in the Piazza del Popolo in Rome. But it was still uninscribed at Seti I's death, and its present inscriptions were placed upon it by his son, Ramses II (§§ 544–49), who reserved for himself one side of the obelisk, where he states the fact. He also affirms that Seti "*filled Heliopolis with obelisks.*"[b] But no others have survived. A doorpost from Heliopolis bears the following dedication:[c]

Seti I, beloved of Shu and Tefnut; he made (it) as his monument for his father, Atum, lord of Heliopolis; making for him a gate of gritstone, the doors thereof of cedar, wrought with —, established as an eternal work, which his majesty made, because he ⌈so much⌉ desired ⌈—⌉ — for the gods of Heliopolis.

246. The building inscriptions on the model are as follows:

[d][He made (it) as] his monument for his father, Re-Atum-Khepri, by making for him an august holy of holies in the likeness of the horizon of heaven, a resting-place of the two horizons, in which the lords of Heliopolis rest, like Atum — — —.

[e]The Good God, making monuments for his father, Re-Harakhte,

---

[a]On the edge, Seti I is eight times shown offering.

[b]See the record of Seti's work on obelisks in the Assuan quarry (§ 201 f.); and an altar of his at Heliopolis (*Annales*, II, 95, 96).

[c]Now in Alexandria; Legrain, *Annales*, V, 121.

[d]Left edge.   [e]Right edge.

making for him in the temple, of good (red) gritstone, two pylons of white costly stone, doorways of bronze, pairs[a] of mesdet (*msd·t*) stone, two obelisks of black basalt (*bḫnw*), established in Heliopolis, the horizon of heaven;[b] the gods of Heliopolis exult at seeing (them).

VIII. MISCELLANEOUS

247. Finally there are two more short dedications: one at Wadi Halfa, and one at Benihasan in the Speos Artemidos.

Wadi Halfa

248. [c][Seti I] seeking monuments for his father, Min-Amon, residing in Bohen; making for him a temple like the horizon of heaven, wherein Re rises.

Benihasan

249. [d]Seti I; he made (it) as his monument for his mother, Pakhet, the great, mistress of Benihasan, in her temple of the secret valley, the ⌜cleft⌝ of the cliff.

250. There are also a dedication inscription from an uncertain monument, possibly an obelisk found at Kantara;[e] and one or two minor references to buildings, of slight importance.

---

[a]The "*pairs*" (here *snsn* or *snwy*) are the tall flagstaves set up against the pylon-towers. In the temples they are of cedar, capped with metal (see II, § 103).

[b]All the preceding contains only participles agreeing with Good God, viz., the king.

[c]Champollion, *Notices descriptives*, II, 705; besides the confirmation of his father's pious works there (§§ 73 ff.).

[d]Champollion, *Notices descriptives*, II, 332; Sharpe, *Egyptian Inscriptions*, II, 60; Lepsius, *Denkmäler*, III, 138, h.

[e]Prisse, *Monuments égyptiens*, 19.

REIGN OF RAMSES II

GREAT ABYDOS INSCRIPTION[a]

251. This is the longest inscription of Ramses II's reign. Together with the Kubbân Stela, it has been regarded as the most important source for his youth and early regency. It shows us the young king in his first year journeying to Thebes,[b] and in mentioning a statue of his father erected by Ramses on that occasion at Thebes, the narrator takes occasion to summarize the king's works in provision for his father (ll. 22–26).[c]

252. Ramses now sails to Abydos (ll. 26–32), where he finds Seti I's beautiful temple (Baedeker, 218–23) unfinished, and its endowments violated (ll. 32, 33). He immediately summons his court and officials (ll. 33, 34), who come in with the usual fulsome adulation demanded by court etiquette (ll. 34–40), after which Ramses announces to them his intention to complete his father's buildings (ll. 40–43), and takes

---

[a]Cut on the wall of the portico behind the colonnade at the rear of the first court in the famous temple of Seti I at Abydos. The inscription is in 116 vertical lines, the first 21 of which accompany a relief and are shorter. Numerous lacunæ break the text. Published by Maspero (from a copy by Devéria): *Essai sur l'inscription dédicatoire du temple d'Abydos*, par G. Maspero (Paris, 1867); again by Mariette in 1880 (*Abydos*, I, 5–9). I also had a collation of Mariette with the original for the Berlin dictionary by Borchardt.

[b]Whence he came is quite uncertain. Maspero (*Struggle of the Nations*, 387) states that he came from Ethiopia, but for this I find no evidence. On the contrary, the mention of the statue erected in Memphis (l. 22) may indicate that he came from the north.

[c]Ll. 1–21 contain only the dialogue between the divinities (ll. 1–17) in the relief and Ramses (ll. 18–21). The translation begins with the words of Ramses (ll. 18–21). The works summarized in ll. 22–26 are (except the statues) not yet undertaken at the time of the visit to Thebes; but, being complete at the time of the composition of this inscription, the narrator inserts the summary here, forgetting that they were not complete at the time of which he is writing.

occasion to recall to his courtiers how his father had him publicly crowned coregent while a mere child, giving him extensive authority and a harem (ll. 43-48). He proceeds to describe his administration as coregent (ll. 48-50), and reiterates in conclusion his determination to complete his father's buildings (ll. 51-55). Hereupon the courtiers fairly outdo themselves in a long-winded eulogy of the dutiful son (ll. 55-69). The narrator now recounts the summons to the architects, artists, and workmen, who are commissioned to complete Seti I's temple. At the same time the king re-enacts and reorganizes his father's endowments for the maintenance of the temple and its mortuary service (ll. 69-75).

253. When all is done, Ramses addresses his deceased father, calling attention to all these pious works for his father's welfare in the hereafter (ll. 75-93), and showing how it will be to his father's interest to ensure unbroken continuance of these favors, by inducing the gods, among whom he now is, to grant Ramses a long reign. Ramses assures his father that his (Seti's) mortuary offerings shall be maintained as long as he (Ramses) continues on the throne (ll. 93-98). To this remarkable compact Seti, in reply, agrees, intercedes with the gods, and assures Ramses that the gods have decreed[a] him an eternal reign, and that he himself enjoys the greatest felicity because of his son's provision for him (ll. 98-116).

254. The inscription, it will be observed, is historically very important, as well as interesting in several respects. The statements regarding Ramses' coregency in youth are detailed and circumstantial. His appearance in public for coronation, in the presence of his father, reminds us of the

---

[a] See similar prayer of Seti, quoted with l. 103, p. 115, n. b.

similar account of Hatshepsut's coronation (II, 215 ff.). But the evidence of the Karnak reliefs (§§ 123 ff.) is so conclusively against his ever having been so chosen by Seti that, like the said story of Hatshepsut's coronation, we must regard it as a fabrication.[a] Such a fiction could hardly have been published immediately on Seti's death, and when we remember Ramses'. extraordinary compact with his deceased father, the question arises whether the inscription is a later product of Ramses' reign, and his long life is the source which suggested the fiction of the compact, to which the narrator now attributes Ramses' remarkable longevity.[b] In any case, the inscription was written after the completion of his works for his father, and after some of his foreign campaigns (l. 93).

255. The king's visit to Thebes in his first year is corroborated by an independent document in the Theban tomb of the High Priest of Amon, Nebunnef (*Nb-wn-nf*).[c] A relief in this tomb shows Ramses II, accompanied by his queen, Mutnofret, and the court, addressing Osiris. Before the god is the following inscription:

256. Year 1, third month of the first season, — —[d] when his majesty went north from the Southern City, ⌈having⌉ celebrated the pleasing ceremonies of his father, Amon-Re, lord of Thebes . . . . . .,[e] [Mut] . . . .,[e] Khonsu in Thebes, Beautiful Rest, and the Divine Ennead

---

[a]See also introduction to Kubbân inscription (§ 283), and my "Ramses II and the Princes in the Karnak Reliefs of Seti I" (*Zeitschrift für ägyptische Sprache*, 37, 138 f.).

[b]Against this is the motive for the account of his appointment as coregent— a motive which would have been influential only immediately after his accession, when he desired to support the legitimacy of his reign.

[c]Champollion, *Notices descriptives*, I, 535, 851, 852; and Lepsius, *Denkmäler*; Text, III, 239.

[d]The space for the day is left vacant in the original.

[e]Further titles of Amon and Mut, omitted by Champollion.

dwelling in Thebes; at his beautiful feast of Opet (named): "Returning-Thence-with-Praise."

257. As Nebunnef was High Priest, this great feast of Amon is naturally recorded in his tomb. It is the same feast, celebrated in the month Hathor, by Thutmose III[a] on his return from his first campaign (II, 541, 550), and, this being the first celebration of it in Ramses' reign, it naturally called him to Thebes, whose powerful priesthood he could not fail to conciliate by appearing at their temple in person on such an important occasion.

258. Returning now to our great document, we find in the relief scene preceding the long inscription that the young King Ramses II appears offering an image of the goddess Mat (Truth) to Osiris, Isis, and his deified father, Seti I. The speeches of the divinities are of solely religious interest. The speech of Ramses, which merges into the long inscription itself, is of historical importance, and begins the following translation:

Speech of Ramses

259. [18]Utterance of the King of Upper and Lower Egypt, Usermare-Setepnere (Ramses II) in the presence of his father, Osiris: "I champion thee, [19]like thy son, Horus; I have done according to [his][b] doing. I repeat for thee monuments in the necropolis, [20]I double offerings for thy ka. I answer on behalf of my father, he being in the Nether World ($Dw^{\jmath} \cdot t$), in the place ⌜— —⌝, [21]for the son becomes the champion of his father, like Horus, when he championed his father, forming him that formed him, fashioning him that fashioned him, making to live the name of him that begat him, the King of Upper and Lower Egypt, Ramses (II), given life, like Re, forever, beloved of Osiris, lord of Abydos."

Voyage to Thebes, Summary of Ramses' Works for His Father

260. [22]When the Lord of the Two Lands arose as king, to act as champion of his father, in the year 1, on his first voyage to Thebes, he fashioned

---

[a]Also by Piankhi (IV, 836).   [b]Cf. l. 43.

statues of his father; King Menmare (Seti I) was he; one in Thebes, another in Memphis, in the temple which he built for them, ²³an addition to the beauty of that which was in Abydos of Towêr, which he loved, which his heart has desired since he was on earth, the soil of Wennofer (Osiris). He repeated the restoration of the monuments of his father, which are in the cemetery, making his name live, fashioning his statues, giving offerings abiding ²⁴for his august ka — his house, supplying his altars, upbuilding that which was fallen in the house which he loved, erecting the seats in his temple, laying its walls, setting up its doorways, erecting the ruins in the seat of[a] his father, in the district of Osiris ——— ²⁵the double façade made therein, in everything which the Great in Victory, the King of Upper and Lower Egypt, Ramses (II), given life, made for his father, Osiris, the King Menmare (Seti I), triumphant. He established for him possessions, supplied with food of the ⌜— —⌝ his heart ²⁶being kindly disposed toward him that begat him, his feelings inclining toward him that brought him up.

Ramses Sails from Thebes to Abydos

261. On one of these days it happened in the year 1, the third[b] month of the first season, the twenty-third day, at the [⌜feast⌝][c] ——— after the return of Amon to Karnak, that he (the king) came forth, favored with might and victory from Amon-Atum in Thebes, and he rewarded him with myriads of years, even to the duration of Re in heaven. Hear ——— ⌜exalted⌝ forever and ever. He raised his hand, bearing the censer, to the horizon of him who abides in the West, his offering being excellent and acceptable to his [⌜father⌝], the lord of love. His majesty departed from the Southern City ——— Re.

(He) began the way,[d] to make the voyage, while the royal barges illuminated the flood, turning down-stream to the seat of might, "House[e]-

---

[a]There is a superfluous *n* here which suggests "*seat of truth, for his father,*" etc.

[b]Borchardt has only one month-sign.

[c]Even in Ramses III's day the Feast of Opet closed at least eight days before this; this must have been the Feast of Hathor, at which Amon also celebrated; but the king must have been at Thebes during the great Feast of Opet, which just preceded.

[d]For the usual form of this phrase, see Amarna Landmarks (II, 960, l. 6), or Scarab of Wild Cattle Hunt (II, 864).

[e]This is the earliest occurrence of the city of "Ramses." It is not clear why it should be mentioned, unless the king was going farther north to the Delta.

of-Ramses-Meriamon-Great-in-Victory." His majesty entered, to see his father, the voyage of the waters of the canal of Abydos[a] (*Nj-wr*), in order to found offerings for Wennofer, consisting of every good thing, that which his ka loves, in order to praise [30]— — — for his brother, Onouris, son of Re in truth, like himself.

Ramses Finds Cemetery Buildings in Ruins

262. He found the buildings of the cemetery belonging to former kings, their tombs[b] in Abydos, beginning to be in ruin. The half of them were in process of construction [31]— — — in the ground, their walls ⌈lying⌉ incomplete, not one brick touching[c] another. That which was only begun[d] had become mere rubbish. There was no one building — — — who was carrying out according to his plans, since their lord had flown to heaven. There was no [32]other son, who renewed the monuments of his father, which were in the cemetery.

Seti I's Temple Unfinished, Its Endowments Violated

263. Lo, the house of Menmare (Seti I), its front and its rear were in process of construction, when he entered into heaven. Its monuments were not finished, its columns were not set up on its ⌈platform⌉, its statue was upon the ground, it was not [33]fashioned after the regulation for it, of the gold-house. Its divine offerings had ceased, the lay priesthood likewise. That which was brought ⌈from⌉ its fields was taken away, their boundaries were not fixed in the land.[e]

Ramses Summons His Court and Officials

264. Said his majesty to the wearer of the royal seal who was at his side: "Speak thou, call [34]the court, the king's-grandees, all the commanders of the army, all the chiefs of works, and the keepers of the

---

[a]Abydos lies seven miles from the river, and is evidently connected with it by a canal which the king here enters. Compare the same voyage of King Neferhotep (I, 763, ll. 16, 17).

[b]These can hardly be anything else than the tombs of the First Dynasty kings. That some of them should be in course of construction may mean that chapels were being erected for these kings (their halls in Seti's temple) or that repairs were going on.

[c]Lit., "*embracing.*"

[d]*Msḫn* means "*birth- or nursing-chamber,*" which may be figurative for "beginning," that which was incipient. Suggested by Erman.

[e]See Seti I's solemn adjuration to respect his endowment of this very temple (§ 180, ll. 11-13, 15-19).

house of rolls (books)." They were brought before his majesty, their noses were bowed in the dust, their knees were on the earth ³⁵in adoration, smelling the earth; their hands were uplifted to his majesty, they praised this Good God, magnifying his beauty in the presence. They told the story according to that which he had done, they likened his brave deeds, as they were; every word which came out of their mouths, was that which the Lord of the Two Lands had actually done. ³⁶They were upon their bellies, ⌈wallowing⌉ upon the earth before his majesty, saying:

The Court Eulogizes the King

265. "We come to thee, lord of heaven, lord of earth, Re, life of the whole earth, lord of duration, of fruitful revolution,ᵃ Atum for the people, lord of destiny, creator of Renenet,ᵇ Khnum ³⁷who fashioned the people ($rḥy\cdot t$), giver of breath into the nostrils of all, making all the gods live, pillar of heaven, support of earth, ⌈—⌉ adjusting the Two Lands, lord of food, plentiful in grain, in whose footsteps is the harvest goddess, ³⁸maker of the great, fashioner of the lowly, whose word produces food, the lord vigilant when all men sleep, whose might defends Egypt, valiant in foreign lands, who returns when he has triumphed, whose sword protects the Egyptians, beloved of truth, in which he lives ³⁹by his laws, defender of the Two Lands, rich in years, great in victory, the fear of whom expels foreign lands, our king, our lord, our Sun, by the words of whose mouth Atum lives. Lo, we are now before thy majesty, that thou mayest decree to us the life that thou givest, ⁴⁰Pharraoh, L. P. H., breath of life, who makes all men live when he has shone on them."

Ramses Announces His Intention to Complete His Father's Buildings

266. Said his majesty to them: "Behold, I have caused that they call you, because of a plan that is before me. I have seen that the buildings of the cemetery, the tombs that are in Abydos, ⁴¹and the works therein, are in an unfinished state, since the time of their lord until this day. When a son arose in the place of his father, the monuments of him that begat him were not restored. Then I conversed with my own heart: 'It is a happy example, to provide for ⁴²them that have

---

ᵃThe king is often called the source of the land's fruitfulness; hence the same here, where he is called Re, the sun.
ᵇGoddess of birth, destiny, and good fortune.

passed away, excellent to behold good — — ⌜Horus who shaped⌝ the thought of the son, that he should incline the heart after his father. My heart leads me in doing excellent things for Merneptah (Seti I). I will cause it to be said forever and ever: ⁴²"It was his son, who made his name live."' May my father, Osiris, ⁴³favor me with the long life of his son, Horus, according as I do that which [he] did; I do excellent things, as he did excellent things, for him who begat me."

Ramses Relates His Appointment as Coregent

267. "I came forth from Re, [⌜although⌝] ye say, from Menmare (Seti I), who brought me up.ᵃ ⁴⁴The All-Lord himself made me great, while I was a child, until I reigned. He gave to me the land while I was in the egg; the great smelled the earth before me, when I was installed as eldest son, as hereditary prince upon the throne of Keb. I reported ⁴⁵— —ᵇ as lord ($ḥry-ḏ\ni ḏ\ni$) of infantry and chariotry. When my father appeared to the public, I being a child between his arms. [He] sa[id] concerning me: "Crown him as king, that I may see his beauty while I live ⁴⁶with him." [⌜Thereupon approached⌝] the courtiers ($ymyw$-$ḥnty$), to set the double diadem upon my head. "Place for him the crown upon his head," so spake he concerning me, while he was upon earth. "Let him organize this land, let him administer —, let him show his face to the people," so spake he ⁴⁷———— because the love of me was so great in his bowels.ᶜ He equipped me with ⌜household⌝ women, a royal harem, like the beauties of the palace, he chose for me wives, after ————, taking the concubines ⁴⁸of ———— his —, seizing ⌜—⌝ᵈ and female companions."

Ramses Describes His Administration as Coregent

268. "Lo, I was Re over the people ($rḥy\cdot t$), those of the South and North were under my feet ———— it was I, who [⌜set⌝] them to ⁴⁹[⌜building⌝] —. I fashioned my father in gold anew, in the first year of my

---

ᵃOr: "*I came forth from Re, [so] say ye, while Menmare brought me up.*"

ᵇMaspero's (Devéria's) text cannot be correct here; Borchardt shows only the canal-sign (mr) with the land-wedge.

ᶜOn the following passage, see Müller, *Liebespoesie*, 5. The different terms for harem-women are not exactly determined as yet.

ᵈMüller, "Abgeschlossene."

appearance (as king).[a] I commanded that his temple be prepared, I established his fields ———. I founded for him offerings for his ka. [50]——— wine, incense, all fruit, I cultivated trees, growing for him. Lo, his house was under my charge, all its works were under my authority, since ——— as a child."

Ramses Repeats His Intention to Complete His Father's Buildings

269. "[51]——— my father; I will enlarge them anew. As for the monuments, I will not neglect his seat, after the manner of those children who forgot [their] father. ——— speak of — [52]——— a son doeth excellent things. My mighty deeds for my father as a child, I will now complete, being Lord of the Two Lands; I will ⌜—⌝ in them in the proper way ——— [53]——— I will lay the walls in the temple of him that begat me. I will charge the man of my choice, to conduct this work therein. I will mason up therein the br[eaches] in its walls [54]———, its pylon-towers of ———. I will cover its house, I will ⌜erect⌝ its columns, I will set stones in the places of the lower foundation, making monument upon monument, two excellent things at one time, bearing my name[b] and the name of my father, for the son [55]is like him that begat him."

The Court Responds with an Eulogy of the King

270. Then spake the royal companions, and they answered the Good God: "Thou art Re, thy body is his body. There has been no ruler like thee, (for) thou art unique, like the son of Osiris, thou hast achieved the like of his designs [56]Isis [hath not loved⌝] a king since Re, except thee and her [⌜son⌝]; greater is that which thou hast done than that which he did when he ruled after Osiris. The laws of the land proceed according to his position. The son is compassionate to him that made him, the divine seed —— [57]him who created him [⌜in the⌝] ⌜e[gg]⌝ — it[c] inclines to the august guardian. None hath done that which Horus did for his father to this day, except thy majesty —. Thou

---

[a]This is evidently the statue of l. 72, and the reference to it by the king here, as a thing of the past, made in the year 1, is an anachronism of which a scribe, composing the inscription at a time when all the events it narrates were past, could easily be guilty.

[b]Ramses II's name is, indeed, upon many portions of the building which Seti built; Seti's name has even been erased to make room for it.

[c]Viz., the egg; that is, the young King Ramses II.

hast increased that which has been done; what ⁵⁸example of excellence ———— that we may introduce it, to tell it in the (royal) presence? Who shall come, that he may recall a thing proposed to thee[a]? (but) thou hast led the ignorant abroad ————. ———— mild, thy heart is kindly toward thy father, Menmare (Seti I), ⁵⁹the divine father, the beloved of a god, Seti-Merneptah, triumphant. Since the time of the god, since the kings have taken the crown, there has been no other like thee, neither seen in face nor heard in speech. [No other] son has repeated monuments for his father. Not one has arisen, ⁶⁰that he might champion his father, (but) every man deals for himself, on behalf of his own name, except thee and Horus, for thou art like the son of Osiris. Behold, thou art a goodly heir like him; as for his kingdom, thou administerest it in like manner. ⁶¹As for him who doeth that which the god did, he shall have the length of life which he enjoyed. Re in heaven [is joyous-] hearted, his divine ennead is glad, the gods are satisfied with Egypt since thy coronation as king of the Two Lands. Beautiful ———— is thy —, excellent is thy truth, it has reached ⁶²heaven, thy plans are right in the estimation of Re, Atum is delighted — —, Wennofer is in triumph at that which thy majesty has done for his ka. He says: '— — — [I give] to thee the duration of heaven, his two heavens;' ⁶³the gods of the secret place of the lord of the nether world say: 'Thou shalt be upon earth like Aton.' Glad is the heart of Merneptah (Seti I), his name shall live again, (for) thou hast fashioned him in gold and real costly stones, ———— his — of electrum ⁶⁴———— his —, thou buildest it anew, bearing thy name. As for every king[b] who is in heaven, whose buildings are in course of construction, there has been no son (of theirs) doing what thou hast done, since Re until ⁶⁵[this day]. ———— Thy majesty — him; that which he did, thou hast remembered, when it was forgotten. Thou hast restored monuments in the cemetery. As for every plan that was neglected, thou hast carried it out in the proper way ———— ⁶⁶———— passes away, another comes. Thy majesty is King of Upper Egypt and King of Lower Egypt, for thou doest excellent things, and thy heart is satisfied in doing truth. Those things which are done in the presence of the gods, shall be heard ———— ⁶⁷———— when [thou] rise[st to] heaven, when thy beauty ascends to the horizon, the eyes see thy excellent deeds before gods and men. Thou art the one

---

[a]The king is the one who originates and proposes.

[b]This is doubtless a reference to the list of kings in the Abydos temple.

who doest it; thou art the one who repeatest monument on monument for the gods, according as thy father, Re, commanded ⁶⁸that thy name should be ⌜known⌝ in every land, from Khenthennofer of the South, northward, from the ⌜shores⌝ of the sea to the countries of Retenu (*Rtnw*), and among the settlements and strongholds of the king, the towns colonized and supplied with people[a] ⁶⁹———— every city ⌜should know⌝ that thou art the god of all people, that they may awake, to give to thee incense at the command of thy father, Atum; that Egypt as well as the Red Land may adore thee."

Ramses Completes and Endows His Father's Temple

271. Now, after ⁷⁰—— these utterances which these nobles [had spoken] in the presence of their lord, his majesty commanded to commission the chiefs of works; he set apart soldiers, workmen, carvers with the chisel, ⁷¹—— draughtsmen, all ranks of artificers, to build the holy place of his father, to erect that which was in ruins in the cemetery, the mortuary house of his father. Lo, ⁷²he [bega]n to fashion his statue in the year 1;[b] while the offerings were doubled before his ka, his temple was properly victualed, and he supplied his necessities. He established his ritual roll of fields, peasant-slaves (*mry·t*) and cattle. ⁷³He appointed priests over their affairs, a prophet to upraise the hands ———— his people under ———— to conduct affairs —— under him; his numerous granaries with grain ⁷⁴———— his possessions. The great officials in South and North are under the authority of his steward, being an act of the King of Upper and Lower Egypt, Usermare-Setepnere; Son of Re, Meriamon-Ramses (II), given life, like Re, forever and ever, for his father, King Menmare (Seti I), triumphant, ⁷⁵——
——[under] the authority of Wennofer. He did it again for his ka in Thebes,[c] Heliopolis, and Memphis[d] (where) his statues rested in their places in all his ⌜stations⌝[e] of the ⌜—⌝.

---

[a]See Müller, *Asien und Europa*, 269, 270.

[b]Doubtless at the same time that he set up one in Thebes and another in Memphis (l. 22).

[c]A reference to Ramses II's work on the Theban mortuary temple of Seti I at Kurna.

[d]If Seti I had temples at Heliopolis and Memphis, they have now utterly vanished; but this remark may apply only to his statues.

[e]Where a statue stopped when carried in festival processions? But Spiegelberg (*Rechnungen*, 58) thinks it means "bazaar, market, or court."

Ramses Addresses His Father, Narrating His Good Deeds to Him

272. Then spake the King of Upper and Lower Egypt, Ramses II,[a] given life, [76]sending up[b] that which he had done for his father, the Osiris, King Menmare (Seti I), triumphant; saying: "Awake thou, (lift) thy face to heaven, that thou mayest see Re, O my father, Merneptah (Seti I), who art a god. Behold, I am making thy name to live, I have protected thee, I give attention to thy temple, [77]thy offerings are established. Thou restest in the Nether World ($Dw\ni\cdot t$), like Osiris, while I shine as Re for the people, being upon the great throne of Atum, like Horus, son of Isis, who protected his father. [78]How [happy] for thee, who begattest me —— since thou comest as one living again. I have fashioned thee, I have built the house thou lovest, wherein is thy statue in the cemetery of Abydos, region of eternity. I have founded offerings [79][for] thy s[tatues], the daily offerings come to thee. [I] am he that doeth that which is lacking to thee; I do it for thee, every desire of thy heart, the excellent thing in thy name. I assess for thee the ⌜officials⌝ ($m\ni dy\cdot w$) [80]—— works for thy ka, in order to offer[c] for thee upon the ground, with bread and drink. I have come myself, myself (sic!), in order to see thy temple beside Wennofer, sovereign of eternity. I have ⌜finished⌝ the work in it, I have laid out the ⌜ground⌝, [81]I — that which thou desirest, making thy every house wherein I have established thy name forever. [I] am he that doeth according to truth, that it (truth) may flourish."

273. "I have given to thee the Southerners, offering gifts to thy temple, and the Northerners, [82](bringing) their tribute before thy beautiful face. I have collected all them that owe thee dues, united in one body, under the administration of the prophet of thy temple, in order to make thy property a permanent whole,[d] to be brought [83][to] thy temple ⌜—⌝ forever."

274. "I made splendid thy treasury, filled with possessions, the heart's desire, which I have given to thee, together with thy dues. I have given to thee a ship ($mn\check{s}$), bearing cargoes upon the sea, conveying to thee [84]the great [⌜marvels⌝] of God's-Land, and the merchants doing merchandising, bearing their wares and their impost therefrom in gold, silver, and copper."

---

[a]Full double name. [b]Viz., to heaven. [c]Lit., "*sprinkle*" or "*sow*." [d]Lit., "*causing thy property to become abiding in one body.*"

275. "I have made for thee calculations of the fields, which had been only verbal [85]——— on high [land], calculated in fields. I equipped them with inspectors, together with husbandmen, to produce clean grain for thy divine offerings. I have given to thee barges with crews, and artisans hewing [86]— without ceasing to sail to thy temple."

276. "I have formed for thee herds of all small cattle, faithfully to supply thy offerings. I levied for thee wild fowl from the ⌈inclosed⌉ marsh; others [87]— — live geese for maintaining those that were hatched. I put fishermen on the waters, on every pool, in order to furnish for thee imposts by the shipload."

277. "I equipped thy temple with every office [88]— — of my majesty. Thy lay priesthood of the temple has its full complement of heads.[a] The peasant-slaves are assessed for woven stuff, for thy wardrobe, and (as for) thy serfs of the fields of every district, every man brings [89]their (sic!) impost, to fill thy house."

278. "Lo, thou hast entered into heaven, thou followest Re, thou minglest with stars and moon. Thou restest in the nether world, like those who are therein, beside Wennofer, lord of eternity; [90]thy two [arms] draw Atum in heaven and in earth, like the unresting stars and the imperishable[b] stars, while thou art on the prow of the barque of myriads of years. When Re rises in heaven, thy two eyes are upon his beauty; [91]when Atum [enters][c] into the earth, thou art among his followers. Thou hast entered into the hidden chamber before its lord; thy going is afar in the midst of the Nether World; thou hast associated thyself with the mortuary gods. Lo, [92][I] pray for the breath of thy august nostrils. I mention thy name many times daily, I — my father ⌈— —⌉ — — — — [93]— I tell of thy valor, when I am in a foreign country.[d] I lay down for thee gifts, my hand bears offerings for thy name, for thy — in thy every place."

---

[a]Viz., "people," often referred to as "*heads*," like our "head of cattle."

[b]The two names literally mean: "*those who cannot rest*," and "*those who cannot perish.*" They are probably the stars of the southern and northern heavens (Brugsch, *Aegyptologie*, 321).

[c]Only the determinative of a verb of going is visible.

[d]There is no indication that this is a reference to a particular campaign, and the statement that it refers to Ramses II's Ethiopic campaign (Maspero, *Struggle of the Nations*, 387), in which it is averred he was engaged at his father's death, lacks foundation.

Ramses Prays His Father to Intercede in His Behalf

279. "Mayest thou speak to Re ———— ⁹⁴— life to his son, Wennofer, with a loving heart. Grant lifetime upon lifetime, united in jubilees for Usermare-Setepnere (Ramses II), given life. It will be well for thee, that I should be king forever, ⁹⁵(for) thou wilt be — by a good son, who remembers his father; (for) I will take counsel for thy temple, every day, and for the affairs of thy ka, in every matter. If I hear of any damage ⁹⁶about to happen, I will command to remove it instantly in every matter. Thou shalt be as if thou livedst, while I reign. I shall look to thy house every day. ⁹⁷— I have —, my heart shall incline after thee, I shall champion thee and thy name, while thou art in the nether world. Excellent indeed shall it be for thee, while I am; while Ramses, given life, like Re, forever, ⁹⁸⌜the son⌝ of Re, lives."

The Deceased Seti I Replies to His Son's Prayer

280. Then was King Menmare (Seti I), triumphant (m ᵓ ᶜ -ḥrw), an excellent soul (b ᵓ), like Osiris, rejoicing over all that which his son, the doer of excellent things, King ⁹⁹Ramses II,ᵃ had done, and praising all his beauty, to Re-Harakhte, and to the gods who are in the nether world, while he spoke in ⌜—⌝ ¹⁰⁰as a father on earth speaks with his son, saying:

281. "Let thy heart be very glad, O my beloved son, Usermare-Setepnere, given life, in ——— giving to thee [myriads] of years, eternity upon the Horus-throne ¹⁰¹of the living. Osiris has besought for thee the duration of heaven, wherein thou risest like Re at early morning. Life and prosperity shall be with thee, — truth, might, and joy of heart, for him who is rich in years. ¹⁰²Thine shall be might and victory, O thou great in victory; health shall be for thy limbs like · (those of) Re in heaven. Joy and rejoicing shall be in thy every abode, O king, defending Egypt, binding the barbarians, spending the eternity ¹⁰³of thy lifetime as King of Upper Egypt, and as King of Lower Egypt, as Atum flourishes at rising and setting. Behold, I say to Reᵇ with a

---

ᵃFull double name, with the usual salutations after it, which have been omitted in the translation, in order to show more clearly the connection.

ᵇA similar prayer of Seti's is found at Kurna (Lepsius, *Denkmäler*, III, 150, a), in which he addresses Amon thus: "*Grant thou to him (Ramses II) eternity, that he may make my name to live, by reason of the command that comes out of thy mouth.*" Here we see the same compact as in the Abydos inscription.

loving heart: 'Grant to him[a] eternity upon earth [104]like Khepri.' I have repeated to Osiris when I entered before him: 'Double thou for him the duration of thy son, Horus.' Behold, Re said in the horizon of heaven: 'Grant eternity, everlastingness, myriads of years [105]of royal jubilees for the son of his body, the beloved Meriamon-Ramses, given life, doer of excellent things.' Atum has decreed to thee his duration as king. Might and victory shall be united [106]behind thee. Thoth writes them at the side of the All-Lord, and the Great Ennead say: 'Re, in his barque, lord of the morning-barque, collects them for him; his eye sees [107]that which thou hast so excellently done. When he sails the heavens with the wind every day, great joy is behind him, because he remembers thy beauty; until Atum [108]sets in the land of the West, thy love is in his body every day.' Behold, Wennofer is lord of triumph ($m^{ c}$-$ḥrw$) through that which thy majesty has done in the place of truth. I [Horus][b] awake him at the reminder of thy goodness; my heart hath joy indeed, because of the eternity which he has decreed for thee. Behold, I have received the things which thou hast given to me: my bread and my water with gladness of heart, breath [110]⌈reaches my nostrils, because of the deeds of a son, whose heart chooses to protect, free from negligence, knowing that which is seemly. Thou hast repeated monument on monument for Osiris under my authority in the presence [111]— — [in] the midst of Abydos (Nfw-wr). I am magnified because of all that which thou hast done for me; I am placed at the head of the abode of the dead, I am transformed, I have become a god more [112]beautiful than before, since thy heart has inclined to me, while I am in the nether world. I am thy true father, who am a god; I have mingled with the gods, following Aton; I [113][know] him who dwells in the barque — — like one in — — — who is in — — —. [114]He [remem]bers thy beauty — — — —. Behold, thou hast a long life, Re has decreed to thee — — — —, forever, like — — —. Thou art the living — of Atum, thy every word [115]comes to pass like (that of) the All-Lord. Thou art the favorite egg of Khepri, the water of a god [which came forth] from him. What thou begettest is that which Re himself has made; he said to thee: '— — — ⌈as the maker of⌉ — — — [116]a guar-

---

[a]Text has "*to thee*," but as Seti here speaks to Re in direct discourse, as the imperative shows, this is clearly an error for "*to him*," as found in the speech to Osiris, in the next line.

[b]Emendation suggested by Erman.

dian, thou comest as living Re to the people; the Southland and Northland [are beneath] thy feet, beseeching myriads of royal jubilees for Usermare-Setepnere, the duration of the All-Lord, when [he] rises ———."'"

KUBBÂN STELA[a]

282. This document records the attempt of Ramses II to supply with water the desert road leading from the Nile at Kubbân to the gold-bearing regions on the east in the great Wadi ʿAlâki.[b] It is similar to the records of like attempts by Seti I at Redesiyeh (§§ 162-98), with which it should be compared. Seti I, indeed, had made a futile attempt to find water on this same road, having dug a well there 200 feet deep, as our document informs us (l. 21). In spite of this fact, Ramses makes another attempt, and sends out the viceroy of Kush for the purpose. He presently reports success at a depth of only 20 feet.

283. A statement in the ceremonious address of the court (ll. 13-19) has always been regarded as of great historical importance. It affirms that Ramses had held important official positions in the land since he was a lad in the tenth year of his age (l. 17). But this statement, we should remember, is found in the midst of a fulsome eulogy abounding

---

[a]This stela was discovered in the ruins on the south of the village of Kubbân, by Prisse d'Avennes. It is now in the château of the Count St. Ferriol at Uriage, near Grenoble. It was published by Prisse (*Monuments égyptiens*, XXI), but his text is excessively incorrect. The first twenty-five lines were then much more accurately published by Chabas (*Les inscriptions des mines d'or*), and again without change by Rheinisch (*Chrestomathie*, Taf. 10). The last fourteen lines (ll. 25-38) have lost the first two-thirds of their length. These have been republished with collation of the Louvre squeeze by Virey (*Recueil*, XIV, 97, 98); his restorations are mostly gratuitous, and often grammatically impossible. An exhaustive copy of the original is very much needed.

[b]See Linant, *Carte de l'Etbaye ou pays habité par des Arabes Bisharis*, comprenant les contrées des mines d'or connues des anciens sous le nom d'Olaki, publiée par le dépôt de la guerre, 1854.

in the most absurd exaggerations. It is probable, in view of these statements, however, that Ramses early developed administrative ability, which he was given opportunity to exercise while still very young. This was doubtless a privilege granted to many princes of the royal house; it does not indicate that Ramses came to the throne while a child, nor do the courtiers here make any such claim,[a] though their words have been so misunderstood.[b]

284. A relief above the inscription shows Ramses II offering incense to "*Horus, lord of Bek (B ɔ k),*" and "*wine to Min residing in the mountain,*" resulting in the usual promises from the god. Then follows below the long inscription:

Introduction

285. [1]Year 3, first month of the second season, day 4, under the majesty of Horus: Mighty Bull, Beloved of Truth; Favorite of the Two Goddesses: Defender of Egypt, Binder of the Barbarians; Golden Horus: Rich in years, Great in Victory; King of Upper and Lower Egypt: Usermare-Setepnere; Son of Re: Meriamon-Ramses (II), given life, forever and ever, beloved of Amon-Re, lord of Thebes, and presider over Karnak; [2]shining upon the Horus-throne of the living, like his father, Re, every day; Good God, lord of the Southland, Horus of Edfu, of brilliant plumage, beautiful hawk of electrum. He protects Egypt with his wing, making shade for the people, as a wall of might and victory. When he went forth [3]from the body,[c] he was (already) terrible for capture, while his might was extending his boundaries; color was given to his limbs like the might of Montu. (He is) the double lord,[d] on the day of whose birth there was exultation in heaven; the gods said: "Our seed is in him." [4]The goddesses said: "He hath come forth from us to exercise the kingship of Re." Amon

---

[a]See *infra*, Figs. 3 and 4, and §§ 123 ff.

[b]E. g., by Wiedemann, *Aegyptische Geschichte*, 419; and by Brugsch, *Zeitschrift für ägyptische Sprache*, 1890, 34 f.

[c]At birth. [d]Written with the figures of Horus and Set.

said: "I am Irsu,[a] I have put justice into its place." The earth is established, heaven is satisfied, the divine ennead is content with his qualities, the Bull, mighty against Kush the wretched, smiting [5]the rebels[b] as far as the land of the Negro. His hoofs trample the Troglodytes, his horn gores into them; his fame is mighty in Khenthennofer; as for his terror, it has reached Karoy ($K\Im ry$). His name circulates among [6]all lands, because of the victories which his two hands have wrought. Gold comes forth from the mountain at his name,[c] like (that of) his father, Horus, lord of Bek ($B\Im\text{-}k\Im$),[d] great in love in the southern countries, like Horus in the land of Miam ($My^c m\Im m$),[e] lord of Bohen ($Bwhn$); the King of Upper and Lower Egypt: Usermare-Setepnere; [7]Son of Re, of his body, Lord of Diadems: Meriamon-Ramses (II), given life forever and ever, like his father, Re, every day.

Investigation of the Land of Akita

286. Now, when his majesty was in Memphis, performing the pleasing ceremonies of his fathers, all the gods of South and North, according as they gave to him might and victory, and long life of myriads [8]of years; on one of these days it came to pass that, lo, his majesty was sitting upon a great throne of electrum, diademed with the double-feathered crown, recounting the countries, from which gold is brought, and devising plans for digging [9]wells on a road lacking in water, after hearing said that there was much gold in the country of Akita ($\Im\text{-}k\Im\text{-}y\text{-}t\Im$), whereas the road thereof was very lacking in water. If a few of [10]the caravaneers of the gold-washing went thither, it was only half of them that arrived there, (for) they died of thirst on the road, together with the asses which they drove before them. There was not found for them their necessary supply of [11]drink, in ascending and descending, from the water of the skins.[f] Hence no gold was brought from this country for lack of water.

---

[a] "*Irsu*" (*Yr-sw*), lit., "*he who made him*," a not uncommon designation of the god as father of the king (II, 985, note).

[b] Cf. Guieysse (*Recueil*, X, 64 ff.), whose rendering is grammatically impossible.

[c] The same remarkable idea referring to Amenhotep IV (II, 946).

[d] District in which the ancient town at Kubbân was situated. See Brugsch, *Zeitschrift für ägyptische Sprache*, 1882, 31 f.

[e] $M\Im m$ as often for $\Im m$. Miam is the ancient name of Derr; see Tomb of Penno (IV, 474 ff.), and Brugsch, *Zeitschrift für ägyptische Sprache*, 1882, 31.

[f] Going from the Nile into the desert is regularly "*ascending*," and the return is

Court is Summoned

287. Said his majesty to the wearer of the royal seal, who was at his side: "Call the princes of the court, [12]his majesty would counsel with them concerning this country, (how) I may take the necessary measures." They were immediately brought before the Good God, their hands uplifted to his ka, acclaiming and smelling the earth before his beautiful face. One (=the king) told them the character of this country, counseling [13]with them concerning the plan of opening a well upon the road thereof.

Address of the Court

288. They said before his majesty: "Thou art like Re in all that thou doest; that which thy heart wishes comes to pass. If thou desirest a matter in the night, in the morning it quickly comes to pass. We have been [14]beholding a multitude of thy marvels, since thy appearance as king of the Two Lands; we have not heard, neither have our eyes seen,[a] (yet) do they come to pass as they are.[a] As for everything that comes out of thy mouth, it is like the words of Harakhte. Thy tongue is a pair of balances, more accurate are thy two lips [15]than the correct weight of Thoth. What is that which thou knowest not? Who is the finisher of it like thee? Where[b] is the place, which thou hast not seen? There is no country which thou hast not trodden. All matters pass through thy ears, [16]since thou hast exercised authority over this land. Thou didst make plans while thou wast (still) in the egg, in thy office of child of a prince.[c] The affairs of the Two Lands were told thee, while thou wert a child wearing the curl;[d] no monument was executed, which was not under thy authority; [17]there was no commission without thy knowledge. Thou wast chief[e] of the army while thou wast

---

"*descending;*" the workmen were unable to carry in the skins sufficient water for the round trip.

[a] See the same idea in l. 22. This method of flattery by courtiers is not unique. The same assumption of a mysterious origin of completed works of the king is found regarding Hatshepsut's obelisks, and the statue of Amenhotep III erected by Amenhotep, son of Hapi.

[b] $Yw-t$ ᵓ = אירא (Bondi, *Lehnwörter*, 31).

[c] $Rp^{c \cdot} ty$. [d] The well-known sidelock of youth.

[e] R ᵓ -ḥry, lit., "*superior mouth;*" this is the phrase used in l. 13 where the king asks for advice = lit., "*mouth*" where "*mouth*" is, of course, a metonymy for "counsel." The exact military rank indicated is not certain. It should be

a boy of the tenth year. Every work that was carried out, it was thy hand which made the foundation thereof. If thou sayest to the water: 'Come upon the mountain,' the flood comes forth [18]quickly after thy word, for thou art Re in limbs, and Khepri with his true form. Thou art the living image on earth of thy father, Atum of Heliopolis. Taste is in thy mouth, intelligence[a] in thy heart; the seat of thy tongue is the shrine of truth, the god sits upon thy two lips.[b] Thy words come to pass every day, [19]thy heart is made into the likeness of (that of) Ptah, the creator of handicrafts.[c] Thou art forever, it shall be done by thy plans, all that thou sayest is heard, O Sovereign, our lord."

Statement of the Viceroy of Kush

289. "As for the country of Akita, this is said concerning it," said the king's-son of Kush the wretched, [20]concerning it before his majesty, "that it has been in this manner lacking in water, since the time of the god. They die therein of thirst, and every earlier king desired to open a well therein, but did not succeed.[d] [21]King Menmare (Seti I) did the like, and caused to be dug a well of 120 cubits[e] depth in his time. It is (however), forsaken on the road, (for) no water came out of it. (But) if thou thyself say to thy father Hapi,[f] [22]the father of the gods: 'Let water be brought upon the mountain,' he will do according to all that thou hast said, like all thy designs, which come to pass before us, (although) they have not been heard in conversation; because thy fathers, all the gods love thee, more than any king, [23]who has been since Re."

---

observed that the courtiers here (ll. 16, 17) make no claim that Ramses became king at ten years of age, as is so often stated. They affirm no more than the assumption of great trusts by Ramses at a very early age; there is no hint of coregency.

[a]This is the same idea as in the Memphite system; ideas come from the heart (=mind). See my "Philosophy of a Memphite Priest" (*Zeitschrift für ägyptische Sprache*, 39, 39 ff.).

[b]This notion is also found in the Memphite system (*ibid.*, pp. 46–48).

[c]In the address of Ptah to Ramses II (Abu Simbel Stela, Lepsius, *Denkmäler*, III, 194, ll. 14, 15), Ptah says: "*I cause the mountains to shape for thee great, mighty, lofty monuments; I cause the highlands to fashion for thee [all] splendid costly stones.*"

[d]Lit., "*Their prosperity* (=success) *did not happen.*"

[e]Two hundred feet. [f] The Nile-god.

Ramses Determines to Dig a Well in Akita

290. Said his majesty to these princes: "How true is all that which ye have said ⌜—⌝, that no water has been dug in this country since the time of the god, as ye say. (But) I will open a well there, ⌜furnishing⌝ water every day as in ²⁴⌜the valley of⌝ the Ni]le, at command of my father, Amon-Re, lord of Thebes, and all the gods of Nubia, according as their heart is satisfied with the things desired. I will cause it to be said in the land —.— — — ²⁵— —."

291. [Then these princes] praised their lord, smelling the ground, throwing themselves upon their bellies in the presence, exulting to the height of heaven.

Said his majesty to the chief king's-scribe —: "²⁶——————— of the road to Akita. Let a month become a day,[a] when [thou] sendest ²⁷———————." [⌜Then the chief king's-scribe communicated to the king's-son of Kush⌝][b] according as it had been commissioned him. Lo, he mustered the people for ²⁸⌜digging the well⌝] ———————. [⌜But they said: "What⌝] then is it which the king's-son shall do? Shall the water ²⁹⌜which is in the nether world hearken to him?"[c] Then they dug the well on⌝] the road to the country of Akita. Never was done the like since the kings who were aforetime ³⁰———————[d] he puts fish in the pools of the regions of ⌜—⌝ of the Delta marshes, pleasing his heart in creating ³¹——————— like a rudder in the wind.[e]

A Letter Announcing Success from the Viceroy of Kush

292. One came, bearing a letter from the king's-son of Kush the wretched, saying: ³²"——————— [⌜The⌝] well ⌜is finished⌝]; that which thy majesty spake with his own mouth has come to pass; the water has come forth from it[f] at 12 cubits, being 4 cubits therein in depth. ³³——————— it outside, as a god does, in satisfying the heart with that

---

[a]That is, let a month of preparation become as short as a day.

[b]This scribe must have communicated the commission to the viceroy of Kush, for it is the latter who executes the task in Akita, as is shown by ll. 28 and 31.

[c]Cf. l. 35.

[d]The subject is uncertain; possibly the Nile-god is meant, being here doubtless the one who brings the water to Ramses' well.

[e]Virey's text has "*shore*" instead of "*wind*."

[f] Feminine pronoun, referring to "*well*" (fem.), which must have been mentioned in the preceding lacuna.

which thou desirest. Never was done ³⁴[the like since the time of the god] ———— Akita rejoices with great joy, those who are far away ³⁵———— the ruler. The water which is in the nether world hearkens to him, when he digs water upon the mountain ³⁶————."

Conclusion

293. ———— to him from the king's-son, announcing that which he had done. They were glad because of ᵃ [it] — ³⁷———— excellent in plans, good in ⌜— —⌝ — —. ³⁸[His majesty ordered to call the name of] this [we]ll: "The-Well-of-Meriamon-Ramses-Mighty-[⌜in-Victory⌝]."

THE ASIATIC WAR

294. Ramses II, with his two predecessors, inherited a very dangerous situation in Syria. Seti I had not succeeded in relieving that situation, and upon Ramses II fell the critical task of confronting and checking the southward advance of the Hittites, in their process of absorbing the Egyptian conquests in Syria. They were the most powerful people which Egypt had ever met, and the conflict lasted nearly twenty years, during which we may discern three periods. In the first of these we find Ramses, after having pushed his Phœnician boundary northward to Beyrut, marching down the Orontes against the Hittites at Kadesh. The remarkable battle which followed was without beneficial result. The second period finds Ramses battling for the recovery of Palestine, where there had arisen a general revolt, undoubtedly incited by the Hittites. This revolt suppressed, the third period finds him again in the Hittite country, conquering Naharin as far north as Tunip, where his progress was such that the Hittites were willing to resign all projects of further conquest in Syria and negotiate a

---

ᵃOr: "*They* (the reports) *were agreeable to* [*the heart of the king*]."

permanent compact in a treaty, in arranging which no mention of the boundary[a] adopted is made.

295. The materials for the three periods are very scanty, except for the battle of Kadesh and the treaty. These materials are as follows:[b]

I. Beginning of the Hittite War.
   1. First campaign: three illegible stelæ on the Nahr-el-Kelb near Beyrut (§ 297).
   2. Second campaign, battle of Kadesh:
      a) Poem on the battle of Kadesh (§§ 305-15).
      b) Official record of the battle of Kadesh (§§ 316-27).
      c) Reliefs of the battle of Kadesh (§§ 328-51).

II. Palestinian revolt.
   1. Reconquest of southern Palestine: a relief at Karnak showing the storming of Askalon (§§ 353-55).
   2. Reconquest of northern Palestine: a short list of towns taken in the eighth year (§ 356); a relief at the Ramesseum, of the storming of Deper (§§ 356-62); a relief in the Hauran (§ 358).

III. Close of the Hittite War.
   1. Conquest of Naharin: a small fragment at the Ramesseum, from an inscription describing the capture of Tunip (§§ 363-65); two short lists of conquered countries (§ 366).
   2. Treaty with the Hittites: entire text of the document (§§ 367-91).

I. BEGINNING OF THE HITTITE WAR

296. Like his great predecessors, Seti I and Thutmose III, Ramses II began his operations for the conquest of northern Syria by first securing the coast and then moving against

---

[a]This boundary will not have been far south of Hamath, which marks the southern limit of Hittite remains.

[b]Besides these materials, see also Nubian War, etc. (§§ 448-91).

the interior, where for the first time he comes into contact with the Hittites.

I. First Campaign

297. Ramses II's first campaign was directed along the Phœnician coast, and extended as far as Beyrut, near which he erected a stela on the Nahr el-Kelb (Dog River) in his fourth year. Another stela, dated "*year 2*"[a] is called uncertain by Lepsius,[b] and is probably to be read "*year 10;*" for the first[c] is clearly 4; and there was but one campaign before that of the "*year 5*,"[d] against Kadesh. A third stela is without date. These stelæ[e] are so weathered that the records of the campaigns which they doubtless contained, are most totally illegible.[f] The location of the stela near the northern boundary of the conquests of Ramses' father, Seti I, is significant. They of course mark the advance boundary of Ramses II's northern conquests.

II. Second Campaign: The Battle of Kadesh[g]

298. This battle, in which Ramses meets the Hittites for the first time, forms the culmination of Ramses II's second

---

[a] Lepsius, *Denkmäler*, III, 197, c.   [b] *Briefe*, 403.
[c] Lepsius, *Denkmäler*, III, 197, b.
[d] Which is called the second campaign, Record, l. 1.
[e] Published by Bonomi, *Transactions of the Royal Society of Literature*, 1st ser., II, pl.; Lepsius, *Denkmäler*, III, 197; see also Boscawen, *Transactions of the Society of Biblical Archæology*, VII, 331 ff.

[f] These stelæ are cut in the limestone of the hillside, and have so weathered that visitors unaccustomed to reading such inscriptions have declared they contained none. One (Boscawen's No. 1, farthest north) was smoothed off by the French, and a record of the French occupation (1860–61) inscribed upon it. The Egyptian inscription was, of course, totally obliterated (Boscawen, *Transactions of the Society of Biblical Archæology*, VII, 336).

[g] Three sources: (1) the so-called "Poem of Pentaur" (referred to above as "Poem"); (2) the Official Record (called "Record"); (3) the Reliefs. The bibliography, etc., will be found with the introduction to each document. In general, see my *Battle of Kadesh*, "Decennial Publications of the University of Chicago," V, 81–127.

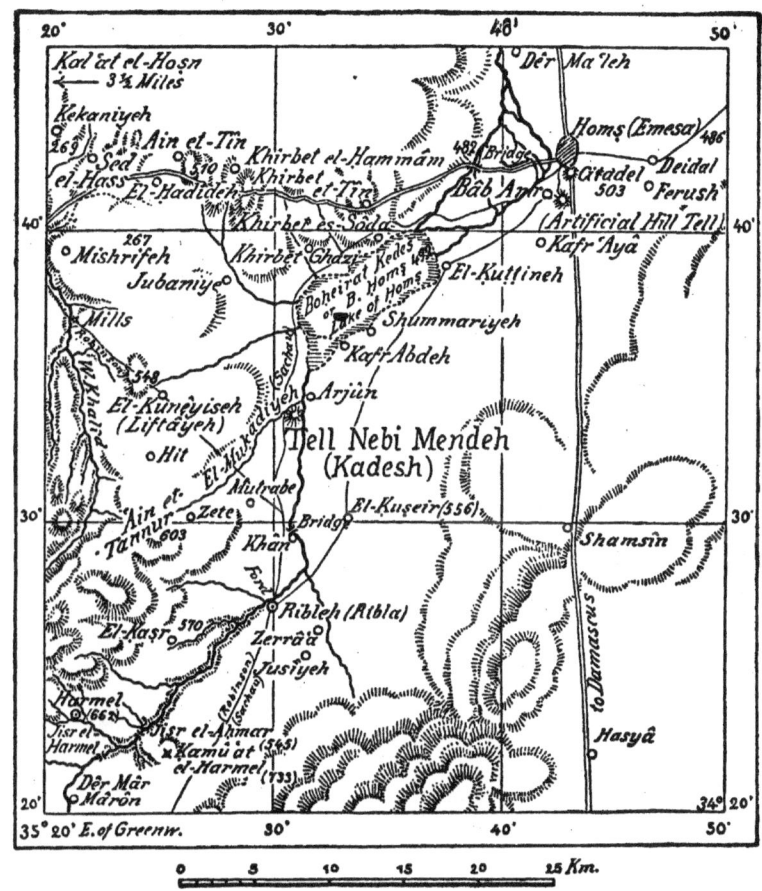

FIG. 7.—Map of the Orontes Valley in the Vicinity of Kadesh, 1:500,000 (after Blanckenhorn)

Syrian campaign, and furnishes nearly all we know of the beginning of his Syrian war. It is of especial interest, being the first battle in history of which we may follow the tactics and the disposition of both armies.[a] About the end of

---

[a] Rev. H. G. Tomkins' study of this battle (*Transactions of the Society of Biblical Archæology*, VII, 390 ff.) was unfortunately made without all the data to be gained from the texts, but shows good use of what he had. Failure to observe the sequence of events made any clear outline of movements impossible. Maspero's account of it in his one volume, *Histoire*, is excellent, but this account was altered in his

April, Ramses marched northward from the fortress of Tharu on the Egyptian frontier, with an army of probably about 20,000 men, in four divisions: the division of Amon, which formed the advance, under the immediate command of the Pharaoh; and the divisions[a] of Re, of Ptah, and of Sutekh, which followed that of Amon in the order given. Marching through Palestine,[b] and along the Phœnician coast road, Ramses passed into Amor, where he formed his van of picked men, on the "*shore in the land of Amor*" (Poem, l. 18). Thereupon he left the coast, perhaps marching up the valley of the Litâny, and reached the last elevation on the east side of the Orontes, where the high valley (the Bukâ ᶜa) drops to the level of the plain around Kadesh, about a day's march south of it.[c] Here he camped (Poem, ll. 11, 12; Record, l. 2), without finding trace of the enemy. He therefore pushed on the next day, and as he reached the ford just south of Shabtuna, later Ribleh,[d] a small town, some seven and a half miles south of Kadesh, he was informed by two Shasu-Bedwin, sent out by the Hittite king for this purpose, that the Asiatics had retreated far northward to the district of Aleppo, beyond Tunip (Record, ll. 2–6). With the division of Amon, therefore, Ramses crossed to the west side of the Orontes at Shabtuna (Poem, l. 12), leaving the other three divisions on the east side, dis-

---

larger history. Meyer is the only later historian who has shown a correct understanding of the general plan of the battle. On the literature of the subject, see my *Battle of Kadesh*, 4, 5.

[a]This word, which I render "*division*," is in Egyptian "*army*" (*mš* ᶜ), but it was probably about the size of a modern army division (see p. 153, note).

[b]The route is uncertain in Palestine (see Müller, *Asien und Europa*, 220), but must have been along the coast when he reached southern Phœnicia. It is barely possible, therefore, that Ramses embarked his army, after leaving Tharu, and landed at some Phœnician port.

[c]*Battle of Kadesh*, 19–21; see *infra*, Figs. 7 and 8.

[d]*Battle of Kadesh*, 21, 22.

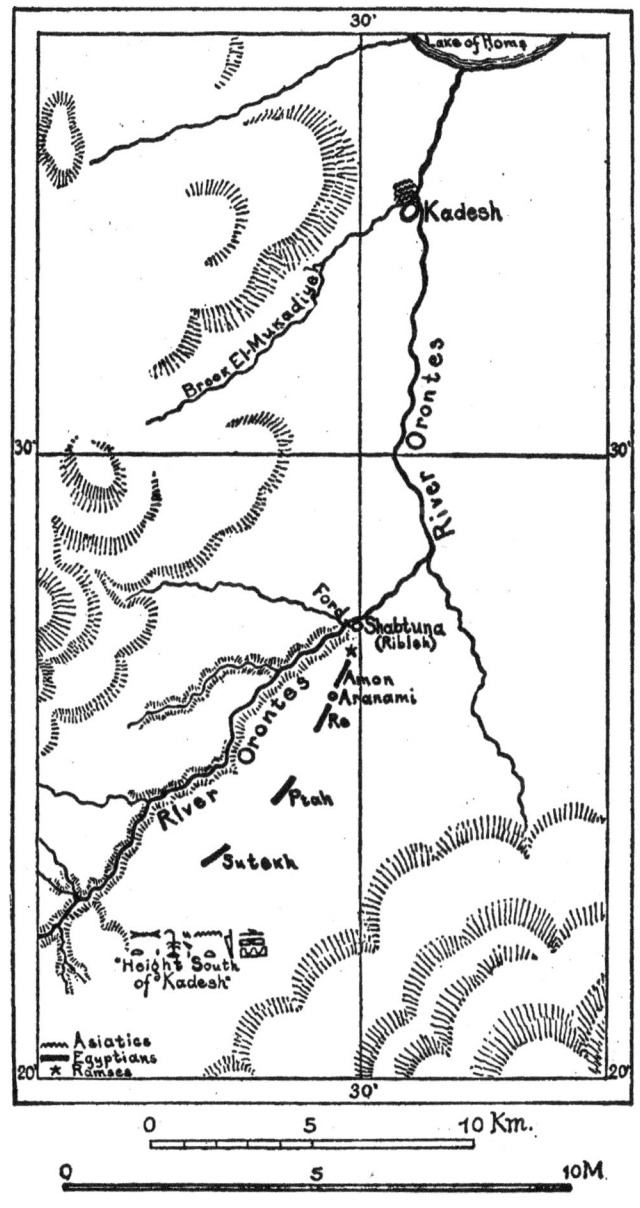

Fig. 8.—March to Kadesh. First Positions

tributed along the road to the south. The division of Re, however, soon crossed at the same ford, with about a mile and a half between its van and the rear of the division of Amon[a] (Fig. 9). With these two divisions following him in a long line, Ramses continued rapidly northward, leaving the other two (Ptah and Sutekh) marching slowly south of Shabtuna, till there was a wide gap between the two halves of his army.

299. Meanwhile the Asiatics (Poem, l. 17), with an army of probably 20,000 men, the combined forces of the north Syrian princes, under the Hittite king, together with a large proportion of mercenaries from states in Asia Minor, adjacent or subject to the Hittites[b]—all these were concealed on the northwest of Kadesh, hidden from the Egyptians by the city. The Hittite king now uses the city to mask his movements, and as Ramses pushes northward on the west side of Kadesh, the Hittite commander shifts his position rapidly eastward and southward,[c] all the time keeping the

---

[a]From this point on consult the battle plans (Figs. 9 to 12). They are taken from my *Battle of Kadesh*. The four Egyptian divisions are marked by their names: Amon, Re, Ptah, and Sutekh.

[b]Poem, ll. 1, 2, 13–16, and 24; Record, ll. 6, 7. The language of the inscriptions puts the Syrian contingents in the same category with those of Asia Minor, but it is clear that the latter are only mercenaries, called "*warriors*" (*tw-hy-r*ꜣ), i. e., professional soldiers, who are in the service of the Hittite king for hire (Poem, l. 16), under their own native commanders, whom the Poem represents as their princes. The Syrians, on the other hand, are real allies of the Hittites, and their kings are really present.

[c]No direct statement of this movement is made in the sources, but after stating that the Hittites are "*on the northwest of Kadesh*" (Poem, ll. 16, 17), while Ramses is still south of Kadesh, they further state that the Asiatics emerged for the attack "*from the southern side of Kadesh*" (Poem, l. 20; Record, l. 20), when Ramses is in camp northwest of Kadesh. The Hittites could not have shifted from the northwest of Kadesh to the south of it, along the west side, for here Ramses was marching northward. They must have passed eastward and southward on the east side of the city (Fig. 10), keeping themselves constantly "*behind Kadesh*," from Ramses' point of view. They could, of course, have passed through Kadesh if the gates were in such positions as to permit. But as they crossed the Orontes

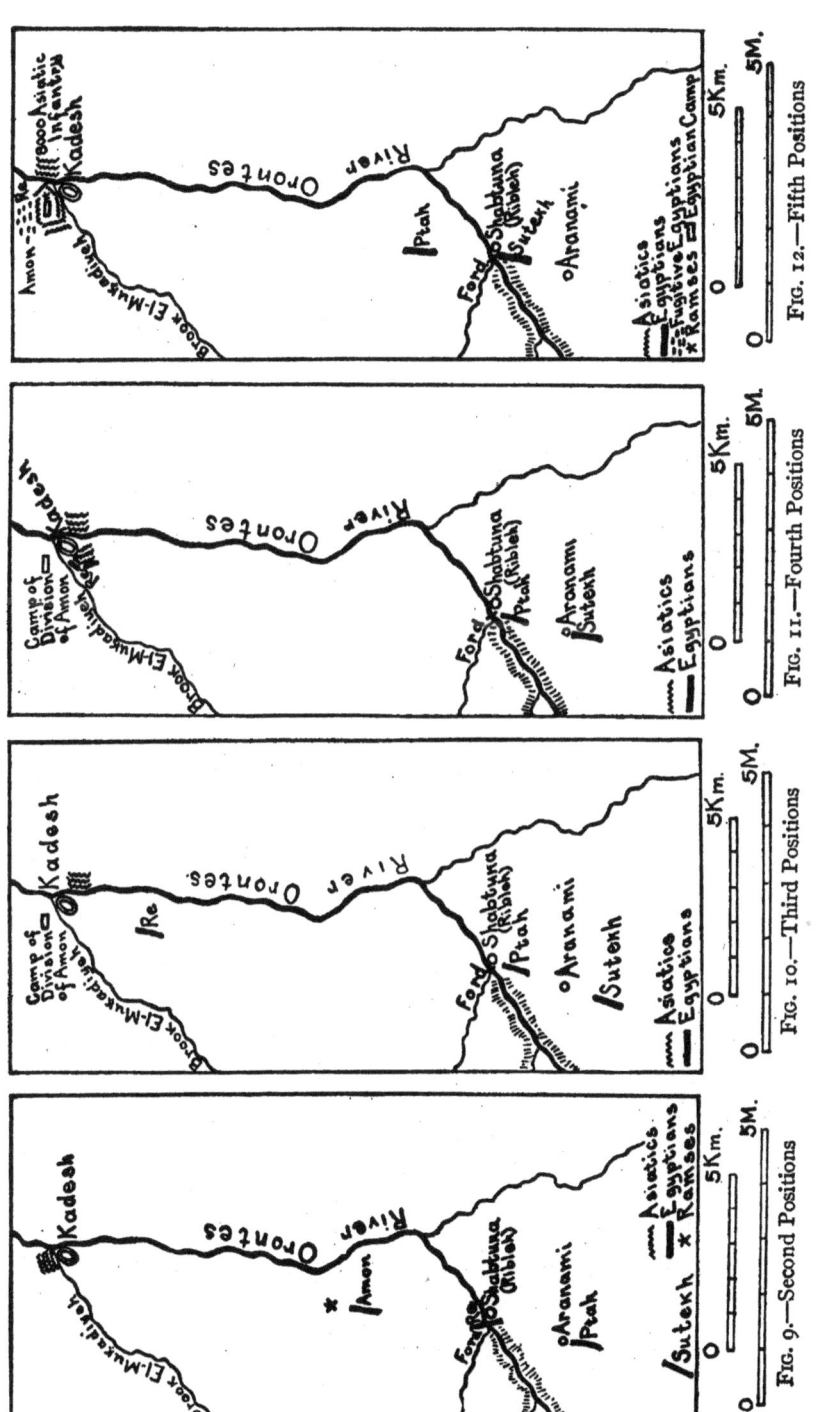

FIG. 9.—Second Positions. FIG. 10.—Third Positions. FIG. 11.—Fourth Positions. FIG. 12.—Fifth Positions.

city between him and the advance of the Egyptians. To do this, he was obliged to transfer his army across the Orontes. Ramses, now quite unsuspicious, advances alone with only his household troops, and deliberately goes into camp northwest of the city (Poem, ll. 12 and 21; Record, ll. 7, 8; Reliefs, § 336, ll. 3, 4; Fig. 10). Thus the Asiatics, with a strong fortress on their right for refuge in case of defeat, by their remarkably skilful maneuvering, have gained a position on Ramses' right flank, which, properly utilized, means his destruction.

300. As the division of Amon comes up and is settling in camp around the tent of Ramses (Reliefs, § 331), an Egyptian scout brings in two of the enemy's scouts, who are beaten (Reliefs, § 330) into confessing the proximity of the foe (Record, § 321). Thoroughly alarmed, Ramses commands the vizier to order up the troops from the south of Shabtuna (§ 324), and the vizier, besides sending a horseman to hasten them, probably goes also himself in a chariot (Record, § 324; Reliefs, §§ 333 f.). Meanwhile the threatening catastrophe becomes a fact: remaining with his infantry, the king of the Hittites sends his chariotry (Poem, ll. 18, 19) to the attack; they *"came forth from the southern side of Kadesh, and they cut through the division of Re in its middle, while they were marching, without knowing, and without being drawn up for battle"* (Poem, § 311). Totally unprepared, caught thus in marching order, the Egyptians fled northward[a] toward Ramses' camp (Record, l. 21), while a messenger was sent to acquaint him with the disaster. But

---

to make the attack (Record, l. 20), they must have come from the east side of the river; and while on the northwest of Kadesh, they were certainly on the west side; hence the two crossings are certain.

[a]This is evidently the northern half of the division of Re, which thus retreats; the southern half apparently fell back southward on the marching division of Ptah.

the Hittite chariotry, which made the attack, pressed the retreating Egyptians northward so rapidly that, while Ramses was sitting in his tent chiding his officers for their ignorance of the enemy's whereabouts, some members of the royal family were driven in headlong flight over the western barricade into the camp by the most advanced of the Hittite chariots (Record, ll. 19, 20; Reliefs, § 332, a, b). These first hostile intruders were dragged from their chariots by the Egyptian foot in the camp and slain.[a] The fleeing troops of the division of Re[b] now arrive and sweep the camping division of Amon into panic and flight, while the advancing Hittite chariotry rapidly enfold Ramses between their extended wings (Poem, l. 23; Record, l. 22; Reliefs, § 336, a, ll. 7. 8, and scene),[c] being 2,500 in number, and representing a force of 7,500 men. Ramses, having with him only his bodyguard,[d] now saw the extended wings of the enemy close completely around him on four sides, seeming like four bodies of chariotry[e] (Poem, l. 23; Record, ll. 21, 22; Reliefs, § 336, a, l. 8). For the moment, he is thus isolated, even from the troops which had accompanied him to the north of Kadesh.

301. On the west side, where the royal fugitives have just

---

[a]*Battle of Kadesh*, Pl. I.

[b]These are the northern portion of the division of Re. As the Hittites succeeded in cutting directly through this division, the southern portion of it should be represented on the plan (Fig. 12) somewhere south of Kadesh between Kadesh and the division of Ptah; but as their position succeeding the attack is quite uncertain, I have not attempted to indicate it.

[c]This enfolding or flanking movement is clearly evident in the relief, where the Hittite chariots, with three men in each, may be easily distinguished from the Egyptian, which carry only two. See also Fig. 12.

[d]It is this circumstance which has given rise to the proud boast, so often repeated in the Poem and in the Reliefs, that he was utterly alone, and won the battle singlehanded.

[e]They can be seen thus in the relief scene (*Battle of Kadesh*, Pl. V); see also Fig. 12.

been driven in, the enemy is already pressing into the camp. On the east the enfolding wing of the enemy is evidently weakest. Ramses did not hesitate an instant, but immediately rallied his household troops and charged into the invaders of his camp, in the endeavor to cut his way out, to rejoin his southern divisions. This unexpected onset gained him a moment's respite, during which he perceived how the enemy was massed against him on the south, and he therefore turned against the enemy's thin line on their extreme right, before they should have time to strengthen it after their rapid advance northward. He charged eastward into the scanty opposing line of chariots so impetuously that he drove them into the Orontes north of the city.[a] In so doing he forsook his camp, which immediately fell into the hands of the enemy. It is unquestionably the rich plunder in Ramses' camp which diverts the Hittites for the moment and saves Ramses from being pushed into the river in his turn.

302. A body of troops, which it is difficult to connect with any of Ramses' four divisions, now unexpectedly arrives and begins his rescue. They are called "*recruits* ($n^c\ ryn$), and are said to arrive from Amor.[b] They enter the camp and slay the plundering Hittites to the last man (§ 340).

---

[a]It is this episode which the reliefs depict so vivaciously in the battle scene (§ 335).

[b]*Battle of Kadesh*, 37, 38. Since reading my account of the incident, Eduard Meyer suggests to me that these troops may be reinforcements from the coast, which have landed at one of the Phœnician harbors, far enough south to be in Amor. It is not possible that these are infantry reinforcements belonging to the troops south of Shabtuna, although they are spoken of as arriving "*from Amor*," for the text mentioning them clearly distinguishes them from the divisions of Re and Ptah. But the course of the battle and the disposition of the troops are from this point quite uncertain. Ramses' desperate assault with his bodyguard is the subject and the *raison d'être* of all these documents, and they depict the whole victory as consisting in this one heroic incident. This over, the subsequent course of the battle between the opposing forces, in which the king is no longer so conspicuous, is of little importance to any of the three documents.

The fleeing troops of Ramses now rallied, and together with the "*recruits*" just mentioned, the Egyptian force engaged was no longer a mere handful.

303. It is apparently at the head of these forces that Ramses now charges six times into the mass of the Hittite chariotry that lies between him and the reinforcements approaching from the south, and brings the enemy to a stand.[a] The Hittite king now sent in an additional thousand chariots from his reserves.[a] Ramses has maintained himself for some three hours and at this juncture, while he is holding his own against fearful odds, the vizier arrives with the division of Ptah, and coming in from the south, quite unexpectedly strikes the Asiatics in the rear.[b] After Ramses' stubborn stand this unforeseen blow in the rear quickly decides the contest, and the Hittite chariotry breaks and flees into the city. Caught between the closing lines of the Egyptians, some of them were taken prisoners and many slain;[c] and the Hittite king was forced to see the day, begun so auspiciously for him, now lost, without being able to throw in against the Egyptian chariots the 8,000 or 9,000 foot which for some reason he held in reserve to the end on the other shore.[d]

304. Whether Ramses attempted an assault upon this Asiatic infantry or not, is a question upon which our documents throw no light. The poem claims that there was another battle on the next day, which is extremely doubtful[e] In any case, it is clear that Kadesh is not taken,[f] and Ramses,

---

[a]*Battle of Kadesh*, 39.

[b]The Luxor relief shows this approach in the rear of the Asiatic chariotry, which is seen retreating into the city. It is clear that the Hittites were forced by Ramses' strong stand to put in all their chariotry against him, and were unable to prevent the advance of the division of Ptah.

[c] Reliefs, *Battle of Kadesh*, Pl. V.

[d]*Battle of Kadesh*, 40.   [e]*Battle of Kadesh*, 46, 47.   [f]See p. 142, note b.

happy in his remarkable escape from destruction, and proud of the personal reputation gained, having won the battle with but a portion[a] of his army, is glad to return to Egypt for a time, where he offers his prisoners to Amon.[b] But Syria as far south as Kadesh, if not farther, remains in the hands of the Hittites.

a. *Poem on the Battle of Kadesh*[c]

305. This poem, long called the "Poem of Pentaur," is our most important document for a study of the battle of Kadesh. It is, fortunately for us, introduced by a sober and careful prose account of Ramses' departure from Egypt, his march to Kadesh, and the position of his four divisions up to the moment of the Asiatic attack. Supplemented by the

---

[a]The entire division of Sutekh was too far away to reach the field in time.
[b]Reliefs, §§ 348–51.
[c]For fuller statement of bibliography, see my *Battle of Kadesh*, 6, 7. The texts are of two kinds: hieroglyphic and hieratic. The hieroglyphic text has been found in three copies on temple walls: at Luxor (Rougé, *Inscriptions hiéroglyphiques*, IV, 232–48; Brugsch, *Recueil de monuments*, II, 40–42; lower ends, Daressy, *Revue égyptologique*, IX, 58); Karnak (Rougé, *ibid.*, IV, 206–31; Brugsch, *ibid.*, II, 29–32; Mariette, *Karnak*, 48–51); and Abydos (Mariette, *Abydos*, II, 4, 5). All these originals are excessively fragmentary, especially the one at Abydos, of which only the lower ends of the vertical lines have survived. Of the publications the Karnak copies of Brugsch and Mariette are so incomplete as to be unusable, and Rougé's copies are neither accurate nor exhaustive. Besides the above publications, I had a collation of Abydos by Borchardt, and photographs of Karnak also by Borchardt, for which I am indebted to the Berlin dictionary. Of the hieratic text there are two papyri, both belonging to the same roll; Papyrus Raifet, containing only one page of ten lines (published by Rougé, *Recueil*, I, and Papyrus Sallier III (select Papyrus I, 24–34), containing eleven pages. Raifet precedes Sallier III, but the beginning is lost. I arranged all the texts in parallel columns, and this quadruplex was then carefully collated with the original Papyrus Sallier III, in the British Museum, by Professor Erman. The texts were once similarly put together by E. de Rougé and published by J. de Rougé (*Revue égyptologique*, III–IX), but without the Abydos copy, the lower part of Luxor, or a collation of the original Papyrus Sallier III. The addition of Abydos has filled a considerable number of lacunæ, and the collation of Sallier III has likewise cleared up many difficulties. As a long passage is misplaced in the hieratic text, and it lacks also the beginning (ten lines), it was necessary to adopt the line numbering from the hieroglyphic for which the Luxor text was chosen. All passages on movements connected with the battle are published in my *Battle of Kadesh*.

official record of the battle (§§ 316 ff.), we are able to trace in it all Ramses' movements, immediately before and leading up to the battle.
The discussion of the poem as a literary composition does not fall within the scope of this volume.ᵃ

Introduction

306. ᵇBeginning of the victory of King Usermare-Setepnere (Ramses II), [who is given life], forever, which he achieved in the land of Kheta ($Ḥt$ ʾ) and Naharin (N-h-ry-n), in the land of Arvad (Y-r ʾ - tw),ᶜ in Pedes (Py-d ʾ -s ʾ), in the Derden (D ʾ -r-d-ny), in the land of ʾMesa (M ʾ -s ʾ), in the land of Kelekesh ([$Ḳ$]ʾ -r ʾ -[k]y-$š$ ʾ ᶜ, sic!), —, Carchemish (K-[r ʾ]-k-my-$š$ ʾ), Kode ($Ḳdy$), the land of Kadesh ($Ḳdš$), in the land of Ekereth (ʾ -k ʾ -r ʾ -t), and Mesheneth (Mw-$š$ ʾ -n-t).
3. . . . . 8 . . . . ᵈ

Preparations and March to the Frontier at Tharu

307. Behold, his majesty prepared his infantry and his chariotry, the Sherdenᵉ ($Š$ ʾ -r ʾ -dy-n ʾ) of the captivity of his majesty from the

---

ᵃIt will be found complete with translation and notes in a later volume of this series.

ᵇThe conventional phrase for beginning a literary composition.

ᶜThis location of the battle in all these lands is probably a loose way of indicating that the land in which it took place was then in the possession of these nationalities. Of the old Syrian enemies of Egypt, we see in this list (also ll. 13-15 and 24): Naharin, Arvad, Carchemish, Kode, Kadesh, Nuges, Ekereth (Ugarit of Amarna Letters), Aleppo, and perhaps Mesheneth. The others, Kheta, Pedes, Derden, Mesa, Kelekesh, Kezweden, and Luka (or Lukat), are the Hittites and their neighbors in Asia Minor. Of the latter the Luka are almost certainly the Lycians, the Kelekesh, probably the Cilicians, the Derden, perhaps the Dardanians, and the Mesa, the Mysians. Kezweden was a part of the Hittite kingdom. The remnant is entirely uncertain, though many identifications have been proposed. See Müller's treatment (*Asien und Europa*, 334 f. and 355 ff.), and Hall (*Annals of British School at Athens*, VIII, 157).

ᵈHymn of praise of the king's valor.

ᵉEarliest mention of these mercenaries in an Egyptian document, although they were used at the close of the Eighteenth Dynasty, as shown by *Amarna Letters*, (ed. Winckler) where they were called Shirdana. They are identified with the Sardinians (Müller, *Asien und Europa*, 372 ff., where the Shirdana, of the *Amarna Letters*, are still unknown).

victories of his sword ⌜— —⌝ ⁹———ᵃ they gave the planᵇ of battle. His majesty proceeded northward, his infantry and his chariotry being with him. He beganᶜ the goodly way, to march. Year 5, the second month of the third season (tenth month), on the ninth day,ᵈ his majesty passed the fortress of Tharu (_T ꜣ -rw_) ¹⁰———ᵉ [like] Montu when he goes forth. Every country trembled before him, [⌜fear⌝] was in their hearts; all the ⌜rebels⌝ came bowing down for fear of the fame of his majesty, when his [army] came ¹¹upon the ⌜narrow⌝ᶠ road, being like one who is upon the highway of —.

March from Tharu to the Region of Kadesh

308. Now, after manyᴳ days after this, behold, his majesty was in "Usermare-Meriamon,"ʰ L. P. H., the city of ———ⁱ cedar. His majesty proceeded northward, and he then ¹²arrived at the highlandʲ of Kadesh (_Ḳdš_). Then his majesty, L. P. H., marched before, like his father, Montu lord of Thebes, and crossed over the channel

---

ᵃLacuna of uncertain length. ᵇCompare Uni, l. 19 (I, 312).

ᶜLit., "_took the head of the goodly way_," a phrase regularly used when a king sets out on an enterprise, like Queen Hatshepsut's expedition to Punt, Amenhotep III's wild cattle hunt, or Amenhotep IV's inspection of the Amarna boundaries (II, 960, l. 6).

ᵈAbout the end of April. ᵉLacuna of uncertain length.

ᶠThis word (_g ꜣ wt_) is a little uncertain; the meaning given is that of Brugsch, who states (_Dictionnaire géographique_, 995) that it designates here the narrow road between the Mediterranean and the lake of Serbonis. The meaning fits this passage well, but there is only one other example of the word (which is not decisive). Müller (_Asien und Europa_, 216) refers it above to the narrow way in the valley (_Buḳaᶜa_) between the Lebanons, but the "many days'" march leading to the Lebanon region is still in the future (ll. 11, 12), not in the past, as Müller states (_ibid._, 216, n. 3).

ᵍPapyrus Raifet begins here.

ʰSome unknown city named after the king, and apparently reached after the departure from the coast. Müller places it near southern Lebanon (_Asien und Europa_, 273, 7).

ⁱLacuna of uncertain length, containing of course, some reference to the arrival among the cedars of Lebanon.

ʲThis highland is "_south of Kadesh_," according to the Record (l. 2), and as he crosses to the west side of Orontes later on (l. 12), where the battle took place, the highland must be some hill on the east side. The plain between Orontes and Anti-Lebanon is here some twenty miles wide (_Palestine Exploration Fund Quarterly Report_, 1881, 166), and the highland referred to is that of Kamûᶜ at el-Harmel (Fig. 7 and _Battle of Kadesh_, 19–21).

of the Orontes[a] (ʾ-r-n-t), there being with him the first division of Amon[b] (named): "Victory-of-King-Usermare-Setepnere-L.-P.-H."

The Coalition of the Prince of Kheta

309. When his majesty, L. P. H., reached the city,[c] behold, ¹³the wretched, vanquished chief of Kheta (Ḫtʾ) had come, having gathered together all countries from the ends of the sea to the land of Kheta, which came entire: the Naharin (N-h-ry-n) likewise, and Arvad (ʾ-rʾ-tw), ¹⁴—, [d]Mesa (Mʾ-sw), Keshkesh (Kš-kš),[d] Kelekesh (Kʾ-rʾ-ky-kšʾ), Luka (Rw-kʾ), Kezweden (Kʾ-ḏʾ-wʾ-dn), Carchemish (K-rʾ-k-my-šʾ),[e] Ekereth (ʾ-kʾ-ry-t), Kode (Ḳdy), the entire land of Nuges (Nw-g-s), Mesheneth (Mw-šʾ-n-t), and Kadesh (Ḳdš). ¹⁵He left not a country which was not brought, to[ᵍether with] their chiefs[f] who were with him, every man bringing his chariotry, an exceeding great multitude, without its like. They covered the mountains and the valleys; they were like grasshoppers with their multitudes. ¹⁶He left not silver nor gold[g] in his land (but) he plundered it of all its possessions and gave to every country, in order to bring them with him to battle.

---

[a]Compare the same phrase on Amenhotep II's Syrian campaign (II, 784, l. 4). This is the crossing at the ford south of Shabtuna, where the Pharaoh was met by the two Shasu-Bedwin, with the false report (Record, ll. 2, 3).

[b]The rest of the army being some distance in the rear on the other side of the river. When the whole army is with him, the usual phrase is: "*his infantry and his chariotry being with him;*" e. g., l. 9. Ramses is therefore already far in advance of the other three divisions, just as he was later when the Hittites attacked him.

[c]Kadesh.

[d]In place of these two names the hieroglyphic texts all have Py-dʾ-sʾ and Yr-wn. Kškš is supposed by Müller to be a corruption of Kʾ-rʾ-ky-šʾ, but as it has a different k and occurs in the Papyrus side by side with Kelekesh, the supposition is doubtful, if not improbable. On the list as a whole, see p. 136, n. c.

[e]Instead of Ekereth, Raifet has Kadesh, which is, of course, senseless repetition, like that of the other texts in repeating Kadesh at the end of the list.

[f]It is incredible that the larger kingdoms of Asia Minor should have been represented at this battle by their kings (wr-w). These mercenaries of the Hittite king had, of course, their commanders; the Syrian princes were some of them really present, and the Egyptians were glad to class the mercenary commanders as similar princes, to the greater glory of the Pharaoh's victory. The close of this section (§ 309) shows clearly how these mercenaries were enlisted.

[g]Karnak, the only hieroglyphic text preserved here, has: "*he left no silver at all (ḥḏ nb)*." This may point to the more plentiful use of silver in Asia Minor, where it was produced.

The Positions of the Two Armies

310. Behold, the wretched, vanquished chief of Kheta, together with the numerous allied countries, were stationed[a] in battle array, concealed on the northwest of the city of Kadesh,[b] while his majesty [17]was alone by himself,[c] [with] his bodyguard,[c] and the division of Amon was marching behind him. The division of Re crossed over the river-bed on the south side of the town of Shabtuna ($Š\ni$-b-tw-n),[d] at the distance of an iter[e] from the [ʳdivision of Amonⁿ]; ——— the division of Ptah was on the south of [18]the city of Aranami[f] ($\ni$-$r\ni$-$n\ni$-m); and the division of Sutekh was marching upon the road.[g] His majesty had formed the first rank of all the leaders of his army, while they were on the shore in[h] the land of the Amor ($\ni$-m-w-$r\ni$ [i]). Behold, the

---

[a]So Raifet. The hieroglyphic texts have: "*were stationed, concealed in battle array,* [ʳ*behind*ⁿ] *the city of Kadesh.*"

[b]See plan (Fig. 9) for the following positions.

[c]Raifet has in place of this phrase: "*none other was with him;*" but the above text (Karnak) is more probably correct.

[d]Raifet has $Š\ni$-bw-dw-n ᵇ, and says "*west side.*" It is the town later called Ribleh (*Battle of Kadesh*, 21, 22). The location of this town is clear from the references given by the Poem and the Record. After camping on the "*highlands south of Kadesh*" (Record, l. 2), Ramses advances toward Kadesh, and on the way thither passes Shabtuna (Record, l. 3), which is near a ford over the Orontes, as our above passage shows. Shabtuna was therefore on the Orontes a few miles south of Kadesh. [Conder (*Palestine Exploration Fund Quarterly Report*, 1881, 169 ff.) was not furnished with proper data from the inscriptions, for the location of Shabtuna.] Ramses, having hitherto advanced on the east side of Orontes, is now moving on the west side, while half his force is still on the east side (Fig. 9).

[e]This variable measure does not exceed $1\frac{2}{3}$ miles (see II, 965).

[f]Raifet has: "*the division of Ptah was opposite them.*" This indicates that Aranami was on the east side of the Orontes. It is certain that Aranami is south of Shabtuna, for the division of Ptah, here marching northward, while just south of Aranami, was still south of Shabtuna when sent for by Ramses after the attack of the Asiatics (Record, ll. 18, 19). See *Battle of Kadesh*, 22, 23.

[g]A very indefinite indication, showing only that this division was far away somewhere on the road. It is not mentioned again, and did not get up in time for the battle.

[h]Raifet has "*of.*"

[i]The "*shore of Amor*" is the Mediterranean coast, at some point in southern Lebanon, where Ramses turned inland. (Cf. Meyer, *Festschrift für Georg Ebers*, 69, n. 2); it was long mistranslated "lake." This detail of Ramses' manipulation of his troops, therefore, refers back to an earlier stage of the campaign like a similar remark on the arrangement of the Hittite king's troops (at end of l. 19).

wretched ¹⁹vanquished chief of ᵃ Kheta was stationed in the midst of the infantry which was with him, and he came not out to fight, for fear of his majesty. Then he made to go the people of the chariotry, an exceedingly numerous multitude like the sand, being three people to each span.ᵇ Now, they had made their combinations (thus): among every three youths was one man of the vanquished of Kheta,ᶜ ²⁰equipped with all the weapons of battle. Lo, they had stationed them in battle array, concealed on the northwestᵈ the city of Kadesh.

The Attack of the Asiatics

311. They came forth from the southern side of Kadesh, and they cut through the division of Re in its middle, while they were marching without knowing and without ²¹being drawn up for battle. The infantry and chariotry of his majesty, L. P. H., retreated before them. Now, his majesty had halted on the north of the city of Kadesh, on the western side of the Orontes (?-r-n-t). Then came one to tellᵉ it to his majesty, L. P. H.

Ramses' Attack

312. His majesty, L. P. H., shone like his father ²²Montu, when he took the adornments of war; as he seized his coat of mail, he was like Baal in his hour. The great span which bore his majesty, L. P. H., called: "Victory-in-Thebes," from the great stables of Ramses (II),

---

ᵃHere Papyrus Raifet ends and Papyrus Sallier begins.

ᵇWith every two of the mercenaries was one Hittite, each three thus formed being in one chariot. This is omitted in the hieroglyphic texts.

ᶜSallier adds: "*without number;*" but this is a misunderstanding by the ancient copyist.

ᵈSo the Papyrus. The hieroglyphic versions have only "*behind*," but as the Egyptian army is south and southeast of Kadesh, "*behind Kadesh*" is for them the north and northwest.

ᵉThis messenger doubtless found the king already engaged in battle. At any rate, the messenger could only confirm what Ramses had already learned from the two Hittite scouts. Had he arrived earlier, the torture of the scouts would have been unnecessary. Their torture, therefore, shows that this messenger had not yet arrived. The attack in the south, therefore, which cut in two the marching division of Re, being at the most not more than a few miles from Ramses' camp, could not have taken place very long before the attack on said camp. This would indicate the rapidity with which the Egyptians were driven northward into Ramses' camp.

ᵃwas in the midst of the leaders.ᵃ His majesty halted in the rout;ᵇ then ²³he charged into the foe, the vanquished of Kheta, being alone by himself and none other with him. When his majesty went to look behind him, he found 2,500 chariotry surrounding him, in his way out, ²⁴being all the youth of the wretched Kheta, together with its numerous allied countries: from Arvad (ʾ-r ʾ-tw), from Mesa (Mʾ-sʾ), from Pedes (Py-dʾ-sʾ), from Keshkesh (Kš-kš), from Erwenetᶜ (Yr-wnˑt, sic!), from Kezweden (Kʾ-ḏʾ-wʾ-dʾ-nʾ), from Aleppo (Ḫy-rʾ-bw), Eketeri (ʾ-kʾ-t-r-y, sic!), Kadesh (Ḳdš), and Luka (Rw-kʾ-tᵈ), being three men to a span, acting in unison.

313. Now follow highly idealized and sometimes purely imaginary incidents, the creation of the poet, in which nothing is historical save the one fact that Ramses holds his own until the arrival of his southern army. He first calls upon Amon for help in his unequal battle. Amon responds and strengthens him against the foe. The king of the Kheta is obliged to summon his allied commanders and send them into the fray. Ramses addresses a scathing rebuke to his own troops, and when his charioteer is dismayed because they are entirely surrounded, he encourages him and charges six times into the hostile ranks, thus holding the enemy in check until his reinforcements from the south can come up.ᵉ

314. At evening the captives of every country are brought to the king's tent, and the next morning the plain is seen

---

ᵃThis phrase is not in Luxor (the only hieroglyphic text preserved at this point), and the connection in the hieroglyphic version was apparently: "*The great span etc.*, ... *was called, etc.*"

ᵇThe same word (y/d) is used of the headlong flight of the Syrians before Thutmose III at the battle of Megiddo (II, 430, l. 4).

ᶜBy Brugsch identified with Ilion! Müller would read the first syllable (Yr) as yᵖ, producing Yawan, or Ionians. For this reading the evidence is insufficient.

ᵈThe last six names are omitted by the hieroglyphic texts; hence the incorrect writings, as the papyrus is inaccurate.

ᵉThere is no reference to the arrival of the "*recruits*," who began the rescue.

covered with the dead, especially of the family of the prince of Kheta.[a] The army comes to the king's tent and celebrates his victory in a hymn of praise. But the king responds, reminding them of their cowardice, and reproaching them that they did not depend upon him to lead and protect them. The next (?) morning Ramses drew up his battle lines and renewed the attack with such effect that the prince of Kheta sent a humble letter suing for peace, which the king read in triumph before his assembled troops, who thereupon gave him another ovation.[b] Pleased with this flattery, he marches southward, and returns in peace to Thebes, where, of course, he is received with triumphant jubilation by the people.

315. The last three lines of Papyrus Sallier III (XI, 9–11), which is the only text in which the conclusion is preserved, furnish the date of "*this writing, in the year 9, second month of the third season, day —, [under the majesty] of King Ramses II.*" This particular copy was one "*which the scribe, Pentewere*[c] (*Pn-t ᵓ -wrˑt*) *made*" (XI, 11), a mere copyist, who was not the author of the poem, as is still usually stated.

b. Official Record of the Battle of Kadesh[d]

316. This document is appended to the wall scenes (§§ 328–47), and seems to have been an official record of

---

[a] This is corroborated by the reliefs.

[b] Even the Poem makes no claim that Ramses captured Kadesh, as is so often stated in the histories. It seems incredible, furthermore, that there should have been a successful battle on the next day, of which the reliefs and inscriptions should show not a single trace. It is possible to conclude with Müller (*Asien und Europa*, 216, n. 1) that the entire conclusion of the poem, recounting the Hittite king's letter proposing peace, is to be referred to the actual arrangements for peace in year 21; but see my *Battle of Kadesh*, 46. In any case, the poem is clearly wrong in placing a treaty of peace after the battle of Kadesh, for Ramses continued the conflict with the Hittites until long after this.

[c] Usually called "Pentaur;" that he was not the author of the poem, as formerly supposed, was shown by Erman (*Neuägyptische Grammatik*, 7).

[d] See my *Battle of Kadesh*, 7, for fuller discussion of bibliography. Three originals:

the battle. It is not as full as the Poem on the marches and positions of the two armies, but it narrates fully the inside history which led to Ramses' incautious advance to the north of Kadesh, furnishing an account of the earliest military ruse known in history. Of all this the Poem says nothing.

Date

317. [1]Year 5, third month of the third season, day 9;[a] under the majesty of Horus: Mighty Bull, Beloved of Truth; King of Upper and Lower Egypt: Usermare-Setepnere; Son of Re; Ramses-Meriamon, given life forever.

Camp South of Kadesh

318. Lo, his majesty was in Zahi (D ᵓ -hy)[b] on his second victorious campaign. The goodly watch[c] in [a]life, prosperity and health, in the tent of his majesty, was on the highland south of Kadesh.

False Message of the Shasu near Shabtuna

319. When his majesty appeared like the rising of Re, he assumed the adornments of his father, Montu. When the king proceeded

---

1. ABU SIMBEL (Champollion, *Monuments*, 27–29; Rosellini, *Monumenti Storici*, 100–102; Lepsius, *Denkmäler*, III, 187, *c–e*. I had also photographs by Grünau, kindly loaned me by Steindorff.

2. RAMESSEUM (Lepsius, *ibid.*, III, 153; Sharpe, *Egyptian Inscriptions*, 2d part, 52).

3. LUXOR (Brugsch, *Recueil de monuments*, II, 53; Champollion, *Monuments*, 127 *bis*; Rosellini, *ibid.*, 106).

Of these Luxor is not given by Champollion and Rosellini, but was copied by Brugsch. Furthermore, the Abu Simbel text is bad, sometimes omitting whole passages. Champollion and Rosellini's copy of this text is unusable, two whole lines being omitted and often the sand-covered lower ends. Although I collated the Abu Simbel text exhaustively, the translation is based chiefly on the Ramesseum. For this text I had only Lepsius, *Denkmäler*; for Sharpe's copy is totally worthless. Though all the originals show lacunæ, I found these disappeared on arranging them in parallel columns. A combined text by Guieysse (*Recueil*, VIII, 126–31) I found unreliable. The line numbers herein refer to the Ramesseum text. All passages on movements of the battle are also published in my *Battle of Kadesh*.

[a]This is about the end of May (see Breasted, *Zeitschrift für ägyptische Sprache*, 37, 129), just one month after leaving the Egyptian frontier at Tharu (Poem, l. 9).

[b]This shows that Zahi was not confined to Phœnicia, this passage making it extend inland over Lebanon and the Orontes valley. See also II, 616, ll. 9, 10.

[c]Compare Thutmose III's camp at Aruna (II, 425, ll. 56, 57).

northward, and his majesty had arrived at the locality south of ³the town of Shabtuna[a] (*Š ͗ -b-tw-n*), there came two[b] Shasu, to speak to his majesty as follows: "Our brethren, who belong to the greatest of the families with the vanquished chief of Kheta, have made us come to ⁴his majesty, to say: 'We will be subjects of Pharaoh, L. P. H., and we will flee from the vanquished chief of Kheta; for the vanquished chief of Kheta sits[c] in the land of Aleppo (*Ḫy-r ͗ -bw*), on the north of Tunip (*Tw-n-p*). He fears ⁵because of Pharaoh, L. P. H., to come southward.'" Now, these Shasu spake these words, which they spake to his majesty, falsely, (for) the vanquished chief of Kheta made them come to spy ⁶where his majesty was, in order to cause the army of his majesty not to draw up for fighting him,[d] to battle with the vanquished chief of Kheta.

Positions of the Two Armies

320. Lo, the vanquished chief of Kheta came with every chief of every country, their infantry and their chariotry, ⁷which he had brought with him by force,[e] and stood, equipped, drawn up in line of battle behind Kadesh the Deceitful, while his majesty knew it not. Then his majesty proceeded northward and arrived on the northwest[f] of Kadesh; ⁸and the army of his majesty ⌈made camp⌉ there.

Examination of Hittite Scouts

321. Then, as his majesty sat upon a throne of gold, there arrived a scout who was in the following of his majesty, and he brought two scouts of ⁹the vanquished chief of Kheta. They were conducted into the pre-

---

[a]On the location of Shabtuna, see *Battle of Kadesh*, 21, 22, and *infra*, p. 139, n. d; and the plans of the battle (Figs. 7, 8).

[b]Abu Simbel has "*two*," but Ramesseum has "*three*," which, of course, may be merely the plural strokes.

[c]So Abu Simbel; Ramesseum has "*is*." The former omits "*the land of*."

[d]That is, to keep the Egyptians in marching order, that he might surprise and find them unprepared for battle, as he actually did.

[e]Or: "*from victories.*"

[f]He had now passed northward along the west side of Kadesh, and camped on the northwest of the city ("*north*," Poem, l. 21). The text over the battle (§ 336, ll. 3, 4) also says he camped on "*the northwest of Kadesh.*" In any case, the general location of his camp is certain. L. 8 perhaps began with some reference to the position of Ramses' three divisions, far in his rear, which is so carefully noted in the Poem (ll. 17, 18), but the restoration above is more probable.

sence, and his majesty said to them: "What are ye?" They said: "As for us, the vanquished chief of the Kheta has caused that we should come to spy out where his majesty is." Said his majesty [10]to them: "He! Where is he, the vanquished chief of Kheta? Behold, I have heard, saying: 'He is in the land of Aleppo ($Ḥy$-r ᵓ -b ᵓ).'" Said they: "See, the vanquished chief of Kheta is stationed, together with many countries, [11]which he has brought with him by force,[a] being every country which is in the districts of the land of Kheta,[b] the land of Naharin (N-hy-r-n), and all Kode ($Ḳd$).[c] They are equipped with infantry and chariotry, bearing their [12]weapons; more numerous are they than the sand of the shore. See, they are standing, drawn up for battle, behind[d] Kadesh the Deceitful."

The Council of War

322. Then his majesty had the princes called into the presence, [13]and had them hear every word which the two scouts of the vanquished chief of Kheta, who were in the presence, had spoken. Said his majesty to them: "See ye the manner wherewith the chiefs'(mr) of the peasantry[e] (yw ᶜ · ty) and [14]the officials under whom is the land of Pharaoh, L. P. H., have stood, daily, saying to the Pharaoh: 'The vanquished chief of Kheta is in the land of Aleppo ($Ḥy$-r ᵓ -b ᵓ y); he has fled before his majesty, [15]since hearing that, behold, he came.' So spake they to his majesty daily. But see, I have held a hearing in this very hour, with the two scouts of [16]the vanquished chief of Kheta, to the effect that the vanquished chief of Kheta is coming, together with the numerous countries [that are with] him, being people and horses, like the multitudes of the sand. They are stationed behind Kadesh the

---

[a]Or: "*in victory.*"

[b]Clearly showing the composite character of the Hittite kingdom at this time.

[c]This is a clear indication of the extent of Kode; all the rest of the countries from Arvad to Asia Minor are included in the term "*all Kode.*" But see Müller, *Asien und Europa*, 242, 48.

[d]"*Behind Kadesh,*" from Ramses' present position in his camp on the north of Kadesh is, of course, south of Kadesh, where the Hittites moved out for the attack on the division of Re.

[e]Or: "*infantry;*" these officials are parallel with "*the governors of the (foreign) countries*" in l. 17. It is clear that the king is chiding the officials in authority both in Asia and Egypt, that is, both his provincial and Egyptian officers.

Deceitful. But [17]the governors of the countries and the officials under whose authority is the land of Pharaoh, L. P. H., were not able to tell it to us."

323. Said the princes who were in the presence of his majesty: "It is a great fault, which the governors of the countries and the officials of Pharaoh, L. P. H., have committed [18]in not informing that [a]the vanquished chief of Kheta was near the king;[a] and (in) that they told his[b] report to his majesty daily."

The Divisions in the South Are Ordered Up.

324. Then the vizier was ordered to hasten[c] [19]the army of his majesty, while they were marching on the south of Shabtuna[d] (Šʾ-b-tw-n), in order to bring them to the place where his majesty was.

The Attack of the Asiatics

325. Lo, while his majesty sat talking[e] with [20]the princes, the vanquished chief of Kheta came,[f] and the numerous countries, which were with him. They crossed over the channel[g] on the south of

---

[a]Lit., "*that the vanquished chief of Kheta was where the king was.*"

[b]Viz., the false report of the Hittite which he sent out by the two Shasu (ll. 3, 4).

[c]The vizier sent the message by a horseman, and probably went also by chariot himself (§§ 333-4).

[d]This is one of the most important statements in the documents on this battle. It shows that, while Ramses is in camp on the north of Kadesh the main body of his army is south of Kadesh on the march in the vicinity of Shabtuna (see Fig. 11). Besides the division of Amon, which is with Ramses, only the division of Re has passed Shabtuna.

[e]The messenger announcing the attack on the division of Re in the south had up to this point not yet arrived, and Ramses apparently receives no notice of the attack until it is upon him.

[f]So Ramesseum; Abu Simbel has: "*with [his] infantry and his chariotry likewise;*" but this is incorrect; the entire battle was one of chariotry, as the reliefs show.

[g]This channel is, of course, that of Orontes, the Hittite king having previously led his forces from the west to the east side, now goes back to the west side, in order to get around the city, while keeping it between him and the Egyptians. Being a city which he commanded, he could, of course, go through it, and emerge for his attack on the south side, unless prevented by lack of gates at the proper points. But this would probably have exposed his issuing forces to the view of the marching division of Re, as the city wall was necessarily clearly in view across the moat. In any case, there must have been some cover south of the city from which the Asiatics emerged for the attack.

Kadesh, and charged into the army of his majesty while they were [21]marching, and not expecting it. Then the infantry and chariotry of his majesty retreated before them, northward to the place where his majesty was. Lo, the foes [22]of[a] the vanquished chief of Kheta surrounded[b] the bodyguard of his majesty, who were by his side.

Ramses' Personal Attack

326. When his majesty saw them, he was enraged against them, like his father, Montu, lord of Thebes. He seized the adornments of battle, [23]and arrayed himself in his coat of mail. He was like Baal in his hour. Then he betook himself to his horses, and led quickly on, being alone by [24]himself. He charged into the foes of the vanquished chief of Kheta, and the numerous countries which were with him. His majesty was like Sutekh, the great in strength, smiting and slaying among them; his majesty hurled them [25]headlong, one upon another into the water of the Orontes.[c]

Ramses' Own Statement

327. "I charged all countries, while I was alone, my infantry and my chariotry having forsaken me. Not one among them stood to turn about. I swear, as Re loves me, as my father, Atum, favors me, that, as for every matter which his majesty has stated, I did it in truth, in the presence of my infantry and my chariotry."

c. The Reliefs of the Battle of Kadesh[d]

328. The pictured story of the battle of Kadesh presented in these reliefs, like the great epic poem on the battle, was a source of such gratification to Ramses, that he had them reproduced six times in the temples of Upper Egypt and

---

[a]Viz., "*belonging to.*"

[b]The Hittite king, having effected the isolation of Ramses and a portion of his troops, now enfolds between his two wings the camp of Ramses, toward, and of course past, which the latter's fleeing troops have retreated (see l. 25).

[c]Ramses evidently attacked the enemy's right wing, before it was sufficiently strong to withstand him, and drove the enemy directly eastward into the river; see Fig. 12.

[d]Cut on the walls of Ramses II's temples at Abydos, Thebes (three times), Derr, and Abu Simbel:

1. ABYDOS.—On the outside of the north, west, and south walls; nearly the whole has perished, and the remains are still unpublished. Short inscriptions

Nubia, and doubtless also several times in the vanished temples of Lower Egypt. As will be seen, owing to the primitive character of Egyptian topographical and architectural drawing, these scenes cannot be made to coincide with the data of the inscriptions, but they furnish invaluable side lights on the battle, and the accompanying inscriptions add facts of the greatest importance.

1. THE COUNCIL OF WAR[a]

329. Ramses sits enthroned, with his officers before him, in consultation. Below, the two Hittite scouts are being beaten, to force them to disclose the location of the enemy.

(Mariette, *Abydos*, II, 10, 11) and three scenes (Mariette, *Voyage dans la haute Egypte*, Pl. 30–32 and p. 72).

2. THEBES.

 a) *Ramesseum*, first pylon: Lepsius, *Denkmäler*, III, 153–55, 157–61; Champollion, *Notices descriptives*, 870–72.

 b) *Ramesseum*, second pylon: Champollion, *Monuments*, 328–30; Champollion, *Notices descriptives*, 585–89, 873, 874; Rosellini, *Monumenti Storici*, 109, 110; Lepsius, III, 164, 165.

 c) *Luxor*, on the first pylon: Champollion, *Monuments*, 323, 324, 327–327 *bis* (last two incorrectly marked Ramesseum); Rosellini, *ibid.*, 104–7; Brugsch, *Recueil de monuments*, 53 (inscriptions only); *Description, Antiquités*, III, 3–6. (None at Karnak, as stated by Guieysse, *Recueil*, VIII, 126, note 1.)

 d) *Karnak*, chiseled out in antiquity: Breasted, *Battle of Kadesh*, Pl. VIII, 45, 46.

3. DERR.—Now destroyed; seen by Champollion (Wiedemann, *Aegyptische Geschichte*, 434, note 5).

4. ABU SIMBEL.—In the great temple, first hall, north wall: Champollion, *Monuments*, 17 *bis*–33; Champollion, *Notices descriptives*, I, 64–66; Rosellini, *ibid.*, 87–103; Lepsius, *Denkmäler*, 187, *c–e*.

The inscriptions from all these reliefs have been combined (from the publications) by Guieysse (*Recueil*, VIII, 120–42) in a handy form for reference, but it is not reliable. An exhaustive publication of the combined originals is very much needed. For the following translations I arranged my own combined text, placing all the publications of all the originals in parallel columns. These are published, in so far as they concern the movements of the armies, in my *Battle of Kadesh*. All the reliefs are also published there, Pl. I–VII.

[a]1. RAMESSEUM, first pylon: Champollion, I, 870; Lepsius, *Denkmäler*, 153.

2. LUXOR: Champollion, *Monuments*, 327 *bis*; Rosellini, *Monumenti Storici*, 106; *Battle of Kadesh*, Pl. IV.

3. ABU SIMBEL: Champollion, *Monuments*, 29; Champollion, *Notices descriptives*, I, 66; Rosellini, *ibid.*, 102; *Battle of Kadesh*, Pl. VI.

The whole scene is evidently located in the tent visible as a rectangle in the center of the camp on the northwest of Kadesh.

Beating Spies

330. [1]The arrival of the scout of Pharaoh, L. P. H., bringing the two scouts of the vanquished chief [2]of Kheta into the presence of Pharaoh, L. P. H. They are beating them, to make them tell [3]where the wretched chief of Kheta is.

Over Horses

Great first span of his majesty: "Victory-in-Thebes," of the great stable: "Usermare-Setepnere-Beloved-of-Amon."

II. THE CAMP[a]

331. In the midst of a rectangular inclosure, barricaded with shields, appears the royal tent,[b] surrounded by the small tents of the officers and the animated life of the camp, which the "*first*[c] *division*," that of Amon, is engaged in arranging. This is the camp north or northwest of Kadesh (Record, l. 7; Poem, l. 21). Within the royal tent, Ramses sits, chiding his officers for their neglect, when suddenly the extreme north end of the Hittite right wing bursts in at the

---

[a]1. RAMESSEUM: Lepsius, *Denkmäler*, III, 154, 155; Prisse, *Histoire de l'art égyptien* (plates unnumbered); *Battle of Kadesh*, Pl. I.

2. LUXOR: Champollion, *Monuments*, 326, 327 (no text); Rosellini, *Monumenti Storici*, 106, 107 (no text); *Battle of Kadesh*, Pl. IV.

3. ABU SIMBEL: Champollion, *Monuments*, 30, 31; Champollion, *Notices descriptives*, I, 65, 66; Rosellini, *ibid.*, 98–99; *Battle of Kadesh*, Pl. VI.

[b]The lion behind the king's tent is his personal pet. He is shown at Luxor fettered; at Abu Simbel (Champollion, *Monuments*, 15) with the Pharaoh on the march; at Bet-Walli beside the Pharaoh's throne (Champollion, *Monuments*, 62); and finally at Derr in two scenes (Lepsius, *Denkmäler*, III, 183, *b*, and 184, *a*), where the king is sacrificing prisoners to Amon-Re. In these last scenes he is accompanied by the inscription: "*The lion, follower of his majesty, slayer of his enemies*" (cf. Champollion, *Notices descriptives*, I, 90); and he is biting one of the prisoners. There is no basis in all this for the current statement that this lion accompanied his master in the battle, where (Champollion, *Monuments*, 25, and Rosellini, *Monumenti Storici*, 87) a lion in the decoration of the chariot has been mistaken for the Pharaoh's pet (see *Battle of Kadesh*, 44, 45).

[c]Evidently so called because of its position in the line of march.

eastern end of the barricade (upper right-hand corner), driving some members of the royal household before them. These hostile intruders are quickly dispatched by the household troops of Ramses, who are to be seen on foot poniarding them.

Over Prince in Chariot

332. ¹Fan-bearer on the king's right hand, —, ²king's-scribe, army commander — ³——— ⁴his majesty the — ⁵on his right hand —.

Over Official in Chariot

·¹Arrival of ²the — of Pharaoh, L. P. H., at —— ³the mother of the royal children, together with the ⁴— of the divine mother ⁵— — — fleeing to ⁶the west [side] of the ⁷camp ᶠ— —ᵈ before the foe.

At Top

The first division of Amon (named): "He-Gives-Victory-to-Usermare-Setepnere (Ramses II)-Given-Life," with which Pharaoh is engaged in making camp.

III. RAMSES' MESSENGERS[a]

333. These messengers are the ones sent southward by the vizier (Record, § 324, ll. 18 and 19) to hasten the forces still in the south near Shabtuna. To carry such a message, they must either make a wide detour westward, to go around the enemy's lines, or hazard the dangerous passage through them. To render the arrival of the orders more certain, the vizier dispatches a horseman, and goes himself[b] in a chariot. Their orders seem to concern only the division of

---

[a]1. LUXOR: Champollion, *Monuments*, 323; Rosellini, *Monumenti Storici*, 106; *Battle of Kadesh*, Pl. IV.

2. ABU SIMBEL: Champollion, *ibid.*, 18; Rosellini, *ibid.*, 95; *Battle of Kadesh*, Pl. VI.

[b]The Luxor relief contains a fragment of inscription showing that the vizier himself probably went. Among the approaching reinforcements hastening up in the rear of the Hittites to relieve Ramses, appear the words: "*Arrival of the vizier to* [ᶠassistᵈ] *the army of* [*his majesty*]" (Champollion, *Monuments*, 324, incorrectly numbered 314). This shows that the vizier got through, and brought up the reinforcements himself.

Ptah. This is because the southern half of the division of Re was, of course, aware of the attack, and the division of Sutekh was evidently too far away for Ramses to hope to bring them up in time.

Before Horseman

334. ¹The scout of the army of Pharaoh, L. P. H., ²going to hasten the division of Ptah, ³saying: "March on! ⁴Pharaoh, L. P. H., your lord, ⁵stands ———."

IV. THE BATTLE[a]

335. We here see the city of Kadesh, by which the battle was fought, so thoroughly moated that it seems to lie in the very Orontes itself, rather than on it. The four drawings of the city preserved show great differences among themselves;[b] and it is evident that no clear idea of the relative positions of city and combatants can be gained from them.[c] We must remember that, according to the inscriptions, the Pharaoh is north of the city. It would seem that a bend in the river enables him to charge directly toward the city, viz., southward, and to drive the enemy into the river. But if the side of the Egyptian drawing where the Pharaoh is, is north, then it represents him as on the east side of the river. Or again, if, as the texts state, he should be on the west side of the river in the Egyptian drawing, then the drawing represents him as south of the city and charging northward.

---

[a]1. RAMESSEUM, first pylon: Champollion, *Notices descriptives*, I, 872; Lepsius, *Denkmäler*, III, 157–61; *Battle of Kadesh*, Pl. II.

2. RAMESSEUM, second pylon: Champollion *Monuments*, 328–30; Champollion, *Notices descriptives*, I, 586–89, 873, 874; Rosellini, *Monumenti Storici*, 109, 110; Lepsius, *Denkmäler*, III, 164, 165; *Battle of Kadesh*, Pl. III.

3. LUXOR: Champollion, *Monuments*, 323, 324; Rosellini, *ibid.*, 104, 105; *Battle of Kadesh*, Pl. V.

4. ABU SIMBEL: Champollion, *Monuments*, 18–26; Rosellini, *ibid.*, 88–95; *Battle of Kadesh*, Pl. VI.

[b]See Müller's useful comparison of the four (*Asien und Europa*, 214, 215).

[c]I have discussed the value of the reliefs fully in my *Battle of Kadesh*, 40–46.

In no way can any of the four ancient drawings of this battle-field be made to coincide with the data of the inscriptions. This is not remarkable when we remember that they do not coincide with each other. In these, as in all Egyptian

Fig. 13.—The Modern Mound of Kadesh (from Koldewey)

drawings, each part is drawn largely irrespective of its relations to any of the other parts. We can here gain no true conception of the plan of the battle. Some facts stated in the inscriptions may be clearly seen in the reliefs however. We observe the Hittite chariotry (above and below) enfolding Ramses within its extended wings. We see also how he drives into the river those in his immediate front, including many prominent allies, officials, and even relatives of the Hittite king. The king of Aleppo is held head downward by his soldiers on the farther shore, that he may disgorge the water which he has swallowed. Here also stands the Hittite king with 8,000 foot,[a] which he makes no effort to bring into action. The inscriptions are these:

Over King's Horses and Chariot

336. [1]The Good God, mighty in valor, great in victory, crushing [2]all countries, King of Upper and Lower Egypt: Usermare-Setepnere; Son of Re; Ramses-Meriamon. [3]The stand which his majesty made while he was camping on the north[4]west of Kadesh. He charged into the midst of the foe [5]belonging to the vanquished chief of Kheta, while he was alone [6]by himself, and no other with him. [7]He found surrounding him [8]2,500 horse in four bodies on his every side. [9]He slaughtered them, making [10](them) heaps beneath his horses. [11]He slew [12]all the chiefs of all the countries, [13]the allies of the vanquished chief of Kheta, together with his own great chiefs, [14]his infantry and his chariotry. He overthrew them [15]prostrate upon their faces, and hurled them down, one upon another into the waters [16]of the Orontes. His majesty was behind them like a fierce-eyed lion [17]——— in their place. Lo, the vanquished chief of Kheta [18]stood extending backward his arms in praise of the Good God.

Among the Fleeing Enemy

337. Tergen — (Ty-r $^{\circ}$-g $^{\circ}$-n —).

Tergenenes (Ty-r $^{\circ}$-g $^{\circ}$-n-n $^{\circ}$-s $^{\circ}$), charioteer of the vanquished chief of Kheta.

The great horse of his majesty: "Victory-in-Thebes;" of the great stable: "Usermare-Setepnere,-Beloved-of-Amon."

---

[a]So Ramesseum; Abu Simbel has: "*Other warriors* (*tw-hy-r* $^{\circ}$) — *before him, 9,000.*" The "*other*" is to distinguish them from the troops in battle. Luxor has merely: "[*The army*] *of the vanquished chief of Kadesh, very numerous in men and horses.*" As the 2,500 Hittite chariots had (three men each) 7,500 men, we get 16,000, to 17,000 men as the total Asiatic force. Ramses will possibly have had about 20,000, and thus each of his four divisions was about 5,000 strong, or about equal to a modern army division. A body of troops mentioned in the Anastasi Papyrus No. 1, as belonging to Ramses II, contained 5,000 men, all foreign mercenaries. See *Battle of Kadesh*, 9.

Kemeth (*K ᵓ-my-ṯ ᵓ*), chief of the Warriors (*Tw-hy-r ᵓ*).

———es (———ᵓ-s ᵓ), charioteer of the vanquished chief of Kheta.

Tergetetethes (*Ty-r ᵓ-g ᵓ-ty-t-ṯ ᵓ-s ᵓ*) chief of the archers of the Thebes (*Ḳbsw*).

Kherpesar (*Ḫy-r ᵓ-p ᵓ-s ᵓ-r ᵓ*), scribe of the vanquished chief of Kheta.

Egem (*ᶜᵓ-g-m*), chief of the archers of the vanquished chief of Kheta.

Teyeder (*Ty-y ᵓ-dw-r ᵓ*), chief of the bodyguard of the vanquished chief of Kheta.

Peyes (*P ᵓ-y-s ᵓ*), charioteer of the vanquished chief of Kheta.

Gerbetes (*G-r-b ᵓ-tw-s ᵓ*), chariot-warrior of the vanquished chief of Kheta.

Semretes (*S ᵓ-my-r ᵓ-tw-s ᵓ*) ———.

Peyes (*P ᵓ-y-s ᵓ*), charioteer of the vanquished chief of Kheta.

Teder (*T ᵓ-d ᵓ-r ᵓ*), chief of the warriors (*Tw-hy-r ᵓ*).

Methrem (*My-ṯ ᵓ-ry-m ᵓ*).

Rebesnen (*R ᵓ-b ᵓ-sw-n-n ᵓ*), chief of the archers of Enenes (*ᵓn-n ᵓ-s ᵓ*).

Septher (*S ᵓ-p ᵓ-ṯ ᵓ-r ᵓ*), brother of the vanquished chief of Kheta.

Thewethes (*Ṯ ᵓ-w ᵓ-ṯ ᵓ-s ᵓ*), chief of the country of Tenes (*T ᵓ-ny-s ᵓ*).

Rebeyer (*R ᵓ-b ᵓ-yw-r*).

The wretched chief of Aleppo (*Ḫy-r ᵓ-b ᵓ*) turned upside down by his soldiers, after his majesty hurled him into the water.

Warriors (*Tw-hy-r ᵓ*), who are in front of the ⌈commander⌉, 8,000. Town of Kadesh.

By the King of Kheta

338. ¹The vanquished, wretched chief of Kheta, ²standing before his infantry and chariotry ³with his face turned round, and his heart afraid. ⁴He went not forth to battle, for fear of his majesty, ⁵after he saw his majesty prevailing [against the vanquished chief] ⁶of Kheta and all the chiefs of all the countries ⁷[who] were with him. His majesty ——— ⁸he overthrew them ———. ⁹[The vanquished chief of Kheta] said: "He is like ¹⁰Sutekh, great in might; Baal is ¹¹in his limbs."

V. THE DEFENSE OF THE CAMP[a]

339. While Ramses was at the front early in the battle, his camp was entered by the Hittite advance; but on the arrival of the "*recruits*" from Amor, the latter fell upon these spoilers and slaughtered them.

In Front of Troops

340. [1]The arrival of the recruits of Pharaoh, L. P. H., from the land of Amor (ʾ-*m-w-r* ʾ). They found that the force of the vanquished chief of Kheta had surrounded the [2]camp of his majesty on its western side. His majesty had been camping alone, no army with him, ⌈awaiting the⌉ arrival of his ⌈officers⌉ [3]and his army and the division with which Pharaoh, L. P. H., was, had not finished setting up the camp. Now the division [4]of Re and the division of Ptah were on the march; they had not (yet) arrived, and their officers were in the ⌈forest⌉ of Bewey (*B*ʾ -*w-y*). Then the recruits [5]cut off the foe belonging to the vanquished chief of Kheta, while they (the foe) were entering into the camp, and Pharaoh's officers[b] [6]slew them; they left not a single survivor among them. Their hearts were filled with the mighty valor of Pharaoh, [7]their good lord; he was behind them like a steward of —, like a wall of iron, forever and ever.

VI. AFTER THE BATTLE[c]

341. This relief shows us the king after the battle is over, enjoying his triumph. As he stands in his chariot, his officers throw down before him the hands of the slain, cut off as trophies. The relief on the Abydos temple (unpublished), though very fragmentary, contained a fuller repre-

---

[a]1. RAMESSEUM: Lepsius, *Denkmäler*, III, 155; *Battle of Kadesh*, Pl. I.
2. LUXOR: Champollion, *Monuments*, 327; Rosellini, *Monumenti Storici*, 107; *Battle of Kadesh*, Pl. IV.
3. ABU SIMBEL: Champollion, *ibid.*, 32; Rosellini, *ibid.*, 97; Lepsius, *ibid.*, 187; *Battle of Kadesh*, Pl. VI.

[b]*Sdm· w-ꜥ š.*

[c]1. ABYDOS: Mariette, *Abydos*, II, 10, 11.
2. ABU SIMBEL: Champollion, *Monuments*, 18; Rosellini, *Monumenti Storici*, 95; *Battle of Kadesh*, Pl. VI.

sentation of Ramses' triumph than the meager scene at Abu Simbel. It showed the king receiving the prisoners, captured according to the accompanying inscriptions, by himself! These inscriptions[a] are as follows:

Ramses' Officers Bringing Captives before Him

342. Bringing in prisoners before his majesty, being those which [he] brought off in the victory of his sword in this wretched land of Kheta, when his majesty caused to be [⌈announced to⌉] his infantry and his chariotry, saying: "[⌈Behold, these are⌉] the prisoners of my own capture, while I was alone, no infantry being with me, nor any prince with me, nor any chariotry."

Beside a Group of Prisoners

343. List (*shwy*) of those countries which his majesty slew, while alone by himself: Corpses, horses, and chariots, bows, swords, all the weapons of warfare.

Beside Another Group of Prisoners

344. Receiving the prisoners which his majesty brought off, in the victory of his sword in this wretched land of Kheta and this wretched land [of] Naharin (*N-h-ry-n*), together with the chiefs of all countries who came with the vanquished chief of Kheta, [b]as living captives.[b]

Over Fleeing Chariots

345. Warriors (*Tw-hy-r⸗*) of ⌈— —⌉ the chariots of the camp of the vanquished chief of Kheta.

The texts at Abu Simbel are not so full; they are the following:

Behind Chariot

346. ¹The Good God, who fought for his army, whose sword repulsed the Nine Bows; king, mighty in victory, ²who hath not his like; charging into the multitudes of every country, making them prostrate bodies. ³His face is fierce-eyed before the chief of Kheta, and the countries of Naharin ⌈— —⌉.

---

[a]Mariette, *Abydos*, II, 10, 11.
[b]This phrase is to be construed with "*brought off.*"

Over Horses

347. Great first span of his majesty (named): "Mut-is-Satisfied," of the great stable: "Usermare-Setepnere-Beloved-of-Amon."

VII. PRESENTATION OF CAPTIVES TO AMON[a]

348. As his father, Seti I, is seen presenting captives and spoil to Amon, on the north wall of the great Karnak hypostyle, so Ramses appears in a like capacity on its south wall. Here he leads and presents to Amon, Mut, and Khonsu, three rows of prisoners, accompanied by inscriptions[b] which show that they are captives taken at the battle of Kadesh:

349. List of the chiefs of Kheta, which his majesty, L. P. H., brought as living captives to the house of his father, Amon: Derden (D-rʾ-d-n-y), Pedes (Py-d-sʾ), Kele[kesh] (Ky-rʾ-[ky-$š$ʾ]) ———.

350. These are followed by four short lines of prisoners, each led by one of Ramses' sons:

a) ——— [behind his majesty, by the] ——— scribe, commander in chief of the army, Amenhirkhepeshef.

b) ——— [behind] his majesty, by the king's-son, Khamwese.

c) ——— behind his majesty, by the king's-son, Meriamon.

d) ——— behind his majesty, by the king's-son, Seti.

351. All these are designated as:

Captives from the northern countries, who came to overthrow his majesty, whom his majesty slew, and whose subjects he brought as living captives, to fill the storehouse of his father, Amon.

III. PALESTINIAN REVOLT

352. At some time between the fifth and eighth years all Palestine, doubtless incited by the Hittites, revolted[c] against

---

[a] Relief on the exterior of the south wall of the hypostyle of the great Amon-temple at Karnak; published by Champollion, *Notices descriptives*, II, 122, 123: accompanying inscription also, Brugsch, *Recueil de Monuments*, I, Pl. 29.

[b] Over the lowermost of the three rows. The inscriptions of the other two, as well as the figures of the captives, have perished. A portion of the middle row is, however, still visible.

[c] It is supposed that Ramses must have met with serious reverses between the fifth and the eighth years, for the Palestinian princes down to the Shephelah to have dared to revolt.

Ramses II, and he was obliged to take up the reconquest of his Asiatic possessions, at his very door, in the later Philistine country with the siege of Askalon.[a]

I. RECONQUEST OF SOUTHERN PALESTINE[b]

353. A relief at Karnak represents the storming of the city of Askalon, and the accompanying inscription refers to its rebellion. Of course, Askalon did not revolt alone, but must have been in league with the other cities of Palestine.

354. In the relief we see the king in his chariot charging the bearded defenders, lined up outside a battlemented city, which is located on an elevation. The storming ladders are up, and an Egyptian officer is demolishing the city gate with an ax, while the inhabitants appear on the walls, beseeching mercy. By the city is the following inscription:

355. The wretched city (dmy), which his majesty captured, when it rebelled, Askalon (?-s-k-rw-n ?). It (the city) says: "It is joy to be subject to thee, and delight to cross thy boundaries. Take thou the heritage, that we may speak of thy valor in all unknown countries."

Over the king's horses appears the usual glorification of his valor.

II. RECONQUEST OF NORTHERN PALESTINE

356. By the eighth year Ramses has reached northern Palestine again, and captures the cities of western Galilee.

---

[a]The place of this siege in Ramses II's wars is uncertain; but as western Galilee revolted in his eighth year, it is not unlikely that the revolt of Askalon is to be connected with that of west Galilee. Indeed, one name in the list of the eighth year may be Askalon (Champollion, *Notices descriptives*, II, 871, I, No. 2 ⌊————⌋ r-n ?). The date "IXth year" (Maspero, *Struggle of the Nations*, 400) for the capture of Askalon is without any documentary support.

[b]Relief and inscription on the exterior of the south wall of the great hypostyle hall at Karnak; Champollion, *Notices descriptives*, II, 195 = Lepsius, *Denkmäler*, III, 145, *c*.

§ 357]   THE ASIATIC WAR   159

The only document is a list[a] showing rows of battlemented cities from which Egyptian officers drive prisoners. Each city bears an inscription beginning: "*City which his majesty plundered in the year 8;*" after which appears the name of a city.[b] Only a few of these names have survived, among which are: a "*city on the mount of Bethanath ($B^{\jmath}$-y-ty-^{c}-n-ty)*," named Kerpet ($K^{\jmath}$-$r^{\jmath}$-pw-[ⁱtⁱ]); Merem ($M^{\jmath}$-$r^{\jmath}$-m, Hebrew, Marôm "Height"); and Sherem ($S^{\jmath}$-$r^{\jmath}$-m, Hebrew, Salôm, "Greeting"). The only place not in the west Galilean region is a city "*in the land of Amor ($^{\jmath}$-m-w-$r^{\jmath}$), Depeř ($D^{\jmath}$-pw-$r^{\jmath}$),*" which carries us over to the region of Tabor.[c] The capture of this city has been depicted with great spirit and much detail in a splendid relief at the Ramesseum.[d] It shows Ramses' sons[e] playing a prominent part in the battle.

357. The accompanying inscriptions unfortunately contain almost exclusively the conventional praise of the king's valor. They disclose, however, the important fact that the

---

[a]On the west side of the northern tower of the first pylon of the Ramesseum; Champollion, *Notices descriptives*, I, 870, 871; Burton, *Excerpta hieroglyphica*, 16; Lepsius, *Denkmäler*, III, 156, and Text, III, 127, 128. Another series of cities, on the outside of the south wall of the great hypostyle at Karnak, evidently bore inscriptions of the same form, though none is now complete; see Lepsius, *Denkmäler*, Text, III, 20, and Champollion, *Notices descriptives*, II, 120.

[b]There were originally at least eighteen, and possibly twenty-four of these cities. They have been studied best by Müller (*Asien und Europa*, 220–22), who is followed above.

[c]But see Müller (*Asien und Europa*, 221), who places it farther north. It seems to me that its place in this list is a good argument for a position farther south.

[d]*Description*, II, 31 = Champollion, *Monuments*, 331 = Rosellini, *Monumenti Storici*, 108 = Lepsius, *Denkmäler*, III, 166 = Mariette, *Voyage dans la haute Egypte*, II, 59 = Prisse, *Histoire de l'art égyptien* = Meyer, *Geschichte*, 290 (colored). Long inscription also Brugsch, *Recueil de monuments*, 54, 1, and the first five lines also, Sharpe, *Egyptian Inscriptions*, II, 51.

[e]On the inhabitants of the city coming forth with their children and household goods, compare the great tablet in front of the Abu Simbel temple (Lepsius, *Denkmäler*, III, 195, a, ll. 11 f.): "*their gifts are of the varieties of the products of their lands, their soldiers and their children are before them, to crave peace from his majesty.*"

Hittites have pushed southward since the battle of Kadesh and temporarily occupied the Tabor region, from which Ramses now ejects them (ll. 11–13). This is the extreme southern limit of the Hittite advance, and was, of course, purely transitory, as their remains are not found south of Hamath. This extreme advance is undoubtedly to be connected with the revolt in Palestine.

358. It was perhaps at this time that the northern trans-Jordan region, the Hauran, again[a] came under the control of Ramses, and some official erected a memorial relief[b] of him there, representing him offering to one of the local gods, with possibly a Semitic name.

The Deper scene, which is our longest document on this period, contains the following inscriptions:

359. ⁱSaid the vanquished of Kheta in praising the Good God: "Give to us the breath that thou givest, O good ruler. Lo, we are under thy sandals; thy terror, ²it has penetrated the land of Kheta. Its chief ³is fallen, because of thy fame; we are like herds ⁴of horses, when the fierce-eyed lion ⁵attacks them."

360. ⁶The Good God, mighty in valor in the countries, stout-hearted ⁷in the array, firm on the steed, ⁸beautiful in the chariot, when he has taken the bow, shooting, ⁹(or) fighting hand to hand, — firm, whom none escapes, — — taking the ⌜beautiful⌝ corselet ¹⁰— — — — in the array, and returning when he has triumphed over ¹¹the vanquished chief of Kheta. When he overthrew him, he scattered him like ¹²straw before the wind, (so that) he forsook his city, ¹³for fear of him. He (Ramses) set his fame therein for every day. His might was in his limbs ¹⁴like fire; a bull fighting upon his boundary, seizing ¹⁵upon the things ⌜which he has captured⌝, a survivor of his hand he has not left. ¹⁶He is a tempest in the countries, great in tumult; bringing ¹⁷the storm-cloud against the chiefs, to desolate their cities, making all their places

---

[a]This region of course revolted with the rest of Palestine.

[b]Known as the "Job-stone;" discovered by Schumacher (*Zeitschrift des Deutschen Palästina-Vereins*, XIV, 142 ff.) at the modern village of Saʿdīyeh, east of the Lake of Genesaret. It was published by Erman (*ibid.*, XV, 205–11).

¹⁸into desert regions. His arrows are behind them like Sekhmet ¹⁹when the wind seizes ᵃ— — — the wretched land ²⁰of Kheta, which is his enemy. King of Upper and Lower Egypt, Usermare-Setepnere, ²¹Son of Re, Ramses-Meriamon.

Over Horses' Heads and again over Their Backs

361. Great first span of his majesty (named): "Meriamon," of the great stable of Ramses-Meriamon.

Six Princes, Beginning at Left

362. 1. King's-son, of his body, his beloved, Khamwese.
2. King's-son, of his body, his beloved, Montu —.
3. King's-son, of his body, his beloved, Meriamon.
4. King's-son, of his body, his beloved, Amenemuya.
5. King's-son, of his body, his beloved, Seti.
6. King's-son, of his body, his beloved, Setepnere.

In City

——— [D]eper [D]ᵓ-*pw-rw*).

IV. CAMPAIGN IN NAHARIN

363. Having thus, in the Palestinian war, recovered Palestine, Ramses again pushed northward and advanced into Naharin.ᵇ

1. CONQUEST OF NAHARIN

364. In a fragmentᶜ at the Ramesseum we find him fighting at Tunip. He has, it would seem, already held this important city of the north, and had set up in it a statue of himself. The city had then revolted, and Ramses is now recapturing it. The inscription evidently narrated some personal exploit of Ramses without his coat of mail.

ᵃOr: "*taking the breath* — — —." Brugsch shows some impossible words in this lacuna.

ᵇAlthough this campaign in Naharin is not dated, it is impossible to place it between the battle of Kadesh (year 5) and the recovery of Galilee (year 8). It can only have followed the campaign of year 8.

ᶜChampollion, *Notices descriptives*, I, 888; Brugsch, *Recueil de monuments*, II, 54, 2; Sharpe, *Egyptian Inscriptions*, II, 51.

365. ¹King of Upper and Lower Egypt: Usermare-Setepnere, Son of Re: Ramses-Meriamon, given life. The king himself, he says: "I swear as Re loves me, as my father Atum favors me, as my nostrils are rejuvenated with satisfying life ²——— the ⌈palace⌉." As for this ⌈overthrow⌉, they stood fighting the city of Kheta, wherein the statue of his majesty, L. P. H., was. His majesty made it ³——— his infantry and his chariotry. His majesty was at the front of his infantry and his chariotry ⁴——— the vanquished of Kheta, who were in the districts of the city of Tunip (Tw-n-p) in the land of N[aharin]. His majesty took his coat of mail ⁵——— twice.[a] He stood fighting the city of the vanquished of Kheta, at the front of his infantry and his ⁶[chariotry] ——— [⌈not having⌉ his] coat of mail upon him. [His] majesty came to take his coat of mail again. It was placed upon him, when ⁷——— [the vanquished] of Kheta, who were in the districts of the city of Tunip (Tw-n-p) in the land of Naharin (N-h-r-n), while his coat of mail was not upon [him].

366. In harmony with this fragment, we find that the lists[b] of cities and countries, which Ramses claims to have conquered, mention Naharin, Lower Retenu, Arvad, Keftyew, and Ketne[c] in the Orontes valley. The fact that these northern regions had to some extent already been under Ramses' control indicates long and arduous campaigning against the Hittites. The revolt of these regions, evident from the Ramesseum fragment just translated, was therefore undoubtedly late in the Asiatic war, and probably had something to do with Ramses' willingness to make peace, later sealed by a treaty of alliance with the Hittites in the year 21, seventeen years after the beginning of the war.

---

[a]The date "*year 12*," usually read here is impossible; it is not supported by any of the three copies.

[b]On a colossus at Karnak (Mariette, *Karnak*, 38) and another at Abydos (Mariette, *Abydos*, II, 2). The list on the north wall of Karnak (Champollion, *Notices descriptives*, II, 119; Brugsch, *Geographische Inschriften*, II, 75; Lepsius, *Denkmäler*, III, 144) attributed by Müller to Ramses II, I have credited to Seti I (p. 57, n. b). See also Daressy, *Recueil*, XX, 119.

[c]The mention of Shinar (Babylonia), Assur, Cyprus, and the like, can, of course, only mean the receipt of gifts from the kings of those countries, as under Thutmose III, who controlled none of them but probably Cyprus.

II. TREATY WITH THE HITTITES[a]

367. After possibly fifteen-years of warfare in Syria, Ramses II consents to a peace with the Hittites. This peace is sealed in a treaty of alliance which forms one of the most remarkable documents which have survived from ancient Egypt. The copy preserved to us is clearly a translation from an original in a foreign language,[b] and in his rendering the Egyptian translator has not always succeeded too well.

368. For recording upon the temple walls, the royal scribe has prefixed: (1) the date (l. 1); (2) the account of the arrival of two Hittite messengers with the treaty on a silver tablet; and (3) the heading of the copy as preserved in the royal archives. In content the treaty which follows is clear and well arranged. After a title or caption, it proceeds with the following eighteen paragraphs:

1. Review of the former relations of the two countries, the immemorial peace of earlier times, and the later war.

---

[a]There are two originals: (1) At Karnak on wall extending south of the great hypostyle, published by Champollion, *Notices descriptives*, II, 195-204 (only 30 lines); Rosellini, *Monumenti Storici*, 116; Burton, *Excerpta hieroglyphica*, 17 (not used); Lepsius, *Denkmäler*, III, 146; Brugsch, *Recueil de monuments*, I, 28 (ll. 1-20); Bouriant, *Recueil*, XIII, 153-60; collation of the geographical names by Sayce, *Proceedings of the Society of Biblical Archæology*, XXI, 194 ff.; Müller, *Vorderasiatische Gesellschaft*, VII, 5, Taf. I-XVI; I had also photographs by Borchardt. (2) At the Ramesseum; only fragments of the last 10 lines; Champollion, *Notices descriptives*, I, 585, 586; Sharpe, *Egyptian Inscriptions*, II, 50; Bouriant, *Recueil*, XIV, 67-70. In spite of the mutilated condition of the two monuments, the frequent repetitions make restoration certain in almost all cases. Müller's edition is the only one which is done with care and accuracy; a number of readings may be added to Müller's text from Sharpe's copy, which seems to have escaped him. The following translation was already in my manuscript when Müller's publication appeared. His text added a few new readings, but otherwise the translation remains unchanged.

[b]In view of Amarna Letter No. 35, from the Hittite king, Seplel (see Knudtzon, *Zeitschrift für ägyptische Sprache*, 35, 141 f.), in Babylonian writing and language, the original of this treaty may have been in the same form.

2. Formal declaration of the new peace pact, which is made binding upon future generations.[a]

3. Mutual resignation of all projects for further conquest in Syria, but without any statement of the boundary adopted.

4. Reaffirmation of the former treaty of the time of Khetasar's grandfather, Seplel,[b] which had continued till interrupted by the war with Khetasar's brother, Metella; but with no restatement of its articles.

5. Egypt makes a defensive alliance with Kheta, depending upon the latter's assistance against all foreign foes.

6. Egypt is to enjoy the co-operation of Kheta in the chastisement of rebellious Syrian (?) subjects.

7. Analogous to 5, in Kheta's favor.

8. Analogous to 6, in Kheta's favor.

9. Extradition of Egypt's political fugitives to Kheta.

10. Extradition of emigrants from Egypt to Kheta.

11. Extradition of Kheta's political fugitives to Egypt.

12. Extradition of emigrants from Kheta to Egypt.

13. The witness of the gods of Kheta and Egypt.

14. Curse on the violator of the treaty.

15. Blessing on the observer of the treaty.[c]

16. Appendix exacting humane treatment of persons

---

[a]It was kept by them in fact, as is shown by the relations of Merneptah with Kheta (§ 580, l. 24).

[b]Knudtzon (*Zeitschrift für ägyptische Sprache*, 35, 141 f.) has found in the Amarna collection a cuneiform letter (No. 35) from this king (called Šu-ub-bi-lu-li-u-ma) to a king of Egypt, called Khuri[ya], who, from the content of the letter, is certainly Napkhurīya, the cuneiform for Neferkheprure (Amenhotep IV). Seplel desires, in this letter, to continue with the Pharaoh the friendly relations hitherto existing between himself (S.) and the Pharaoh's father, who has just died. This is clearly Amenhotep III, to whom we may therefore carry back the first treaty between Egypt and Kheta. But the Amarna letters show how badly the Hittites observed the treaty. On the chronological difficulty, see p. 167, n. c.

[c]These two paragraphs form a frequent conclusion of documents intended to be valid in perpetuity, and they mark the logical conclusion here.

extradited from Kheta, who are to suffer no injury in person, family, or property.

17. The same regarding those extradited from Egypt.

18. This final paragraph belongs only to the copy, and not to the treaty. It describes the figures and seals on the silver tablet, and records the words accompanying these seals.

369. Space does not permit further discussion of this remarkable document,[a] but it will be evident that, notwithstanding Ramses' conquest of such northern cities as Tunip in Naharin (§§ 344 f.), he never succeeded in breaking the power of the Hittites. Evidently his complete success in stopping the further southward advance of so powerful an invader was no small reason for congratulation.

Date

370. [1]Year 21, first month of the second season, twenty-first day, under the majesty of the King of Upper and Lower Egypt: Usermare-Setepnere, Son of Re: Ramses-Meriamon, given life, forever and ever, beloved of Amon-Re-Harakhte, Ptah-South-of-His-Wall, lord of "Life-of-the-Two-Lands," Mut, mistress of Ishru, and Khonsu-Neferhotep; shining upon the Horus-throne of the living, like his father, Harakhte, forever and ever.

Arrival of the Hittite Messengers

371. [2]On this day, lo, his majesty was at the city (called): "House-of-Ramses-Meriamon," performing the pleasing ceremonies of his father, Amor-Re-Harakhte-Atum, lord of the Two Lands of Heliopolis; Amon[b] of Ramses-Meriamon, Ptah[b] of Ramses-Meriamon, "— great in strength, son of Mut," according as they gave to him eternity in jubilees, everlastingness in peaceful years, all lands, and all countries being prostrate beneath his sandals forever. [3]There came the king's-messenger,

---

[a]See discussion of special points by W. M. Müller (*Vorderasiatische Gesellschaft*, VII, 215–40).

[b]Forms of Amon and Ptah, worshiped in Ramses' temple at Tanis.

the deputy and butler —,[a] together with the king's-messenger —[a] [⌈bringing⌉ to the king] Ramses II [⌈the messenger⌉] of [Kheta⌈,Ter]teseb and the ⌈second messenger⌉ of Kheta [ᵇ⌈bearing⌉ a silver tablet[b] ⁴which the great chief of the Kheta, Khetasar ($Ḫ$-t ᵓ -$š$-r ᵓ) [caused][b] to be brought to Pharaoh, L. P. H., to crave peace [fro]m [the majesty] of the King of Upper and Lower Egypt, Ramses II,[c] given life, forever and ever, like his father, Re, every day.

Heading of the Copy

372. Copy of the silver tablet, which the great chief of Kheta, Khetasar ($Ḫ$-t ᵓ-s ᵓ -r ᵓ) caused to be brought to Pharaoh, L. P. H., by the hand of his messenger, ⁵Terteseb (T ᵓ -r ᵓ -ty-$š$-bw), and his messenger, Ramose, to crave peace from the majesty of Ramses II, the Bull of rulers, making his boundary as far as he desires in every land.

Caption of the Treaty

373. The treaty which the great chief of Kheta, Khetasar, the valiant, the son of Merasar (M-r ᵓ -s ᵓ -r ᵓ), ⁶the great chief of Kheta, the valiant, the grandson[d] of Seplel (S ᵓ -p ᵓ -[rw-rw]), [the great chief of Kheta, the val]iant, made, upon a silver tablet for Usermare-Setepnere (Ramses II), the great ruler of Egypt, the valiant, the son of Menmare (Seti I), the great ruler of Egypt, the valiant, the grandson of Menpehtire (Ramses I), ⁷the great ruler of Egypt, the valiant; the good treaty of peace and of brotherhood, setting peace [⌈between them ᵉ⌉], forever.

---

[a]The names of two Egyptian envoys have here disappeared. Whence they came is not clear. They may have gone out to meet the two Hittite envoys a day's journey or two; or they may have been the Egyptian commissioners who had negotiated the treaty at the court of Kheta.

[b]The restoration is based on l. 4, where we have a verbatim repetition of this connection.

[c]Double name.

[d]There is no word for "grandson" in Egyptian; text has "*son of the son*."

[e]The loss is greater than this by several words. In view of the preceding words ("*setting peace*") and similar phrases frequent in the treaty (e. g., ll. 9, 10), it seems to me that Müller (*Vorderasiatische Gesellschaft*, VII, 215–21) overemphasizes the alliance side of the document. It is not only a treaty of alliance, but also a treaty of peace, and the war evidently continued until the negotiations for the treaty began, which could hardly have been earlier than a year before the date of the arrival of the messengers in Egypt. They reached Egypt in late winter or early spring (twenty-first of Tybi), somewhere around the first of February; and the preceding summer may have seen the last of the hostilities. The treaty distinctly states (ll. 8, 9) that it marks the beginning of a relation designed by the gods to conclude hostilities between the two nations.

Former Relations of the Two Countries

374. 1. Now, at the beginning, since eternity, the relations of the great ruler of Egypt with the great chief of Kheta were (such) that the god prevented hostilities between them, by treaty. Whereas, in ⁸the time of Metella ($Mw\text{-}t\text{-}n\text{-}r$ ɔ), the great chief of Kheta, my brother, he fought w[ith Ramses II],[a] the great ruler of Egypt, yet afterward, beginning with this day, behold, Khetasar, the great chief of Kheta, is [in] a treaty-relation for establishing the relations which the Re made, and which Sutekh made,[b] for the land of Egypt, ⁹with the land of Kheta, in order not to permit hostilities to arise between them, forever.

The New Peace Pact

375. 2. Behold then, Khetasar, the great chief of Kheta, is in treaty relation with Usermare-Setepnere (Ramses II), the great ruler of Egypt, beginning with this day, in order to bring about good peace and good brotherhood between us forever, ¹⁰while he is in brotherhood with me, he is in peace with me; and I am in brotherhood with him, and I am in peace with him, forever. Since Metella ($Mw\text{-}t\text{-}n\text{-}r$ ɔ), the great chief of Kheta, my brother, succumbed to his fate,[c] and Khetasar sat as

---

[a] A cartouche is visible.

[b] Re and Sutekh are here the gods of Egypt and Kheta respectively.

[c] Lit., "*departed* (*ḥnn*) *after his fate;*" this, of course, indicates his death. The succession of his brother justifies the suspicion that his death was due to his brother; but this is not certain. Furthermore, this death of Metella is clearly the occasion of the peace, and not the occasion of the war with Ramses II, as often stated (Maspero, *Struggle of the Nations*, 389). Thus the opponent of Ramses II was Metella (l. 8), and Khetasar hastens to make peace soon after his accession (l. 10). We may roughly reconstruct thus:

Amenhotep III, end of reign	} Seplel, father of	
Ikhnaton		
Ikhnaton's ephemeral successors		
Harmhab	} Merasar, father of	
Ramses I		
Seti I	} Metella	} brothers
Ramses II to about year 20		
Ramses II from year 20 on	Khetasar	

The three generations of Hittite kings ruled accordingly over 110 years—over 37 years each—an exceptionally high average for three successive kings in the orient. This would indicate some uncertainty as to the identity of Seplel and Šubbiluliuma of Amarna Letter No. 35, which carries him back to Amenhotep III (see note, p. 164). He may therefore possibly be no earlier than Harmhab, and, as Müller has suggested (*op. cit.*, 226), the Amarna letter may be from an earlier Seplel.

¹¹great chief of Kheta upon the throne of his father, behold, I am together with Ramses-Meriamon, the great ruler of Egypt, and he is [ʳwithᵃ me inʳ] our peace and our brotherhood. It is better than the former peace and brotherhood which were in the land. Behold, I, even the great chief of Kheta, am with ¹²[Ramses II], the great ruler of Egypt, in good peace and in good brotherhood. The children of the children of the great chief of Kheta shall be in brotherhood and peace with the children of the children of Ramses-Meriamon, the great ruler of Egypt, being in our relations of brotherhood and our relations ¹³[of peace], that the [land of Egypt] may be with the land of Kheta in peace and brotherhood like ourselves, forever.

Mutual Renunciation of Further Conquests

376. 3. There shall be no hostilities between them, forever. The great chief of Kheta shall not pass over into the land of Egypt, forever, to take anything therefrom. Ramses-Meriamon, the great ruler of Egypt, shall not pass over into the land ¹⁴[of Kheta, to take anything] therefrom, forever.

Reaffirmation of the Former Treaties

377. 4. As for the formerᵇ treaty which was in the time of Seplel (*Sʾ-pʾ-rw-rw*), the great chief of Kheta, likewise the formerᵇ treaty which was in the time of Metella (*Mw-t-n-rʾ*), the great chief of Kheta, my father,ᶜ I will hold to it. Behold, Ramses-Meriamon, the great

---

ᵃSo Müller, but he does not give room for "*with*."

ᵇThis word (*mty*) has not been hitherto understood in this connection; there is no doubt about its meaning, "*customary, usual, habitual*," and then "*former*." Compare Amâda Stela (II, 798), where a new four-day list of offerings is established for Anuket "*as an increase upon the 3 days of her customary (mty) feast;*" or II, 619; after new offerings are presented, the old ones are to be offered "*according to the measure of the customary (mtt) offering which is in this temple;*" after a feast a god returns to his "*customary (mt(t)) seat*" (*Recueil*, 16, 56, l. 6, above).

ᶜ"*Father*" is either used here as in Egypt, where any predecessor on the throne is called "*father;*" or the name "*Metella*" is an error for Merasar, who was certainly the father of Metella and Khetasar. Now, as Khetasar has already (ll. 7, 8) referred to the ancient peace as continuing down to, but broken under, Metella, a new treaty under Metella above mentioned (l. 14) is surprising. He may be marking the beginning and end of the same treaty: beginning under Seplel and ending, because broken, under Metella. The Pharaoh with whom Metella's treaty was maintained can hardly be any other than Seti I. (See "*it*," ll. 14, 15.)

ruler of Egypt, will hold ¹⁵[to it] with us ⌜together⌝, beginning with this day. We will hold to it, and we will deal in this former manner.ᵃ

Egypt's Defensive Alliance with Kheta

378. 5. If another enemy come against the lands of Usermare-Setepnere (Ramses II), the great ruler of Egypt, and he shall send to the great chief of Kheta, saying: "Come with me as reinforcement against him," the great chief of Kheta shall ¹⁶[come], and the great chief of Kheta shall slay his enemy. But if it be not the desire of the great chief of Kheta to come, he shall send his infantry and his chariotry, and shall slay his enemy.

Chastisement of Syrian Subjects

379. 6. Or if Ramses-Meriamon, ¹⁷[the great ruler of Egypt], be provoked against ⌜delinquent⌝ subjects,ᵇ when they have committed some other fault against him, and he come to slay them, then the great chief of Kheta shall act with the lord of Egypt ⌜— —⌝.

Kheta's Defensive Alliance with Egypt

380. 7. If another en[emy come] against the great chief of Kheta, [and he shall send] to the great chief (sic!) [of Egypt], Usermare-Setepnere ¹⁸⌜ᶜfor reinforcements⌝ then he] shall come to him as reinforcement, to slay his enemy. But if it be [not]ᵈ the desire of Ramses-Meriamon, the great ruler of Egypt, to come, he shall [send his infantry and his chariotry ⌜and shall slay his enemy⌝]. ⌜Or⌝ ———— ¹⁹— seeing them, besides returning answer to the land of Kheta.ᵉ

ᵃThe stipulations of the former treaty, as known to both parties, are not stated.

ᵇThis word (modified by *s ᵖ· w*, which Müller regards as a conjunction) must refer to Asiatic subjects of Egypt, who rebel or fail to pay tribute. Kheta is not, in such a case, to interfere in Egypt's attempts at punishment, but is to act in harmony with Egypt. Egypt's obligation in the corresponding clause is much more elaborate, but is unfortunately not clear, owing to its fragmentary condition. Evidently the two clauses mean that both are to act in harmony in Syria; each is to assist the other there, and not take advantage of any revolt in the other's dependencies, for self-aggrandizement.

ᶜThere is not room for the message, as in the corresponding paragraph.

ᵈOmitted in original.

ᵉThere is evidently a second alternative of some kind here, to which the Egyptian king may resort, which is not found in the corresponding clause defining the Hittite obligation.

Chastisement of Syrian Subjects

381. 8. Now if subjects of the great chief of Kheta transgress against him, and Ramses-Meriamon, the great ruler of Egypt, shall ———— the land of Kheta and the land of Egypt ²⁰— — — ⌜— —⌝, that is to say: "I will come after ⌜their punishment,⌝[1a] to Ramses-Meriamon, the great ruler of Egypt, living forever, — — — the land of Kheta. . . . .[b] their appointing him for them, to be lord, to cause that Usermare-Setepnere, the great ruler of Egypt, shall be silent from his speech forever.[c] If he — his — — the land of Kheta, and he shall turn back [⌜again to⌝] the great chief of Kheta ————.

Extradition of Political Fugitives in Kheta

382. 9. [If any great[d] man of the land of Egypt shall flee and shall come to] the great chief of Kheta, from either a town ²²[or] — of the lands of Ramses-Meriamon, the great ruler of Egypt, and they shall come to the great chief of Kheta, then the great chief of Kheta shall not receive them, (but) the great chief of Kheta shall cause them to be brought to Usermare-Setepnere, the great ruler of Egypt, t[heir] lord therefor.

Extradition of Emigrants to Kheta

383. 10. Or if there flee a man, or two men who are unknown ²³—, and they shall come to[e] the land of Kheta, to become foreign subjects, then they shall not be settled in the land of Kheta, but they shall be brought to Ramses-Meriamon, the great ruler of Egypt.

---

[a]Or: "*fate;*" have we here: $ḥr$-s ᵓ -p ᵃ yf (or p ᵓ ysn) $š$ ᵓ y, as in l. 10?

[b]A few unintelligible fragments are omitted; about one-fifth line.

[c]This last is the legal phraseology of receipts, by which all future claim is renounced. From the end of l. 19 on we have additional enactments not found in the corresponding clause of the Hittite obligations.

[d]The persons who flee are of two classes: "*great men*" and "*men who are not known*," viz., people of no consequence from the Egyptian point of view, but merely mechanics, artisans or servants.

[e]These, being people of no rank, come only "*to the land of Kheta;*" but the "*great men*" go personally "*to the great chief of Kheta.*" The verb used for the "*great men*" shows also the distinction between the two classes; it is *šsp*, "*receive,*" whereas, referring to the unknown persons, we find w ᵓ $ḥ$ (possibly "*admit*"), probably "*settle,*" that is, allow them to settle down (but w ᵓ $ḥ$ is also used once of the "*great men,*" l. 24).

Extradition of Political Fugitives in Egypt

384. 11. Or if any great man shall flee from the land of Kheta, [and he shall come to] Usermare-Setepnere, the great ruler of Egypt, (from) either a town or a district,[a] or [24][any region of] those belonging to the land of Kheta, and they shall come to Ramses-Meriamon, the great ruler of Egypt, then Usermare-Setepnere, the great ruler of Egypt, shall not receive them, (but) Ramses-Meriamon, the great ruler of Egypt, shall cause them to be brought to the great chief of Kheta. They shall not be settled.

Extradition of Emigrants to Egypt

385. 12. Likewise, if there flee a man, or two, or three, [25][who are not] known, and they shall come to the land of Egypt, to become foreign subjects, then Usermare-Setepnere, the great ruler of Egypt, shall not settle them, (but) he shall cause them to be brought to the great chief of Kheta.

The Witness of the Gods of Kheta and Egypt

386. 13. As for the words of this ⌜contract⌝[b] of the great chief of Kheta, with Ramses-Meriamon, the great ruler [26][of Egypt], written upon this silver tablet; as for these words, a thousand gods of the male gods and of the female gods, of those of the land of Kheta, together with a thousand gods, of the male gods and of the female gods of those of the land of Egypt, they are with me as witnesses [⌜to⌝] these words: the Sun-god, lord of the heavens, the Sun-god, of the city of Ernen[c] (ʾ-r-n-nʾ), [27]Sutekh, the lord of the heavens, Sutekh of Kheta, Sutekh of the city of Ernen, Sutekh of the city Zepyerened (Dʾ-pw-yʾ-rʾ-n-dʾ), Sutekh of the city of Perek (Pʾ y-rʾ-kʾ), Sutekh of the city of Khesesep (Hy-sʾ-sʾ-pʾ), Sutekh of the city Seres (Sʾ-ry-sw), Sutekh of the city of Aleppo (Hy-rʾ-pʾ), Sutekh of the city of Rekhsen (Rʾ-hʾ-sy-nʾ), Sutekh [28][of the city of —], ——— ⌜—⌝, Sutekh of the

---

[a]Cf. the use of this word (kʿh, "*corner*") for a distant region in Harkhuf (I, 335), and for any district as here, in the Twenty-second Dynasty, Dakhel stela (IV, 726, l. 2), and two more examples (*ibid.*, note).

[b]We expect here the name of the Hittite king; hence the above (Müller) is very uncertain.

[c]A city in the district called by the Assyrians "Kammanu . . . . on the border of the territory of the Cappodocian Comana," according to Sayce (*Proceedings of the Society of Biblical Archæology*, 23, 98).

city of Sekhpen (Sᵓ-y-$ḫy$-pᵓ y-nᵓ), Antheret (ᶜnᵃ-$ṯ$-rᵓ-ty) of the land of Kheta, the god of Zeyethekhrer ($Ḏ$ᵓy-yᵓ-$ṯ$-$ḫy$-r-ry), the god of Kerzet — (Kᵓ-r-$ḏ$ᵓ·y-tᵓ- —), the god of Kherpenteres ($Ḫ$-r-pᵓ-n-ty-ry-sᵓ), ²⁹the goddess of the city of Kerekhen — n — (Kᵓ-r-$ḫ$-n- — -n — - —), the goddess of ⌜Khewek⌝ (⌜$Ḫ$⌝-wᵓ-⌜kᵓ⌝ᵇ), the goddess of Zen — ($Ḏ$ᵓ-y-n —), the god of Zen — wet (⌜$Ḏ$⌝-n- — -ᶜnw⌜-ty),ᶜ the god of Serep (Sᵓ-rᵓ-pᵓ),ᵈ the god of Khenbet ($Ḫ$-n-bᵓ-tᵓ),ᵉ the queen of the heavens, gods, lords of swearing, the goddess, the mistress of the soil, the mistress of swearing, Teskher (Tᵓ-sᵓ-$ḫ$-rᵓ), the mistress of ³⁰the mountains, and the rivers of the land of Kheta, the gods of the land of Kezweden (Ky-$ḏ$ᵓ-wᵓ-dᵓ-nᵓ), Amon, the Sun-god, Sutekh, the male gods and the female gods of the mountains and the rivers of the land of Egypt, of the heavens, the soil, the great sea, the wind, and the storms.

Curse on the Violator of the Treaty

387. 14. Now, these words, ³¹which are upon this silver tablet, are for ᶠthe land of Kheta and for the land of Egypt. As for him who shall not keep them, the thousand gods of the land of Kheta, and the thousand gods of the land of Egypt shall desolate his house, his land, and his subjects.

Blessing on the Observer of the Treaty

388. 15. Now as for him who shall keep these words, which are upon this silver tablet, whether theyᵍ be of Kheta, or whether they be people ³²of Egypt, and they shall not devise (aught) against them; the thousand gods of the land of Kheta, together with the thousand gods of the land of Egypt, shall preserve his health, and his life, together with his issue, with his land,ʰ and his subjects.

ᵃMüller corrects to s and reads Astarte, which is probable.

ᵇSayce's reading $ḫ$ᵇ, with $ḫ$ and ᵓ is, of course, impossible.

ᶜSo Bouriant and Müller; Sayce has $Ḏ$ᵓ-y-ty-ty.

ᵈSo the old texts; Müller has a lacuna for Sᵓ.

ᵉUncertain.

ᶠThe fragments of the Ramesseum duplicate begin here; but Bouriant's reconstruction begins with l. 33.

ᵍThe change of number is in the original.

ʰAccording to Müller, this word is omitted in the original, and he is corroborated by the photograph.

Treatment of Extradited Persons by Kheta

389. 16. If a man flee from the land of Egypt, or two or three, and ³³come[a] to the great chief of Kheta, the great chief of Kheta shall seize upon them, and shall cause them to be brought back to Usermare-Setepnere, the great ruler of Egypt. Now, as for the man who shall be brought (back) to Ramses-Meriamon, the great ruler of Egypt, let not his crime be set up against him; let not ³⁴his house be injured, nor his wives, nor his children, [let] him [not be killed], and let no injury be done to his eyes, to his ears, to his mouth, nor to his feet. Let not any crime be set up against him.

Treatment of Extradited Persons by Egypt

390. 17. Likewise if a man flee from the land of Kheta, be it one, be it two, (or) be it three, and they shall come to Usermare-Setepnere, ³⁵the great ruler of Egypt, let Ramses-Meriamon, the great ruler of Egypt, seize [upon them, and let him cause] that they be brought to the great chief of Kheta; and the great chief of Kheta shall not set up their crime against them; let not his house be injured, nor his wives, nor his children, let him not be killed, and let no injury be done to his ears, ³⁶to his eyes, to his mouth, nor to his feet. Let not any crime be set up against him.

Figures and Seals on the Front of the Silver Plate

391. 18. ᵇThat which is in the middle of this silver tablet: on its front side is a figureᶜ in the likeness of Sutekh embracing the likeness of the great chief of Kheta, surrounded by the following ⌜words⌝: "The seal of Sutekh, the ruler of the heavens; the seal of the treaty which Khetasar, the great chief ³⁷of Kheta, the valiant, the son of Merasar (M-r ᵓ -s ᵓ -r ᵓ), the valiant, the great chief of Kheta, the valiant, made."

ᵃFrom here on, see Bouriant's reconstruction, *Recueil*, XIV, 68, 69.

ᵇThat this phrase begins the description of the silver plate is self-evident; but is rendered still more clear by the parallel phrase in l. 37 and l. 38.

ᶜThis word ($ḥpyw$) is the usual one for inlay-figures in descriptions of Egyptian monuments; it may equally well mean "*design*" or "*device*." The sculptures of Boghazköi show a figure of the Hittite ruler embraced by his god (see Messerschmidt, *Corpus Inscriptionum Hettiticarum*, Taf. 27 E; di Cara, *Proceedings of the Society of Biblical Archæology*, 13, 196; and Müller, *Vorderasiatische Gesellschaft*, VII, 233 f.). [Later: Krall's review of Müller's publication of the text contains the same explanation of the figures on the plate.]

That^a which is in the midst of the surrounding design^b is the seal [of Sutekh, the ruler of the heavens]. [That which is ⌜in the middle⌝ on] its other side is a figure, in the likeness of ⌜——⌝^c of Kheta, embracing the figure of the princess of Kheta, surrounded by the following words: "The seal of the ³⁸Sun-god of the city of Ernen (ʾ-r-n-nʾ), the lord of the land; the seal of Petkhep (Pw-tw-ẖy-pʾ), the princess^d of the land of Kheta, the daughter of the land of Kezweden (Ky-ḏʾ-wʾ-d-n), the — — — of Ernen, the mistress of the land, the votress of the goddess. That which is in the midst of the surrounding design is the seal of the Sun-god of Ernen, the lord of every land."

RELATIONS OF EGYPT WITH THE HITTITES AFTER THE WAR

392. Ramses II regarded the conclusion of his war with the Hittites as a triumph for himself. Peace once established, he referred to himself continually as the conqueror of the Hittites.^e Especially at Abu Simbel is this noticeable, where his inscriptions speak of him as one:

"Who has made the land of Kush as if it had not existed; who has caused the land of Kheta to cease the contradiction of its mouth . . . . . smiter of the land of Kheta . . . . . . smiter of the land of Kheta, which is made heaps of dead."^f

This attitude is also evident in his obelisk inscriptions, e. g., at Tanis he is spoken of as "*carrying off the chiefs of Retenu as living prisoners, crushing the land of Kheta;*"

---

^aSo here and in l. 38, as the duplicate (Sharpe's copy) shows.

^bLit., "*the surrounding of the design;*" the same also in the last line.

^cSome female divinity, as the word for figure (rpyˑt) shows.

^dLit., "*chieftainess,*" being the feminine (wrˑt) of the word which we render "*chief*" (wr), lit., "*great one.*"

^eBesides the following, it should be noticed that the latest copies of the Kadesh Poem represent Ramses in the same light (see Müller, *Asien und Europa,* 216, n. 1; and *infra,* § 314, n.).

^fStela on the front of the Abu Simbel temple (Lepsius, *Denkmäler,* III, 195, *a*, portions of ll. 2–9).

and again, "*penetrating this land of Kheta, capturing it with valor, making a great slaughter among his heroes.*"[a]

393. This is the light then, in which the Egyptians chose to represent their relations with Kheta. But the peace was not broken, and we are able to trace the amicable relations between the two nations through the thirty-fifth year of Ramses' reign, and we know it continued also into that of his successor. The documents are:

I. Blessing of Ptah (§§ 394-414).
II. Marriage Stela (§§ 415-24).
III. Message of the Chief of Kheta to the Chief of Kode (§§ 425, 426).
IV. Coptos Stela (§§ 427, 428).
V. Bentresh Stela (§§ 429-447).

I. THE BLESSING OF PTAH[b]

394. This remarkable document contains a long address of Ptah to Ramses II, which promises him all possible good fortune (ll. 3-28). To this Ramses replies by enumerating some of his good works for the god (ll. 29-37). The document is chiefly of religious interest, but both addresses contain references to historical events of importance.

395. The speech of Ptah mentions his building of the

---

[a]All of Ramses II's obelisks were erected at least nine years after the close of the Hittite war; the above texts are translated from Petrie, *Tanis*, I, VII, No. 45, and VIII, No. 49.

[b]Engraved on a large stela in the first hall of the great Abu Simbel temple, and is published by Champollion, *Monuments*, 38 (without relief at top); Lepsius, *Denkmäler*, III, 194, from which Rheinisch, *Chrestomathie*, XIII, is copied; Naville, *Transactions of the Society of Biblical Archæology*, VII, 119 ff. and plate, made from a squeeze. The document was later appropriated by Ramses III and engraved by him upon the first pylon of the Medinet Habu Temple, published by Dümichen, *Historische Inschriften*, I, 7-10; Rougé, *Inscriptions hiéroglyphiques*, II, 131-38. The translation herein is made with constant reference to the later version (called M), which is very useful, as the older text (called A) omits the first person singular ending frequently and is in places corrupt. Important variants from M are given in the notes.

residence city, Tanis (ll. 16–18), and the visit of the Hittite king (ll. 24–28), bringing his eldest daughter, which had occurred in the year 34, a year before the erection of our stela. It furnishes us with a shorter account of the incident than the Marriage Stela (§§ 415–24). It is interesting to note that the visit is attributed to the influence of Ptah (ll. 15 and 25), just as in the Coptos Stela (§§ 427, 428), which refers to the same or a similar incident.

396. The reply of Ramses mentions in particular his temple buildings at Memphis (ll. 32–34) and their endowment (ll. 34, 35).

397. A relief at the top of the stela shows Ramses II smiting three Asiatic enemies before Ptah-Tatenen, who is leading to him six captives, one of whom is a Negro, and the rest are bearded; but, as the names show, the latter should be Negroes (p. 202, n. c). The inscription below, of thirty-seven lines, is as follows:

Date

398. [1]Year 35, first month of the second season, day 13, under the majesty of ...... [2]...... Ramses II,[a] given life.

Introduction

399. Utterance of Ptah-Tatenen, of lofty plumes and ready horns, begetter of the gods, to his son, his beloved, [3]firstborn of his body, the divine god, sovereign of the gods, great in royal jubilees like Tatenen, King Ramses II, given life:[b]

Speech of Ptah; Birth of Ramses

400. "I am thy father, who begat thee as the gods, all thy limbs are of the gods. I assumed my form as the Ram, lord of [4]Mendes,[c] and begat thee in thy august mother,[c] since I knew that thou wouldest be

---

[a]Full fivefold titulary. [b]Double titulary.

[c]M has: "*I cohabited with thy august mother, in order to fashion thy form (ky) as lord of* [*the Two Lands*¹]."

my champion, that thou wouldst indeed do profitable things for my ka. I fashioned thee to rise like Re, exalted thee before the gods, King Ramses II, given life. The companions of ⁵Ptah jubilate,ᵃ thy Meskhenetᵇ rejoices in jubilation since ᶜthey have seen me, ⌈a likeness to⌉ᶜ my august, great, and mighty body. The priestessesᵈ of the house of Ptah, the Hathorsᵇ of the house of Atum are ⁶in festivity, their hearts are in joy. Their hands are uplifted in acclaim since they have seen thy beautiful form. Thy amiability is like my ⌈majesty⌉; the gods and goddesses acclaim thy beauty, praising, ⁷and assigning to me laudation, saying: "Thou art our august father, who hast fashioned for us a god like thee, Ramses II, given life."

Ptah Promises Happiness

401. "When I see thee my heart rejoices, and I receive thee in an embrace of gold, I enfold thee with ⁸permanence, stability and satisfaction; I endow thee with health and joy of heart; I immerse thee in rejoicing, joy, gladness of heart, and delights, — forever."

Ptah Promises Wisdom

402. "I make thy heart divine like me, I choose thee, I weigh thee, I prepare thee, that thy heart may discern, that thy utterance may be profitable. There is nothing ⁹whatever which thou dost not know, (for) I have completed thee ᵉthis day and before, that thou mayest make all men live by thy instruction,ᵉ O King Ramses II, given life."

Ptah Promises Power

403. "I have set thee as everlasting king, ruler established forever. I have wrought ¹⁰thy limbs of electrum, thy bones of copper, thy organs of iron. I have given to thee the divine office, that thou mayest rule the Two Lands ᶠlike the King of Upper and Lower Egypt."ᶠ

ᵃFollowing M, which the parallelism shows to be more probably correct, A has: "*The companions of Ptah are (thy) nurses.*"

ᵇGoddess of birth.

ᶜFollowing M; a lacuna makes A unintelligible. M would mean that in seeing Ramses they see Ptah.

ᵈLit., "*great, august ones,*" a title of these priestesses.

ᵉM has: "*in the counsels of life, that thou mayest make others live by thy designs.*"

ᶠM: "*as thy kingdom.*"

Ptah Promises Agricultural Wealth

404. "I give thee a great Nile, I endow for thee the Two Lands with wealth, produce, food, and luxuries, giving ¹¹plenty[a] in every place where thou treadest. I give to thee constant harvests, to feed the Two Lands at all times; the sheaves[b] thereof are like the sand of the shore, their granaries approach heaven, and their grain-heaps are like mountains. There is joy and laudation ¹²at seeing thee, (for) plenty of fish and fowl are under thy feet.[c] The South and North are satisfied with thy ka.[c] Heaven is given to thee and that which is in it; earth[d] is led to thee and that which is in it; [e]the pool comes to thee bearing its fowl.[e] Harsekha[f] ¹³bears her provisions, the best of the ka of Re; Thoth has set them on thy every side, that thou mayest open thy mouth, to enrich whom thou pleasest, according as thou art the living Khnum, and thy dominion is in victory and might like (that of) Re when he ruled ¹⁴the Two Lands, O King Ramses II, given life."

Ptah Promises Mineral and Industrial Wealth

405. "I cause the mountains to shape for thee great, mighty, perfected monuments; I cause the countries to fashion for thee [all] splendid, costly stone, for ⌜employment⌝ in monuments in thy name. ¹⁵I make profitable for thee all works;[g] I cause all labor[h] to serve thee, everything that goes on two legs, (or) upon four legs, everything that flies, and all that soars. I put it into the heart of every land ¹to offer and to labor for thee[i] themselves;[j] [k]chiefs, great and small,[k] with ¹⁶one accord do profitable things for thy ka, King Ramses II, given life."

---

[a]Read *sḏf*ᵃ. [b]M: "*grain.*" [c]M.
[d]Original has "*Keb,*" the earth-god.
[e]In M the word "*pool*" is determined with a wild fowl, and it reads: "*the (bird-) pools lead to thee the fowl of heaven*" (*yry·w-pt*). A similar notion is found in IV, 265, l. 2.
[f]A rare goddess of unknown functions.
[g]Perhaps: "*workmen.*"
[h]Lit., "*all artisanship*" (fem.); but M shows as determinative a man.
[i]M: "*to offer their labor (impost) to thee.*"
[j]The same idea is found in the Coptos stela of Ramses II (§ 428).
[k]Possibly: "*chiefs and petty kings;*" M has only "*great and small.*"

Ramses' Residence City and its Buildings

406. "Thou hast made an august residence, to make strong the boundary of the Two Lands (named): "House-of-Ramses-Meriamon-Given-Life," [a]that it may flourish on earth like the four pillars [17]of heaven — — — a sovereign therein,[a] that thou mayest celebrate the royal jubilees that I celebrated therein. I put on thy crown with my own two hands, when thou appearest upon the great double staircase. Men and gods acclaim thy name [18b]like mine when thou celebratest the royal jubilees.[b] Thou fashionest the statues, thou buildest their holy places as I[c] did at the first beginning."

Ptah Promises Long Life and Prosperity

407. "I give to thee years of royal jubilees, my rule, my place, my throne. I endow thy limbs with life, satisfaction and protection behind thee, [d]with [19]prosperity and health. I protect Egypt under thy authority, the Two Lands are diffused with the satisfying life of[d] Ramses II, given life."

Ptah Promises Power

408. "I have set for thee the might, victory, and strength of thy sword in every land, I have bound for thee the hearts of all lands,[e] [20]I have set them beneath thy feet. When thou appearest every day, [f]the captives of the Nine Bows[f] are brought to thee, the great chiefs of every land present to thee their children, I assign them to thy mighty sword, to do what thou pleasest with them, [21]O King Ramses II, given life. I have put thy terror in every heart, thy love in every body; I have set thy might in every country, thy fear encircles the mountains, and the

---

[a]M has: "*plentiful in provisions for Egypt, flo[urishing] like [the four pillars of] heaven; thy majesty abides in its palace, that I may build the wall of my seat therein.*"

[b]M has: "*when thou appearest at the jubilees, like me.*"

[c]Compare the great Ptah inscription of Memphis, which says of him: "*He made likenesses of their (the gods') bodies to the satisfaction of their hearts, he made the gods enter into their bodies of every wood, of every costly stone, of every [t]metal[t]*" (l. 60); also: "*He formed the gods . . . . he set the gods in the holy places*" (ll. 59, 60; Zeitschrift für ägyptische Sprache, 1901, Taf. I, II).

[d]M has: "*As the protection of ([t]thy[t]) limbs. Victorious art thou, every land is under thee, Egypt is diffused with thy beauty.*"

[e]M has: "*the lands of the Asiatics (S'ṭ·tyw).*"

[f]M has: "*the captives of thy two hands.*"

chiefs tremble at the mention of thee. Thy majesty flourishes, [22]steadfast as their head; they come to thee, crying out together, to crave peace from thee. Thou lettest live whom thou wilt, and thou slayest whom thou wilt. Lo, the throne of every land is under thy authority."

Ptah the Author of Ramses' Prosperity

409. "I cause to befall thee [23]thy [a]great[a] wonders, and every good thing to happen to thee. The Two Lands[b] under thee are in acclamation, Egypt flourishes, rejoicing, O Ramses II, given life. I have transferred my dignity to thee; thy great and marvelous [24]excellence approaches heaven; the Two Lands are in joy, they who are therein rejoice at that which has happened to thee. As for the mountains, the waters, and the buildings upon the land, they remove at thy good[c] name, when they behold this command."

Visit of the Hittites

410. "I have made [25]for thee the [d]land of Kheta[d] into subjects of thy palace; I have put it into their hearts to present themselves, with fearful steps to thy ka, bearing their impost which their chiefs have captured, all their possessions as tribute to [26]the fame of his majesty, L. P. H. His eldest daughter is in front thereof, to satisfy the heart of the Lord of the Two Lands, King Ramses II, given life. ⌜It⌝[e] is a mysterious marvel; she knows not the excellent matter which I have done at thy desire, [27]that thy great name should be excellent forever. The success of the victorious hero is a great mystery for which he prays. It has not been heard since (the time of) the gods; the mysterious records have been in the house of books from the time of Re until thy majesty, [28]L. P. H., (but) the relation of Kheta in one accord with Egypt has not been known. Lo, it was commanded to slay them beneath thy feet, in order to make thy name live forever, O King Ramses II, given life."

---

[a]M. [b]M has: "*the lands.*" [c]M has: "*victorious.*"

[d]M modifies these statements to suit the times of Ramses III; it has: "*every land*" here; and in place of "*his eldest daughter, etc.*" (l. 26), it has: "*their sons and their daughters as slaves to thy palace.*"

[e]Possibly: "*she;*" all this is omitted in M.

Reply of Ramses

411. ²⁹Utterance of the divine king, Lord of the Two Lands, ᵃlord of the form ofᵃ Khepri, in whose limbs is Re, who came forth from Re, whom Ptah-Tatenen begat, King Ramses II, given life; to his father, from whom he came forth, Tatenen, ³⁰father of the gods: "I am thy son whom thou hast placed upon thy throne. Thou hast assigned to me thy kingdom, thou hast fashioned me in thy likeness and thy form, which thou hast assigned to me and hast created. I shall do again every good thing that thou desirest, while I am sole lord, as thou wast, to settle the ⌈affairs⌉ᵇ of the land. I have created Egypt for thee anew, I have made it as at the beginning, I have wrought the gods' forms from thy limbs, even to their color and to their bodies; I have equipped Egypt according to their desire, I have built it up with ³²temples."

Building of Memphis Temple

412. "I have enlarged thy house in Memphis,ᶜ protected with everlasting works, with excellent labor, in stone, wrought with gold and genuine costly stones, I constructed thy forecourt ³³on the north with an august double façade before thee. Their doors are like the horizon of heaven, causing (even) strangers to praise thee. I made for thee an august temple in the midst of the inclosure. Thou god, ⌈whom I have⌉ fashioned, art in its secret chapel, ³⁴resting upon its great throne."

Endowment of Memphis Temple

413. "It is equipped with priests, prophets, peasant-slaves, lands, and cattle. It is made festive with innumerable divine offerings consisting of all things. I have celebrated thy great feast of royal jubilees, ³⁵as thou commandest them me. All things that are, are brought to thee in great offerings, at thy desire: bulls (*wn-dw*), cattle beyond limit. I have brought all their number in millions; as for the fat thereof, it has reached heaven, and the dwellers in heaven have received it."

ᵃSo M; A has: "*becoming as* (= *like*, or merely introducing the predicate) *Khepri*."

ᵇSee Ineni, l. 17, note (II, 341).

ᶜSee §§ 530–37.

Foreign Conquests

414. ³⁶" I have caused every land to see the beauty in the monuments which I have made for thee. I have branded the people of the Nine Bows and the whole land with thy name, they belong to thy ka, forever, for thou art the creator of them; by command of this thy son, who is upon thy throne, ³⁷lord of gods and men, sovereign celebrating the jubilees like thee ᶠwhen thou¹ bearest the two sistrums, ªson of the white crown, heir of the red crown,ª possessing the Two Lands in peace, Ramses II, given life, forever and ever."

II. MARRIAGE STELA ᵇ

415. This monument enables us to trace more fully the further relations between Egypt and the Hittites after the peace had been negotiated. A relief at the top shows the king of the Hittites and his daughter in the presence of Ramses. Before the daughter are the words: "*Matneferure*,ᶜ *daughter of the chief of Kheta.*" A mutilated inscription accompanying the two visitors contained their words of praise to Ramses II. The beginning is entirely lost for five lines, where it proceeds:ᵈ

Speech of King of Kheta

Thou didst command the land of Kheta, thou takest captive the people — with all their possessions, the eldestᵉ daughter being at their

---

ªAmend so; see Naville's commentary.

ᵇCut in the face of the south wall of the excavated court in front of the temple of Abu Simbel. The lower half being covered by sand, Lepsius saw only the relief at the top and eighteen lines (of the forty-one lines) below; this much he published (Lepsius, *Denkmäler*, III, 196), but without indication that it was not the whole. The entire inscription, without the relief, was published by Bouriant (*Recueil*, XVIII, 164–66). In ll. 36–39, I was able to control Bouriant's publication by the copy of Steindorff, which he kindly placed at my disposal. The original is much mutilated, and so indistinct that some passages have been omitted as too uncertain in text for translation.

ᶜMisread by Lepsius; for proper reading, see § 417.

ᵈBouriant did not copy this; the following translation is made from Steindorff's copy of the original.

ᵉAs the Hittite king is speaking, one expects "my daughter" as in l. 32 of the long inscription, which repeats these words.

head, to ——— before thy beautiful face. Thou commandest them —— —— under thy feet forever and ever, together with the whole land of Kheta. While thou shinest upon the throne of Re, every land is under [thy] feet, forever.

416. Below the relief is a long inscription of forty-one lines beginning with the date "*year 34*," Three-fourths (twenty-nine lines) of this inscription are devoted to an extravagant encomium of the Pharaoh, containing only the hackneyed phrases of conventional praise, relieved by two references to the defeat of Kheta. The last fourth of the document (ll. 30–41) then proceeds with an incident, of which the mutilated condition of the monument and the excessively inaccurate publication permit us to gain only the meagerest outline. After a reference to the treaty of peace, the king of the Hittites is represented as reverting to their defeat by Ramses, and he apparently proposes that they proceed to Egypt. This they do, bringing rich gifts, and the news soon reaches Ramses, who is filled with delight, and prepares to receive his visitors; the chiefs of Kheta, Kode, and "*the chiefs of every land.*" He seems to be concerned for their arrival in the uncertainties of winter travel, and offers an oblation to Sutekh on their behalf. When finally, with the escort he had sent to meet them, they arrive in safety, they appear with the Hittite king's eldest daughter at their head, the troops of Egypt "*mingling with the foot and horse of Kheta.*" A great feast seems to have been immediately held, where those who had once faced each other in combat now eat and drink together, while the Asiatic princes approach the Pharaoh in audience.

417. It is probably at this feast that the Hittite princess thus brought to Egypt was married to Ramses. The historical character of this marriage is further evidenced by the colossus of Ramses II at Tanis, attached to which is a statue of a queen bearing the inscription:[a]

---

[a]Mariette, *Recueil*, IX, 13; Rougé, *Inscriptions hiéroglyphiques*, 74; Petrie, *Tanis*, I, 24, Pl. 5, 36 B.

"Great king's-wife, mistress (ḥn·t) of the Two Lands: Mat-nefrure (M ꜣ·t-nfr·w-R ᶜ),[a] daughter of the great chief of Kheta."

This inscription, therefore, renders unquestionable the main facts of the following narrative on the Marriage Stela.

The Treaty of Peace

418. ³⁰....... The chief of Kheta sent, asking of me permanent[b] peace. Never did he — for them. Now ⌈afterward⌉....... ³¹under the great fame of the Lord of the Two Lands, King Ramses (II).

The Chief of Kheta Counsels with His Officers

419. Then spake the chief of the land of Kheta to his ⌈army⌉[c] and his nobles, saying: "Now is our land devastated; Sutekh ⌈is⌉ our lord to ⌈protect us⌉, (but) ⌈he has⌉ not........ ³²fighting with them. We have been taken captive with all our possessions; my eldest daughter being before them[d]........"

They Proceed with Gifts to Egypt

420. Then they ⌈came⌉ with [their] possessions, and [their] splendid ⌈gifts⌉ before ³³them, of silver and gold, marvels many and great, horses to — them, — living things.....

The News Reaches Ramses

421. ..... to delight the heart of his majesty, saying: "Behold, the great chief of Kheta comes, ³⁴bringing his eldest daughter, bearing much tribute, being everything........ The chief of Kheta, together with the chief of ⌈Kode[e] and people⌉ of Kheta, are bringing them. They have traversed many mountains and difficult ways, that they

---

[a]Meaning: "*She who sees the beauty of Re*" (the sun). It is the name of the last hour of the night (Brugsch, *Thesaurus*, IV, 845; Petrie, *Proceedings of the Society of Biblical Archæology*, XXVI, 36).

[b]*N rnp·t n rnp·t*, "*year by year?*"

[c]The word is lost except the determinative of men and plural strokes; of course, the first *f* is a misread *n*.

[d]These words are among those used by the chief of Kheta in addressing the Pharaoh in the relief above (§ 415).

[e]This restoration, in view of the letter in *Anastasi*, II (§§ 425, 426), is exceedingly probable.

might reach the boundaries of his majesty. . . . ³⁵. . . . . ." His majesty received the ⌈word⌉ — — [in] the palace, with joy of heart.

Ramses Makes Preparations to Receive Them

422. When he heard such strange and unexpected matters . . . . . . he commanded ³⁶the army and the princes to receive in front of them in haste.

Ramses' Sacrifices to Sutekh for Good Weather

423. Then his majesty took counsel ⌈for⌉ the army[a] with his own heart, saying: "What are these newcomers like! When there goes not a messenger[b] to Zahi (D ⸴-h ⸴) in these days of flood ³⁷on the upper ⌈heights⌉[c] in winter."[d] Then [he] offered an oblation for ⌈—⌉ and for Sutekh. Then he came [⌈pray⌉]ing, saying: "Heaven is — and earth is under ⌈thy feet⌉. That which thou commandest is all that happens. Thou — to make the flood and the cold upon the ⌈heights⌉ . . . . . ³⁸. . . . which thou hast assigned to me, King Ramses (II)." Then his father, Sutekh, heard every [wor]d . . . . . .

Arrival of Ramses' Escort with the Visitors

424. . . . . . . his army came, their limbs being sound, and they were long in stride ³⁹. . . . . The daughter of the great chief of Kheta marched in [⌈front⌉] of the army . . . . of his majesty in following her. They were mingled with foot and horse of Kheta; they were ⁴⁰warriors[e] as well as regulars; they ate and they drank ⌈not⌉ fighting face to face . . . . between them, after the manner of the

---

[a]This is probably the "*army*" escort of the visitors, by which term ("*army*") Ramses refers to the whole expedition now on the way to Egypt.

[b]Lit., "*they go not by messenger*," or "*as a messenger*."

[c]Bouriant has miscopied the word, as is shown by its second occurrence in this same line; it is perhaps k ⸴, "*height*."

[d]It is evident that Ramses expresses to himself here his wonder that these visitors are coming in the winter rainy season, when hardly a state messenger could reach Zahi; though the language he uses is obscure and difficult. He now offers to Sutekh a gift for the sake of good weather and the safe arrival of the visitors. The similar reference in the poem (§ 426) on the same occasion to Ramses' power over rain and storm is hardly accidental. The author of the poem knew of the Abu Simbel Stela. For a similar offering for favorable weather on a voyage, see Punt Expedition (II, 252).

[e]Mercenaries.

god himself, King Ramses (II). The great chiefs of every land came; they were bowed down, turning back in fear, when they saw [This majesty; the chief of⌐] Kheta [⌐came⌐] among them, [⌐to seek the favor⌐] of King Ramses (II).

III. MESSAGE OF THE CHIEF OF KHETA TO THE CHIEF OF KODE[a]

425. This poetic fragment perhaps indicates that Ramses II invited the chief of Kheta and other Asiatic chiefs, at least the chief of Kode, to Egypt, and this invitation a court poet of course regards as a command (Poem below, l. 2). To this invitation the Abu Simbel stela (§§ 415–24) makes no reference, and the whole ten-line poem, being of course only the fancy of a court poet to embellish his description of the glories of Ramses' capitol, to which the Hittite visitors came, may have no foundation in fact. Such a visit, however, and the marriage alliance which it consummated, as we know from the Amarna Letters, must have occasioned much preliminary correspondence, of which this poem offers us a hint.

426. The great chief (*wr-*⌐ᵒ⌐) of Kheta sent to the chief (*wr*) of Kode (saying):

"Equip thyself that we may proceed to Egypt,
That we may say: 'The behest of the god comes to pass;'
Let us make overtures to Ramses II, L. P. H.,
For he gives breath to whom he will,
And every country lies at his disposition.
Kheta is in his power alone,
If the god accepts not his offering,
It (Kheta) sees no rain,[b]
For it is in the power of Ramses (II), L. P. H.,
The Bull, loving valor."

---

[a]Papyrus Anastasi II, Pl. II. ll. 1–5 = *ibid.* IV, Pl. VI, ll. 7–10. Their connection with the Hittite king's visit was first noted by Erman, *Aegypten*, 707.

[b]Lit., "*water of heaven;*" it can hardly be an accident that the prose account (§ 423) also narrates an instance of Ramses' power with the god in respect of rain and storm.

IV. COPTOS STELA[a]

427. This document recorded the visit to Egypt of a number of the Asiatic princes bearing gifts for the Pharaoh. It is a visit precisely like that of the Hittite king (§ 410) and his neighbors, and reference is made to "*his other daughter,*" as if another princess were being brought to Ramses in marriage. As the mention of this princess occurs directly after a reference to Keshkesh, one of the allies of the Hittite king; as the envoys are later (l. 13) said to be "*the children of the great chiefs of the land of Kheta,*" and as there is a reference to a coming "*to Egypt for the second time,*" this may possibly be the account of Ramses' marriage to a second Hittite princess. The pious priests attribute both the visit and the gifts, to the gods (l. 9), and particularly, among the gods of Egypt, to Ptah, precisely as is done in the Blessing of Ptah in referring to the visit of the Hittite king with his daughter (§ 410, l. 25).

428. ³ᵇ——— [chiefs of]ᶜ all countries conveying their tribute, ⁴——— of much gold, of much silver, of all costly stones, ⁵——— very many captives of Keshkesh ($K\check{s}$-$k\check{s}$), many captives ⁶[of] ——— in writing for King Ramses (II) ⁷——— many [herds] of goats, many herds of small cattle[d] before his other daughter ⁸——— Ramses II, given life, to Egypt for the second time. It was not troops who brought them; it was not ⁹——— [the god]s of the land of Egypt,

---

[a] A "black quartzose" stela found by Petrie in the Coptos temple; it had contained an older, probably Middle Kingdom, inscription, which Ramses II had dressed off for the reception of his own inscription (Petrie, *Coptos*, 15). It has been broken so that about half the document is missing, the line of breakage being from the beginning of the first to the end of the last line. Text, *ibid.*, XVIII; I had also a copy by Schaefer, which added a little at the broken edge, and furnished one correction.

[b] The extreme ends of the first two lines show remains of the titulary.

[c] Both the following context and the remains seen by Schaefer render this restoration probable, if not certain.

[d] The published ꜥnḫ·t, "*goats*," is an error; original has yꜣw·t (Schaefer's copy).

the gods of every country, while they caused the great chiefs of every country to convey ¹⁰——— their — themselves to King Ramses (II), given life. ¹¹——— to convey their gold, to convey their silver, to convey their vessels of green ¹²[stone to King] Ramses (II), given life; to bring their herds of horses, to bring their herds of ¹³——— their herds of goats, to bring their herds of large cattle. The children of the great chiefs of the land of Kheta ¹⁴cameᵃ bearing them themselves, from the boundaries of the lands of King Ramses (II), given life, ¹⁵— themselves. It was not a prince who came to bring them, it was not the infantry who came to bring them, it was not the chariotry who came to bring them, it was not ¹⁶the ⌜mercenaries⌝ who went to bring them; it was Ptah, father of the gods, who has put all lands, and all countries under the feet of this Good God, forever and ever.

V. BENTRESH STELAᵇ

429. It is clear that the visit of the Hittite king to Egypt was for the purpose of personally presenting his daughter to Ramses II in marriage. This marriage made a great impression upon the people, and the story of it circulated among them as the introduction to a legend which had grown up from another incident closely connected with the marriage. In the Eighteenth Dynasty, Dushratta, king of Mitanni, sent to Egypt the goddess Ishtar of Ninevah, in the year 35 or 36 of Amenhotep III,ᶜ doubtless for the sake

---

ᵃRemains of the determinative of the verb of going may be seen.

ᵇDiscovered by Rosellini in a small temple of Græco-Roman age now perished, which stood by the Khonsu-temple at Karnak (Erman, *Zeitschrift für ägyptische Sprache*, 1883, 58; Rosellini, *Monumenti Storici*, II, 48 f.; but when first seen by Champollion it was in the "ruines du Sud-Est" (Champollion, *Notices descriptives*, II, 280). It was carried to Paris by Prisse, and is now in the Bibliothèque Nationale. It was published by him (*Monuments égyptiens*, XXIV) afterwards from Champollion's copy (*Notices descriptives*, II, 280–90); Birch, *Egyptian Texts*, 77–81; Rougé, *Etude sur une stèle égyptienne appartenant à la Bibliothèque Impériale*, Paris, 1858 (*extrait du Journal Asiatique*, August, 1856; August, 1857; June and August to September, 1858; Rheinisch, *Chrestomathie*, Taf. 12; finally Ledrain, *Les monuments Eg. de la Bib. Nat.*, Pl. 36–44. The publications contain a number of inaccuracies, and it was possible to correct a good many errors from my own copy of the original, now in the Bibliothèque Nationale at Paris.

ᶜ*Amarna Letters*, ed. Winckler, 20, 13–29.

of the old king's health;[a] she had likewise gone to Egypt in the time of Dushratta's father. The chief of Kheta sent in like manner to Egypt, desiring that Khonsu be brought to Kheta for the purpose of healing his daughter, the younger sister of Ramses' queen, Matnefrure. This was done,[b] and although no contemporary record of the incident has survived, it gradually found place among the folk-tales of the time.

430. Some eight or nine hundred years later, in Persian or early Greek times, the priests of Khonsu at Thebes determined to record the story to the greater glory of their god. They put the current tale into language as archaic as they could command, and engraved it upon a stela, which is now our source for the document.[c] In doing this they evidently found some difficulty. The current version, of course, spoke of the king only as Ramses or Ramses-Meriamon. The priests, desiring to lend an official air to their stela, attempted to prefix to the king's name his full titulary, and in doing so used that of Thutmose IV! Nor was their knowledge sufficient to correct the errors or remove the absurdities of the popular version of the story. They consistently carry through seventeen months as the length of time necessary to go from Egypt to Bekhten[d] (*Bḫtn*), a land otherwise unknown; Nefrure, a corruption of Matnefrure, the real name of the Hittite chief's daughter; a date before the year 23 for the marriage of Matnefrure, which

---

[a] See Meyer, *Festschrift für Georg Ebers*, 65, 66.

[b] A tradition of the visit of an Egyptian god in Syria is preserved in Macrobius; see Birch, *Zeitschrift für ägyptische Sprache*, 1874, 67 f.

[c] The real age and origin of the Bentresh Stela were first noticed by Erman (*Zeitschrift für ägyptische Sprache*, 1883, 54 ff.), but as the earlier case of Ishtar (*Amarna Letters*, ed. Winckler, 20) was then unknown, Erman naturally denied the content of the stela much of an historical basis.

[d] A corruption of Bactria?

really took place in the year 34—these and other errors, which will be evident to the reader, were calmly accepted by the priestly editors. Incidentally, this document therefore shows clearly how utterly ignorant of earlier Egyptian history were these late priests; and suggests caution in the use of the priest Manetho's work, who lived at about the time when this tale was put into writing.

431. The upper fourth of the stela is occupied by a relief, showing on either side the two sacred barques of the Khonsu's borne on the shoulders of priests. That on the right is Khonsu-in-Thebes-Beautiful-Rest, to whom Ramses II is offering incense; while that on the left belongs to "*Khonsu-the-Plan-Maker-in-Thebes, Great God, Smiter of Evil Spirits.*" Before him his priest, offering incense, is accompanied by the inscription:

432. The name of the prophet, priest of Khonsu-the-Plan-Maker-in-Thebes, is Khonsuhetneterneb ($Hnsw-h\cdot t-ntr-nb\cdot t$, sic!).[a]

Below the relief is the long inscription, as follows:

Introduction

433. ¹Horus: Mighty Bull, Likeness of Diadems, Abiding in Kingship, like Atum; Golden Horus: Mighty of Strength, Expelling the Nine Bows;[b] King of Upper and Lower Egypt, Lord of the Two Lands: Usermare-Setepnere; Son of Re, of his Body: Ramses-Meriamon, ²beloved of Amon-Re, lord of Thebes, and all the gods of Thebes. . . . .
4. . . . .[c]

Tribute in Naharin

434. Lo, his majesty was in Naharin ($N\text{-}h\text{-}r\text{-}[n]$) according to his yearly custom, while the chiefs of every country came bowing down in

---

[a]Meaning: "*Khonsu is chief of all gods.*" The form, both of this name and this short inscription, is unknown in the time of Ramses II.

[b]These three names (the second title, "*Favorite of the Two Goddesses,*" has been omitted before "*Abiding, etc.*") are those of Thutmose IV! The last two, however, show clearly that Ramses II is meant.

[c]The usual epitheta of the kings, running through ll. 2–4 (beginning).

peace, because of the fame of his majesty. From the marshes[a] was their tribute; silver, gold, lapis lazuli, [5]malachite and every sweet wood of God's-Land were upon their backs, each one leading his neighbor.

Marriage of Ramses and Chief of Bekhten's Daughter

435. Then the chief of Bekhten ($B\underline{h}tn$) caused his tribute to be brought, and he placed his eldest daughter in front thereof,[b] praising his majesty, and craving life from him. Now, [6]she was exceedingly beautiful to the heart of his majesty, beyond everything. Then they affixed[c] her titulary as: "Great King's-Wife, Nefrure ($Nfr\cdot w\text{-}R^c$)."[d] When his majesty arrived in Egypt, she fulfilled all the functions of king's-wife.

Arrival of the Messenger from Bekhten

436. When the year 23, the tenth month, the twenty-second day, came, while his majesty was in Thebes, the victorious, the mistress of cities, performing [7]the pleasing ceremonies of his father, Amon-Re, lord of Thebes, at his beautiful feast of Southern Opet (Luxor), his favorite seat, of the beginning (of the world), came one to say to his majesty: "A messenger of the chief of Bekhten has come, bearing many gifts for the King's-Wife." Then he was brought [8]before his majesty together with his gifts. He said, praising his majesty: "Praise to thee, Sun of the Nine Bows! Give us life from thee." So spake he, smelling the earth before his majesty. He spake again before his majesty: "I come to thee, [9]O king, my lord, on account of Bentresh ($B\text{-}n\text{-}t\text{-}r\text{-}\check{s}$), thy great[e] sister of the King's-Wife, Nefrure. Sickness has penetrated into[f] her limbs. May thy majesty send a wise man to see her."

---

[a]At the northern limits of the earth. The division may be wrong here; "*from the marshes*" goes better with the verb "*came*," but too much seems to intervene. The following would then be: "*Their tribute, silver, etc., were upon their, etc.*"

[b]Exactly as in the documents on the coming of Matnefrure, especially the Ptah Stela (§ 410), with which the above passage is also in verbal agreement.

[c]To all seals and documents; that is, she takes an official Egyptian name on becoming a queen. On the use of this word "*affix*" (*wd*), see my *New Chapter* (Sethe, *Untersuchungen*, II, 2, 19, 20).

[d]This is, of course, an error of the late priests for $M\cdot t\text{-}nfr\cdot w\text{-}R^c$, the real name of the Hittite king's daughter (§ 417).

[e]Possibly to be rendered "*oldest.*"

[f]Lit., "*has mingled with.*"

Dispatch of the Wise Man to Bekhten

437. Then said his majesty: "Bring to me the sacred scribes[a] and the officials [10]of the court." They were led to him immediately. Said his majesty: "Let one read to you, till ye hear this thing. Then bring to me one experienced in his heart, who can write with his fingers, from your midst." The king's-scribe, [11]Thutemhab,[b] came before his majesty, and his majesty commanded that he go to Bekhten together with this messenger.

Arrival of the Wise Man in Bekhten

438. The wise man arrived in Bekhten; he found Bentresh in the condition of one possessed of a spirit. He found [12]her[c] ⌜unable⌝ to contend with him.

Message of the Chief of Bekhten to Ramses

439. The chief of Bekhten repeated in the presence of his majesty,[d] saying: "O king, my lord, let his majesty command to have this god brought ———."[e] [⌜Then the wise man whom his majesty had sent, returned⌝] [13]to his majesty in the year 26, the ninth month, at the feast of Amon,[f] while his majesty was in Thebes.

---

[a]$Tt\ nt\ pr\ ^c\ nh$=lit., "*those in charge of the writings of the house of life*," a title especially common in Ptolemaic times. In the Canopus Decree it is rendered by the Greek οἱ ἱερογραμματεῖς.

[b]A man of this name and of the same office lived in the time of Ramses II, and his stela is in Leyden (Lieblein, 884; Erman, *Zeitschrift für ägyptische Sprache*, 1883, 55).

[c]*Sw* for *sy*; several words, now no longer visible on the stone here, were seen and copied by Prisse, but more correctly by Rheinisch.

[d]This alone would indicate that the chief of Bekhten, finding the wise man unable to cast out the spirit, went himself to Egypt to ask that the god be sent to do so. The loss between the two parts of the stela, just below this point, makes it difficult to trace the connection, but it seems more probable that the words of the chief of Bekhten are a message, sent by the returning wise man to Ramses, for it is clear that he received some message at the beginning of l. 13; and, further, the chief of Bekhten is found in Bekhten by the god on his arrival there. The chief therefore certainly remained in Bekhten.

[e]Lacuna of uncertain length, between the two fragments of the stela.

[f]As the god later consumes one year and five months (l. 17) in going to Bekhten, the round trip between Egypt and Bekhten should take some thirty-four months. This exactly suits the above passage, according to which the returning wise man has been absent nearly three years, which allows for a short stay in Bekhten.

Ramses' Interview with the Two Khonsu's

440. Then his majesty repeated (it) before Khonsu-in-Thebes-Beautiful-Rest, saying: "O my good lord, I repeat before thee concerning the daughter of the chief of Bekhten." [14]Then they led Khonsu-in-Thebes-Beautiful-Rest to Khonsu-the-Plan-Maker, the great god, smiting the evil spirits. Then said his majesty before Khonsu-in-Thebes-Beautiful-Rest: "O thou good lord, if thou inclinest thy face to Khonsu-[15]the-Plan-Maker, the great god, smiting the evil spirits, he shall be conveyed to Bekhten." There was violent nodding. Then said his majesty: "Send thy protection with him, that I may cause his majesty[a] to go to Bekhten, to save the daughter of the chief of Bekhten." [16]Khonsu-in-Thebes-Beautiful-Rest nodded the head violently. Then he wrought the protection of Khonsu-the-Plan-Maker-in-Thebes, four times.

Departure of Khonsu-the-Plan-Maker

441. His majesty commanded to cause Khonsu-the-Plan-Maker-in-Thebes to proceed to a great ship, five transports ($kk \cdot t$), numerous chariots [17]and horses of the west and the east.

Arrival of the God in Bekhten

442. This god arrived in Bekhten in a full year and five months. Then the chief of Bekhten came, with his soldiers and his nobles, before Khonsu-the-Plan-Maker. He threw himself [18]upon his belly, saying: "Thou comest to us, thou art welcome with us, by command of the King Usermare-Setepnere (Ramses II)."

Cure of Bentresh

443. Then this god went to the place where Bentresh was. Then he wrought the protection of the daughter of the chief of Bekhten. She became well [19]immediately.

Conciliation of the Spirit

444. Then said this spirit which was in her before Khonsu-the-Plan-Maker-in-Thebes: "Thou comest in peace, thou great god, smiting the barbarians. Thy city is Bekhten, thy servants are its people, I am thy servant. [20]I will go to the place whence I came, to satisfy thy

---

[a]Meaning the god.

heart concerning that, on account of which thou comest. (But) let thy majesty command to celebrate a feast-day with me and with the chief of Bekhten." Then this god nodded to his priest, saying: [21]"Let the chief of Bekhten make a great offering before this spirit." While these things were happening, which Khonsu-the-Plan-Maker-in-Thebes wrought with the spirit, the chief of Bekhten stood with his soldiers, and feared very greatly. Then [22]he made a great offering before Khonsu-the-Plan-Maker-in-Thebes and the spirit; and the chief of Bekhten celebrated a feast-day ⌜with⌝ them. Then the spirit departed in peace to the place he desired, by command of Khonsu-the-Plan-Maker-in-Thebes, [23]and the chief of Bekhten rejoiced very greatly, together with every man who was in Bekhten.

Retention of the God in Bekhten

445. Then he took counsel with his heart, saying: "I will cause this god to remain with me in Bekhten; I will not permit that he return to Egypt." [24]Then this god tarried three years and nine months in Bekhten.

Vision of the Chief of Bekhten

Then the chief of Bekhten slept upon his bed, and he saw this god coming to him, to forsake his shrine; he was a hawk of gold, and he flew upward toward Egypt. [25]He (the chief) awoke in fright.

Departure of the God for Egypt

446. Then he said to the priest of Khonsu-the-Plan-Maker-in-Thebes: "This god, he is still with us; let him depart to Egypt; let his chariot depart to Egypt." [26]Then the chief of Bekhten caused this god to proceed to Egypt, and gave to him very many gifts of every good thing, very many soldiers and horses.

Arrival of the God in Egypt

447. They arrived in peace at Thebes. Then came the city of Thebes, and [a]the-Plan-Maker-in-Thebes [27]to the house of Khonsu-in-Thebes-Beautiful-Rest. He set the gifts which the chief of Bekhten had given to him, of good things, before Khonsu-in-Thebes-Beautiful-Rest, (but) he gave not every thing thereof into his house. Khonsu-the-

---

[a]Khonsu has probably been omitted by mistake.

Plan-Maker-in-Thebes arrived ²⁸[at] his [plac]e in peace in the year 33, the second month, the ninth day,ᵃ of King Usermare-Setepnere; that he might be given life like Re, forever.

NUBIAN WARS AND REFERENCES TO NORTHERN WARS

448. The temples of Nubia contain many references of an indefinite character to Ramses II's Nubian wars, from which it is impossible to gain any idea of them, the localities conquered, or the date of the campaigns. These references are often so mingled with those of the northern wars against the Asiatics and Libyans that it is not possible to separate and classify them all. They are continued through the temples of Egypt also.ᵇ Of the Libyan war we learn little more than the fact, though the Tanis Stela furnishes an important hint of an alliance of the Libyans with the Sherden and a naval battleᶜ (§ 491). To our knowledge of

---

ᵃThe round trip consumed 34 months (1 year and 5 months each way, l. 17), and he had remained in Bekhten 45 months (l. 24), a total absence of 79 months, or 6 years and 7 months. As he left Egypt in the ninth month of the year 26 (l. 13, date of wise man's return to summon him), if that date be late in the year 26, an absence of 6 years and 7 months would put his return in the year 33, as the priestly author of the inscription has done.

ᵇScenes showing Ramses sacrificing foreign captives of the north and south are found in practically all his temples; e. g., at the Ramesseum (Lepsius, *Denkmäler*, III, 159, b), where we find beside the scene the words: "*Slaying their chiefs, making them as if they had not been;*" and again: "*The chiefs of the countries of the south and the north, whom his majesty carried away as living captives.*" On his obelisks also there are very general references to his wars; thus at Tanis (Petrie, *Tanis*, I, VII, No. 45) he is called one, "*capturing Nubia by his valor, wasting Tehenu;*" and "*great in valor like a bull in Retenu;*" again (*ibid.*, No. 47): "*carrying off the chiefs of Retenu as living prisoners, crushing the land of Kheta.*" At Kurna, in the temple, some divinity addressed Ramses thus (Piehl, *Inscriptions*, I, 145 A): "——— *the gods of Khenthennofer and Wawat in their nomes, and lands; the chiefs of God's-Land, who fashion every splendid costly stone for their son, Ramses II ——— lapis lazuli of Tefrer, every costly stone that is in the two mountains, the products of Nun. The subjects of the Negroes come to thee ⌜by land and water, bringing⌝ down-stream all the reckonings of Nubia in the records of Thoth, in order to make festive the temple of thy father, Amon, lord of gods.*" (See also Dümichen, *Historische Inschriften*, II, 38.)

ᶜThe hymn to Ramses II, in Papyrus Anastasi II, says: "*Libya falls before his] sword*" (III, 4).

the Asiatic wars nothing definite is added. The materials are:
  I. Abu Simbel Temple (§§ 449–57).
  II. Bet el-Walli Temple (§§ 458–77).
  III. Assuan Stela (§§ 478, 479).
  IV. Luxor Temple (§§ 480–84).
  V. Abydos Temple (§§ 485, 486).
  VI. Tanis Stelæ (§§ 487–91).

I. ABU SIMBEL TEMPLE

449. The following scenes[a] in the great temple at Abu Simbel contain references to Ramses II's Asiatic wars, a war against the Libyans, and the Nubian war.

Scene[b]

450. Ramses II, with bow and sword in hand, rides slowly in his chariot, evidently accompanying his army on the march. Beside his horses runs his tame lion, while an orderly with bow, quiver, and staff, his sandals strung on his arm, marches at the horses' heads. Before them are driven two lines of bound Negro prisoners.

Inscription

451. Good God ⌈—⌉, who smites the south, who crushes the north; king, fighting with his sword, carrying off the furthest ends[c] of those who transgress his inviolable ⌈places⌉. When his majesty arrives in the countries, he overthrows myriads; he desolates them. He has — Retenu, slaying their chiefs; he causes the Negroes to say: "Away! He is like flame, when it comes forth, and there is no water to quench

---

[a]The publications will be found with each scene. The great battle scene of Kadesh will be found in §§ 335–38.

[b]Champollion, *Monuments*, 15, 16 = Rosellini, *Monumenti Storici*, 84, 85: Champollion, *Monuments*, also adds (Pl. 16 *bis*) two Negro heads, in full size of original.

[c]There is possibly a lacuna here.

it." He makes the rebels to cease the contradiction which their mouths offered, when he took them.

Scene[a]

452. Ramses II, with bow in hand, leads two lines of captive Negroes, and presents them to Amon, Mut, and Khonsu.

Inscription over Ramses and Negroes

453. The bringing of the tribute, by the Good God, to his father, Amon-Re, lord of Thebes, after his arrival from the country of Kush, overthrowing the rebellious countries, crushing the Asiatics in their place; consisting of silver, gold, lapis lazuli, malachite, and every splendid costly stone, according as he decreed for him might and victory against every country.

The wretched chiefs of Kush, whom his majesty brought from his victories in the country of Kush, in order to fill the storehouse of his august father, Amon-Re, lord of Thebes, according as he gave might against the south, victory against the north, forever and ever.

Scene[b]

454. Ramses II, with drawn bow, stands in his chariot, charging a Syrian city, situated on a hill. The inhabitants on the city walls are nearly all pierced with arrows; just outside, a fleeing Syrian drives off his cattle to refuge in the city. Behind Ramses, three princes dash forward, each in his chariot.

Inscription over Ramses

455. Good God, valiant son of Amon, lord of the sword, protector of his army ⌜in⌝ battle, mighty in strength, knowing where to place his hand, firm in the chariot like the lord of Thebes, lord of victory, fighting millions, mighty Bull among multitudes, piercing through the allies,

---

[a]Champollion, *Monuments*, 35 = Rosellini, *Monumenti Storici*, 86 (both without inscription over Ramses and Negroes); Champollion, *Notices descriptives*, I, 66; Lepsius, *Denkmäler*, III, 188, a.

[b]Champollion, *Monuments*, 12–14 = Rosellini, *Monumenti Storici*, 80–82 = Gau, *Antiquités de la Nubie*, 61.

crushing the rebellious upon the mountains; they enter into their valleys like grasshoppers. Thou makest the sword to cut off their place, ⌜where⌝ thy enemies come forth, O king, mighty of sword.

Over Three Princes

456. King's-son, of his body, his beloved, Amenhirkhepeshef.
King's-son, of his body, his beloved, Ramses.
King's-son, of his body, his beloved Perehirunamef.

Scene[a]

457. Ramses II, standing over a fallen Libyan, hurls backward another Libyan, whom he is thrusting through with his spear.

Inscription

The Good God, slaying the Nine Bows, crushing the countries of the north, — valiant in the countries, a mighty swordman, like Montu, bringing the land of the Negroes to the land of the north, the Asiatics ($\ulcorner\supset m \cdot w$) to the land of Nubia. He has placed the Shasu ($\check{S} \supset -s \supset$) into the land of —, he has settled the Tehenu on the heights, filling the strongholds, which he built, with the captivity of his mighty sword, ⌜slaying⌝ Kharu ($\underline{H} \supset -rw$), ⌜wasting⌝ Retenu ($R\underline{t}nw$), which his sword overthrew.

II. BET EL-WALLI TEMPLE[b]

458. The impressive reliefs in this temple represent the northern and southern wars of Ramses II: the northern wars, against Asiatics and Libyans, are on the northern wall of the forecourt, and the southern wars, against the

---

[a]Champollion, *Monuments*, 17 = Rosellini, *Monumenti Storici*, 83. The scene is copied from that of Seti I on the north wall of Karnak (Scene XIII, §§ 123-32).

[b]These scenes are cut on the rock side-walls of the excavated forecourt of the Bet el-Walli temple. Young published the complete series from drawings by Wilkinson (*Hieroglyphics*, 81–87, *b*) An effective colored reproduction of the ensemble is given by Bonomi-Arundale, *Antiquities*, Pl. 38, Figs. 155, 156; the separate scenes are published by Champollion, *Monuments*, 63–73, 92, No. 4 Champollion, *Notices descriptives*, I, 154; Rosellini, *Monumenti Storici*, 65–75; Gau, *Antiquités de la Nubie*, 12, 14, 15; and fragments, Lepsius, *Denkmäler*, III, 176, *a, b, d, e, f, g*.

Nubians, are on the southern wall. Thus each series indicates by its position the locality where the wars it depicts took place. In each series the movement of events is toward the temple door, where the king sits in both final scenes, receiving the captives from his wars.

I. NORTHERN WARS

459. The scenes in this series are chiefly, if not exclusively, symbolical, and therefore do not depict specific events. They were evidently devised to form a pendant to the other series on the southern wall, which does depict an actual Nubian campaign.

Scene[a]

460. Ramses II, charging in his chariot, leans over and seizes two of the enemy by the turban, and cuts them down with his sword; before him the mass of the enemy flees. They are bearded, and are undoubtedly Semites.

Inscription

461. ———— valiant son of Amon, lord of the sword, protector of his army in battle, mighty against ——— his hand, firm in the chariot, like the lord of Thebes, ———— victorious, fighting millions, mighty Bull among myriads, ———— smiting the rebellious ————.

Scene[b]

462. A symbolic scene showing an Asiatic city, on the walls of which the inhabitants gather, with hands uplifted, beseeching mercy. The city chief or petty prince in the citadel is seized by the gigantic Ramses, who stands over him with upraised sword. A prince (with sidelock) advances to the gate with a battle axe.

---

[a]Champollion, *Monuments*, 64 = Rosellini, *Monumenti Storici*, 67 = Bonomi-Arundale, *Antiquities*, Pl. 38, Fig. 156 = Gau, *Antiquités de la Nubie*, 12, 14, 3.

[b]Champollion, *Monuments*, 65 = Rosellini, *Monumenti Storici*, 68 = Bonomi-Arundale, Pl. 38, Fig. 156 = Gau, *Antiquités de la Nubie*, 12, 14, 3.

Inscriptions

463. The inscriptions have all perished[a] except the words of the captured chief:

By the Citadel

Said the wretched chief,[b] in magnifying the Lord of the Two Lands: "⌈— —⌉ there is no other like Baal, O ruler, his real son, forever."

Scene[c]

464. Ramses II slays with the sword a Libyan[d] whom he has seized by the hair and forced to the knees. A hound leaps upon the Libyan's hip. Approaching Ramses in front, with uplifted arms, are two rows of officials, now almost vanished.

Inscription behind Ramses

465. O Good God, great in terror, victorious lion, lord of the sword, embracing the rebellious lands of Tehenu (*Ṯḥnw*); thy sword has overthrown the Nine Bows, slaying him who is beneath thy sandals, like Re, every [day] forever and ever.

Before Officials, Upper Row

466. Said the princes who are in the presence of his majesty, in magnifying the Lord of the Two Lands: "— — — [migh]ty in valor, victorious when thou hast shown thy might among the rebellious — — the sun shines not because of thy rage therein ...... ⸺."

Before Official, Lower Row

467. Said the fan-bearer on the right of the king, prince, — real king's-scribe, his beloved, king's-son, Amenhirunamef, in [⌈celebrating⌉]

---

[a]Fragments of three columns over the city show the main inscription to have been of the usual conventional character.

[b]The absence of the name shows the purely typical character of the scene.

[c]Champollion, *Monuments*, 63 = Rosellini, *Monumenti Storici*, 66 = Bonomi-Arundale, *Antiquities*, Pl. 38, Fig. 156 = Gau, *Antiquités de la Nubie*, 12, 14, 2.

[d]A similar scene within the temple (rear wall, Champollion, *Notices descriptives*, I, 151; Lepsius, *Denkmäler*, III, 176, c) bears the words: "*Good God, slaying Tehenu.*"

the praise of his lord, in magnifying his might: "———— in the countries. Thou hast slain their chiefs ————."

Over Hound

Anath (ᶜ*nty*)-is-Protection.

Scene[a]

468. Ramses II, standing, battle axe and bow in hand, grasps three Syrians by the hair, as they kneel before him. A king's-son (from his dress), doubtless Amenhirunamef, leads up a line of prisoners, consisting of a Libyan and three Asiatics.

Inscriptions

469. The inscriptions have all disappeared except two short lines:

Behind Ramses

Thy might and thy victory are in all lands and all countries; thy terror is in their hearts.

Scene[b]

470. Ramses II, enthroned in state, with his tame lion by his side, gives audience to his vizier (from the costume), followed by six officers; and to his son, Amenhirunamef, leading Asiatic prisoners.

Inscription before Vizier

471. Said the princes, who are in the presence of his majesty: "Praise to thee, O good and amiable ruler, son of Amon, who came forth from his limbs. When thou camest forth upon earth, thou wast like Re on high ......[c] Black land (Egypt) and Red land (desert)

---

[a]Champollion, *Monuments*, 66, 67 = Rosellini, *Monumenti Storici*, 69, 70 = Bonomi-Arundale, *Antiquities*, Pl. 38, Fig. 156 = Gau, *Antiquités de la Nubie*, 12, 14, 1.

[b]Champollion, *Monuments*, 62 = Rosellini, *Monumenti Storici*, 65 = Bonomi-Arundale, *Antiquities*, Pl. 38, Fig. 156 = Gau, *Antiquités de la Nubie*, 12, 14, 2.

[c]Conventional praise.

are under thy sandals; Palestine and Kush are in thy grasp. Egypt rejoices, O ⌜good⌝ ruler, because thou hast extended their borders, forever."

Over King's-Son

The fan-bearer on the right of the king, prince, real king's-scribe, his beloved, Amenhirunamef.

II. SOUTHERN WAR

472. This series evidently depicts particular events in Ramses II's Nubian war. When this war took place it is difficult to say with certainty,[a] but it was under the administration of Amenemopet as viceroy of Kush, and must, therefore, have fallen in the first half of Ramses' reign.[b] The scene of the war is equally uncertain. The three lists[c] of conquered Nubian countries consist of unfamiliar names, from which little can be obtained as to the locality of the war. Brugsch thinks that the Abu Simbel list does not extend above Napata.[d]

Scene[e]

473. Ramses, standing in his chariot with drawn bow, charges the Negroes, who flee in a horde before him into a palm grove, in which two Negroes lead away a wounded

---

[a]There is a current statement that Ramses II was viceroy of Ethiopia before Seti I's death, and that the battle depicted in our reliefs took place then. Not only is there no evidence that Ramses II was ever viceroy of Kush, but our reliefs further show that Amenemopet was viceroy at this time.

[b]The Assuan stela (§§ 478, 479), which is dated in the year 2, may possibly have been erected on this campaign.

[c]Mariette, *Abydos*, II, Pl. 2, *a*, *b*, Pl. 3; and a list of six names at Abu Simbel (Lepsius, *Denkmäler*, III, 194), which are those of Negro peoples, in spite of the beards (see Brugsch, *Geschichte*, 529, and 346 f. Nos. 25, 28, and 77). Southern countries are also mentioned on the Karnak wall (Lepsius, *Denkmäler*, III, 148, *d*).

[d]Brugsch, *Geschichte*, 529, note.

[e]Champollion, *Monuments*, 71, 72 = Rosellini, *Monumenti Storici*, 74, 75 = Bonomi-Arundale, *Gallery*, Fig. 155; and Lepsius, *Denkmäler*, III, 176, *a*, *b*.

comrade to his family. Behind him charge two princes in their chariots.[a]

Inscriptions

474. An inscription over the enemy has disappeared, except the words: "———— those who transgress his boundaries." Two others have survived:[b]

Over First Prince

Said the fan-bearer on the right of the king, the hereditary prince, the king's-son, of his body, his beloved, Amenhirunamef: "......... in the South; I rejoice, my heart is joyful, (for) my father smites his enemies; he puts forth the might of his strength against the Nine Bows."

Over Second Prince

The king's-son, of his body, his beloved, the divine water that came forth from the Mighty Bull, Khamwese.

Scene[c]

475. On the right sits Ramses enthroned; approaching from the left are two long lines of Negroes, bringing furniture of ebony and ivory, panther hides, gold in large rings, bows, myrrh, shields, elephants' tusks, billets of ebony, ostrich feathers, ostrich eggs, live animals, including monkeys, panthers, a giraffe, ibexes, a dog, oxen with carved horns, an ostrich. At the end are also two Negro women, one carrying her children in a basket. Led by two Egyptians

---

[a]A scene inside the temple shows Ramses II smiting a Negro, with the words: "*Good God, repulsing the Nine Bows, smiting the chiefs of Kush, the wretched.*" (Lepsius, *Denkmäler*, III, 176, d.)

[b]In Bonomi-Arundale are the fragments of a text over the palm grove in which one may discern: "———— *ruler like Baal*," probably belonging to words of the Negroes.

[c]Champollion, *Monuments*, 68–70 = Rosellini, *Monumenti Storici*, 71–73 = Bonomi-Arundale, Fig. 155; and Lepsius, *Denkmäler*, III, 176, e, f = Gau, *Antiquités de la Nubie*, 15.

at the head of the lower line are two bound Negroes. The lower line is introduced by the vizier, and two officials, followed by the viceroy of Kush, bearing a table hung with skins and decorated with flowers. At the head of the upper row (which represents the scene a moment after that of the lower row) is the king's-son, Amenhirunamef, presenting the gifts which together with the splendid table have been placed on the ground. Behind the table which he has just set down appears the viceroy of Kush, receiving decorations for good service.

Inscriptions

476. Behind Ramses are four columns containing an elaborate titulary, in which is the phrase: "*making boundaries as he pleases in Retenu.*" The other texts are brief and fragmentary.

Over Viceroy of Kush, Lower Row

477. King's-son of Kush, Amenemopet, son of Peser, triumphant.

Over King's-Son, Top Row

The fan-bearer on the right hand of the king, real king's-scribe, his beloved, hereditary prince, first king's-son, of his body, Amenhirunamef, triumphant, revered (sic!).

Over Viceroy of Kush, Top Row

King's-son of Kush, Amenemopet, son of Peser, triumphant.

III. ASSUAN STELA[a]

478. This monument contains only a fulsome eulogy of Ramses II, in which reference is made to all his wars. Its position at the Nubian frontier would indicate that it was

---

[a]Cut on the rocks at Assuan; published by Lepsius, *Denkmäler*, III, 175, g = Rougé, *Inscriptions hiéroglyphiques*, 252, 253, = de Morgan, *Catalogue des monuments*, 6.

erected on some Nubian expedition of Ramses II, and its date, "*year 2*," may, therefore, be that of the Nubian war, recorded at Bet el-Walli.

479. 1. Year 2, eleventh month, twenty-sixth[a] day, under the majesty of [2]Ramses II,[b] beloved of Amon-Re, king of Gods, and Khnum, lord of the cataract region.

[3]Live the Good God, Montu of millions, mighty like the son of Nut, fighting for ⟦—⟧, strong-hearted lion. He has overthrown [4]myriads in the space of a moment; great wall of his army in the day of battle, whose fear has penetrated all lands. [5]Egypt rejoices when the ruler is among them (i. e., the lands); he has extended its boundaries forever, plundering the Asiatics (*Sṭ·tyw*) and capturing their cities. [6]He has crushed the foreigners of the north, the Temeh[c] have fallen for fear of him, the Asiatics are anxious for breath from him, [7]who sends Egypt on campaigns; their hearts are filled with his designs, as they sit in the shadow of his sword, and [8]they fear not any country. He plunders the warriors (*ʿḥ ʾ·w*) of the sea, the great lake of the north,' while they lie sleeping. [9]A vigilant king, accurate in design; there fails not anything that he has said. The foreigners come to him carrying their children, to ask [10]the breath of life; his battle-cry is mighty ⌈in⌉ the land of Nubia (*T ʾ -pd·t*), his strength repels the Nine Bows; Babylon (*S ʾ -[n-]g ʾ -r ʾ*), Kheta and A— (?—)[d] come to him, bowing down, because of his fame.

IV. LUXOR TEMPLE

480. Besides the reliefs and inscriptions relating to the battle of Kadesh (§§ 305–51), the Luxor temple contains a number of references to Ramses II's wars, conquests, and relations with foreign countries. On a granite statue,[e] under a list of northern and southern countries, is the usual statement of the extent of Pharaoh's power, including the

---

[a]Rougé, *Inscriptions hiéroglyphiques*, has 27.
[b]Full titulary.
[c]Text has *Ty-m-ḥ-nw!* It may be that Tehenu is meant.
[d]Probably Arvad or Isy-Cyprus.
[e]*Recueil*, 16, 50, 51.

"Great Circle (šn wr), the sea, the southern countries of the land of the Negro as far as the marsh lands, as far as the limits of the darkness, even to the four pillars of heaven."

481. More important is a scene among the reliefs which portrays the presentation of annual dues[a] by the king's sons and the chief officials of the kingdom. These dues consist of both "*tribute*" (*yn-w*) and taxes or impost (*bk·w*), besides "*dues*" (*ḥsb·t*); and they come from Nubia, Asia, and Egypt. At the head of the procession are seventeen sons of Ramses, of whom the first four are:

482. 1. Hereditary prince, king's-son, crown prince, of his body, commander in chief of the army, Amonhirkhepeshef.

2. King's-son, of his body, commander of the army[b] of the Lord of the Two Lands, Ramses.

3. Captain of archers, master of horse, Perehirunamef.[c]

4. Khamwese.

483. These are all well known elsewhere, especially Khamwese, as they took part in the king's wars (§ 362). The thirteenth in the row is Merneptah, who, on the death of his twelve elder brothers and his father, became king.

Behind the princes is a line of men bearing "des offrandes, conduisant des bœufs à cornes singulières comme à Abydos." Above them all is an inscription, designating them as:

484. The hereditary prince ⌜of the palace⌝, king's-son, crown prince; [⌜the king's-sons⌝], the grandees of the palace ⌜—⌝[d] their lord, their father, Ramses II, given life. The governors of the city and

---

[a]Relief and accompanying inscriptions in the first court of the Luxor temple, south side; *Recueil*, XIV, 31, L, but without the reliefs.

[b]Personal troops of the king.

[c]A list of seventeen daughters is on the west wall of this court (*Recueil*, XIV, 32). They are preceded by the first three sons above, but No. 3 has the title, "*First charioteer of his majesty.*" The queen Nefretiri heads the line.

[d]Some verb like "come to" has here been miscopied, as is evident from the parallelism with the second group, also followed by the name of Ramses after a verb of coming.

viziers,[a] companions, treasurers of the palace, overseers of the silver- and gold-house, commanders of the army, commanders of ⌜infantry⌝ (*mnfy·t*), captains of archers, ⌜master builders⌝, governors of southern and northern countries, chief treasurers, chief mayors, stewards, leaders of leaders, and town commandants, overseers of horns,[b] overseers of hoofs,[b] overseers of feathers,[b] ⌜—⌝ of Egypt, the marshal of the two thrones of Upper and Lower Egypt, the counts, and superior prophets, coming with bowed head, bearing their tribute of the impost of Nubia (*T ɜ -pd·t*), every product of Asiatic countries, the dues (*ḥsb·t*) of Egypt, to behold the beauty of their lord, King Ramses II.

V. ABYDOS TEMPLE[c]

485. Ramses II's mortuary temple at Abydos, as we have already noted, contains reliefs from the Kadesh series (§ 328), as well as a copy of the Kadesh poem (§§ 305–15). Besides these, the mortuary reliefs also contain references to his wars.[d] These reliefs show a long procession of priests and officers, bringing an immense and varied array of offerings for Ramses II's mortuary temple, in which these reliefs appear. Like others of their class, these scenes are of purely religious and mortuary significance, except the last.[e] This represents a section of the procession headed by a superb bull, and an ibex; these animals, with their attendants and some lesser offerings, face a long procession in a double line of Egyptian troops who are summoned by a

---

[a]"*Governors*" is clearly plural, but "*vizier*" is not so written; the relief would probably determine whether we have here the two viziers.

[b]Live-stock and poultry.

[c]A series of mortuary reliefs on the walls of the first court; published by Mariette, *Abydos*, II, 6–10.

[d]Mariette indicates other historical materials in this temple; he says: "La face antérieure du pylône semble présenter un résumé des campagnes de Ramsès. Le roi a la hache, la masse d'armes, et l'enseigne de victoire. Des officiers lui amènent des prisonniers. Aucun personnage n'est visible en entier. On croit cependant reconnaître des Lybiens, des nègres et des Asiatiques."

[e]Mariette, *Abydos*, II, Pl. 10; long inscription also Brugsch, *Thesaurus*, V, 1222, 1223.

trumpeter. Four men at the head of the troops are followed by a royal span drawing an empty chariot, accompanied by an orderly with sandals strung on his arm as usual. Behind the troops who follow the chariot are Negroes, Asiatics, Puntites, and perhaps Libyans. Over the whole is an inscription in one long line, the beginning of which is very fragmentary; scattered among the figures were also some inscriptions, most of which have now disappeared:

Over Chariot Horses

486. Great span of his majesty, L. P. H., (named): "Beloved-——————."

Over Asiatics

Chiefs of the countries ————.

Long Inscription

........[a] Utterance of the Son of Re, Ramses-Meriamon: "O ye Kings of Upper and Lower Egypt, who shall come after, who shall assume the double crown upon the throne of Horus, who shall desire Abydos, region of eternity; may your ka's exist for you without ceasing, may your time be happy like my time, may the full Nile come for you at his season, may valor be yours without flinching, like the victories of my sword in every country, may ye take captive those that rebel against Egypt, may ye put those whom ye capture in them, into my august temple. Lo, as for a king, he is the divine seed,[b] while he is a dweller in heaven, as when he was on earth; he assumes the forms, which he desires, like the Moon-god. Establish ye the offerings of this my temple of Osiris, whose august image rests therein, the divine ennead which follows him, being united at his side; (then) shall favors be craved from them, making sound your limbs: An excellent reward shall be his who doeth it, according as ye protect my house for its gods, and hearken to the Good God, Ramses II, given life."

---

[a]The mutilated beginning contained an address to Ramses II.
[b]Lit., "*divine water.*"

VI. TANIS STELÆ

487. The Tanis temple contained at least four large granite stelæ commemorating Ramses II's prowess in war. Of two[a] of these only insignificant fragments have survived; and the third[b] contains a conventional encomium much mutilated. At the end was the narrative of some specific event, of which the following is discernible:

He (Ramses II) said to the king's-messenger ——— fortresses equipped with everything for ———.

488. The fourth stela[c] is almost entirely the conventional praise of the king's valor;. but the last three lines contained a reference to rebellious Sherden and ships of war, which would indicate a naval battle in connection with the Libyan war, with whom the Sherden were, of course, allied.

Ramses' Valor

489. [1]Live the Horus, Mighty Bull.......... Ramses (II), given life, [2]forever, victorious king, valiant in the array, mighty, fighting myriads, overthrowing on his right, slaying on his left, like Set in his hour of rage, [3]mighty Bull, shaking every opposing country with the victories of his sword; protector of Egypt, repulsing the Nine Bows. Every land fears before him; he is like [4]a lion when he has tasted combat; no land can stand before him, King Ramses II; charging into the array, [5]he turns not back, he is the first of the front rank of his army; valiant upon the steed, when he takes his bow, shooting on his right, and he who stands in the rear[d] escapes him not; mighty in strength, [6]with victorious arm, bearing the mace and the shield; crushing the chiefs beneath his feet; no one is able to sustain the combat, every country flees before him, the terror of him is like fire behind them.[e]

---

[a]Petrie, *Tanis*, II, Pl. II, 76, 77.   [b]*Ibid.*, 78, bis.

[c]Rougé, *Inscriptions hiéroglyphiques*, 68–70 = Petrie, *Tanis*, II, Pl. II, 78. Both publications show many errors, for which each furnishes control of the other; Rougé has even omitted half a line (l. 8).

[d]Lit., "*behind the land.*"   [e]*Tanis*, II, has: "*in their heart.*"

Triumphs in Asia and Nubia

490. ⁷King Ramses II, given life; capturing the lands of the Asiatics (*S*ṭ·*tyw*) with his sword, carrying off their chiefs as living captives; ⁸great ruler, — — — — by the might of his youthful strength; ᵃbraveʳheartedⁱ before the mighty, valiant like Montu, defender of the land, ⁹husband of Egypt, rescuing her from every country. His fame is mighty in — — — — — the land of the Negro, with valor, slaying the Troglodytes of wretched Kush ¹⁰in the victories of his mighty sword. He causes Egypt to be joyful, and sets gladness of heart in Tomeri (Egypt), King [Ramses II] ⸺⸺; ¹¹plundering the chiefs of the Asiatics in their land. He has wasted the inheritance of —, making them to be ⸺⸺, ¹²slain under his feet, whose great sword is mighty among them.

Triumphs in the West

491. He has captured the countries of the West, causing them to be as that which [is] not ⸺⸺ ¹³[Sute]kh on his right, of the battle, King Ramses II. [He] has ferried overᵇ ⸺⸺ [come] ¹⁴to him, bearing their tribute; [his] fear [ʳpenetratesʳ] their heart. The rebellious-hearted Sherdenᶜ (*Š*ʾ-*r*ʾ-*d-ny*) ⸺⸺ ¹⁵them; mighty — — — — — ships of war in the midst of the [ʳseaʳ] ¹⁶⸺⸺ before them.

BUILDING INSCRIPTIONS

492. Although the name of Ramses II is more widely found upon the monuments of Egypt than that of any other king, no comprehensive building record of his, such as those

---

ᵃThe remainder of l. 8 from this point on was omitted by Rougé, who passes to the second half of l. 9 which he represents as the beginning of l. 9 ("*the land of the Negro, etc.*").

ᵇThis is the word used for crossing a river; it probably refers to a crossing of one of the branches of the Nile in the western Delta by Ramses or his western foes (see IV, p. 49, n. b).

ᶜThe Kadesh poem refers to the capture of Sherden before that campaign (§ 307); and Papyrus Anastasi II mentions "*the Sherden whom thou hast taken in thy might*" (V, 2), who have been sent as Egyptian mercenaries against the "*tribes of the desert.*" The reference to the "*Sherden of the sea, who are of the captivity of his majesty,*" may belong to the reign of Merneptah (Anastasi II, verso of Pl. 8, l. 1).

of the Eighteenth Dynasty, has survived to us. The great inscription of Abydos concerns almost solely Seti I's temple there, which is chiefly the work of Seti himself. The account of Ramses I's buildings preserved in his inscriptions is therefore but a slight indication of the vast extent of his building achievements; and this fact must be clearly borne in mind, in using the following inscriptions.[a]

493. They comprise:
I. Great Temple of Abu Simbel (§§ 495–99).
II. Small Temple of Abu Simbel (§§ 500, 501).
III. Temple of Serreh (§ 502).
IV. Temple of Derr (§ 503).
V. Temple of Sebûᶜa (§ 504).
VI. Temple of el Kab (§ 505).
VII. Temple of Luxor (§§ 506–8).
VIII. Temple of Karnak (§§ 509–13).
IX. The Ramesseum (§§ 514, 515).
X. Temple of Kurna (§§ 516–22).
XI. Seti I's Temple at Abydos and Great Abydos Inscription (§§ 262–77).
XII. Ramses II's Temple at Abydos (§§ 524–29).
XIII. Memphis Temples (§§ 530–37) and further:
  1. Great Abydos Inscription (§ 260, l. 22).
  2. Blessing of Ptah (§§ 412–413, ll. 32, 35).
XIV. City of Tanis (Blessing of Ptah, § 406, ll. 16–18).[b]

---

[a]For example, in Nubia Ramses II built at least six new temples: (1) Bet el-Walli; (2) Gerf Husen; (3) Es-Sebûᶜa; (4) Derr; (5) Abu Simbel (large temple); (6) Abu Simbel (small temple). Of these I was able to find the dedication inscriptions of the last four only.

[b]Poetical description of the city by an Egyptian scribe: Papyrus Anastasi II, Pl. I, l. 1–Pl. II, l. 5 = *ibid.*, IV, Pl. V, Pl. VI, ll. 1–10. It is in this passage that the message of the chief of Kheta (§§ 425, 426) to the chief of Kode is found (cf. Chabas, *Mélanges égyptologiques*, 2ᵉ sér., 151. Maspero, *Du genre épistolaire*, 102; Erman, *Aegypten*, 242). A longer description of the city in a similar vein is found in Papyrus Anastasi III, Pl. I, l. 11–Pl. III, l. 9 (cf. Chabas, *op. cit.*, 132–34, Maspero, *op. cit.*, 103–6; Brugsch, *Geschichte*, 545–48).

494. Besides the above, there are occasional unimportant doorway inscriptions, giving the building record in the conventional form as at Bet el-Walli, Kalabsheh[a] or a similar statue dedication as at Sebûᶜa. There must also be a number of architrave dedication inscriptions, like those of the Ramesseum, which are still unpublished.

I. GREAT TEMPLE OF ABU SIMBEL[b]

495. This, the most remarkable of the grotto temples of Egypt, was already far advanced in its construction, in the reign of Seti I. It is impossible to find any other explanation of the fact that an inscription of Ramses II's first year[c] is found in the doorway at the rear of the first hall, which connects it with the second hall.

496. The building inscription accompanies a relief[d] showing Ramses II enthroned, with an official named Ramses-eshahab (R^c-ms-sw-$^c\check{s}^{\,\text{ɔ}}$-hb) bowing before him. The inscription shows that Ramses II is instructing him to build a temple in honor of Horus of He,[e] which may be some other temple than that of Abu Simbel. There is no mention of any previous work by Seti I; and the interesting references to the use of foreign prisoners in the work might imply that it was done after the wars of Ramses had begun.

---

[a]Sharpe, *Egyptian Inscriptions*, II, 59.

[b]See Champollion, *Monuments*, 3–37; *Notices descriptives*, 43–77; Rosellini, *Monumenti Storici*, 114; Gau, *Antiquités de la Nubie*, 57–61; Lepsius, *Denkmäler*, III, 185–193; Dümichen, *Der ägyptische Felsentempel von Abu Simbel*, 1869.

[c]Lepsius, *Denkmäler*, III, 189, *a*.

[d]This relief has been published (with inscription) only in Champollion, *Monuments*, 9, where the text is plainly very badly copied. Wiedemann (*Aegyptische Geschichte*, 452, 453) would refer this inscription to some other as yet undiscovered building.

[e]This may be the temple of Ramses II at Serreh (called Aksche, Lepsius, *Denkmäler*, III, 191, *m*, *n*), ten miles north of Wadi Halfa (Sayce, *Recueil*, XVII, 163). It occurs also in the Middle Kingdom; see I, 602.

Before the said officer are the words:

King's-butler of his majesty, L. P. H., Ramses-eshahab, triumphant; he says: "As for all that comes out of thy mouth, it is like the words of Harakhte."

497. A longer inscription above and behind him is introduced by the full fivefold titulary of Ramses II, accompanied by poetic epithets, such as "*he who spreads out his wings over his army,*" and closing appropriately with "*maker of monuments in the house of Horus, his august father.*" The inscription then proceeds:

498. Behold, as for his majesty, L. P. H., he is vigilant in seeking [11]every profitable occasion, by doing excellent things for his father, Horus, [12]lord of He (H°),[a] making for him his house of myriads of years, by excavating in this mountain of He, ⌜which no⌝ one before ⌜did⌝, except the son of [13]Amon, lord of —. His might is in all lands; bringing for him multitudes of workmen from the captivity of his sword in every country. He has filled the houses ($pr \cdot w$) of the gods [14]with the children of[b] Retenu ($Rtnw$). ⌜Afterward he⌝ gave orders[c] to the king's-butler, Ramses-eshahab, to equip the land of Kush anew in the great name of his majesty, L. P. H. He said: "Praise to thee! O valiant king of Egypt, sun of the Nine Bows. There is no rebel in thy time, every land is pacified. Thy father, Amon, has decreed for thee that every land be beneath thy feet; he gives to thee south as well as north, west and east, and the isles in the midst of the sea.

499. A dedication[d] to Harakhte is as follows:

Ramses II; he made (it) as his monument for his father, Harakhte,[e] great god, lord of Nubia ($T^{\circ}\text{-}pd\cdot t$).

II. SMALL TEMPLE OF ABU SIMBEL

500. The smaller grotto temple on the north of the large temple was made by Ramses II for his queen, Nefretiri, as the divinity to whom it was dedicated:

---

[a]Name of the region in which Abu Simbel is located (see I, 602).
[b]"*The chiefs of,*" is probably omitted.   [c]Read *rdy m ḥr n.*
[d]Sharpe, *Egyptian Inscriptions*, II, 29; Lepsius, *Denkmäler*, III, 187, a, b.
[e]Variant: "*Amon-Re, king of gods.*"

ᵃRamses II; he made (it) as his monument for the Great King's-Wife, Nefretiri, beloved of Mut —, a house hewn in the pure mountain of Nubia (Tᵓ-$pd·t$), of fine, white and enduring sandstone, as an eternal work.

Its origin is sometimes also ascribed to the queen herself.

ᵇThe Great King's-Wife, Nefretiri, beloved of Mut; she made a house in the pure mountain.

501. Other references to the construction of the monument are these:

ᶜRamses-Meriamon, beloved of Amon, like Re, forever, made a house of very great monuments, for the Great King's-Wife, Nefretiri, fair of face — —.

His majesty commanded to make a house in Nubia (Tᵓ-$pd·t$), hewn in the mountain. Never was done the like before.

III. TEMPLE OF SERREH[d]

502. "Southward of the village of Serreh, ... on the western bank of the Nile, and about ten miles north of Halfa, are the foundations of a temple built by Ramses II." The architrave dedications have perished, but one of the doors still bears the words (twice):

Great door of Usermare-Setepnere; he made (it) as his monument for his living image in the land of Nubia (Tᵓ-$pd·t$); its beautiful name, which his majesty made, is: "Usermare-is-Splendid-in-Strength."

Ramses II was thus himself the god of this temple, as Amenhotep III was at the Nubian temple of Soleb.

IV. TEMPLE OF DERR

503. This temple was dedicated to Re-Harakhte by Ramses II. On its later history, see IV, §§ 474–83.

ᵃDedication from the hypostyle (Lepsius, *Denkmäler*, III, 192, *d*); variations of it in abbreviated form appear on the front, between the statues.

ᵇSharpe, *Egyptian Inscriptions*, II, 58; Lepsius, *Denkmäler*, III, 192, *c*.

ᶜOn façade; Lepsius, *Denkmäler*, III, 192, *b*.

ᵈSayce, *Recueil*, XVII, 163 f.

ªRamses II; he made (it) as his monument for his father, Harakhte; making for him the "House-ᵇof-Usermare-Meriamon-in-the-House-of-Re."

Ramses II; he made (it) as his monument for his father, Amon-Re, lord of Thebes (*Ns·wt-t>wy*); making for him a temple in the House of Re.

V. TEMPLE OF SEBÛᶜA

504. A so-called hemispeos, by the village of Sebûᶜa, built by Ramses II, who called it "*House of Amon.*" He was himself one of the deities worshiped in it.

The dedications are as follows:

ᶜRamses II; he made (it) as a monument for his father, Amon-Re, king of gods.

A pillar in the forecourt bears the following:ᵈ

Ramses-Meriamon in the House of Amon; he made (it) às his monument for his father, Amon-Re, making for him a great and august pillar, adorned with every splendid costly stone; that he might be given life, stability, and satisfaction, like Re, every day.

VI. TEMPLE OF EL KAB

505. A small temple to Nekhbet, built within the city wall by Ramses II, bears the following dedication:

ᵉ⌈Ramses II⌉; he made (it) as his monument for his mother, Nekhbet], making for her a great pylon, — ⌈— —⌉ of fine white sandstone, its length is 15 cubits; its door is of cedar, the ⌈mounting⌉ thereof of copper, ⌈with⌉ the great name of ⌈my majesty⌉ ———.

ªChampollion, *Notices descriptives*, I, 94 (first 94, there are two!); Lepsius, *Denkmäler*, III, 183, *a*.

ᵇAlso called "*Temple-of-Ramses-in-the-House-of-Re;*" Champollion, *Notices descriptives*, I, 91.

ᶜTwice in the cella; Lepsius, *Denkmäler*, III, 180.

ᵈLepsius, *Denkmäler*, III, 182, *b*.

ᵉAlong bottom of the left pylon of sandstone; Lepsius, *Denkmäler*, Text, IV, 37.

VII. TEMPLE OF LUXOR[a]

506. Ramses II built a peristyle court in front of the Eighteenth Dynasty Luxor temple, with a façade of two large pylon-towers. To do this, he destroyed a beautiful granite chapel of Thutmose III, which had stood in front of the Eighteenth Dynasty temple. The architect was the High Priest of Amon, Beknekhonsu, who has left a brief record of the building on his statue (§§ 561–68). The king's only building record, as far as published, is contained in the following dedication inscriptions:

507. [b]Mighty Bull, exalter of Thebes, Favorite of the Two Goddesses, establishing monuments in Luxor for his father, Amon, who placed him upon his throne; Golden Horus, seeking excellent things for him who fashioned him; King of Upper and Lower Egypt: Usermare-Setepnere. He made (it) as his monument for his father, Amon-Re, king of gods, making for him the "Temple ($ḥt$-ntr)-of-Ramses-Meriamon[c]-in-the-House (pr)-of-Amon," of fine white sandstone, which the Son of Re, Ramses-Meriamon, given life, like Re, forever, made for him.

508. The other two dedications are substantially the same as far as the words: *"house of Amon;"* one[d] then proceeds:

In front of Luxor, erecting for him a pylon ($bḫn·t$) anew; its flagstaves approach heaven; which the Son of Re, etc. (as above).

The other continues:[e]

Its beauty is unto the height of heaven, a place of the appearance for the lord of the gods, at his feast of (Luxor).

---

[a]On the history and construction of this temple, see the paper by Borchardt (*Zeitschrift für ägyptische Sprache*, 1896, 122–38); and Daressy, *Notice explicative des ruines du temple de Louxor* (Le Caire, 1893).

[b]Lepsius, *Denkmäler*, III, 149, a.

[c]The words "*Possessed of Eternity*" are added to Ramses' name in the name of this temple in at least one other occurrence of it (northwest corner, letter from Borchardt).

[d]Champollion, *Monuments*, 338, and Brugsch, *Thesaurus*, 1241.

[e]Brugsch, *Thesaurus*, 1242; verified from a photograph.

VIII. TEMPLE OF KARNAK

509. Ramses II brought to completion at Karnak the works begun by his two predecessors. He erected all of the columns in the southern half of the great hypostyle hall, except the two short rows immediately south of the nave, Seti I having completed the northern half, the nave with both rows of flower-columns and the first row of bud-columns of the southern half. Ramses II further built a girdle wall entirely around the Eighteenth Dynasty temple, to widen it to the increased width of the new hall in front. The Nineteenth Dynasty Karnak temple thus became the largest temple ever erected in the history of building, whether ancient or modern.

510. Although the conception, and for the most part the erection, of the great hall belong to Seti I and his father, the dedication inscriptions were largely added by Ramses II in his own name.

[a]Ramses II, mighty king, making monuments in the house of his father, Amon, building his house in eternal work, established forever. Lo, the Good God inclined his heart to make monuments, sleeping or waking, he ceased not seeking to do excellent things. It was his majesty who gave the regulations, and led the work on his monuments. All his plans come to pass immediately, like those of his father, Ptah-South-of-His-Wall, a likeness indeed of that which the excellent maker, the maker of excellent things, made, which his majesty made ——————— of excellent and eternal work. Every country is beneath thy feet, O king, ruler of the Nine Bows, Lord of the Two Lands, Ramses II. He made (it) as his monument for his father, Amon-Re, lord of Thebes ($Ns \cdot wt\ t \ni wy$), making for him the "Temple-of-the-Spirit-($Y \ni \d{h}$)-of-Ramses-Meriamon-in-the-House-of-Amon-over-against-Karnak ($Yp \cdot t\text{-}ys \cdot wt$)," of fine white sandstone; a resting-place for the lord of gods, a beautiful refuge for the divine ennead; surrounded by — columns; the walls thereof are like the two mountains of Aphroditopolis,

---

[a]Champollion, *Notices descriptives*, II, 66–68.

established, made very ⌜—⌝; its beauty (reaches) to the height of heaven.

Amon Speaks to the Gods

511. ᵃ"Behold ye, this beautiful, pure and enduring monument, which my son, of my body, my beloved, King Ramses II, hath made for me; whom I brought up from the womb, to make excellent things for my house; whom I have begotten in the fashion of my (own) limbs, to celebrate the 'Going Forth' of my ka. Ye shall endow him with satisfying life, ye shall form his protecting suite, and be his associate when he is with you. He shall be a spirit as ye are spirits; his name shall flourish as your names flourish to the end of the two periods (of sixty years) and forever; according to that which he has built for Karnak for the first time, of fine white sandstone. He hath given joy to my dwelling more than (his) predecessors have done......"

512. Ramses II; he made (it) as his monument for his father, Amon-Re, lord of Thebes, making for him the "Temple-of-the-Spirit-of-Ramses-Meriamon-in-the-House-of-Amon," of fine white sandstone. Its beauty (reaches) to the height of heaven, over against Karnak; its august columns are of electrum, made like every place that is in heaven. (It is) mistress of silver, queen of gold, it contains every splendid costly stone. "I have made it for thee with a loving heart, as a profitable son does for his father, by enlarging the monuments of him that begat him, and establishing the house of him that caused him to take the whole land."

ᵇLive the Good God, who makes monuments for his father, Amon-Re.

513. The dedications on the architravesᶜ of the nave, above the windows, are also of Ramses II, and only repeat the above dedications. The architect who erected the gigantic columns of the hypostyle was Hatey, who reverts to his achievement among his titlesᵈ thus:

ᵃArchitrave of first row of columns on the right; Champollion, *Notices descriptives*, II, 83, 84.

ᵇColumns of the first row on the left, Champollion, *Notices descriptives*, II, 79.

ᶜChampollion, *Notices descriptives*, II, 85.

ᵈStatue in Lady Meux's collection; see *Some Account of the Collection of Egyptian Antiquities in the Possession of Lady Meux*, by E. A. Wallis Budge, 143. I am indebted to Mr. Alan Gardiner for the reference.

Great chief of works on all the monuments of his majesty, erecting great columns in the House of Amon.

IX. THE RAMESSEUM

514. The beautiful mortuary temple of Ramses II on the west side at Thebes, known as the Ramesseum, was combined with a palace[a] which has since perished. The temple itself, while it has preserved some of the most important historical records of Ramses II's reign contains no building inscription except the usual dedication[b] on the architraves:

515. Ramses II; he made (it) as his monument for his father, Amon-Re, making for him a great and august broad-hall ($wsḫ·t$) of fine white sandstone, its nave[c] of great flower-columns, surrounded by bud-columns: a place of rest for the lord of gods at his beautiful "Feast of the Valley;" that he might, through him, be given life ———[d] shaping his sacred barque like the horizon-god, founding daily offerings, doing the things which please his father, causing that his house should be for him like Thebes, supplied with every good thing, granaries reaching heaven, an august treasury containing silver, gold, royal linen, every real costly stone, which King Ramses II brought for him.

---

[a]Lepsius, *Denkmäler*, III, 159, shows an "*Appearance of the king, like Re, in his palace* (c ḫ c) *which is in the temple* (ḥ·t ntr)." This fact was already noticed by Erman, *Aegypten*, 107, 108.

[b]Sharpe, *Egyptian Inscriptions*, II, 53; Brugsch, *Recueil de monuments*, 53, No. 2; Lepsius, *Denkmäler*, Text, III, 134 (see also 133). The name of the Ramesseum was: "*The-House* (ḥ·t)-*of-Usermare-Setepnere* (*Ramses II*),-*L.-P.-H.,-in-the-House-of-Amon*" (Wiedemann, *Zeitschrift für ägyptische Sprache*, 1883, 34); also mentioned on a stela at Vienna (*Recueil*, IX, 50, 51). An architect of the Ramesseum is mentioned on his fragmentary statue at Cairo (Daressy, *Recueil*, 22, 143); its treasurer (Lepsius, *Denkmäler*, Text, III, 249); and its deputy (*ibid.*, 250).

[c]The text has ḫft ḥrs, evidently meaning "*its center*," as the columns of the Ramesseum hypostyle are so arranged, and no other colonnades are thus placed in this temple. It is not an error, for it is repeated on another architrave (Lepsius, *Denkmäler*, Text, III, 134, with a slight mistake).

[d]The connection has been omitted by Sharpe, but it is evidently the conclusion of a second dedication.

X. TEMPLE OF KURNA

516. This mortuary temple of Seti I was left unfinished by him, and his son, Ramses II, states the fact in his inscriptions, narrating also that he completed it for his father; in doing which he made his own dedication inscriptions more prominent than those of his father.

517. ᵃHe made (it) as his monument for his father, Amon-Re, king of gods, lord of heaven, ruler of Thebes, restoring the house of his father, King Seti I, triumphant. Behold, he went to his retreat, he attained heaven, he joined Re in heaven; while this his house was in course of construction. Its doors were in ruin at their stations, and all its walls of stone and brick; no work therein was finished, neither inscriptions nor sculpture. Then his son, the Lord of the Two Lands, Ramses II, commanded to build the works in his house of millions of years, over against Karnak, and [to fashion] hisᵇ image resting in his house, gilded with electrum, when the god sails in ⌜person⌝ at his feast of the valley to rest inᶜ his house, as the first of the kings.

518. ᵈUtterance of the gods and goddesses who are in the Northland, to their son, King Ramses II, given life: "We have come to thee, our arms bearing offerings, and supplied with provision and food. We have gathered to thee every good thing of all that grows upon earth,ᵉ in order to make festive the house of thy father. As thou art his beloved son, so art thou like Horus, the protector of his father, in taking the inheritance of the Two Lands. How goodly is the [⌜son⌝] who restores what is ruined! Thou hast built the house of thy father, completed in its work, thou hast fashioned his image for ——— of gold ——— thou hast — divine offerings ——— I have — that

---

ᵃDevéria, *Bibliothèque égyptologique*, IV, 292, 293; Champollion, *Notices descriptives*, I, 694; Brugsch, *Recueil de monuments*, 51, 3; Lepsius, *Denkmäler*, III, 152, *a*; beginning also Lepsius, *Denkmäler*, Text, III, 91.

ᵇFrom here on, this text is found also in Devéria, *Bibliothèque égyptologique*, IV, 293, 294.

ᶜSee Piehl (*Zeitschrift für ägyptische Sprache*, 1887, 38), whose reading is confirmed by the duplicate.

ᵈSee also Champollion, *Notices descriptives*, I, 693.

ᵉThe following, to the word "*gold*," is also in Devéria, *Bibliothèque égyptologique*, IV, 294, 295.

which thou hast done ⌜again for⌝ the house of their father. Thou hast endowed it with satisfying life; as a benevolent son is, so art thou.

519. ᵃRamses II; he made (it) as his monument for his father, Amon-Re, lord of Thebes, presider over Karnak; restoring the house of his father, King Seti I. ———— they erected all its walls of — stone; no work therein was finished,ᵇ neither inscriptions nor sculpture ....ᶜ

520. ᵈRamses II; he made (it) as his monument for his father, Amon-Re, restoring for him the house of his father, King Seti I. Lo, (he is) in heaven ———— its doors are of real cedar, surrounded with walls of brick established forever, which the Son of Re, Ramses-Meriamon, made for him.ᵉ

521. Ramses II recognized the temple, however, as sacred also to his grandfather, as he indicates in these dedications:

ᶠRamses II; he made (it) as his monument for his father's father, the Good God, Ramses I, triumphant.

ᶠRenewal of the monument which King Ramses II made for his father's father, the Good God, Ramses I, in the monument of his father, the Lord of the Two Lands, Seti I.

ᵍRamses II; he made (it) as his monument for his father, the Good God, Menpehtire (Ramses I), making for him a house of millions of years on the west of Thebes, of good white sandstone, wherein Amon rests, like Re, in the horizon of heaven.ʰ

ᵃPiehl, *Inscriptions*, I, 145 A f.

ᵇRestored from the duplicate passage in § 517.

ᶜFrom here on, as in duplicate (§ 517).

ᵈChampollion, *Notices descriptives*, I, 296; Lepsius, *Denkmäler*, III, 152, *b;* Brugsch, *Recueil de monuments*, 51, 1.

ᵉAnother fragmentary dedication, Lepsius, *Denkmäler*, Text, III, 100; and a fragmentary door-dedication, Brugsch, *Recueil de monuments*, 51, 2.

ᶠChampollion, *Notices descriptives*, I, 307 and 704; Brugsch, *Recueil de monuments*, 52, 5; Lepsius, *Denkmäler*, III, 152, *g;* Lepsius, *Denkmäler*, Text, III, 94, 95.

ᵍChampollion, *Notices descriptives*, I, 705; Lepsius, *Denkmäler*, III, 152, *f*, also *e* with slight variant.

ʰSee further, Wilkinson, *Materia hieroglyphica*, Pl. I.

522. While acknowledging thus the original dedication of the temple to the mortuary service of his father and grandfather, Ramses added also a series of dedications in his own name alone. These are as follows:

ªRamses II; he made (it) as his monument to his father, for his father, Amon-Re, lord of Thebes, making for him a house of millions of years on the west of Thebes, (of) fine white sandstone, the doors thereof of real cedar, which [the Son of Re], Ramses-Meriamon, given life, like Re, made for him.

. . . . . . .ᵇ making for him a oroad-hall of appearance in front of his Great House, a place of appearance for the lord of gods at the "Feast of the Valley" ―――.

XI. SETI I'S TEMPLE AT ABYDOS

523. See Great Abydos Inscription (§§ 262–77).

XII. RAMSES II'S TEMPLE AT ABYDOSᶜ

524. This inscription contains a brief record of the building and endowment of Ramses II's mortuary temple at Abydos.

525. Lo, his majesty, L. P. H., was "Son-Whom-He-Loves," the champion of his father, Wennofer, by making for him a beautiful, august temple, established for eternity, of fine limestone of Ayan; a great double pylon of excellent work; portals of granite, the doors thereto of copper, wrought with figures in real electrum; a great seat of alabaster, mounted in granite, his excellent seat of the beginning; a meskhen-chamber for his divine ennead, his august father who rests therein, and Re when he has reached heaven. His protecting image is beside him that fashioned him, like Horus, upon the throne of his father.

526. (He) established for him permanent daily offerings, at the beginnings of the seasons, all feasts at their times, offered to his ka.

ªChampollion, *Notices descriptives*, I, 696.

ᵇOmitting introductory formula, which is as in preceding.

ᶜInscription engraved on the exterior of the south wall of Ramses II's temple at Abydos; published by Mariette, *Abydos*, II, Pl. 3 (cf. *ibid.*, II, § 139); see also Mariette, *Voyage dans la haute Egypte*, I, 29.

He filled it with every thing, overflowing with food and provision, bulls, calves, oxen, geese, bread, wine, fruit; (it) was filled with peasant-slaves, doubled in fields, made numerous in her_ds; the granaries were filled to bursting, the grain-heaps approached heaven, —[a] for the storehouse of divine offerings, from the captivity of his victorious sword.

527. His treasury was filled with every costly stone, silver, gold in blocks; the magazine was filled with every thing from the tribute of all countries. He planted many gardens, set with every (kind of) tree, all sweet and fragrant woods, the plants of Punt. The Son of Re, Lord of Diadems, Ramses-Meriamon, beloved of Osiris, First of the Westerners, great god, lord of Abydos, made (it) for him.

528. The dedications of the temple doors are as follows:[b]

1. He made (it) as his monument for his father, Osiris, residing in "House ($ḥ·t$)-of-Ramses-Meriamon-Possessing-Abydos;" making for him a doorway of black granite, the doors mounted with copper, and gilded with electrum,[c] which his son, Ramses II, made for him.

2. Live the god, the Lord of the Two Lands, Ramses II. He made (it) as his monument for his father, Osiris, lord of Abydos, making for him a great doorway of pink granite, the doors of bronze in beaten work (called): "Portal-of-Usermare-Setepnere-Raiser-of-Monuments-in-Abydos."

529. The dedication inscription of the shrine-chamber is partially preserved on a fragment of alabaster, thus:

He made (it) as his monument for his father, Osiris, making for him a "Great Seat" of pure alabaster ———.

XIII. MEMPHIS TEMPLES[d]

530. Ramses II built largely at Memphis, and a temple on the south of the sacred lake was chiefly due to him.

---

[a]There is a sign for "*slave*" here, but a verb (?) is lacking in the lacuna.

[b]Brugsch (*Recueil de monuments*, I, Pl. XII), who does not state (p. 22) in which temple he found them. The numbers refer to those on his plate.

[c]These doors are said to be "*of electrum*" in an inscription at the base of the same door. Its name is also given there as the "*Portal-of-Usermare-Setepnere-Possessed-of-Eternity.*"

[d]See Maspero, *Struggle of the Nations*, 422, 423; Wiedemann, *Aegyptische Geschichte*, 445, note 3; H. Brugsch, (*Zeitschrift für ägyptische Sprache*, VII, 2),

One of his temples there was called "*The-House-of-Millions-of-Years-of-King-Usermare-Setepnere-in-the-House-of-Amon-in-Memphis.*"[a] But Ramses' works in Memphis have perished with the city. The chief literary references to them are in the Great Abydos Inscription (§ 260, l. 22), and the Blessing of Ptah (§§ 412, 413, ll. 32–35). A paragraph in a letter of instructions from an official to his subordinate refers to Ramses II's Thoth-temple in Memphis, and mentions repairs on the Sphinx, which may be of later date:

531. [b]I have heard that thou hast taken the eight laborers ($h^3 y$) who were working in the "House-of-Thoth-of-Ramses-Meriamon,-L.-P.-H.,-Satisfied-with-Truth" in Memphis. Thou shalt deliver them to draw stone for[c] the Sphinx in. Memphis.

532. References to Ramses II's Ptah-temple are rare. The following interesting building inscription[d] is so fragmentary that the name of the king is uncertain. As it lies in the temple chiefly due to Ramses II, he is the most probable king to whom we may refer it. It was upon a great stela which marked the "*Station of the King*," or ceremonial station occupied by the Pharaoh during the official ritual ceremonies. Like similar stelæ at Thebes in the temples

---

gives brief mention of Mariette's excavations here (see also Mariette, *Monuments divers*, 31). De Morgan's later excavations are briefly described by E. Brugsch (*Egypt Exploration Fund Archæological Report*, 1892–93, 24, 25). Daressy studied the remains exhumed in 1887–8 and 1892 by the Service, with plan of the temple of Ramses II (*Annales*, III, 22–31).

[a]*Ynbw-ḥd*, Mariette, *Monuments divers*, 62, b = Rougé, *Inscriptions hiéroglyphiques*, XXX; cf. also Mariette, *Monuments divers*, 63 f.

[b]Spiegelberg, *Recueil*, 17, 158. Papyrus Turin, 19, 2.

[c]Or: "*to.*" Vyse found an incomplete stela of Ramses II between the feet of the Sphinx.

[d]Fragment of a large stela of gritstone still 13 feet high and over 2½ feet wide. The beginnings of 12 horizontal lines are preserved. It was found in the ruins of Ramses II's Memphite temple of Ptah; published by Daressy, *Annales*, III, 27, 28. Fragments of two other similar stelæ, too scanty for use here, were also found by Daressy in this temple (*ibid.*, 28).

of Amenhotep III (II, 904, 910), Elephantine (II, 791), and Amâda (II, 791–97), it bore an account of the erection of the building in which it stood. As in the building inscriptions of Thutmose III (II, 131 ff.), Amenhotep III (II, 878–92), and others, it is introduced by an account of the king's coronation. Enough of the fragmentary inscription is preserved, to show that, as in the coronations of Thutmose III and Harmhab, Amon appeared in public, delivered an oracle proclaiming him king, and proceeded to the palace to crown him. In all probability, therefore, the oracle and the crowning by Amon, were the regular custom at the accession of every king in the Empire. Hence the innumerable conventional references to Amon's having fixed the diadem upon the Pharaoh's head designate an actual ceremony. That this prerogative of Amon was not originally his, but was usurped from Re, is evident. Undoubtedly a similar ceremony took place at Heliopolis at the accession of every Pharaoh, from the Fifth Dynasty on, to the assumption of the rite by Amon at an uncertain date after the rise of Thebes.

Amon and His Gods Come Forth

533. [1]———— [2]— his house of Luxor, with his ennead ($psd\cdot t$) behind him. When the land brightened again, and day came ————.

Oracle Naming King

534. ———— [3]Thou art my son, the heir who came forth from my limbs. As I am, shalt thou be, with none except thee ————. [4]Their offerings shall be doubled, they shall recognize thee as my son who came forth from my limbs. I have gathered ————.

Coronation in the Palace

535. ———— [5]coming to him, to the palace. He placed himself before him in the shrine of his august son ———— [6]Amon ⌜—⌝. Lo, Amon came, with his son before him, to the palace, to fix his diadem upon his head, to exalt the two plumes ————.

Character of Reign

536. ——— ⁷that he might do what satisfies thee. He has avoided deceit, and expelled lying from the land, while his laws are firm, in the administration of the regulations of the ⌈ancestors⌉ ——— ⁸diadem ⌈—⌉. He has ⌈—⌉ the circuit of the sun, all lands are together doing the ⌈service⌉ of this great god, ⌈—⌉ like ———.

Station of the King, and Building Inscription

537. ⁹He made (it) as his monument for his father, Ptah-South-of-His-Wall, making for him a "Station of the Ruler"ᵃ of gritstone, over against ⌈—⌉ᵇ ——— ¹⁰ᶜdoors upon themᶜ of real cedar, in order to make splendid the house of ⌈—⌉,ᵈ in order to purify the way which his father, Ptah, treads. He gave to him a house anew ——— ¹¹of — cubits, of every splendid costly stone; its flagstaves are of real cedar, wrought with Asiatic copper, their tips of electrum. A broad-hall was made ⌈—⌉ ——— . . . . . . .ᵉ

XIV. CITY OF TANIS

See Blessing of Ptah (§ 406, ll. 16–18); see also above note on XIV, p. 211.

STELA OF THE YEAR 400ᶠ

538. This monument was erected at Tanis by an important official of Ramses II, named Seti. He had been dispatched thither to erect a stela in honor of Seti I, and improved the

---

ᵃThe determinative is a stela, as elsewhere. The place meant is the same as at Thebes, Elephantine, and Amâda, see II, 140, note. The material above mentioned, "*gritstone*," is that of the stela bearing the inscription, which is here meant. It stood therefore in the holy of holies, and not at the front of the temple, as Daressy thought (*Annales*, III, 28).

ᵇ$Y \cdot dr \cdot t$, with determinative of a house.

ᶜProbably ⸤ ⸥ $w\ hr\cdot sn$.

ᵈPossibly Daressy has omitted R ⸢, and we should read "*Ramses;*" or *mss* is vulgar writing for *ms-sw* = "*He who begat him.*"

ᵉThe last line is obscure, but it is clear that the account of the building is concluded in l. 11.

ᶠGranite stela discovered at Tanis by Mariette and reburied there by him. It could not be found at the excavation of Tanis by Petrie (*Tanis*, II, 32); hence

opportunity to place a stela of his own, bearing a record of his visit in the temple, to which he appended prayers for the favor of the god, as so many officials did in Abydos. Although headed with the full titulary of Ramses II, the document is dated in the four hundredth year of King Opehtiset-Nubti, a Hyksos ruler. This remarkable fact shows that the reign of this king began an era—the only one known in Egypt—which had survived in use at Tanis into the Ramessid times.[a] Unfortunately, the stela does not give the year of Ramses II in which it was erected. Wiedemann dates it, as it seems to me with probability, at Ramses II's death. In any case, the knowledge of the lapse of 400 years between the Hyksos Nubti and some year of Ramses II is of great value.

539. At the top of the monument is a relief, showing Ramses II offering wine to Set. Behind the king stands Seti, the author of the monument, praying, as follows:

— — — thy ka, O Set, son of Nut, mayest thou grant a happy life following thy ka, to the ka of . . . .[b] [Seti].

540. Below the relief is Seti's record of his commission, with the appended prayer, as follows:

Live . . . .[c] King Ramses II, sovereign, who equips the Two Lands with monuments in his name, so that Re rises in heaven for love of him, King Ramses II.

541. His majesty commanded to make a great stela of granite

---

it has never been in Bulak, as stated by Birch (*Records of the Past*, IV, 33). A notice of the discovery was published by de Rougé (*Revue archéologique*, N. S., IX, 1864, 128–36), and the monument itself by Mariette (*ibid.*, N. S., XI, 1865, Pl. IV and pp. 169–90); and Bunsen, *Egypt's Place*, 2d ed., V, 734 f. See also Chabas, *Zeitschrift für ägyptische Sprache*, 1865, 29 ff.; Wiedemann, *ibid.*, 1879, 138 ff.; and Piehl, *Recueil*, II, 121, 122.

[a]Wiedemann thought that it was still later in use, and that Manetho, as excerpted by Africanus, dates the death of Bokkhoris in the year 990 of this era (see *Zeitschrift für ägyptische Sprache*, 1879, 138 ff.); but this conclusion is due to a misunderstanding.

[b]Seti's titles as below. [c]Full fivefold titulary.

(*ynr-n-m ᴐ · t*), in the great name of his fathers, in order that the name of his grandfather,[a] King Menmare, Son of Re: Seti-Merneptah, might be exalted, enduring and abiding forever, like Re, every day.

542. In the year 400, in the fourth month of the third season, on the fourth day, of the King of Upper and Lower Egypt: Opehtiset (*Cᴐ-phty-St*); Son of Re, his beloved: Nubti,[b] whom Harakhte desires to be forever and ever; came the hereditary prince, governor of the (residence) city, vizier, fan-bearer on the right of the king, chief of bowmen, governor of foreign countries, commandant of the fortress of Tharu (*T ᴐ -rw*), chief of the foreign gendarmes, king's-scribe, master of horse, chief priest of the Ram-god, lord of Mendes, High Priest of Set, ritual priest of Buto-Upet-Towe, chief of prophets of all gods, Seti, triumphant, son of the hereditary prince, governor of the (residence) city, vizier, chief of bowmen, governor of foreign countries, commandant of the fortress of Tharu, king's-scribe, master of horse, Peramses, triumphant; born of the lady (*nb·t-pr*), the musician of Re (*P ᴐ -R ᶜ*), Teya (*Ty-ᴐ*), triumphant. He said: "Hail to thee, O Set, son of Nut, great in strength in the barque of millions of years, ⸢overthrowing enemies⸣ in front of the barque of Re, great in terror, ——— [grant m]e a happy life following thy ka, while I remain in ———."

ROYAL JUBILEE INSCRIPTIONS

543. The sources for the jubilee celebrations of Ramses II are fuller than for those of any other king. Unfortunately, his obelisks, although far more numerous[c] than those of his

---

[a]Seti I was not the grandfather, but the father, of Ramses II; hence Wiedemann has suggested (*Zeitschrift für ägyptische Sprache*, 1879, 142) that when the upper part of the stela containing the titulary, etc., of Ramses II had been completed, Ramses died, and "*his majesty*" refers to his son and successor, who sent confirmatory orders for the erection of the monument in Seti I's honor. Seti I could then be referred to as his majesty's grandfather. The rendering "*grandfather*" is, however, open to objection; it is possible that we should render: "*father of his fathers*," although it is a question how much attention should be paid to the plural strokes after "*father*" in a text of this age.

[b]This name is thought by some to refer to the god Set, but, of course, no one in the time of Ramses II believed that Set ruled 400 years before! [Later: See the same view by Ed. Meyer, *Aegyptische Chronologie*, 66.]

[c]Ramses II erected no less than fourteen obelisks at Tanis alone (Petrie, *Tanis*, I, Pl. VII–XI; Rougé, *Inscriptions hiéroglyphiques*, 194–97); then the well-

ancestors, bear inscriptions of a very vague and general nature, extolling the king's power and glory,[a] and containing no references to the royal jubilees, to celebrate which they were erected. Indeed, they do not, for the most part, show even the former conventional dedication inscription.[b]

544. A good example of this, is the Heliopolis obelisk, left uninscribed by Seti I, which was then inscribed by Ramses II, who with, for him, unusual generosity, appropriated only one side for his own inscription. Its inscriptions are as follows:[c]

North Side

545. . . . .[d] (Seti I), whose monuments are excellent in Heliopolis seat of eternity, like the four pillars of heaven, abiding, enduring at

---

known pair in Luxor (one now in Paris); a pair in Karnak (Lepsius, *Denkmäler*, III, 148, *a*); four now in Rome (one a forgery); one now in Florence; besides usurping those of his predecessors, particularly that of his father, Seti I, at Heliopolis. A Berlin scarab (No. 1947, *Ausführliches Verzeichniss des Berliner Museums*, 420), commemorates the erection of obelisks by him. A pair of obelisks taken out of the Elephantine quarry, probably by Ramses, are commemorated by the official in charge in an inscription on the island of Sehel, thus: "*Real king's-confidant, his beloved, conducting the work on two great obelisks, High Priest of Khnum, Anuket, and Satet, Amenhotep.*" (Mariette, *Monuments divers*, V, 70, No. 17 = Brugsch, *Thesaurus*, V, 1214 = de Morgan, *Catalogue des monuments*, 94, 140 = Lepsius, *Denkmäler*, Text, IV, 125, [6]. Not in Petrie, *Season in Egypt*, but see No. 58, *ibid.*)

[a]The historical references in the obelisk inscriptions will be found in § 392 and § 448, note.

[b]As the obelisks at Tanis are all prostrate, there may be dedications on the hidden sides, which have never been turned up. The only dedication to be found on any of Ramses II's obelisks thus far is on the two Luxor obelisks. The one still in Luxor reads (Sharpe, *Egyptian Inscriptions*, II, 60): "*He made (it) as his monument for his father, Amon-Re, erecting for him two great obelisks of granite.*" The other one, now in Paris, reads: "*Ramses II; he made (it) as his monument for his father, Amon-Re, making for him a great obelisk (called): 'Ramses-Meriamon-is-the-Beloved-of-Atum.'*" (Sharpe, *Egyptian Inscriptions*, I, 42, 43; Saint-Maur, *Voyage du Luxor en Egypte* [Paris, 1835], Pl. II; Champollion-Figeac, *L'Obélisque de Louqsor transporté à Paris* [Paris, 1833].) For Beknekhonsu's record of the erection of these Luxor obelisks, see his statue inscription (§§ 561–68).

[c]*Interpretatio Obeliscorum Urbis* . . . . . . digesta per A. M. Ungarellium (Romæ, MDCCCXLII), Tab. II; Sharpe, *Egyptian Inscriptions*, II, 66; *Transactions of the Royal Society of Literature*, 2d ser., I, opp. p. 176 (drawings by Bonomi), Marucchi, *Gli Obelischi Egiziani di Roma* (Rome, 1898), Tav. III, IV.

[d]Full titulary, except fifth name.

the forecourt of Re. The ennead of gods is satisfied with his deeds. (May) the Son of Re, Seti-Merneptah, beloved of the gods of Heliopolis, [live] like Re.

South Side

546. .... (Seti I), who adorned Heliopolis for him who is therein, who purified it for Re, its lord; the lords of heaven and earth rejoice; his favor is doubled because of his deeds. May the Son of Re, Seti-Merneptah, beloved of Harakhte, live through him, like Re.

West Side

547. .... (Seti I), who filled Heliopolis with obelisks, shining with rays; the house of Re is flooded with his beauty, and the gods of the Great House rejoice. May the Son of Re, Seti-Merneptah, beloved of the ennead of gods which is in the Great House, be given life through him (*nf*).

East Side

548. .... Ramses (II), who has made his monuments like the stars of heaven, whose works mingle with the sky, rejoicing over which Re rises in his house of millions of years. It was his majesty who beautified[a] this monument for his father, in order to cause that his name should abide in the house of Re. May Ramses (II)-Meriamon, beloved of Atum, lord of Heliopolis, be given life through him (*nf*).

549. It will be seen that the obelisk has become more and more a monument of a general character in celebration of the king's glory, and has lost its exclusive significance as a memorial of the royal jubilee. This is indicated also by the fact that memorial inscriptions commemorating the celebration of the royal jubilees are to be found in Upper Egypt from el Kab to Philæ, as if other record than the obelisks were necessary. From these commemorative inscriptions the following table of jubilees may be reconstructed:[b]

---

[a]That is, added the inscriptions. "*Beautifying*" is used in the same way by Thutmose IV on the obelisk of his grandfather, Thutmose III (II, 833).

[b]The Roman numerals in the following footnotes refer to the nine inscriptions (§§ 552–60). My list (*Zeitschrift für ägyptische Sprache*, 39, 60, note), which follows Brugsch, is to be corrected as herein.

550. Year 30,[a] first jubilee.
Year 33,[b]
Year 34,[c] } second jubilee.
Year 37,[d] third jubilee.
Year 40,[e] fourth jubilee.
Year 41,[f]
Year 42, } fifth jubilee.
Year 44,[g] sixth jubilee.
Year [47?],[h] seventh jubilee.
Year [50?],[i] eighth jubilee.
Year [53?],[i] ninth jubilee.

551. Most of these celebrations, at least as far as the year 41, were in charge of Ramses II's favorite son, Khamwese,[j] assisted by another son, Khay, who continued later.

I. FIRST GEBEL SILSILEH INSCRIPTION[k]

552. Year 30. First occurrence of the royal jubilee of the Lord of the Two Lands, Usermare-Setepnere, given life forever.

[His majesty commanded] to celebrate the royal jubilee in the whole land.

King's-son, (sem-) priest, Khamwese, triumphant.[1]

---

[a]I, II, III, IV, V.   [b]II, p. 232, n. b.   [c]II, III, IV, V.

[d]II, III, IV (called by mistake the fourth jubilee), V (so Champollion; Brugsch has 36).

[e]III, IV, V, VI.   [f]Year 41, VII; year 42, VIII.

[g]VIII.

[h]Year unknown; its celebration is rendered certain by the certainty of eighth and ninth.

[i]Berlin scarabs, No. 3549 (*Ausführliches Verzeichniss des Berliner Museums*, 420) and No. 5081 (*Zeitschrift für ägyptische Sprache*, 1891, 128), giving only number of jubilee without date.

[j]On the monuments of this son, which are too fragmentary for insertion here, see Wiedemann, *Aegyptische Geschichte*, 464–66.

[k]Lepsius, *Denkmäler*, III, 175 f.; Brugsch, *Thesaurus*, V, 1127 (without relief); and Champollion, *Notices descriptives*, I, 252.

[1]Relief showing Khamwese in the costume of a high priest of Memphis.

II. BIGEH INSCRIPTION[a]

553. Year 30. First occurrence of the royal jubilee. Year 34.[b] Repetition of the royal jubilee. Year 37.[c] Third occurrence of the royal jubilee.

Of the Lord of the Two Lands: Usermare-Setepnere, Lord of Diadems: Ramses-Meriamon, given life forever. His majesty commissioned the (*sm-*) priest, the king's-son, Khamwese, to celebrate the royal jubilees in the whole land.

III. SECOND GEBEL SILSILEH INSCRIPTION[d]

554. Year 30. First occurrence of the royal jubilee.
Year 34. Repetition of the royal jubilee.
Year 37. Third occurrence of the royal jubilee.
Year 40. Fourth occurrence of the royal jubilee.

Under the Lord of the Two Lands, Usermare-Setepnere, Lord of Diadems, Ramses-Meriamon, given life forever.

His majesty commanded to commission the (*sm-*) priest, king's-son, Khamwese, to celebrate the royal jubilees in the whole [land] in South and North.

IV. THIRD GEBEL SILSILEH INSCRIPTION[e]

555. This inscription is a duplicate of the preceding, the lacuna in which it supplies. It shows an incorrect variant, calling the jubilee of year 37, the fourth.

---

[a]On the rocks of the island of Bigeh: Champollion, *Notices descriptives*, I, 162; Sharpe, *Egyptian Inscriptions*, II, 58; Young, *Hieroglyphics*, 42; Lepsius, *Denkmäler*, Text, IV, 175; Brugsch, *Recueil de monuments*, II, 83, 3. De Morgan (*Catalogue des monuments*) has omitted this inscription.

[b]Another inscription on the island of Sehel (Bigeh, Brugsch, *Thesaurus*, V, 1128; but Mariette, *Monuments divers*, 71, No. 32, and de Morgan, *Catalogue des monuments*, 88. No. 62, give Sehel) has: "*Year 33; repetition of the royal jubilee of the Lord of the Two Lands, Ramses II.*"

[c]The "39" given by Wiedemann (*Aegyptische Geschichte*, 465) is taken from Brugsch, *Recueil de monuments*, which has 39; but it is an error, as all the other publications have 37, except Champollion, *Notices descriptives*, which has 36.

[d]At the right of the entrance of the great rock temple of Harmhab at Gebel Silsileh (Champollion, *Monuments*, 116). Over the inscription Ramses II and Khamwese appear in a relief, worshiping Ptah and Sebek of Gebel Silsileh.

[e]At the left of the entrance of the great rock temple of Harmhab at Gebel Silsileh: Champollion, *Monuments*, 115. Above the inscription is a relief in which Ramses II and Khamwese appear in worship before Ptah-Tatenen and Amen-rasonther.

V. FOURTH GEBEL SILSILEH INSCRIPTION[a]

556. Year 30. First occurrence of the royal jubilee.
Year 34. Repetition of the royal jubilee.
Year 37.[b] Third occurrence of the royal jubilee.
Year 40. Fourth occurrence of the royal jubilee.

Under the Lord of the Two Lands, Usermare-Setepnere, Lord of Diadems: Ramses-Meriamon, given life, like Re, forever.

His majesty commanded to commission the hereditary prince, (*mry-ntr-*) priest, attached to Nekhen, prophet of Mat, chief justice, judge, governor of the (residence) city, vizier, Khay, triumphant, to celebrate the royal jubilees [in the] whole [land], in South and North.

VI. SEHEL INSCRIPTION[c]

557. Year 40. Came the king's-son, (*sm-*) priest of Ptah, satisfying the heart of the Lord of the Two Lands, Khamwese, to celebrate the [fourth] royal jubilee [in the who]le [land in South and North].

VII. EL KAB INSCRIPTION[d]

558. Year 41. Came the king's-son, (*sm-*) priest of Ptah, satisfying the heart of the Lord of the Two Lands, Khamwese, to celebrate the fifth royal jubilee [in the wh]ole [lan]d.

---

[a]Large stela at the right of the door of the great rock chapel of Harmhab at Gebel Silsileh, published by Champollion, *Monuments*, 118; Brugsch, *Recueil de monuments*, II, 83; and Brugsch, *Thesaurus*, V, 1128 (without relief and quite incorrectly). Over the inscription, before the dates, kneels Khay, and still higher appears Ramses II before Amon-Re, Harakhte, Mat, Ptah-Tatenen, and Re-Sebek of Gebel Silsileh.

[b]Brugsch has 36.

[c]On the rocks of the island of Sehel at the first cataract: Mariette, *Monuments divers*, 71, No. 33, and de Morgan, *Catalogue des monuments*, 103, No. 33, where de Morgan's copyists have evidently reproduced Mariette's copy, without finding the original. The second jubilee is also referred to on Sehel (see II, p. 232, n. b).

[d]According to Lepsius, this inscription is in the temple of Amenhotep III (Lepsius, *Denkmäler*, III, 174, *d*); whereas Brugsch puts it in the tomb of Setau (*Thesaurus*, V, 1128). Wiedemann (*Aegyptische Geschichte*, 465, n. 5) evidently thinks there are two such inscriptions; one in the temple, and one in the tomb; but that given by Lepsius, *Denkmäler*, is certainly the same as that placed by Brugsch in the tomb of Setau. A relief over the inscription shows Khamwese in obeisance to his father, enthroned as Osiris.

VIII. FIFTH GEBEL SILSILEH INSCRIPTION[a]

559. Year 42, first month of the second season, day 1, of King Ramses II, given life, forever and ever. His majesty commanded to commission the vizier Khay ($Ḫ ͑ y$), to inaugurate the fifth royal jubilee of King Ramses II, in the whole land.

IX. SIXTH GEBEL SILSILEH INSCRIPTION[b]

560. Year 44.[c] First month of the second season, day 1, under the majesty of the king, the Lord of the Two Lands, Usermare-Setepnere, given life forever — —; Son of Re, Lord of Diadems, Ramses-Meriamon, given life, like Re, forever.

His majesty commanded to com[mission] the hereditary prince (*mry-ntr-*) priest, chief justice, judge, governor of the (residence) city, vizier, Khay, [triumphant, to celebr]ate the sixth royal jubilee, in the whole land, in the districts of South and North.

INSCRIPTION OF BEKNEKHONSU[d]

561. The most important of Ramses II's officials who has transmitted a mortuary autobiography to us, was Beknekhonsu, the High Priest of Amon. He tells us every step in his career, with the length of each office, as follows:

---

[a]Legrain, *Recueil*, XXVI, 219, n. 3.

[b]Stela on the right of the entrance of the great rock chapel of Harmhab at Gebel Silsileh; published by Champollion, *Monuments*, 119; Brugsch, *Recueil de monuments*, 83, 2: Brugsch, *Thesaurus*, V, 1128, IV. A relief above the inscription shows Ramses II accompanied by Mat, before Amon, Mut, Khonsu, Harakhte, and Sebek of Gebel Silsileh. Below the inscription is Khay kneeling, with a few lines of adoration before him.

[c]So Brugsch; Champollion, *Monuments*, has 45.

[d]On the back of a squatting statue of Beknekhonsu, now in the Glyptothek at Munich (No. 30). It was carefully published by Devéria, *Mémoires de l'Institut égyptien*, 1862, I, 701–54; reprinted in *Bibliothèque égyptologique*, IV, 276–323 (plate opposite p. 288). A collation with a photograph showed the text to be without error. It was again inaccurately published by Brugsch (*Thesaurus*, 1240 f., where even a year is incorrect: 6 for 27! l. 3). The tomb of Beknekhonsu was found by Champollion (*Notices descriptives*, I, 538) at Thebes in Assasif; smaller objects from his tomb are noted by Devéria (*Bibliothèque égyptologique*, IV, 295, 296).

Infancy, 4 years, from 1 to 4.

Youth, 12 years, from 5 to 16. (Being chief of the stable at least a part of this time.)

Priest, 4 years, from 17 to 20.

Divine father, 12 years, from 21 to 32.

Third prophet, 15 years, from 33 to 47.

Second prophet, 12 years, from 48 to 59.

High Priest,[a] 27 years, from 60 to 86.

562. Beginning under Seti I, he must have been of about the same age as Ramses II, and was likewise the only official known to us who survived almost if not quite, as long as the aged Ramses himself.[b] In addition to his sacerdotal duties, he was also chief architect, and as such built a temple for Ramses II, "*at the upper portal of the house of Amon,*" which can only be the Luxor temple of Ramses II. He also refers to its obelisks, its flagstaves, its lake, its gardens, and other accessories which he provided for the temple. He is further found serving as judge in a civil suit in the forty-sixth year of Ramses II.[c]

Titles

563. [1]Hereditary prince, count, High Priest of Amon, Beknekhonsu, triumphant; he says:

Career

564. "I was a truthful witness, profitable to his lord, extolling the instruction of his god, proceeding upon his way, performing the excellent

---

[a]Lit., "*First prophet.*" Brugsch's six years as the length of service in this office (*Thesaurus* and *Geschichte*, 566) is an error; I have especially compared the photograph on this point.

[b]The statue of a Beknekhonsu, High Priest of Amon under Ramses III, found in the temple of Mut (Benson and Gourlay, *The Temple of Mut in Asher*, 343-47), cannot, for reasons of chronology, as well as because at least two high priests held office in the interim, be identified as that of our Beknekhonsu.

[c]Papyrus Berlin No. 47, l. 4; *Zeitschrift für ägyptische Sprache*, XVII, 1879, 72, and Taf. I.

ceremonies in the midst of his temple. I was chief overseer of works in the house of Amon, satisfying the excellent heart of his lord. O all ye people, take account in ²your hearts; ye who are on earth, who shall come after me, in millions of millions of years, after old age and infirmity, whose hearts are versed in discerning worth; I will inform you of my character while I was upon earth, in every office which I administered since my birth."

565. 1. "I passed four years in extreme childhood (*nḏs*).

2. I passed twelve years as ³a youth (*ḥwn*), while I was chief of the training-stableᵃ of King Menmare (Seti I).

3. I acted as priest (*w ͨ b*) of Amon, during four years.

4. I acted as divine father of Amon, during twelve years.

5. I acted as third prophet of Amon during fifteen years.

6. I acted as second prophet of Amon during twelve years.

7. Heᵇ favored me, he distinguished me, because of my rare merit. He appointed me to be High Priestᶜ of Amon during twenty-seven years."

Character

566. "I was ⁴a good father to my serf-laborers, training their classes, giving my hand [to] him who was in trouble, preserving alive him who was in misfortune, performing the excellent duties in his temple. I was chief overseer of works before Thebes for his son, who came forth from his limbs, King Ramses II, given life, maker of monuments for his father, Amon, ⁵who placed him on his throne."

The assistant, the High Priest of Amon, Beknekhonsu, triumphant, made (it).

Building of Luxor Temple

567. He says as follows: "I performed the excellent duties in the house of Amon, being chief overseer of works of my lord. I made for him a temple (called): 'Ramses-Meriamon-Hearer-of-Petitions,' at

---

ᵃ*Š· ḥpr.* See Erman, *Festschrift für Georg Ebers,* 444, 445.

ᵇThis may refer to either the king or the god, but it probably refers to the god, as in l. 4.

ᶜLit., "*first prophet of Amon,*" being in direct succession from the rank of third and second prophet.

the upper[a] portal of the house (*pr*) of Amon. I erected obelisks[b] therein, of granite, whose beauty approached heaven. A wall ⁶was before it of stone over against Thebes; it was flooded;[c] and the gardens were planted with trees. I made very great double doors of electrum; their beauty met the heavens. I hewed very great flagstaves, and I erected them in the august forecourt in front of his temple."

Sacred Barges

568. "I hewed great barges of the 'Beginning-of-the-River,' for Amon, Mut, and Khonsu; by the hereditary prince, High Priest of Amon, Beknekhonsu."

---

[a]This is the southern gate of the temenos of the Karnak temple toward Luxor, to which the four southern pylons of Karnak led. At this portal the great obelisk of Thutmose III was erected by Thutmose IV (Lateran Obelisk, II, 835), who also calls it the "*upper portal of Karnak*." The only temple of Ramses II at this portal is the Luxor temple; but the name given it by Beknekhonsu does not accord with the name of Luxor temple (see § 507).

[b]These are the two Luxor obelisks of Ramses II, of which one is still in situ, and the other in the Place de la Concorde, Paris.

[c]He means that the wall surrounded or gave access to a temple lake. Cf. the work of Ramses IX (Mariette, *Karnak*, 40, l. 7), whose wall ($d \supset d \supset$ as here) gave access to the Karnak lake. There is certainly no reference to the Kurna temple and the Ramesseum, as some have thought.

REIGN OF MERNEPTAH

THE INVASION OF LIBYANS AND MEDITERRANEAN PEOPLES

569. For this, one of the most serious invasions which have ever threatened Egypt, we possess a series of four documents, which furnish a fairly full account of its course, the ensuing battle, and the resulting relief in Egypt. They are the following:
I. The Great Karnak Inscription (§§ 572–92).
II. The Cairo Column (§§ 593–95).
III. The Athribis Stela (§§ 596–601).
IV. The Hymn of Victory (§§ 602–17).

570. These sources enable us to see the already aged Merneptah facing the evil conditions on his Libyan frontier, inherited from the decades of neglect which concluded his great father's reign. The Libyans have for years past been pushing into and occupying the western Delta.[a] They pressed in almost to the gates of Memphis, eastward to the district of Heliopolis, and southward to the two oases nearest the Fayûm. Worse than this, they had made a coalition

---

[a]Golénischeff's interesting and suggestive letter (*Zeitschrift für ägyptische Sprache*, 40, 101–6) draws geographical data from a new papyrus in his possession, on the basis of which he would place this immigration and invasion (as well as those under Ramses III) south of the Fayûm near Ehnas. His arguments are not without force, but the conclusion seems to me to be refuted by the statement that this invasion and the battle which repelled it occurred in the "*western rwd*" (Karnak Inscription, l. 30, where "*western*" is omitted, and Athribis stela, l. 7). *Rwd* is a term used only of the Delta, the two halves of which are called the eastern and western *rwd* (Spiegelberg, *Rechnungen*). The invasions under Ramses III were also in the "*western rwd*" (IV, 405). See also Harris, 10, 8 (IV, 224). Furthermore, the improbability that the Libyans would enter Egypt by way of the northern oases, going around the south side of the Fayûm, to reach the region of Memphis, is evident.

with the maritime peoples of the Mediterranean, who now poured into the Delta from Sardinia on the west to Asia Minor on the east. The mention of these peoples in these documents is the earliest appearance of Europeans in literature, and has always been the center of much study and interest.[a] With the sympathy, if not the direct assistance of the Kheta, the Libyan king, Meryey, put himself at the head of these combined allies and invaded the Delta, bringing his wives and belongings, and apparently intending a permanent occupation. Some time during the first half of the tenth month (late in March), in Merneptah's fifth year, a messenger reached him with the news. Rallying his forces immediately, Merneptah met the enemy on the third of the eleventh month (about April 15) at Perire in the western Delta, and in six hours' fighting routed their combined forces with immense slaughter. He pursued them from Perire to the rise of the Libyan desert, called the "*Mount of the Horns of the Earth.*"

571. It is difficult to understand the exact interrelation of the numbers given in the Great Karnak Inscription and the Athribis Stela, but over 9,000 of the enemy were slain, possibly as many more taken prisoners, while many horses and cattle, and vast numbers of weapons were captured. The Libyan king was forced to ignominious flight, his camp, his wives, and his personal belongings falling into the hands

---

[a]The layman has long been misled regarding this event by such titles for it as "Invasion of the Greeks," although there is now no doubt that the early peoples of southern Europe participated in this invasion. Since the study of Sardinian art by Perrot and Chipiez, as Müller has shown, we must accept the Sherden as Sardinians; the Teresh may then equally well be the Etruscans (Tyrsenoi), and the Shekelesh might be the Sikeli (if *š* be an ethnic termination in these western names; but see IV, 59). Maspero has suggested Sagalassos in Asia Minor. The Ekwesh are not impossibly the Achæans, and from Asia Minor are the Luka or Lycians. Compare Müller, *Proceedings of the Society of Biblical Archæology*, X; and *Asien und Europa*, 335–59; 371–84; and Hall, *Annual of the British School at Athens*, VIII, 157.

of the Egyptians. After setting fire to the camp, the Egyptians carried the plunder in triumph to the king, who viewed the trophies of the dead, the prisoners, and the spoil. He then returned home, and in the royal palace, probably at Memphis, he delivered a triumphal address, to which the court responded with acclamation. The people of the Delta, on hearing the news, break out into rejoicing that peace and safety are restored to them.

I. GREAT KARNAK INSCRIPTION[a]

572. This, one of the longest documents preserved on the temple walls of Egypt, gives the fullest account which has survived to us of the great victory of Merneptah over the Libyans. The prominence of Ptah in the narrative betrays the Memphite origin of the document, but the original which doubtless once existed in Memphis has now perished.

573. The document does not offer us any idea of the

---

[a]A long inscription of originally eighty lines, engraved on the inside (west) of the eastern wall connecting the main Karnak temple with Pylon VII (Baedeker's plan), the northernmost of the southern pylons. The upper ends of the lines have lost the space of one course of masonry, equivalent to about four to five words. The text, noted first by Champollion, was partially published by Lepsius (*Denkmäler*, III, 199, a; only ll. 44–77 and list of names, Text, III, 43); Brugsch then purposed to publish the first half, omitted by Lepsius, and inserted ll. 8–43 in his *Geographische Inschriften*, II, Pl. 25 (not Pl. 85, as stated in *Records of the Past*, IV, 37, nor 35, as given in Maspero, *Struggle of the Nations*, 432). Brugsch numbered his lines 1 to 36, but he really omitted ll. 1–7. It was finally completely published by Dümichen (*Historische Inschriften*, I, 2–6), Mariette (who copies Dümichen's mistakes, *Karnak*, 52–55), and de Rougé (*Inscriptions hiéroglyphiques*, 179–98). None of these publications is very exact; both Lepsius and Brugsch omit the lower ends of the lines, doubtless still covered in their day, without any indication of the fact. Rougé found the upper ends of ll. 36–41 (on a block rediscovered by Legrain in 1901, see l. 36, p. 246, n. a), and properly placed them; I arranged all the publications in parallel columns, and the resulting text, while tolerably close to the original and preserving some signs now lost, was not sufficiently accurate. Later I secured good photographs of the inscription through the kindness of Borchardt, which added some readings of importance. The new fragments found by Legrain (*Annales*, IV, 2–4) contain nothing of importance except the reference to the "*western rdw;*" they arrived too late to be available in the following text.

[§ 576]   LIBYAN-MEDITERRANEAN INVASION

course of the battle, beginning the account of the conflict itself almost immediately with the rout of the Libyans; but it is gratifyingly full regarding the conditions which led up to the battle and the immense plunder which resulted from it. In style it is often so highly colored, and effuse in poetic figures, that the translation is rendered difficult.

Title

574. ¹[ʿBeginning of the victory which his majesty achieved in the land of Libyaⁿ]ᵃ ———— i, Ekwesh (ʾ-ḳʾ-wʾ-šʾ), Teresh (Tw-rw-šʾ), Luka (Rw-kw), Sherden (Šʾ-rʾ-d-n), Shekelesh (Š-k-rw-šʾ), Northerners coming from all lands.

Valor of Merneptah

575. ²— — — — —ᵇ his valor in the might of his father, Amon; King of Upper and Lower Egypt: Binre-Meriamon; Son of Re: Merneptah-Hotephirma, given life. Lo, this Good God, flourishing — — — ³— — — — — his [fathers] all the gods, as his protection. Every country is in fear at the sight of him, King Merneptah.ᶜ ←— — — — — desolated, made a waste, commanding that the invader of his every boundary of Egypt bow himself down in his time, ⁵— — — — — all his ⌜plans⌝ (whose) verdict is the breath of life. He causes the people to be care-free, sleeping while the terror of his strength is in ⁶— —.

Preparation of Defenses

576. — — —, to protect Heliopolis, city of Atum, to defend the stronghold of Ptah-Tatenen, to save — from evil ⁷— — — — — tentsᵈ

ᵃThe presence of the list of hostile allies at the beginning of the inscription would indicate with great probability that the opening words were the same as in the Kadesh Poem, which likewise begins with a list of the allied foes.

ᵇThe loss is one course of masonry at the top—at most four or five words at the beginning of each line.

ᶜDouble name, as also in all other places in the inscription.

ᵈHebrew אֹהֶל. This remark may possibly refer to the Libyans and indicate the distribution of their immigrants from Per-Berset on the west to the Heliopolitan canal on the east.

before Per-Berset (Pr-b ⁾ -r ⁾ -$ys˙t$),ᵃ ⌜reaching⌝ᵇ the Sheken ($Š$ ⁾ -k ⁾ -n ⁾) canal on the ⌜——⌝ᶜ of the Eti (⁾ -ty)ᵈ canal.

Libyan Aggression

577. ⁸— — — — — not cared for, it was forsaken as pasturage for cattle because of the Nine Bows, it was left waste from the times of the ancestors. All the kings of Upper Egypt abode in their pyramids ⁹— — — — —; the kings of Lower Egypt [rested]ᵉ in the midst of their cities, inclosed in the state palace, for lack of troops; they had no bowmen to answer against them.

Accession of Merneptah, and His Preparations

578. It happened ¹⁰ ᶠ— — — — — he [⌜assumed⌝] the throne of Horus, he was appointed to preserve the folk ($p^{c}˙t$) alive, he hath arisen as king to protect the people ($rḫy˙t$). There was might in him to do it, because of — — —ᵍ in ¹¹— — — — — Meber (M ⁾ -b ⁾ -r ⁾),ʰ the choicest of his bowmen were mustered, his chariotry was brought up from every side, his scouts were in — — — — his ⌜—⌝ in ¹²— — — — — his —. He considered not hundreds of thousands in the day of the array. His infantry ($mnfy˙t$) marched out, the heavy armedⁱ troops arrived, beautiful in appearance, leading the bowmen against every land.

ᵃThis town has nothing to do with modern Belbês on the eastern margin of the Delta (classic Byblos? See Brugsch, *Dictionnaire géographique*, 197); but was in the western Delta (see IV, 370).

ᵇRougé, *Inscriptions hiéroglyphiques*, has yr (the eye) = "*do, make*," perhaps used as in Uni (I, 322, ll. 41, 42, note) with the meaning "*reach, visit.*"

ᶜText has not "*north*," but either $šd$ or ᶜ nd with the d written out alphabetically, and a long horizontal determinative lost in a joint of the masonry.

ᵈA canal leaving the Nile by Heliopolis; the Sheken canal is otherwise unknown (see Brugsch, *Dictionnaire géographique*, 77).

ᵉThe parallelism demands a verb similar in meaning to "*abode.*"

ᶠThere is here a reference to the accession of Merneptah, as Brugsch has noticed (*Geschichte*, 569).

ᵍFragments of words; Brugsch's "weil er war das Ebenbild des [schön] gesichtigen" (= Ptah) is quite impossible.

ʰA syllable or two may be lost at the beginning; it is the name of an unknown foreign country. The connection before it is not clear, but it is evident that the practical preparations for the campaign begin here.

ⁱLit., "*those who bear the hand-to-hand fighting;*" these are heavily armed foreign mercenaries.

News of Coalition of Libyans and Sea-Peoples against Egypt

579. ᵃ— — ¹³— — — — — the third season, saying: "The wretched, fallen chief of Libya, Meryey ($M\text{-}r\text{?-}y\text{'-}yw\text{-}y$), son of Ded ($Dy\text{-}d$), has fallen upon the country of Tehenu with his bowmen ¹⁴— — — — — Sherden ($[\check{S}]\text{'-}r\text{'-}d\text{-}n$), Shekelesh ($\check{S}\text{'-}k\text{-}rw\text{-}\check{s}\text{'}$), Ekwesh ($\text{'}^b\text{-}k\text{'-}w\text{'-}\check{s}\text{'}$), Luka ($Rw\text{-}kw$), Teresh ($Tw\text{-}ry\text{-}\check{s}\text{'}$), taking the best of every warrior and every man of war ($p\d{h}rr$) of his country. He has brought his wife and hisᶜ children ¹⁵— — — — — leaders of the camp, and he has reached the western boundary in the fields of Perire."ᵈ

Merneptah's Speech

580. Lo, his majesty was enraged at their report, like a lion; ¹⁶[The assembled his court], and said to th]em: "Hear ye the command of your lord; I give — — as ye shall do, saying: I am the ruler who shepherdsᵉ you; I spend my time searching out ¹⁷— — — — you, as a father, who preserves alive his children; while ye fear like birds, and ye know not the goodness of that which he does. Is there none answering in ¹⁸— — — — — ['Shall the land be¹ wa]sted and forsaken at the invasion of every country, while the Nine Bows plunder its borders, and rebels invade it every day? Every — takes ¹⁹— — — — — to plunder these fortresses. They have repeatedly penetrated the fields of Egypt ⌜to⌝ the [great]ᶠ river. They have halted, they have spent whole days and

---

ᵃThis announcement was made in the tenth month, as is shown by the Cairo column (§ 595), which fills out the lacuna at the beginning of the above section. Allowing the fourteen days for the muster of the troops (l. 28), and remembering that the armies met in battle on the third of the eleventh month, it will be seen that the news must have reached the king during the first half of the tenth month.

ᵇThe first syllable is omitted by Dümichen, *Historische Inschriften*, Mariette, *Karnak*, and Brugsch, *Geographische Inschriften;* being given only by de Rougé, *Inscriptions hiéroglyphiques*, where it is probably a correction by de Rougé himself.

ᶜSo Rougé, *Inscriptions hiéroglyphiques;* Dümichen, *Historische Inschriften*, and Mariette, *Karnak*, have "*their.*"

ᵈ$Pr\text{-}yr$ misread by Brugsch as $Pr\text{-}Yr\text{-}\check{s}ps\text{·}t$, and then identified with Prosopis. This is shown to be incorrect by the short version (§ 600, l. 9). See Müller (*Asien und Europa*, 357, n. 3), who would identify it as the $Y\text{'}rw$ of the Pyramid Texts (Mernere, 182 = Pepi, 145; cf. also Teti, 351 = Pepi, II, 174), "a border town of the natron district."

ᵉLike Seti I in making the well on the Redesiyeh road (Third Inscription, § 195, l. 2).

ᶠThe restoration is certain, the determinative (papyrus roll) is clear, and there is just room for the "*great*"-sign (ᶜ') above it. In exactly the same connection it is used in Ramses III's Libyan wars (IV, 405, see note).

months dwelling [20]— — — — —. They have reached the hills of the oasis,[a] and have cut off the district[b] of Toyeh ($T^\jmath$-yh).[c] ⌜Sold⌝ it has been since the kings of Upper Egypt, in the records of other times. It was not known [21]— — — — — as worms, not considering their bodies, (but) loving death and despising life. Their hearts are exalted against the people[e] [22]— — — — — their chief. They spend their time going about the land, fighting, to fill their bodies daily. They come to the land of Egypt, to seek the necessities of their mouths; their desire is [23]— — — — — my bringing them like netted fish on their bellies. Their chief is like a dog, a man of ⌜boasting⌝, without courage; he does not abide — [24]— — — — — bringing to an end[f] the Pedetishew ($Pd\cdot ty$-$šw$),[g] whom I caused to take grain in ships, to keep alive that land of Kheta.[h] Lo, I am he whom the gods —, every ka [25]— — — — — under me, King Merneptah, given life. By my ka, by the —, as I flourish as ruler of the Two Lands ⌜the land shall be made⌝ [26]— — — — — Egypt. Amon nods approval, when[i] one speaks in

[a]The usual designation of the oasis otherwise called by the Egyptians the "Northern Oasis," and by the Greeks "The Lesser." It lies exactly southwest of the Fayûm, in N. 28°, less than one hundred miles west of the Nile valley.

[b]Brugsch (*Dictionnaire géographique*, 70) has $n\ ḥr\ n$ (for $m\ ḥr\ n$) = "*in front of*," that is, "*cut off in front of*," which does not alter the meaning.

[c]This is the oasis now called "Farafrah," about seventy-five miles west of south of the "Northern Oasis." The Libyans had thus taken the two oases nearest them, south of the natron district.

[d]Mty; it must in some way indicate the customary and habitual thing in former times. See § 377, n. b. $Ḥrtw$ = "*one says;*" hence the whole, probably, literally is: "*The customary thing*," say they, "*since, etc.*"

[e]Of Egypt ($rḫy\cdot t$). [f]$S^c rk$.

[g]Asiatics, or: "*the Pedetishew bring to an end.*"

[h]The king evidently regards Kheta as included in the coalition of northern peoples against Egypt, and the logic of the reference seems to be Kheta's ingratitude in joining a combination against the Egyptians, who had sent grain for her maintenance, as if such grain had not been sent in a commercial way, but from philanthropic motives, which, of course, was probably not the case. In view of the mention of Kheta among the defeated peoples in the Hymn of Victory (§ 617, l. 26), the question arises whether Kheta already in the year 3 had not been in such close sympathy with the plans of these allies that Merneptah had extended against the Kheta also the campaign on which the Asiatic peoples and towns mentioned in the Hymn of Victory (§ 617, ll. 26–28) were pillaged. I can only answer this question in the affirmative. The plunder of a few towns on the Hittite border in Syria would be quite sufficient, in the eyes of an oriental, to justify the boast in l. 26.

[i]Or: "*say they in Thebes.*"

[§ 583]   LIBYAN - MEDITERRANEAN INVASION   245

Thebes. He has turned his back against the Meshwesh (M-$š$ ͗ -w ͗ -$š$ ͗), and looks [not] on the land of Temeh (T-m-$ḥ$), when they are ²⁷——."

Beginning of the Campaign

581. — — — —ᵃ the leaders of the bowmen in front thereof to overthrow the land of Libya. When they went forth, the hand of the god was with them; (even) Amon was with them as their shield. The land of Egypt was commanded, saying: ²⁸"— — — — [rea]dy to march in fourteen days."

Merneptah's Dream

582. Then his majesty saw in a dream as if a statue of Ptah were standing before Pharaoh, L. P. H. He was like the height of ²⁹— — — — —. He spake to him: "Take thou (it)," while he extended to him the sword,ᵇ "and banish thou the fearful heart from thee." Pharaoh, L. P. H., spake to him: "Lo, ³⁰— — — — —."ᶜ

Approach of the Two Armies

583. — infantry and chariotry in (great) numberᵈ were camped before them on the shore (rwd)ᵉ in front of the district of Perire (Pr-yr). Lo, the wretched chief of ³¹[Libya] — — — — — in the night of the second day of the third month of the third season (eleventh month) when the land grew light (enough) for advancing with them. The wretched fallen chief of Libya came at the time of the third day of the third month of the third season (eleventh month), and he brought ³²— — — — — until they arrived. The infantry of his majesty went forth together with his chariotry, Amon-Re being with them, and the Ombite (Set) giving to them the hand.

ᵃIt is clear that the king's speech is concluded in the lacuna, and that the march of the troops now begins.

ᵇCompare the frequent reliefs in which the god extends a sword ($ḫpš$) to the king. There is not in this speech any warning to Merneptah to withhold himself from the battle, and remain at home, as indicated in the translation of Chabas (*Etudes sur l'antiquité historique*, 195). This old misunderstanding of Chabas has gained general currency in the histories. [Later: See W. M. Müller (*Orientalistische Litteraturzeitung*, V, December, 1902, 477) for the similarity of this dream story to that in Herodotus, II, 141.]

ᶜThe answer of the Pharaoh was evidently very short.

ᵈM $rḫ$·t, lit., "*in a list or statement.*"

ᵉSee § 570, note.

The Battle

584. ⌈Every⌉ man ³³— — — — — their blood, there was none that escaped among them. Lo, the bowmen of his majesty spent six hours of destruction among them; they were delivered to the sword upon ³⁴— — — — — of the country. Lo, as they fought — —; the wretched chief of Libya halted, his heart fearing; withdrew (again), stopped, knelt, ³⁵— — — — ⌈leaving⌉ sandals, his bow, and his quiver in haste behind [him], and every [thing] that was with him. ⌈— —⌉ his limbs, great terror coursed in his members. ³⁶ᵃLo, ⌈they⌉ slew — — — of his possessions, his ⌈equipment⌉, his silver, his gold, his vessels of bronze, the furniture^b of his wife, his throne, his bows, his arrows, all his works, which he had brought ³⁷from his land, consisting of oxen, goats, and asses, ⌈and all were carried away⌉ to the palace, to bring them in, together with the captives. Lo, the wretched chief of Libya was in speed to flee ⌈by himself⌉, while all ³⁸the people among the captains — — — among the wounded of the sword. Lo, the officers (*snn*), who were upon the horses of his majesty, set themselves after them — — felled with ³⁹arrows, carried off, slain, — —.

Retrospect

585. No [man] has seen it in the annals of the kings of Lower Egypt; lo, this land of Egypt was in [the]ir power, in a ⌈state⌉ of weakness in the time of the kings of Upper Egypt, ⁴⁰so that their hand could not be repelled, — — — — these — out of love of their beloved son, in order to protect Egypt for her lord, that the temples of Egypt might be saved, and in order to announce ⁴¹the mighty power of the [Good] God — — — —.

Escape of Libyan Chief

586. [The commandant] of the fortress of the West^c [sent] a report to the Court, L. P. H., saying, as follows: "The fallen Meryey (*Mw-*

ᵃDe Rougé found a block containing the beginnings of ll. 36–41; they are to be found in place only in his publication. Later (1901) Legrain found the same block under the débris, and published it (*Annales du service*, II, 269), without recognizing that it had long before been seen and copied by de Rougé. The recovery of this block, however, shows that the loss at the beginnings of the lines is, for the main part of the inscription, only the space of one course of masonry.

ᵇOr: "*ornaments*."

ᶜThis is the fort or station referred to by Ramses III (IV, 340; Harris, 51*b*, 3).

r ͗ -y ͗ -y) has come, his limbs have fled because of his ⌈cowardice⌉, and (he) passed by me, by favor of night, in safety.ᵃ ⁴²— — — — — want; he is fallen, and every god is for Egypt.ᵇ The boasts which he uttered, have come to naught; all that his mouth said has returned upon his (own) head. His condition is not known (whether) of death ⁴³[⌈or of life⌉] — — —. Thou hast — him of his fame; if he lives, he will not (again) command, (for) he is fallen, an enemy ofᶜ his (own) troops. It is thou who hast taken us, to cause to slay ⁴⁴— — — — —ᵈ in the land of Temeh (*Ty-m-ḥ-w*) [and of Libyaᵉ]. They have put another into his place, from among his brothers, another who fights him,ᶠ when he sees him. All the chiefs are ⌈disgusted⌉ ⁴⁵— — —."

Triumphal Return

587. [⌈Then returned⌉] the captains of archers, the infantry (*mnfy·t*), and chariotry; every contingent of the army, whether recruits, or heavy armed troops,ᵍ ⁴⁶[⌈carried off the plunder⌉] — — [⌈driving⌉] asses before them, laden with the uncircumcisedʰ phalli of the country of Libya, together with the hands of every country that was with them, ⌈like fish

---

ᵃ*M rwd*.

ᵇThe rendering is grammatically uncertain; it may possibly also be: "*every god has overthrown him for Egypt's sake.*"

ᶜBrugsch's text ends here.

ᵈLepsius' text begins here.

ᵉOnly the foreign determinative is preserved.

ᶠThis pronoun is omitted by Dümichen, *Historische Inschriften*, and Mariette, *Karnak*.

ᵍOwing to the connection in the following line, *ḥr kf ͨ w* is possibly to be rendered "*bore the captures.*" But see l. 12. In any case, some such statement must have introduced l. 46, or is to be found in the closing words of l. 45.

ʰLit., "*phalli with the foreskins*" (*Ḳrn·t*=ערלה). Müller's objections (*Proceedings of the Society of Biblical Archæology*, 1888, 147 ff.) to this rendering, it seems to me, do not take full account of the use of the word in this text. He maintains that *ḳrn·t*="*horn*" (long ago suggested by Chabas, *Etudes sur l'antiquité historique*, 234, n. 2) means simply phallus, because Athribis Stela uses it in the same place where our long text has "*phallus*," or interchangeably with "*phallus.*" But *ḳrn·t* is something which the Sherden and the other allies did not have (l. 54)! Moreover, it is something connected with the phallus which they did not have. As the phonetic equivalence *ḳrn·t* = ערלה is unexceptionable, it seems to me the rendering "*foreskin*" is very probable. The question of the homes of these people is in greater uncertainty than the rendering of *ḳrn·t*, and should be decided by this rendering rather than the reverse.

on the grass¹, and the possessions ⁴⁷— — — — — the enemies of their land. Lo, the whole land rejoiced to heaven; the towns and the districts acclaimed these wonders which had happened; the Nile ⁴⁸— — — — their — as tribute under the balcony,ᵃ to cause his majesty to see his conquests.

List of Captives and Slain

588. List of the captives carried off from this land of Libya and the countries which he brought with him; likewise the property ⁴⁹— — — — —ᵇ [betwee]n the ⌜château⌝ᶜ of Merneptah-Hotephirma [destroyer of]ᵈ Tehenu (Ty-[$ḥ$]-nw) which is in Perire (Pr-yrr), as far as the upper towns of the country, beginning with "— of Merneptah-Hotephirma."

⁵⁰[Children of the chief of Libya whose]ᶠ uncircumcised phalli [were carried off]	6 men
Children of chiefs, and brothers of the chief of Libya, slain, whose [uncircumcised] phalli were carried off	⁵¹— —
— — Libyans, slain, whose uncircumcised phalli were carried off	6,359
Total, children of great chiefsᵍ	⁵²— —

ᵃThis is the palace balcony on which the Pharaoh appeared to the people. It is also mentioned in a similar connection in Papyrus Harris (*infra*, IV, 408), and is several times depicted in the Amarna tombs (e. g., Lepsius, *Denkmäler*, III, 103–9). Cf. also Harmhab Decree (II, 66, l. 9).

ᵇAthribis Stela, l. 8 (§ 600).

ᶜ$Pr\ m$ ². It occurs also in the parallel passage in the Athribis Stela (§ 600, l. 8), and twice in Papyrus Harris (5, 2, and 31, 6, one of which was north of Heliopolis). It is clear that the limits of the flight and pursuit are being given as in the battle under Ramses III; they are given in the Athribis Stela (ll. 8, 9) as the château in Perire and the "*mount of the Horns of the Earth;*" this terminus is the same as under Ramses III, and of course is the rise of the Libyan desert, or some elevation near it, upon which Ramses III had built a town. (The term, "*Horns of the Earth,*" is also used of the southern limit of territory known to the Egyptians.) Whether the beginning point of the flight, viz., Perire, is the same as $Ḥ\ ˙t$-$š\ ^c\ ˙t$, where the flight began under Ramses III, is perhaps uncertain, but the above facts concerning the $pr\ m$ ², and the parallel character of the two invasions would certainly at least place them near together, and it is probable that they are identical. (See also Pr-m ᵒ y, *Zeitschrift für ägyptische Sprache*, 40, 102.)

ᵈBrugsch has "*destroyer of*" in this lacuna, but it is in none of the texts.

ᵉProbably another place-name.

ᶠ§ 601, l. 10.

ᵍProbably continued by l. 12 of the extract.

— — [Sher]den (— — *dy-n*ꜣ), Shekelesh (*Š*ꜣ*-k*ꜣ*-rw-š*ꜣ), Ekwesh (ꜣ*-k*ꜣ*-y-w*ꜣ*-š*ꜣ) of the countries of the sea,[a] who had no fore-[53b]skins:

Shekelesh (*Š*ꜣ*-k*ꜣ*-rw-š*ꜣ)	222[c] men
Making.	250[d] hands
Teresh (*Tw-rw-š*ꜣ)	742[e] men
Making	790[d] hands
Sherden (*Š*ꜣ*-r*ꜣ*-d-n-n*ꜣ)	54— —
[Making]	— —
[Ek]wesh (— —ꜣ*-y-w*ꜣ*-š*ꜣ) who had no foreskins, slain, whose hands were carried off, (for) they had no [55][foreskins]	— - -
— — in heaps, whose uncircumcised phalli were carried off to the place where the king was	6,111[f] men
Making uncircumcised phalli	56— —
— — whose hands [were carried off]	2,370[g] men
Shekelesh (*Š*ꜣ*-k*ꜣ*-rw-š*ꜣ) and Teresh (*Tw-rw-š*ꜣ) who came as enemies of[h] Libya	57— —
— — Kehek, and Libyans, carried off as living prisoners	218 men

[a]It is noticeable that this designation, both here and in the Athribis Stela (l. 13), is inserted only after the Ekwesh. In the Athribis Stela Ekwesh is cut off by a numeral from the preceding, showing that the designation there belongs only to them.

[b]All the texts indicate a lacuna here at the top of l. 53, and yet the half of the word "*foreskin*" at the bottom of l. 52 fits exactly the other half at the top of l. 53. This may be an accident, but if correct, then there is no lacuna at top of l. 53, and no place for a number between. The number corresponding to this place in the Athribis Stela (viz., 2201 +x) is not found in this text till l. 56.

[c]Müller's 212 (*Asien und Europa*, 358) is an error; all four texts have 222.

[d]Why the number of hands cut off should exceed the number of men, when one hand was cut from each man, does not appear.

[e]Lepsius, *Denkmäler*, has 750.

[f]Apparently only 6,111 of the 6,359 mentioned in l. 51 were carried before the king.

[g]So Dümichen, *Historische Inschriften*, and Lepsius, *Denkmäler;* but Mariette, *Karnak*, and Rougé, *Inscriptions hiéroglyphiques*, have 2,362 (none has 72 as in Müller, *Asien und Europa*, 358).

[h]"*Of*" is here possessive = "*belonging to*," not in a hostile sense.

Women of the fallen chief of Libya, whom he brought with him, being alive	12 Libyan women
Total carried off ⁵⁸— — — — —	9,376 people[a]

List of Spoil

589. Weapons of war which were in their hands, carried off as plunder: copper swords of the Meshwesh (*M-š ᵓ -w ᵓ -š ᵓ*)	9,111
⁵⁹— — — —[b]	120,214
Horses which bore the fallen chief of Libya and the children [of the ch]ief of Libya, carried off alive, pairs	12[c]
⁶⁰Possessions — — — —[d] Meshwesh — —[e] which the army of his majesty, L. P. H., who fought the fallen of Libya, captured: various cattle	1,308[f]
Goats	61—
— — various —	64[g]

---

[a]This is probably the total of the slain, Libyan and non-Libyan, for the corresponding number in the Athribis Stela (l. 17) has before it: "*fallen of Libya, total number;*" the non-Libyan foreigners being thus merely designated as of the Libyan party. Of the actual Libyans slain we have a total of 6,359 (l. 51), and of non-Libyan foreigners at least 2,370 (l. 56). This makes a total of 8,729, omitting a few hundred non-Libyans, who would doubtless bring the total up to 9,376, as given in our text above. But it is possible that this number refers only to captives, in this case, as the Athribis Stela gives at least 9,300 killed (l. 17), the total of killed and captured would be over 18,000! See also Müller, *Asien und Europa*, 358, n. 5.

[b]Probably smaller weapons; at the end is the determinative of a foreign country, probably Libya.

[c]Dümichen, *Historische Inschriften*, shows an uncertain 100, and a 1; Mariette, *Karnak, idem*; Rougé, *Inscriptions hiéroglyphiques*, a 10 and a 1; Lepsius, *Denkmäler*, remains of the same; Brugsch (*Geschichte*, 576) has 113. But the photograph is practically certain as 12.

[d]The last word indicates men, as shown by the determinative.

[e]This space was left empty on the monument; Rougé, *Inscriptions hiéroglyphiques*, says: "Cette partie n'a pas été gravée;" Lepsius, *Denkmäler*, "leer."

[f]So Dümichen, *Historische Inschriften*, and Mariette, *Karnak*; Rougé, *Inscriptions hiéroglyphiques*, and Lepsius, *Denkmäler*, have 1,307.

[g]So Rougé, *Inscriptions hiéroglyphiques*, and Lepsius, *Denkmäler*; Dümichen, *Historische Inschriften*, and Mariette, *Karnak*, have 54.

Silver drinking-vessels ($tb\cdot w$) —a
($t^{\flat}$-pw-r)-vessels, ($rhd\cdot\hat{\imath}$)-vessels, swords, armor,
knives,[b] and various vessels   3,174[c]

They were taken away [62]— — — — fire was set to the camp and their tents of leather.

Triumph in the Palace

590. Their lord, the king, appeared, L. P. H., in the broad-hall of the palace, while [63][ꞇthe court acclaimedꞁ] his majesty, L. P. H., rejoicing at his appearance, which he made. The servants [of his majesty] exulted to heaven; the suite on both sides — —.

Merneptah's Speech

591. [64][His majesty said]: "— — —[d] because of the good which Re has done for my ka I have delivered their utterance, speaking as a god, who giveth might, whose [ꞇdecreeꞁ][e] has caused that King Merneptah, L. P. H., [65]— — — should unite — as subjects[f] in the midst of their town; Kush likewise bears the tribute of the conquered. I cause him to see (it) in my hand in — [66]— — — — his chief, bringing his impost each year, in — a great slaughter being made among them. He that lives shall fill the temples [67]— — — —. Their fallen chief, fleeing before me, I have put into — — — slay him. He is made a roast, snared like a wild fowl.[g] I have given the land [68]— — — — for every god. They are born ꞇof the mouthꞁ of the sole lord of Egypt. Fallen is the transgressor — .... — — .... [69]— — — — —, victorious is Re, mighty against the Nine Bows; Sutekh giveth victory and might to Horus, rejoicing in truth, smiting —, King Merneptah, L. P. H. I am [70]— — — — mighty, he is not taken. The Libyans plotted evil things, to do them in Egypt. See! their ꞇprotectorsꞁ are fallen!

---

[a]Left empty on original, as in l. 60; after it are the fragmentary names of the two sorts of vessels, and it is possible that the lacuna did not contain a numeral. In that case, the miscellaneous list begins with the silver vessels.

[b]With determinative of copper.

[c]So Dümichen, *Historische Inschriften*, Mariette, *Karnak*, and Lepsius, *Denkmäler*; Rougé, *Inscriptions hiéroglyphiques*, has 3,175.

[d]The lacuna here is evidently longer than usual at the beginning of the lines.

[e]The word has the determinative of speech.

[f]$Bk\cdot w$, viz., "*tax-paying subjects.*"

[g]Ramses III makes use of the same figure (IV, 41).

I have slain them, and they are made ⌜— —⌝ ⁷¹— — — — — I have made Egypt to flow with a river; the people love me, as I love them, and give to them breath for their cities. There is rejoicing over my name in heaven and earth ⁷²— — — — — they found. My time hath achieved beautiful things in the mouth(s) of the youth, according to the greatness of the excellent things which I did for them. It is true throughout ⁷³— — — — — adoring the excellent lord, who has taken the Two Lands, King Merneptah, L. P. H."

Reply of the Court

592. They said: "How great are these things which have happened to Egypt! — — ⁷⁴— — — — — Libya is like a petitioner, brought as a captive. Thou hast made them to be like grasshoppers, for every road is strewed with their ⁷⁵[⌜bodies⌝]ᵃ — — — — [⌜bestowing⌝] thy provision in the mouth of the needy. We lie down with joy at any time;ᵇ there being no ⁷⁶— — — —ᶜ . . . .

II. THE CAIRO COLUMNᵈ

593. This document first furnished the date of Merneptah's great Libyan victory, and was therefore formerly of greater importance than at present.

It contained a shorter account of the announcement of the invasion to the king, which fills out the lacuna in the great Karnak Inscription (§ 579, ll. 12, 13), preceding the announcement. The historical content of the document is as follows:

ᵃBrugsch, *Wörterbuch*, Supplement, 894.

ᵇThere is perhaps a reference to this in the Athribis Stela (recto, l. 4), where the king is called: one *"who causes Egypt to sleep until the morning."* Ll. 76, 77 contain only scanty fragments of conventional phrases; ll. 78 and 79 have each only two signs visible at the bottom. They must be near the end of the inscription, but the exact number of lines lost at the end is uncertain.

ᶜThese are the last two lines of text preserved; they are too fragmentary for use here. Mariette, *Karnak* (Texte, 75), states that there are two more lines, but his plate (55) gives ll. 78–80, without any visible signs.

ᵈSection of a granite column now in the Cairo Museum, first noticed in the court of the building of the minister of public instruction in Cairo by Brugsch (*Geschichte*, 577, note); then removed to the museum and published (without the reliefs) by Maspero (*Zeitschrift für ägyptische Sprache*, 1881, 118).

[§ 597] LIBYAN-MEDITERRANEAN INVASION

594. Above is a scene showing Merneptah receiving a sword from a god,[a] who says to him: "I cause that thou cut down the chiefs of Libya whose invasion thou hast turned back."

595. Below was an inscription in vertical lines, of which only the following is now visible:

¹Year 5, second month of the third season (tenth month). One came to say to his majesty: "The wretched [chief] of Libya has invaded ⁽with⁾ —,[b] being men and women, Shekelesh ($\check{S}$ ꜣ-k-rw-$\check{s}$ ꜣ) ² ———."[c]

III. THE ATHRIBIS STELA[d]

596. This monument contains a shorter account of Merneptah's Libyan campaign, closing with a list of the killed, the captured, and the spoil. It forms a useful supplement to the Karnak document, furnishing, among other data, the exact date of the battle in Merneptah's fifth year.

Recto

597. A relief at the top shows Atum at the left and Amon-Re at the right, both seated. The scene before Atum is lost; before Amon-Re appears Merneptah, who receives the sword from the god, and leads to him at the same time seven captives.

---

[a]Called only "dieu innommé" by Maspero, who has not published the relief; but he states that the heads are lost, and the god therefore unrecognizable.

[b]Name of a country, of which only "— -n-r ⸍—" is now visible.

[c]Only a few traces.

[d]A granite stela from Athribis in the southern Delta, now in Cairo; published without reliefs by Maspero (*Zeitschrift für ägyptische Sprache*, 1883, 65–67). It is inscribed on both sides. A piece broken off vertically through the ends of the horizontal lines is now lost, depriving us of several words at the end of each line of the recto, and at the beginning of each line of the verso. The exact amount of the loss is determined on the verso at the beginning of l. 9, by comparison with the Karnak Inscription (§ 588, l. 49). As Maspero has published only from the squeeze, his text (used here) is sometimes uncertain; and a collation of the original is much needed.

Below is an inscription of sixteen lines, mostly conventional praise of the king. It contains the following references to the campaign against the Libyans:

Introduction; Valor of Merneptah

598. Year 5, third month of third season (eleventh month), third day, under the majesty of King [Merneptah] ——— achieving his fame against the land of Temeh .... ⁴..... they speak of his victories in the land of Me[⌈shwesh⌉] .... ⁶..... who puts Libya under the might of his terror. .... ——— ⁷making their camps into wastes of the Red Land, taking ——— ⁸every herb that came forth from their fields. No field grew, to keep alive[a] ... ⁹... ¹⁰Re himself has cursed the people since they crossed into [⌈Egypt⌉] ¹¹with one accord. They are delivered to the sword in the hand of Merneptah-Hotephirma. .... ¹². ... The families of Libya are scattered upon the dykes like mice ——— ¹³seizing among them like a hawk, (while) there is found among them no place of [⌈refuge⌉] ——— ¹⁴like Sekhmet. His arrows fail not among the limbs of his enemies; every survivor[b] among them [⌈is carried off as a living captive⌉] ¹⁵They live on herbs like [⌈wild⌉] cattle ——— ¹⁶........

Verso

599. The other side of the stela shows, at the top, another relief like the first, except that the two gods are here Harakhte and Sutekh. Below it is an inscription of nineteen lines, of which the first four contain only the customary fulsome laudation of the king. Specific references to the Libyan campaign begin with l. 5, as follows:

List of Slain, Captives, and Spoil

600. ⁵——— the Meshwesh, desolated forever by the might of the valiant warrior, the Mighty Bull, who gores the Nine Bows. ⁶——— [List of] the captives which the mighty sword of the Pharaoh, L. P. H., carried off from the fallen of Libya ⁷——— who were on

---

[a]There is an obscure reference in l. 9 to the wells.
[b]Of course read *sp nb*.

the western shore,ᵃ whom Amon-Re, king of gods, Atum, lord of the Two Lands of On, Harakhte, Ptah-South-of-His-Wall, lord of the life of the Two Lands, and Sutekh, gave ⁸[to] King Merneptah; (and of) the slain in ⌜—⌝ between the ⌜château⌝ᵇ ⁹Merneptah-Hotephirma — — [Tehenu, which is in]ᵇ Perire (*Pr-yrw*) and the mount of the "Horns of the Earth." Statement thereof:

601. Children of the wretched fallen chief of Libya, ¹⁰[whose uncircumcised phalli were carried off]ᶜ	6 men
Children of chiefs, brothers of the wretched, fallen chief of Libya, carried offᵈ as the ¹¹_____	— —
— —ᵉ of Libya, slain, whose phalli were carried off	6,200 [+x] ᶠmen
¹²_____ of the families of Libya, slain, whose phalli were carried off	— men
¹³_____	200 men
Ekwesh (ʾ-*ḳ-w*ʾ-*y-š*ʾ) [of]ᵍ the countries of the sea, whom had brought the wretched ¹⁴[ʰfallen chief of Libya,ʰ ⁱwhoseⁱ] hands [were carried off]ʲ	2,201 [+x]ᵏ men
Shekelesh (*Š*ʾ-*ḳ*ʾ-*rw-š*ʾ)	200ˡ men
Teresh (*Tw-rw-š*ʾ)	722 [+x]ᵐ men
¹⁵_____ Libya, and Sherden (*Š*ʾ-*r*ʾ-*d-n*ʾ), slain	— men
¹⁶_____	32 men

ᵃ*Rwd;* see Karnak Inscription (§ 583, l. 30).

ᵇSee Karnak (§ 588, l. 49 and note).

ᶜKarnak (§ 588), l. 50.

ᵈKarnak differs, having: "*whose [uncircumcised] phalli were carried off.*"

ᵉWith the determinative of people, probably belonging to "*families,*" now lost in the lacuna.

ᶠKarnak (§ 588, l. 51) has 6,359.   ᵍKarnak (§ 588, l. 52).

ʰRestored from context; Egyptian order of words; "*chief*" is the subject.

ⁱKarnak (§ 588, l. 54).

ʲRestored from parallel passages in Karnak, e. g., l. 54.

ᵏKarnak (§ 588, l. 56) has 2,370.

ˡKarnak (§ 588, l. 53) has 222.   ᵐKarnak (§ 588, l. 53) has 742.

Women of the wretched chief of Libya	[12 Libyan][a] women
17——— the fallen of Libya, total number	9,300 [+x][b]
18———	5,224 [+x][c]
Bows, — — —	2,000 [+x]
19——— gold ———.	

IV. HYMN ON THE VICTORY OVER THE LIBYANS[d] (ISRAEL STELA)

602. This composition is one of a class common in the Nineteenth Dynasty. It is a poetic encomium in celebration of the great victory of Merneptah over the Libyans in the fifth year of his reign. It adds nothing to the facts furnished by the Karnak inscription (§§ 572–92) concerning this victory, except the picturesque description of the joy and relief among the Egyptians (ll. 21–26, § 616). Without the Karnak inscription little could have been gathered from this document of the importance of Merneptah's victory, or the gravity of the danger from which it brought relief; for, as Spiegelberg has remarked, it never even mentions the northern allies of the Libyans. Many of the descriptive passages too, are so figurative and highly colored as to be unintelligible.

---

[a]Karnak (§ 588, l. 57).   [b]Karnak (§ 588, l. 58) has 9,376.
[c]This numeral refers to the weapons, etc., beginning in l. 58 (Karnak, § 589).
[d]On a stela discovered by Petrie in the ruins of Merneptah's mortuary temple at Thebes, in 1896. The inscription occupies the back of the stela of Amenhotep III, taken from his mortuary temple by Merneptah (see II, § 878). It was first published by Spiegelberg (*Zeitschrift für ägyptische Sprache*, 34, 1 ff.), and again by him (*Six Temples*, Pls. XIII, XIV). I had also photographs, kindly sent me by E. Brugsch-Bey, made by him on a large scale from a squeeze. There is a duplicate original in Karnak, of which only a fragment has survived. It is published by Dümichen (*Historische Inschriften*, I, 1), and by Erman (*Zeitschrift für ägyptische Sprache*, 34). I have collated it for the accompanying translation. A considerable literature on the Israel passage has arisen, which will be found on p. 257, note. On the elucidation of the text in general, besides Spiegelberg's commentary (with his publication of the text), see: Piehl, *Sphinx*, IV, 125; Müller, *Recueil*, XX, 31, 32; Griffith, *Proceedings of the Society of Biblical Archæology*, XIX, 1897, 293–300.

603. The monument has attracted wide attention, because of the reference to Israel in the last section. This is the earliest mention of Israel known to us in literature, not excluding the Hebrew Scriptures themselves. It occurs in a clear-cut strophe (§ 617) of twelve lines, which forms the conclusion of the composition. This strophe opens and closes with a couplet containing a universal statement of the subjugation of foreign peoples in general, while the eight lines between are a rapid list of certain of the defeated foreigners, among whom is Israel. The assertion of the defeat of Israel is so brief and bald that little can be drawn from it. Moreover, it is made up of conventional phrases, applied also to other peoples. Much has been made of the second phrase, "*his seed (pr·t) is not.*" It has been applied to the seed[a] of Israel and referred to the slaying of the male children of the Israelites by the Egyptians! But this phrase is

---

[a] The treatment which this phrase has received by some biblical scholars furnishes another curious example of the totally misleading use of such evidence, where it is received at second hand. Thus in the *Expositor* (March, 1897, 161, note) we find the statement that Spiegelberg renders this phrase ("*his seed is not*") thus: "*without fear*" (!). An examination shows that Spiegelberg, translating into German, quite properly rendered the phrase: "ohne Frucht" ("without fruit"). The German "Frucht" was then misread by the writer in the *Expositor* as "Furcht" = "fear"! From the *Expositor* this absurdity then passed into other articles and gained currency. Some of the essays on the passage are therefore to be used with the greatest caution; but see: Hommel, *Neue Kirchliche Zeitschrift*, VII, 581–86; Müller, *Independent*, July 9, 1896, 940; Sellin, *Neue Kirchliche Zeitschrift*, VII, 502–14; Molandre, *Revue des religions*, September–October, 1897, Steindorff, *Zeitschrift für alttestamentliche Wissenschaft*, XVI, 1896, 330–33; and *Mittheilungen des Deutschen Palästina-Vereins*, 1896, 45, 46; Marshall; *Expositor*, July, 1896; Petrie, *Contemporary Review*, May, 1896, 617–27; and *Century Magazine*, August, 1896; Spiegelberg, *Sitzungsberichte der Preussischen Akademie*, 1896, 593 ff.; Naville, *Recueil*, XX, 32–37; Brandt, *Theologische Tijdschrift*, 1896, 505–12; Fries, *Sphinx*, I, 208 ff.; Daressy, *Revue archéologique*, XXXIII, 263 ff.; Wiedemann, *Le Muséon*, XVII, 89–107; Halévy, *Revue sémitique*, 1896, 285 ff. Breasted, *Biblical World*, January, 1897, 62–68. A useful presentation of the various views on the passage is given by Moore, *Presbyterian Quarterly*, January, 1898.

found five times[a] elsewhere in the inscriptions referring to a number of other peoples as follows:

604. 1. "*Those who reached my border are desolated, their seed is not*" (referring to northern invaders).[b]

2. "*The Libyans and the Seped are wasted, their seed is not.*"[c]

3. "*The fire has penetrated us, our seed is not*" (words of defeated Libyans).[d]

4. "*Their cities are made ashes, wasted, desolated; their seed is not*" (referring to the Meshwesh).[e]

5. "⌈*Gored*⌉ *is the chief of* ⌈*Amor*⌉, ... *his seed is not.*"[f]

605. The words, "*his (their, our) seed is not*," are, therefore, a conventional phrase applicable to any defeated and plundered people, and cannot possibly designate an incident peculiar to the history of Israel, like the slaying of the male children(!). Israel, clearly located among Palestinian peoples by the inscription, was defeated and plundered by Merneptah. This inscription is not the only evidence of a campaign by him in Palestine, although the fact seems to have been entirely overlooked in the discussion of the Israel passage. Merneptah was in Asia in his third year, as the journal of a border commandant shows (§ 633, VI. 9; § 635, V, 5).

606. An invasion of Palestine by Merneptah is further

---

[a] See Breasted, *Biblical World*, January, 1897, 66. Three of these examples were quoted also by Spiegelberg (*Zeitschrift für ägyptische Sprache*, 34, 23). I have there rendered *pr·t* as "*grain*," but further study of the parallel texts has led me to modify that rendering.

[b] War of Ramses III's eighth year against sea-peoples (IV, 66, l. 23).

[c] Dümichen, *Historische Inschriften*, I, XXXIV, l. 36.

[d] Libyan war of Ramses III's fifth year (IV, 43, l. 47).

[e] Dümichen, *Historische Inschriften*, I, XX, l. 2.

[f] Libyan war of Ramses III's fifth year (IV, 39, ll. 13, 14).

evident from the epithet assumed by him among his titles: "*Binder of Gezer* ($k^{\jmath}$ -$d^{\jmath}$ -$r^{\jmath}$),"[a] which town he must have captured and punished after revolt, as indicated also in our Hymn of Victory (l. 27). For the mention of a specific town, or even nation, in such an epithet, in a titulary must refer to some definite occurrence. In the same way Ramses III called himself in his titulary "*Conqueror of the Meshwesh* (IV, 84), and had the records of his defeat of the Meshwesh perished, we should still be justified in concluding that he had overthrown them.[b] It is certain, therefore, that Merneptah campaigned in Palestine, and there can be no doubt that Israel there suffered defeat and pillage at his hands.

Date and Introduction

607. [1]Year 5, third month of the third season (eleventh month), third day, under the majesty of Horus: Mighty Bull, Rejoicing[c] in Truth; King of Upper and Lower Egypt: Binre-Meriamon, Son of Re: Merneptah-Hotephirma, magnifying might, exalting the victorious sword of Horus, mighty Bull, smiter of the Nine Bows, whose name is given forever and ever.

The Great Deliverance

608. His [2]victories are published in all lands, to cause that every land together may see, to cause the glory of his conquests to appear; King Merneptah,[d] the Bull, lord of strength, who slays his foes, beautiful upon the field of victory, when his onset[e] occurs; the Sun,[f] driving

---

[a]From an inscription of thirteen lines in the temple of Amâda, published by Bouriant (*Recueil*, 18, 159, 160). It records a revolt in Wawat, which Merneptah subdued, "*seeking out the enemy in this entire land, to prevent their ⌈—⌉ to revolt a second time*" (l. 10). The publication is so inaccurate that a translation of the whole is quite impossible.

[b]See a similar epithet applied to Thutmose IV (II, 822).

[c]The sign is $k^{\jmath}$ ("*be high*"), but, as Piehl has remarked (*Sphinx*, IV, 126), the variants show that $h^c y$, "*rejoice*," is to be read.

[d]The double name in the text is from here on abbreviated as above.

[e]A word (*hnd*) used especially of the charge of a bull. (See Piehl, *Sphinx*, IV, 128.)

[f]Text has "*Shu*," a sun-god. See Piehl, *ibid.*, 127.

away ³the storm which was over Egypt, allowing Egypt to see the rays of the sun, removing the mountain of copper from the neck of the people so that he might give breath to the people who were smothered. He gratified the heart of Memphis on their foes, making Tatenen rejoice over his enemies. He opened the gates of the walled city[a] which were stopped up, and caused ⁴his temples to receive their food (even), King Merneptah, the unique one, who establishes the hearts of hundreds of thousands of myriads, so that breath enters into their nostrils at the sight of him. He has penetrated the land of Temeh in his lifetime, and put eternal fear ⁵in the heart of the Meshwesh. He has turned back Libya, who invaded Egypt, and great fear of Egypt is in their hearts

The Rout of the Libyans

609. Their advanced columns[b] they left behind them, their feet made no stand, but fled. Their archers threw down their bows, and the heart of their fleet ones was weary ⁶with marching. They loosed their water skins[c] and threw them to the ground, their ⌜—⌝[d] were taken and thrown out.

The Fall of the Libyan Chief

610. The wretched, fallen chief of Libya, fled by favor of night alone,[e] with no plume upon his head, his two feet ⌜failed⌝. His women were taken ⁷before his face, the grain of his supplies was plundered, and he had no water in the skin to keep him alive. The face of his brothers was hostile to slay him, one fought another among his leaders.[f] Their camp was burned and made a roast,[g] all his possessions were food ⁸for the troops. When he arrived in his country, he was the complaint of every one in his land. ⌜Ashamed⌝, he bowed himself[h] down, an evil

---

[a]Memphis. [b]Lit., "*their marchers forward.*"

[c]Not "tents" (Müller, *Recueil*, XX, 31), which is a masculine noun (see Harkhuf, I, 353, l. 20, and Karnak, § 589, l. 62), while ḫnˑt, "*water skin,*" above, is feminine. Tents were not borne by the troops on the march.

[d]Spiegelberg has: "ihre Säcke (?) wurden genommen und ausgeschüttet (?)."

[e]Cf. Karnak, § 586, l. 41.   [f]Compare Karnak, l. 44.

[g]The figure is that of a snared bird in Karnak (l. 67), where the same phrase occurs (see also Rosellini, *Monumenti Storici*, 139, l. 4, for the same phrase). The figure is continued above in the next parallel phrase.

[h]Read šspˑf ksw, as in Sinuhe (ll. 17, 18, I, 493).

fate removed (his) plume. They all spoke against him, among the inhabitants of his city: "He is in the power of the gods, the lords of Memphis; ⁹the lord of Egypt has cursed his name, Meryey (*m-w-r ᾿ - y ᾿ -y*), the abomination of Memphis, from son to son of his family, forever. Binre-Meriamon is in pursuit of his children; Merneptah-Hotephirma is appointed to be his fate."

Merneptah's Fame in Libya

611. He has become a ¹⁰proverb[a] for Libya (*R ᾿ -bw*); the youth say to youth, concerning his victories: "It has not been done to us ⌜before⌝ since the time of Re," say they.[b] Every old man says to his son: "Alas for Libya!" They have ceased to live in the pleasant fashion of walking in the field; their going about is stopped in a single ¹¹day. The Tehenu are consumed in a single year. Sutekh has turned his back upon their chief; their settlements are desolated with his ⌜consent⌝. There is no work of carrying ⌜—⌝[c] in these days. Concealment is good; there is safety in the cavern.[d] The great lord of Egypt, possessor of might ¹²and victory! Who will fight, knowing his stride? The fool, the witless is he who receives him;[e] he shall not know the morrow, who transgresses his boundary.

Divine Protection of Egypt

612. Since the time of the gods, say they, Egypt has been the only daughter of Re; his son is he who ¹³sits upon the throne of Shu. No one can make a design to invade her people, for the eye of every god is behind him who would violate her; it (the eye)[f] captures the rear of her foes. ⌜————⌝[g] ¹⁴A great wonder has happened for Egypt, [h]the

---

[a]Lit., "*he has become the striking of a proverb* (*sḏd·t*);" compare the Arabic ضرب مثلا.

[b]It is the Libyan youth who speak, in spite of their reference to Re. The Puntites are also made to refer to Re in Hatshepsut's reliefs.

[c]Spiegelberg suggests "Körbe."

[d]See Müller, *Recueil*, XX, 31.

[e]Meaning his onset in battle.

[f]The feminine pronoun (*nts*, "*she*") above translated "*it*," might refer to Egypt, but the parallelism shows that it must refer to "*eye*," which is feminine.

[g]This phrase, to the end of l. 13, is corrupt.

[h]Lit., "*the hand of which*."

power of which has made her invader a living prisoner. The divine king ⌈exults⌉ over his enemies, in the presence of Re. Meryey (*M-r ᵓ - y ᵓ -y*), the evil-doer, whom the god, the lord who is in Memphis, has overthrown, he has been judged ¹⁵with him in Heliopolis, and the divine ennead declared him guilty of his crimes.

Merneptah Divinely Appointed

613. The All-Lord has said: "Give the sword to my son, the upright of heart, the good and kindly Merneptah, the ⌈champion⌉ on behalf of Memphis, the advocate of ¹⁶Heliopolis, who opens the towns that were closed up. Let him set free multitudes who are bound in every district, let him give offerings to the temples, let him send in incense before the god, let him cause the princes to ⌈recover⌉ their possessions, let him cause the poor to ⌈re-enter⌉ their cities."

Heliopolis Praises Merneptah

614. They say among the lords of Heliopolis ¹⁷regarding their son, Merneptah: "Give to him duration like Re, let him be advocate of him who is oppressed in every country. Egypt has been assigned to him as the portion of ⌈him who has gained it⌉ for himself forever. His strength is its people. Lo, when one dwells in the time of this hero, the breath ¹⁸of life[a] comes immediately. . . . . so they say.

The Gods Delivered Meryey to Merneptah

615. Meryey (*M-w-r ᵓ -wy-y*), ¹⁹the wretched, vanquished chief of Libya, came to invade the "Walls-of-the-Sovereign" (Memphis), ⌈who is its lord,⌉ whose son shines on his throne, the King Merneptah. Ptah[b] said concerning the vanquished (chief)[c] of Libya: "All his crimes shall be gathered ²⁰and returned upon his (own) head. Deliver him into the hand of Merneptah, that he may make him disgorge what he has swallowed, like a crocodile. Behold, the swift is the captor of the swift; and the king shall snare him, (though) his strength be known; for Amon shall bind him in his hand and shall deliver him to his ka ²¹in Hermonthis, (to him) the King Merneptah."

---

[a] It is regularly the king who furnishes his people with the breath of life; cf. also l. 4.
[b] The Karnak fragment has "*Amon.*"
[c] Karnak fragment has: "*concerning him of Libya (p-n-Rbw).*"

Rejoicing of the Egyptians

616. Great joy has come in Egypt, rejoicing comes forth from the towns of Tomeri.[a] They converse of the victories which Merneptah has achieved among the Tehenu: "How amiable [22]is he, the victorious ruler! How magnified is the king among the gods! How fortunate is he, the commanding lord! Sit happily down and talk, or walk far out upon the way, (for) there is no fear in the heart of the people. [23]The strongholds are left to themselves, the wells are opened (again). The messengers ⌜skirt⌝ the battlements of the walls, shaded[b] from the sun, until their watchmen wake.[c] The soldiers lie sleeping, and the border [24]scouts are in the field at their (own)[d] desire. The herds of the field are left as cattle sent forth, without herdmen, crossing (at will) the fulness of the stream. There is no uplifting of a shout in the night: 'Stop! Behold, one comes, one comes with the speech of strangers!'[e] One comes [25]and goes with singing, and there is no lamentation of mourning people. The towns are settled again anew; as for the one that ploweth his harvest, he shall eat it. Re has turned himself to Egypt; he was born, destined to be [26]her protector, the King Merneptah"

Concluding Strophe

617. "The kings are overthrown, saying: "Salâm!"[f]
Not one holds up his head among the Nine Bows.
Wasted is Tehenu,
Kheta[g] is pacified,
Plundered is Pekanan[i] ($P^{\jmath}$-$k^{\jmath}$-n^{c}-n^{c}, sic!), with every evil,
[27]Carried off is Askalon ($^{\jmath}$-s-$k^{\jmath}$-r-ny),
Seized upon is Gezer ($K^{\jmath}$-$\d{d}^{\jmath}$-$r^{\jmath}$),

---

[a]Another name for Egypt.

[b]Lit., "*cool from the sun.*"

[c]The watchmen who should receive the messenger's news are asleep, and the messenger walks in the shade of the wall till they wake, as his message is not in haste as in time of war.

[d]That is, whether they like or not; they may patrol or not as they wish.

[e]Meaning the cry of the sentinels that men of foreign speech (viz., Libyans) are coming.

[f]The Libyans are represented as also using this Semitic word in Ramses III's war with them (fifth year, IV, 43, l. 50, and IV, 45, l. 56).

[g]See Great Karnak Inscription (§ 580, l. 24).

[h]Lit., "*the Canaan.*"

Yenoam (Y-nw-^{c} $^{\prime}$-mw) is made as a thing not existing.
Israel ($^{\prime}$-s-r-$^{\prime}$-r) is desolated, his seed is not;
Palestine (H $^{\prime}$-rw) has become a widow[a] ²⁸for Egypt.
All lands are united, they are pacified;
Everyone that is turbulent is bound by King Merneptah, given life like Re, every day.

INSCRIPTIONS OF THE HIGH PRIEST OF AMON, ROY

618. The documents left by Roy are of the greatest importance as showing when the office of High Priest of Amon was for the first time transmitted from father to son, and thus came to be regarded as hereditary. Moreover, an examination of them discloses the fact that this arrogation of power by the High Priest of Amon took place under Merneptah, not at the close of the Nineteenth Dynasty, as commonly supposed, but at the latest in the reign of Merneptah, and possibly still earlier, in the reign of Ramses II. Roy lived in the reign of Merneptah (§§ 628 ff.), and inherited the high priesthood of Amon from his father, Rome, heretofore considered his son.[b] Roy's father, Rome, therefore lived under Ramses II, and must have been the successor of Beknekhonsu[c] (§§ 561–68). Roy's son was named Bekne-

---

[a]The meaning of this phrase is rendered evident by an epithet applied to Ramses II on his Tanis stela (§ 490, l. 9), viz., "*husband of Egypt*," meaning, of course, "*protector of Egypt*." Hence a land may be widowed (= without a "*husband*," = without a protector), and Palestine had no protector against Egypt.

[b]Since the above was written Wreszcinski's very useful list of the high priests of Amon has appeared (*Die Hohenpriester des Amon*, von W. Wreszcinski, Berlin, 1904), in which he also makes Rome the elder, and probably the father of Roy (*ibid.*, 14, note).

[c]Beginning sixty years from some point in the reign of Seti I, Beknekhonsu was High Priest of Amon for twenty-seven years. This brings the close of his term to at least the sixtieth year of Ramses II's reign, so that Rome must have succeeded him. It can hardly be an accident that one of the prophets of Amon in Ramses II's forty-sixth year, under the high priesthood of Beknekhonsu, was named Rome (Berlin legal papyrus No. 3047; *Zeitschrift für ägyptische Sprache*, 1879, l. 5).

khonsu;[a] hence, as the name thus appears in Roy's family, he (Roy) may have been the grandson of the Beknekhonsu of Ramses II's reign, in which case the hereditary character of the office began with Beknekhonsu. Roy survived into the reign of Seti II; but already under Merneptah he succeeded in gaining high office for his son, with prospects of succeeding to the high priesthood. According to Legrain, his statue recently found in the great Karnak cache bears the following statement:

"Le roi a donné que mes enfants soient rassemblés en corporation (tribu) de mon sang, les établissant parmi les prophètes qui sont sous sa direction. Moi, je suis premier prophète d'Amon, et mon fils est établi à côté de moi en qualité de second prophète et de sous-directeur du palais du roi à l'occident de Thèbes; le fils de mon fils recevra les titres de quatrième prophète d'Amon, de père divin, d'officient et de prêtre."[b]

Legrain has accepted the current conclusion that Roy was the father of Rome, and hence identifies Roy's son above, who became second prophet, with Rome. The narrative of Roy, however, does not give the name of his son; but it is given in the Karnak relief (§ 620) as Beknekhonsu, who must therefore be the son referred to on this new Karnak statue.[c]

---

[a] Brugsch, *Thesaurus*, 1321.

[b] *Recueil*, 27, 72. Legrain gives no text.

[c] As now published (*Recueil*, 27), Legrain's data furnish no evidence that Roy was the father, and Rome his son. The fact that he is able to reconstruct from Twenty-second Dynasty statues a genealogy reaching back to a second prophet, Rome, has no bearing. We know that our Rome is called High Priest of Amon on contemporary monuments; hence the second prophet, Rome, who heads Legrain's genealogy (*Recueil*, 27, 73), was evidently a different person. The monuments found by Legrain, when published *in extenso*, may contain evidence that Rome was the son and Roy the father; for I admit that some difficulties attend the supposition that the reverse was true; but the evidence now accessible is certainly strongly in favor of this conclusion.

I. KARNAK INSCRIPTION[a]

619. This document is of importance, first, because of its place, viz., on the walls of the Karnak temple of Amon, where heretofore none but the Pharaoh's name might appear. At the east end of Pylon VIII, built by Thutmose I, was the kitchen[b] or refectory of the high priests of Amon. In view of the extensive household of the high priests at this time, it must have been a considerable building. In Roy's time it had fallen into ruin; and in the reign of Merneptah (§ 625) Roy rebuilt and enlarged it. On the east end of Pylon VIII, near the entrance to the building, where all who went in would see it, he left a record of his pious work, calling upon all the bakers, confectioners, and the like, who daily entered there, to remember him for it and to pray to Amon for him. To this record he prefixed a hymn of praise to Amon, which he placed in the mouth of his deceased father, Rome. Rome recounts his own long life accorded him by Amon, and adds: *"My son is in my place, my office is in his hand, in hereditary succession, forever"* (l. 6). Rome is thus represented as regarding the hereditary character of the office of High Priest as a matter of course; which would indicate that the beginning of the hereditary succession was earlier, as indicated above (§ 618). The use of the temple wall, and the restoration of one of its connected buildings by the High Priest of Amon, are significant symptoms of the tendency which two hundred years later placed the High Priest on the throne of Egypt.

---

[a]On the east end of Pylon VIII, overlooking the sacred lake; published: Lepsius, *Denkmäler*, III, 237, c; Stern, *Zeitschrift für ägyptische Sprache*, XI, 74 ff. (partially); and Brugsch, *Thesaurus*, VI, 1321, 1322 (partially). I had a photograph (for which I am indebted to Borchardt) which filled out many of the lacunæ in Lepsius, *Denkmäler*, and made possible the study of the document as a whole, which, as it has not been done since Stern (1873), furnishes new and important facts.

[b]The dwelling of the High Priest was farther east, south of the lake.

620. Beside the inscription, in relief, are two priests in the attitude of prayer; the first must be Roy, though no name is appended; for the second figure is not Roy (as shown by the accompanying inscription). The second figure is accompanied by the words:[a] "*His son, the second prophet of Amon, Beknekhonsu.*" This second figure and the name have been chiseled out by political enemies, probably at the fall of Seti II, into whose reign Roy survived.

The inscription is as follows:

Praise by Rome

621. Giving praise to Amon-Re, smelling the earth to his beautiful face, by the High Priest of Amon, Rome (R°-*m*). He says: . . . . . .

Here follows conventional praise of the god, with a prayer for the king,[b] after which Rome proceeds:

Speech of Rome

622. "⁴Thou didst grant[c] me long life carrying thy image, while my eye beheld thy two uraei every day, and my limbs were endued with health . . . . . ⁵ . . . . . Thou didst prolong my existence during a pleas-

---

[a]Brugsch, *Thesaurus*, 1321; I cannot see any traces of the name on the photograph, but the title is legible as above.

[b]Lepsius, *Denkmäler*, gives the name as that of Seti II, like the two scenes on the left; but I cannot read this name on the photograph. It was not read by either Stern or Brugsch. If Lepsius has not introduced it from the neighboring adoration of Amon by Seti II, and it actually stands in our passage, it must be a prayer for the king put into the mouth of the deceased Rome; just as the deceased Seti I is made to pray for Ramses II at Abydos. Our inscription in that case dates from the reign of Seti II. The matter can be settled only by an examination of the original; but historically the reasons against reading Seti II are strong, for Roy would then have been High Priest through the reigns of successive kings hostile to each other, Merneptah, Amenmeses, Siptah, and Seti II, in whose quarrels the High Priest of Amon was, of course, involved. It is not likely that the same High Priest continued under them all.

[c]The tense of the original permits translating all the following as a prayer until l. 6, where the nominal sentence, "*my son is, etc.*," cannot be optative. Hence the whole is historical, and not a prayer. Again, as both Rome and Roy are given the title High Priest of Amon, one of them must be dead; and the deceased is of course he whose son has succeeded him. Hence we must conclude that Rome is the father, and not the son (otherwise Maspero, *Momies royales*, 666).

ant life, abiding in thy temple, while my limbs were ⌜sound⌝, following thy ka, while my eye beheld the way, until I arrived at the West[a] of Thebes, satisfied with seeing Amon. ⁶My son is in my place, my office is in his hand, [b]in hereditary succession[b] forever, as is done for a just man, profitable in the house of his lord."

Introduction of Roy's Speech

623. For[c] the ka of the only excellent and just one, the favored of his god, Amon, profitable to Mut, and amiable to Khonsu, pleasing the heart of the Lord of the Two Lands; ⁷hereditary prince, divine father, pure of hands, master of secrets of heaven, earth, and the nether world, ⌜—⌝ of Kamephis (Amon), sem priest in the eternal horizon,[d] great seer of Re-Atum in Thebes, third prophet of Amon, second prophet of Amon, High Priest[e] of Amon, Roy, triumphant. He saith:

Roy's Speech

624. ⁸"O ye priests and scribes of the house of Amon, good servants of the divine offerings,[f] bakers, mixers,[g] confectioners, makers of cakes, and loaves,[h] those who perform their every duty for their lord; who shall enter into this refectory,[i] which is in [⌜the house of Amon⌝]. ⁹——— daily; ⌜pray⌝ for me because of my good and great deeds."

Roy's Restoration

625. "I found this house (ᶜ·t) in complete ruin; its walls falling, the woodwork wretched, the doorposts of wood perishing, the paint ⌜faded⌝.

---

[a]The cemetery; meaning till he died.

[b]Lit., "*one, son of another forever*" (*w ᶜ s ᵓ w ᶜ*), which is a phrase for hereditary succession. Only the second *w ᶜ* is here clearly preserved, but on the photograph I can see the feet of the *s ᵓ*-goose and one end of the first *w ᶜ*-harpoon. In view of the occurrence of the same phrase in l. 12, there can be no doubt about the reading here. The hereditary character of the high priesthood of Amon is thus proven.

[c]It is possible that this still belongs to Rome's speech, which does not alter the conclusions drawn from the inscription; "*for the ka, etc.*," being then a second dative after "*done.*"

[d]The king's tomb.   [e]Lit., "*first prophet.*"

[f]Temple income; servants who handle the naturalia of the temple income are meant.

[g]Or: "*kneaders*" (ᶜ*tḥ*).

[h]Three sorts of loaves are given: *sn·t, by·t,* and *prsn.*

[i]Or: "*kitchen*" (*w ᶜ b·t*).

I [ˈlaid it outˈ] ¹⁰with increase throughout, heightened and widened and ˈestablishedˈ. I made its doorposts of sandstone, I mounted upon them doors of real cedar; a [pla]ce for the bakers and mixers who are in it. I made it a better work than before, for the protection [ˈof the servantsˈ] ¹¹of Amon, lord of gods."

Roy's Admonition

626. "Give ye heed and hear ye what I say! Trespass not against any thing which I have made; prosper my name, — my virtues (*sp*), speak favorably for me in the presence of Amon; then shall he favor you, — according as he does — — [ˈye shall attainˈ] ¹²old age in his house, his food shall be yours, ye shall bequeath (your offices) to your children ᵃin hereditary succession*ᵃ* in his house forever. Place offerings ¹³before my statue,ᵇ pour out libations upon the ground for my name, set flowers before me when ye enter, ¹⁴bespeak for me his favor with a loving heart for my god, Amon, lord of gods. Then shall be given to you ¹⁵other things which — —. Cause [this writing] to be read, in order to do according to my sayings ¹⁶which are before you. Put my good reputation in the mouth of the youth, according as I have done excellent things in the House of Amon ¹⁷on every occasion, — — Amon, because of these my —. May he grant me 110 years bearing ¹⁸[his] image — — — forever. I said ¹⁹in my heart — — — his ka." For the ka of the High Priest of Amon, Roy.ᶜ

II. SILSILEH STELAᵈ

627. The building which Roy erected at Karnak was partially of sandstone, and as the High Priest of Amon was regularly chief architect of the buildings at Karnak, it is

---

ᵃ*W ꜥ s ꜣ w ꜥ*, as restored in l. 6 above, *q. v.*

ᵇHis statue must have been in the temple near this place.

ᶜA relief (Lepsius, *Denkmäler*, 237, *c*) beside this long inscription shows Rome and Roy kneeling with upraised hands before two royal cartouches, the names in which are chiseled out. Lepsius' notebook offers no help as to their reading. The two men have each the title "*High Priest of Amon.*" There is no sign of the relationship between them, and both are *m ꜣ ꜥ ḫrw* ("*triumphant*")! Below are the words: "*The assistant whom his majesty taught, the High Priest of Amon, Rome, made (it).*" If made in the lifetime of Rome, the expunged names will be those of Merneptah. Over this scene is one showing Seti II worshiping Amon; it has no necessary connection with that of Rome and Roy.

ᵈChampollion, *Monuments*, 102 = Lepsius, *Denkmäler*, III, 200, *a*.

probable that Roy went to Silsileh himself to superintend the quarrying of the sandstone for his building at Karnak. Our inscription does not state the object of his visit, but nothing else is known to us which would bring the High Priest of Amon to Silsileh. This dates Roy's building in Merneptah's reign.

628. The stela shows King Merneptah and Roy worshiping before Amon. Below are the name and titles of Roy as in above Karnak inscription (§ 625, ll. 6, 7). Down each side is a prayer, one for Roy, and the other for Rome, with no statement of the relationship between them. Both bear the title, "*High Priest of Amon*," which they could not have borne simultaneously. One is, therefore, already deceased in Merneptah's reign, and as Roy appears assisting the king in the relief, it is Rome who is the deceased father. Hence the old supposition that Rome was the son and still lived under Seti II is incorrect, as we found was indicated also by the Karnak inscription. Rome, therefore, if deceased in Merneptah's short reign, must have been High Priest of Amon during the latter part of Ramses II's reign, and possibly survived into the reign of Merneptah.[a]

DAYBOOK OF A FRONTIER OFFICIAL[b]

629. On the blank backs of a few pages of a school copybook an official in some town[c] on the Palestinian frontier, in the days of Merneptah, has noted for temporary reference

---

[a]The other inscriptions mentioning Roy are of no historical importance: a carnelian buckle with his name and titles is in Paris (*Bibliothèque Nationale*, No. 1468, *bis*), and a mortuary stela of one of his subordinates is in Leyden (V, 8). I owe the first reference to Dr. Wreszcinski.

[b]Papyrus Anastasi III, British Museum, 10246, Pls. VI and V, verso, of the "*Select Papyri.*" I had also a collation of the original for the Berlin *Dictionary* by Steindorff. See Erman, *Zeitschrift für ägyptische Sprache*, 29, 32, and *Life in Ancient Egypt*, 538 f.

[c]Erman thinks he was in the well-known frontier town of Tharu.

the names and the business of the messengers who passed through the place on their way to Syria. In addition to the important and interesting glimpse of the active intercourse between Egypt and Syria in the thirteenth century B. C., which the document affords us, it is of importance also as showing that Merneptah in his third year was in Syria, undoubtedly on the campaign during which he plundered Israel, as related in his Hymn of Victory of the year 5 (§ 617).

The notes are of the most hurried character, and so abbreviated that the prepositions are omitted.

Fifteenth Day

630. VI¹Year 3, first month of the third season (ninth month), fifteenth day:

There went up the servant of Baal, Roy ($R^{\flat}$-y), son of Zeper ($D^{\flat}$-pw-$r^{\flat}$) of Gaza ($G^{\flat}$-$d^{\flat}$-y, sic!), ²who had with him for Syria ($H^{\flat}$-rw) two different letters, to wit: (for) the captain of infantry, Khay ($H^{c}y$), one letter; ³(for) the chief of Tyre, Baalat-Remeg (B-^{c}-l-tw-$R^{\flat}$-m-g-w), one letter.

Seventeenth Day

631. Year 3, first month of the third season (ninth month), seventeenth day:

⁴There arrived the captains of the archers of the Well of Merneptah-Hotephirma, L. P. H., ⁵which is (on) the highland, to ⌈report⌉ in the fortress which is in Tharu ($T^{\flat}$-rw).

Uncertain Day

632. ⁶Year 3, first month of the third season (ninth month), ⌈—⌉th[a] day:

There returned the attendant, Thutiy, son of Thekerem ($T^{\flat}$-$k^{\flat}$-rw-m) of Geket ($G^{\flat}$-$k^{\flat}$-ty);[b] ⁷Methdet (M-$t^{\flat}$-dw-ty-w), son of Shem-Baal ($S^{\flat}$-m-B-^{c}-$r^{\flat}$) (of) the same (town); ⁸Sutekhmose, son of Eperdegel (^{c}-pr-d-$g^{\flat}$-$r^{\flat}$) (of) the same (town), ⁹who had with him,

---

[a]The original looks like 12!

[b]Perhaps an error for $G^{\flat}$-$d^{\flat}$-ty=Gaza.

for the place where the king was, (for) the captain of infantry, Khay ($Ḫ ^c y$),[a] ⌈gifts⌉ ($yn·tw$, sic!) and a letter.

633. V¹There went up the attendant, Nakhtamon, son of Thara ($T ^ɔ -r ^ɔ$) of the Stronghold of Merneptah-Hotephirma, L. P. H., ²who journeyed (to) ⌈Upper⌉ Tyre ($Ḍ ^ɔ -r ^ɔ -Rw-m$),[b] who had with him for Syria ($Ḫ ^c -rw$), two different letters, to wit: ³(for) the captain of infantry, Penamon, one letter; (for) the steward, Ramsesnakht, of this town, one letter.

634. ⁴'There returned the chief of the stable, Pemerkhetem ($P ^ɔ - mr-ḫtm$), son of Ani, of the Town of Merneptah-Hotephirma, ⁵which is in the district of the Aram ($^ɔ -r ^ɔ -m$),[c] who had with him (for)[d] the place where the king was,[d] two letters, to wit: ⁶(for) the captain of infantry, Peremhab ($P ^ɔ -R ^c -m-ḥb$), one letter; ⁷for the deputy, Peremhab, one letter.

Twenty-fifth Day

635. ⁸Year 3, first month of the third season (ninth month), twenty-fifth day:

There went up the charioteer, Enwau ($Ynw-w ^ɔ ww$), of the great stable of the court of Binre-Meriamon, (Merneptah), L. P. H.[e]

LETTER OF A FRONTIER OFFICIAL[f]

636. This remarkable document is a communication in the usual official style, in which some frontier official informs his superior that certain Edomite Bedwin, doubtless in ac-

---

[a]As this Khay has already gone up to Syria (according to VI, 2, § 630), and his address is now the king's camp, the king must be somewhere in Syria.

[b]Müller inclines to place this town on the Jordan (*Asien und Europa*, 272); but he reads $Ḍ ^ɔ -r ^ɔ -d(?)w-m$.

[c]As the article shows, the scribe has miswritten Aram for Amor. Cf. Müller, *Asien und Europa*, 222, and 234.

[d]Müller, (*Asien und Europa* 270 f.) would regard this as the place from which the letter came, and not the address. That this is impossible is shown by the fact that the source of the letters is never given in the entire list; and, further, by the parallel in VI, 9, which is of itself quite enough to show that the king was in Asia; but he was not necessarily in his royal town in Amor, which is only mentioned as the home of the officer bearing the letter.

[e]Here follows a list of fifteen names of unofficial persons, whose connection with the preceding is not indicated.

[f]Papyrus Anastasi VI in the British Museum; Pl. IV, l. 13–Pl. V, l. 4. Cf. Müller, *Asien und Europa*, 135.

cordance with instructions, have been allowed to pass the fortress in the district of Succoth in the Wadi Tumilât, to pasture their cattle near Pithom. The instance is paralleled by the similar case under Harmhab (§§ 10–12), and that of the Israelites (Gen. 47:1–12).

637. The papyrus is very fragmentary, and some of the uncertain portions are omitted below.

Pl. 4

638. [13]Another matter for the satisfaction of my lord's heart [14][to wit]:

We have finished passing the tribes of the Shasu ($Š^{\jmath}$-sw) of [15]Edom through the Fortress of Merneptah-Hotephirma, L. P. H., in Theku,[a] (T-kw) [16]to the pools of Pithom, of Merneptah-Hotephirma [1]in

Pl. 5

Theku, in order to sustain[b] them and their herds in the domain of Pharaoh, L. P. H., the good Sun [2]of every land. . . . . . . ———— I have caused them to be brought [3]. . . . . . . other names of [4]days ⌈when⌉ the fortress of Merneptah-Hotephirma may be passed, [5]————.

---

[a]Succoth ?

[b]Causative of the verb "*to live*" (as in Hebrew), regularly used to indicate preservation and sustenance in time of famine.

REIGN OF SIPTAH

NUBIAN GRAFFITI

639. The only inscriptions of important historical content from the reign of Siptah are the graffiti of his viceroys in Nubia, especially those at Wadi Halfa.[a] They show that he was at first called Ramses-Siptah, and later Merneptah-Siptah. He went out to Nubia apparently in his first year, as far as Abu Simbel, to appoint Seti his new viceroy of Kush (No. 1), and Neferhor the official who brought the new viceroy out to his post, recorded his arrival at Wadi Halfa (No. 2). The "*reward*" brought by Neferhor on this occasion for the officials of Nubia can be nothing else than the new king's attempt to win and hold them to his support. He evidently succeeded, for in the year 3 the treasury official, Piyay, records his visit at Wadi Halfa to receive the tribute of Kush (No. 3).

640. In the same year Seti is still viceroy, recording his devotion to the king on the rocks at the first cataract (Nos. 5 and 6). He is now also "*governor of the gold-country of Amon*" and "*chief steward of the king.*" Siptah ruled at least three years longer, for one of his messengers visited Wadi Halfa in the year 6 (No. 8). Another of his supporters to whom much interest attaches in these graffiti is his treasurer, Bay. This man was chief treasurer, and a man of some power, or he could not have excavated a tomb in the Valley of the Kings; but a mistranslation of Brugsch has

---

[a]On pillars of the southern temple of Thutmose III; they are published by Sayce, *Recueil*, XVII, 161, 162, and are referred to under his numbers. For most of them I had also the copies of Steindorff, which he very kindly placed at my disposal.

given currency to a totally false idea of Bay's position. In both the graffiti (Nos. 6 and 7) commemorating Bay, there is attached to his name a relative clause: "*whom the king established in the seat of his father*," a not uncommon statement, indicating that a man has inherited his father's office. Brugsch's rendering, following de Rougé,[a] "in dem er (Seti) den König auf den Thron seines Vaters setzte," is grammatically untenable;[b] hence the prevailing interpretation in all the histories since de Rougé's time, that the king owed his throne to Bay, is without foundation. On the contrary, the old hypothesis of Rougé,[c] that the powerful noble of this reign was the viceroy of Kush, Seti, who became King Seti II, succeeding Siptah, is supported by these graffiti. Seti becomes "*governor of the gold-country of Amon*," which places him in close communication with the powerful priesthood of Amon,[d] from whom so many usurpers drew their strength.

641. The succession of the kings of the time, supposed to be against Rougé's supposition, is clearly in support of it; but the evidence either has been overlooked or has only recently been published. There is space here to note only some of the main points in the evidence. Amenmeses, the successor of Merneptah, was a usurper and persecuted the memory of Merneptah, for example at the Ramesseum, where he set his own name over that of Merneptah.[e] Amenmeses was in turn treated in the same way by his successor, Siptah, who inserted his own name over that of Amenmeses

---

[a] *Etude sur une stèle égyptienne*, 186.

[b] See note on No. 7, § 649.

[c] *Ibid.*, 187.

[d] Indeed, there is a definite connection between the High Priest of Amon and Nubia, for he became viceroy of Nubia as his power increased (*Annales*, IV, 9).

[e] Lepsius, *Denkmäler*, III, 219, c, A; *ibid.*, Text, III, 130.

in a relief^a at Kurna, showing Amenmeses worshiping the Theban divinities, who are associated with Ramses II and Seti I, from whom Amenmeses was probably descended. The succession of Amenmeses-Siptah is therefore certain. On examining the position of Seti II with reference to the said two kings, the evidence of his first tomb in the Valley of the Kings is conclusive. Lepsius' careful and exhaustive examination^b of the royal names in the tomb of Siptah's queen, Tewosret, shows conclusively that Seti II usurped this tomb. He therefore followed Siptah, and may very well have been that king's powerful viceroy of Nubia, Seti, whom we find commemorated in the following graffiti. In Ramses III's time he was looked upon as the only legitimate king between Merneptah and Setnakht.^c

642. ^d1. Praise to Amon! May he grant life, prosperity and health to the ka of the king's-messenger to every country, companion of the feet of the Lord of the Two Lands, favorite of Horus in the palace (the king), first charioteer of his majesty, Rekhpehtuf (Rh-$phtw$· f). His lord came to establish the king's-son of Kush, Seti, upon his seat, in the year 1 of the Lord of the Two Lands, Ramses-Siptah.

---

^aLepsius, *Denkmäler*, III, 201, *c;* Text, III, 91, 92; so Rougé, *op. cit.*, 185. The Horus-name of Amenmeses in the body of the text below (l. 1), was overlooked and not changed by Siptah, thus betraying the identity of the original king to whom the monument belonged. The mythological reference on this monument, to the rearing of Amenmeses by Isis in Khemmis is, of course, applied to any king in the inscriptions (e. g., Thutmose III; II, 138), and does not at all show the actual birthplace of the king. This ancient misunderstanding appears again in *Proceedings of the Society of Biblical Archæology*, 1904, 37.

^bLepsius, *Denkmäler*, III, Text, 209–14; *Mémoires de la mission française au Caire*, III, 123–36. Seti II did not use the tomb after his usurpation of it, but hewed another and larger one (Lepsius, *Denkmäler*, Text, III, 214 ff.; *Mémoires de la mission française au Caire*, III, 146 ff.). The empty tomb of Tewosret was then usurped by Setnakht, who enlarged it (*loc. cit.*).

^cLepsius, *Denkmäler*, III, 212.

^dSouth wall of the Abu Simbel temple; unpublished, so far as I have been able to ascertain; the rendering above is based on Steindorff's copy. It was known to Brugsch (*Geschichte*, 587 f.).

643. 2.ᵃ Year 1 of the Good God, Ramses-ᵇSiptah, given life. Praise to thy ka, O Horus, lord of Bohen! May he grant life, prosperity, health, fitness for service, favor and love, to the ka of the king's-messenger to every country, priest of the Moon-god, Thoth, the scribe (named) Neferhor, son of Neferhor, scribe of the archives of Pharaoh, L. P. H., when he came with rewards for the officials ($ḥ\,\text{ᵓ}\,tyw$) of Nubia ($T\,\text{ᵓ}\,\text{-}pd\cdot t$), and to bring the king's-son of Kush, Seti on his first expedition.

644. 3.ᶜ Year 3 under the majesty of King Siptah.ᵈ The fanbearer on the king's right hand, king's-scribe, overseer of the treasury, king's-scribe of the archives of Pharaoh, steward in the houseᵉ in the house of Amon, Piyayᶠ ($Pyy\,\text{ᵓ}\,y$) came to receive the tribute of the land of Kush.

645. 4.ᵍ Year 3 of King Siptah. The first charioteer of his majesty, king's-messenger to every country, to establish the chiefs upon their thrones, satisfying the heart of his lord, Hori, son of Kem ($K\,\text{ᵓ}\,m$), triumphant, of the great stable of Seti-Merneptah, of. the court. He made it in the year 3.

646. 5.ʰ (Name of Siptah). Year 3, first month of the third season, day twenty. Praise to thy ka! O mighty king! May he grant favor to the ka of theⁱ fan-bearer on the king's right hand, king's-son of Kush, governor of south countries, Seti.

ᵃHalfa temple, Sayce's 14; Steindorff's manuscript.

ᵇThis unusual form of Siptah's name occurs also at Abu Simbel (No. 1, § 642)— a fact overlooked in proposing to identify this king with Amenmeses (*Recueil*, XVII, 162, note), who never has Siptah as the second part of his given name. We must therefore accept two forms of Siptah's name; (1) Ramses-Siptah, used at the beginning of his reign; (2) Merneptah-Siptah, introduced not later than the year 3 (No. 4, § 645). The change is paralleled, e. g., by the alteration in Seti II's name (Lepsius, *Denkmäler*, Text, III, 214).

ᶜHalfa temple, on a large ram, Sayce's, 11.   ᵈDouble name.

ᵉAs this word "*house*" ($ḥ\cdot t$) is at the bottom of a line, something has evidently escaped the copyists below; we have here the official name of an Amon-temple, with the name of the king lacking before "*in the house of Amon.*"

ᶠA third graffito of the year 3 in this temple was made by this same Piyay, Steindorff's manuscript.

ᵍHalfa temple; Sayce's second 12; Steindorff's copy.

ʰRock inscription on the island of Sehel; Lepsius, *Denkmäler*, III, 202, b = Mariette, *Monuments divers*, 71, No. 44 = de Morgan, *Catalogue des monuments*, I, 86, No. 29 = Brugsch, *Thesaurus*, V, 1215, *t*.

ⁱHis titles are repeated below, with "*hereditary prince*" prefixed.

647. 6.[a] A relief shows King Siptah enthroned, with his treasurer, Bay, behind him; Seti, the viceroy of Kush, is before him in the attitude of praise. The inscriptions are:

Over Bay

Wearer of the royal seal, sole companion, casting out lying, presenting truth; whom the king established [in][b] the seat of his father, great chief treasurer of the whole land, Ramses-Khementer[c]-Bay.

Over Seti

Praise to thee! O mighty king! By the king's-son of Kush, governor of the gold countries of Amon, fan-bearer on the king's right hand, chief steward of the king, king's-scribe of the records of Pharaoh, L. P. H., Seti.

648. [d]7. Another similar relief shows King Siptah offering flowers to Amon; Bay appears behind the king, and over them both are the words:

King's Prayer

Giving praise to Amon-Re, doing obeisance to his ka. May he protect his son, Lord of the Two Lands, Ikhnere-Setepnere (Siptah).

Bay's Prayer

649. May they[e] grant recognition to truth, and reward to him who doeth it (truth), a prosperous life with a happy heart, joy of heart, possession of health; for the ka of the great chief treasurer of the whole land,

---

[a]Rock inscription near Assuan; Lepsius, *Denkmäler*, III, 202, c = Champollion, *Notices descriptives*, I, 214 = de Morgan, *Catalogue des monuments*, I, 28, No. 6 (copied from Lepsius, *Denkmäler*, with all the mistakes).

[b]The original is to be corrected from No. 7.

[c]A compound name, meaning: "*Ramses-Shining-Among-the-Gods-Bay.*"

[d]In a rock grotto at Gebel Silsileh; Champollion, *Monuments*, 120, 4 = Lepsius, *Denkmäler*, III, 202, a.

[e]"*They*" means Amon and Siptah.

whom^a the king established in the seat of his father, whom he loved, Bay.^b

650. 8.^c Year 6 of the king of Upper and Lower Egypt, Ikhnere-Setepnere; Son of Re: Merneptah-Siptah.

The first charioteer of his majesty, king's-messenger to every country, Ubekhu ($Wbḫ \cdot w$). His^d son, the king's-son of Kush, Hori, made (it).

651. 9.^e (Name of Siptah).

Fan-bearer on the king's right hand, king's-messenger to Kharu and Kush, ———— (name lost).

---

^aThat this is a relative clause is shown by the second relative, "*whom he loved*," which shows that we should not render *smn* as a participle. The *n*-form, which we should expect in earlier times, is perhaps involved in the *n* of *smn* (Sethe, *Verbum*, I, § 226); but more probably the form is simply in accord with the prevailing tendency of the old *n-form* to give way to *sdm·f* at this time.

^bA third inscription of the reign of Siptah, containing the same phrase, is at Wadi Halfa (Steindorff's manuscript), and is, of course, to be assigned to Bay, although his name is lost.

^cHalfa temple; Sayce's 1. Steindorff's copy.

^dSo Steindorff; Sayce has "*son of*."

^eHalfa temple; Sayce's 3.

www.ingramcontent.com/pod-product-compliance
Lightning Source LLC
Chambersburg PA
CBHW061244230426
43662CB00020B/2414